The Continental Ethics Reader

The Continental Ethics Reader

Edited by
Matthew Calarco and Peter Atterton

Routledge
New York and London

Published in 2003 by
Routledge
29 West 35th Street
New York, NY 10001
routledge-ny.com

Published in Great Britain by
Routledge
11 New Fetter Lane
London EC4P 4EE
routledge.co.uk

10 9 8 7 6 5 4 3 2 1

Cataloguing-in-Publication-Data is available from the Library of Congress.

ISBN 0–415–94329–9 (hb)
ISBN 0–415–94330–2 (pb)

CONTENTS

CONTENTS

CONTENTS

ACKNOWLEDGMENTS

We thank the copyright holders for granting permission to reproduce the following material in this book:

G.W.F. Hegel, "Lordship and Bondage," *Phenomenology of Spirit*, trans. A.V. Miller (Oxford: Oxford University Press, 1977), 111–9. © Oxford University Press, 1977. Reprinted from *Phenomenology of Spirit* by G.W.F. Hegel, trans. A.V. Miller (1977) by permission of Oxford University Press.

Edmund Husserl, extract from "Fifth Meditation," *Cartesian Meditations*, trans. Dorion Cairns (Dordrecht: Kluwer, 1991), 91–6, 105–6. © Kluwer Publishers. Reprinted with kind permission of Kluwer Academic Publishers.

Max Scheler, extract from *Formalism in Ethics and Nonformal Ethics of Values*, trans. Manfred S. Frings and Roger L. Funk (Evanston: Northwestern University Press, 1973), 87–109. © Northwestern University Press.

Martin Heidegger, extract from *Being and Time*, © 1962 by SCM Press Ltd. Translated by John Macquarrie and Edward Robinson (New York: Harper & Row, 1966), 153–63. Reprinted by permission of HarperCollins Publishers Inc.

Emmanuel Levinas, "Philosophy and the Idea of Infinity," *Collected Philosophical Papers*, trans. Alphonso Lingis (Pittsburgh: Duquesne University Press, 1998), 47–59. © Kluwer Publishers. Reprinted with kind permission of Kluwer Academic Publishers.

Søren Kierkegaard, "Is There a Teleological Suspension of the Ethical?" *Fear and Trembling*, trans. Howard V. Hong and Edna H. Hong (Princeton: Princeton University Press, 1983), 54–67. © 1983 by PUP. Reprinted by permission of Princeton University Press.

Friedrich Nietzsche, extract from *On the Genealogy of Morals and Ecce Homo*, ed. Walter Kaufmann, trans. Walter Kaufmann and R.J. Hollingdale, 24–39. © 1967 by Random House, Inc. Used by permission of Random House, Inc.

Jean-Paul Sartre, "Existentialism Is a Humanism," extract from *Existentialism and Humanism*, trans. Philip Mairet (London: Methuen, 1982), 23–37. © Methuen Publishing Limited.

Martin Heidegger, extract from "Letter on Humanism," trans. David Farrell Krell, *Basic Writings* (San Francisco: Harper, 1993), 217–34, 248–59. English translation © 1977 Harper & Row, Publishers, Inc. General introduction and Introduction to each Selection Copyright © 1977 by David Farrell Krell. Reprinted by permission of HarperCollins Publishers Inc.

Walter Benjamin, "Critique of Violence," *Reflections: Essays, Aphorisms, Autobiographical Writings by Walter Benjamin*, trans. Edmund Jephcott (New York: Schocken Books, 1978), 277–300. English translation © 1978 by Harcourt, Inc., reprinted by permission of the Publisher.

Max Horkheimer and Theodor Adorno, extract from *Dialectic of Enlightenment*, trans. John Cumming (New York: Continuum, 1995), 81–99. English translation © 1972 by Herder and Herder, Inc. Reprinted by permission of The Continuum International Publishing Group.

Jürgen Habermas, "On the Pragmatic, the Ethical, and the Moral Employments of Practical Reason," *Justification and Application: Remarks on Discourse Ethics*, trans. Ciaran Cronin (Cambridge: MIT Press, 1993), 1–17. © Massachusetts Institute of Technology.

Georges Bataille, "The Notion of Expenditure," *Visions of Excess: Selected Writings, 1927–39*, trans. Allan Stoekl (Minneapolis: University of Minnesota Press, 1985), 116–29. © 1985 by the University of Minnesota.

Emmanuel Levinas, "Substitution," trans. Peter Atterton and Graham Noctor, *Basic Philosophical Writings*, eds. Adriaan T. Peperzak, et al. (Bloomington: Indiana University Press, 1996), 80–95. The French edition of this article originally appeared in *La Revue philosophique de Louvain* 66 (1968), 487–508. Reprinted with kind permission of *La Revue philosophique de Louvain*.

Jean-François Lyotard, extracts from *The Differend: Phrases in Dispute*, trans. Georges Van Den Abbeele (Minneapolis: University of Minnesota Press, 1988), 3–5, 107–10. Copyright 1988 by the University of Minnesota.

Michel Foucault, "On the Genealogy of Ethics: An Overview of Work in Progress," *Michel Foucault: Beyond Structuralism and Hermeneutics*, Hubert L. Dreyfus and Paul Rabinow (Chicago: The University of Chicago Press, 1982), 229–52. © 1982, 1983 by the University of Chicago.

Jacques Derrida, extract from "Passions: An Oblique Offering," *On The Name*, trans. David Wood (Stanford: Stanford University Press, 1995), 15–31. © 1993 by Editions Galilee; English translation © 1995 the Board of Trustees of the Leland Stanford Jr. University. With permission of Stanford University Press, www.sup.org.

Richard Rorty, extracts from "Private Irony and Liberal Hope," *Contingency, Irony, and Solidarity* (Cambridge: Cambridge University Press, 1989), 73–8, 82–9, 92–5. © Cambridge University Press 1989. Reprinted with permission of Cambridge University Press.

Gilles Deleuze and Félix Guattari, extract from *Anti-Oedipus: Capitalism and Schizophrenia*, trans. Helen Lane, Mark Seem, and Robert Hurley (Minneapolis: University of Minnesota Press, 1989), 1–16. © 1977 by Viking Penguin Inc., English language translation. Used by permission of Viking Penguin, a division of Penguin Putnam.

Luce Irigaray, "Sexual Difference," *Ethics of Sexual Difference*, trans. Carolyn Burke and Gillian C. Gill (Ithaca: Cornell University Press, 1993), 5–19. © 1993 Cornell University. Also used by permission of the publisher, Cornell University Press. Reprinted by permission of the Continuum International Publishing Group Ltd.

Hélène Cixous, extracts from "The Laugh of the Medusa," trans. Keith Cohen and Paula Cohen, *Signs* 1, 4 (1976), 875–8, 886–93. © 1976 by the University of Chicago.

Julia Kristeva, extracts from "Women's Time," trans. A. Jardine and H. Blake, *Signs* 7, 1 (1981), 18–25, 30–5. © 1981 by the University of Chicago.

Sigmund Freud, extract from *Civilization and Its Discontents,* trans. James Strachey. (New York: W. W. Norton, 1961). Copyright © 1961 James Strachey, renewed 1989 by Alix Strachey. Used by permission of W. W. Norton & Company, Inc.

Jacques Lacan, *Seminar Book VII—The Ethics of Psychoanalysis*, ed. Jacques-Alain Miller, trans. Dennis Porter (New York: W. W. Norton, 1992). Copyright © 1986 by Les Editions Du Seuil. English translation © 1992 by W. W. Norton & Co. Used by permission of W. W. Norton & Company, Inc.

While every effort has been made to secure permissions prior to publication, in some cases it was not possible to trace the copyright holder or to obtain a reply. The editors and publishers apologize for any errors and omissions, and if notified, the publisher will endeavor to rectify these at the earliest opportunity.

We wish to thank Robin Prior for his suggestions and advice in the preparation of this volume. We also wish to extend our gratitude to Damon Zucca at Routledge for his help in bringing the project to fruition.

INTRODUCTION

The following anthology is a collection of primary readings in the newly emerging field of Continental ethics. This is the first comprehensive gathering of such readings, and should prove enormously valuable to students and professors working in fields as diverse as modern European philosophy, ethics, cultural studies, literary theory, and women's studies. It includes selections from key thinkers in the areas of phenomenology, existentialism, critical theory, postmodernism, psychoanalysis, and feminism, offering the reader a well-rounded view of historical and contemporary ethical trends in Continental thought.

The aim of the anthology is to make available for the first time a single text dedicated to meeting the needs of students, professors, and independent scholars across the disciplines who are interested in Continental philosophy with a focus on ethics. This audience has been ill served by previous ethics anthologies, whose Continental component is typically restricted to Kierkegaard, Nietzsche, and Sartre. We have sought to remedy this lack by incorporating selections from other key figures in the Continental tradition, including Freud, Heidegger, Levinas, Lyotard, Habermas, Foucault, Irigaray, and Derrida, who are crucial to contemporary debates in ethics.

Quot homines tot sententiae ("As many people, as many opinions"—Terence). It is inevitable that some readers will disagree with our decision to include certain authors and not others. Due to the limitations of space, we have been forced to exclude a number of thinkers whom, in an ideal world, we would have liked to include. Perhaps the most significant omissions are Bergson, Jaspers, Marcel, Gadamer, Arendt, Blanchot, Merleau-Ponty, de Beauvoir, Ricoeur, Badiou, and Agamben. Let us simply say that our decision regarding which thinkers to include in the volume was based on the originality and approach of their work as well as the balance and relation of each thinker with respect to one another. We have tried to select works that most readily lend themselves to classroom use while also providing seminal works for scholarly research. The decision to offer multiple selections from Heidegger and Levinas is justified by the fact that Heidegger is without doubt the most influential thinker within twentieth-century Continental philosophy in general, while Levinas is arguably the most original thinker within Continental ethics in particular.

Our fivefold classification ("Phenomenology," "Existentialism," "Critical Theory," "Postmodernism," and "Psychoanalysis and Feminism") inevitably involves a certain amount of simplification. We have adopted it, however, because it designates the customary methods, approaches, and schools within Continental philosophy and thereby serves to orient the reader who is new to the field. The short headnote at the beginning of each selection will help to familiarize the neophyte further by introducing the reading and situating it within the context of the author's overall thought. We have also appended at the end of each introduction a select bibliography of major works available in English.

To be sure, the field of Continental ethics is bound to appear somewhat baffling to Anglo-American philosophers who see the major task of ethics as one of analyzing and constructing rational arguments in order to offer practical guidance for moral agents. For Continental philosophers, all these *philosophemes*—"reason," "practice" (in opposition to "theory"), and "agency"—are contestable. In the main, they share with Hegel the view that *ratio* is historically constituted and in this sense cannot act as the final arbiter for ethical truth. The classical opposition between theory and practice is also called into question inasmuch as they are shown mutually to inform and support each other. Last—but certainly not least—the vast majority of Continental philosophers have long treated with suspicion the notions of agency and freedom, which are the very hallmarks of the humanist subject under attack since Marx, Nietzsche, and Freud.

So what is Continental ethics? For us, the term designates a family-resemblance concept referring to a network of ideas and texts within the Continental tradition that bear on the question of ethics without being reducible to a common doctrinal essence. These ideas include the thought of intersubjectivity, human finitude, the Other, responsibility, language, domination, the gift, desire, and sexual difference. It is important to note that while many of the authors (Hegel, Husserl, Bataille, and Deleuze and Guattari) included in this volume do not address ethical thought directly, they are important because of the implications of their work for a critique of ethics from a Continental perspective. Others (Derrida, Lyotard) are here included because of their deconstructive retrieval of ethical discourse. Still others (Levinas, Irigaray) have a place in this volume because of their attempt to develop a new ethical theory from within a postmetaphysical framework.

We hope that this anthology will serve to dispel the widespread myth that Continental philosophy has little to offer philosophers who are engaged in a sober and rigorous reflection on ethics. Both challenging and stimulating, frustrating and rewarding, Continental ethics is seldom disappointing to the reader who is willing to have his or her traditional ethical views called into question in what is perhaps the most radical manner so far attained in the West.

Matthew Calarco and Peter Atterton
Pacific Beach, California
June 2002

Part 1

PHENOMENOLOGY

1

GEORG WILHELM FRIEDRICH HEGEL
(1770–1831)

One of the most influential of the German idealist philosophers, Hegel was born in Stuttgart, Germany, in 1770. He entered the theological seminary at the University of Tübingen in 1788 and began his career as a university teacher in 1801. His career was interrupted in 1806 by Napoleon's victory at Jena and resumed ten years later at Heidelberg. In 1818, Hegel became professor of philosophy at the university of Berlin, where he remained until his death in 1831.

Despite their extreme difficulty, Hegel's writings changed the course of subsequent philosophy and exerted a profound influence on thinkers as diverse as Marx and Heidegger. He wrote voluminously in nearly every area in philosophy, including epistemology, logic, religion, ethics, aesthetics, politics, and—most important—the philosophy of history. Hegel's ambitious goal was nothing less than an attempt at a complete system of philosophy, beginning with the *Science of Logic* (1812–1816) and followed by the tripartite *Encyclopaedia of the Philosophical Sciences* (1817) (revised in 1827 and 1830). Hegel's various lecture courses on aesthetics, religion, history of philosophy, and philosophy of history are generally regarded as the most accessible of his often baffling and obscure prose and provide an excellent entry point into his work.

Hegel's most famous work, *Phenomenology of Spirit* (1807), seeks to describe philosophy as a historical development in which the inconsistencies and contradictions of previous philosophy are "overcome" (*aufheben*) through a process known as "dialectics." As thinking proceeds through the various stages of consciousness, self-consciousness, reason, spirit, and religion, it eventually comes to know itself as the absolute subject-object of history—which Hegel calls Absolute Knowledge. Our selection begins with Hegel's famous description of the emergence of self-consciousness from "consciousness"—a quasi-solipsistic state in which the self has not yet attained a genuine sense of selfhood. Hegel's claim here is that one cannot be fully conscious of oneself unless one is in relation with other selves, who are also in search of "recognition" (*Erkennung*). To obtain such recognition, says Hegel, each individual must be willing to risk his or her biological existence in a battle fought for pure prestige's sake. Only thus does one prove oneself capable of subordinating one's natural or animalistic instincts to creative and rational purposes. The outcome of this primitive struggle is either death, in which case the victor is still bereft of the desired recognition, or the capitulation of one of the combatants, giving rise to the unequal relation Hegel calls "Lordship and Bondage." This struggle is sometimes referred to as the "master-slave dialectic." For Hegel, it forms the basis of all further social relations—including ethics.

Select Bibliography of Hegel's Works in English

Hegel's Lectures on the History of Philosophy. Trans. E.S. Haldane and Frances H. Simson. Lincoln: University of Nebraska Press, 1995.

GEORG WILHELM FRIEDRICH HEGEL (1770–1831)

Hegel's Philosophy of Nature. Part Two of the Encyclopaedia of the Philosophical Sciences. Trans. A.V. Miller and William Wallace. Oxford: Clarendon Press, 1970.

The Hegel Reader. Ed. Stephen Houlgate. Oxford: Blackwell, 1998.

Hegel's Science of Logic. Trans. A.V. Miller. Atlantic Highlands, NJ: Humanities Press, 1989.

Logic. Part One of the Encyclopaedia of the Philosophical Sciences. Trans. William Wallace. Oxford: Clarendon Press, 1975.

Phenomenology of Spirit. Trans. A.V. Miller. Oxford: Oxford University Press, 1977.

Philosophy of Mind. Part Three of the Encyclopaedia of the Philosophical Sciences. Trans. William Wallace and A.V. Miller. Oxford: Clarendon Press, 1971.

The Philosophy of History. Trans. J. Sibree. Buffalo, NY: Prometheus, 1991.

LORDSHIP AND BONDAGE

178. Self-consciousness exists in and for itself when, and by the fact that, it so exists for another; that is, it exists only in being acknowledged. The Notion of this its unity in its duplication embraces many and varied meanings. Its moments, then, must on the one hand be held strictly apart, and on the other hand must in this differentiation at the same time also be taken and known as not distinct, or in their opposite significance. The twofold significance of the distinct moments has in the nature of self-consciousness to be infinite, or directly the opposite of the determinateness in which it is posited. The detailed exposition of the Notion of this spiritual unity in its duplication will present us with the process of Recognition.

179. Self-consciousness is faced by another self-consciousness; it has come *out of itself*. This has a twofold significance: first, it has lost itself, for it finds itself as an *other* being; secondly, in doing so it has superseded the other, for it does not see the other as an essential being, but in the other sees its own self.

180. It must supersede this otherness of itself. This is the supersession of the first ambiguity, and is therefore itself a second ambiguity. First, it must proceed to supersede the *other* independent being in order thereby to become certain of *itself* as the essential being; secondly, in so doing it proceeds to supersede its *own* self, for this other is itself.

181. This ambiguous supersession of its ambiguous otherness is equally an ambiguous return *into itself*. For first, through the supersession, it receives back its own self, because, by superseding *its* otherness, it again becomes equal to itself; but secondly, the other self-consciousness equally gives it back again to itself, for it saw itself in the other, but supersedes this being of itself in the other and thus lets the other again go free.

182. Now, this movement of self-consciousness in relation to another self-consciousness has in this way been represented as the action of *one* self-consciousness, but this action of the one has itself the double significance of being both its own action and the action of the other as well. For the other is equally independent and self-contained, and there is nothing in it of which it is not itself the origin. The first does not have the object before it merely as it exists primarily for desire, but as something that has an independent existence of its own, which, therefore, it cannot utilize for its own purposes, if that object does not of its own accord do what the first does to it. Thus the movement is simply the double movement of the two self-consciousnesses. Each sees the *other* do the same as it does; each does itself what it demands of the other, and therefore also does what it does only in so far as the other does the

same. Action by one side only would be useless because what is to happen can only be brought about by both.

183. Thus the action has a double significance not only because it is directed against itself as well as against the other, but also because it is indivisibly the action of one as well as of the other.

184. In this movement we see repeated the process which presented itself as the play of Forces, but repeated now in consciousness. What in that process was *for us* is true here of the extremes themselves. The middle term is self-consciousness, which splits into the extremes; and each extreme is this exchanging of its own determinateness and an absolute transition into the opposite. Although, as consciousness, it does indeed come *out of itself*, yet, though out of itself, it is at the same time kept back within itself, is *for itself*, and the self outside it, is for *it*. It is aware that it at once is, and is not, another consciousness, and equally that this other is *for itself* only when it supersedes itself as being for itself, and is for itself only in the being-for-self of the other. Each is for the other the middle term, through which each mediates itself with itself and unites with itself; and each is for itself, and for the other, an immediate being on its own account, which at the same time is such only through this mediation. They *recognize* themselves as *mutually recognizing* one another.

185. We have now to see how the process of this pure Notion of recognition, of the duplicating of self-consciousness in its oneness, appears to self-consciousness. At first, it will exhibit the side of the inequality of the two, or the splitting-up of the middle term into the extremes which, as extremes, are opposed to one another, one being only *recognized*, the other only *recognizing*.

186. Self-consciousness is, to begin with, simple being-for-self, self-equal through the exclusion from itself of everything else. For it, its essence and absolute object is "I"; and in this immediacy, or in this I [mere] being, of its being-for-self, it is an *individual*. What is "other" for it is an unessential, negatively characterized object. But the "other" is also a self-consciousness; one individual is confronted by another individual. Appearing thus immediately on the scene, they are for one another like ordinary objects, *independent* shapes, individuals submerged in the being [or immediacy] of *Life*—for the object in its immediacy is here determined as Life. They are, *for each other*, shapes of consciousness which have not yet accomplished the movement of absolute abstraction, of rooting out all immediate being, and of being merely the purely negative being of self-identical consciousness; in other words, they have not as yet exposed themselves to each other in the form of pure being-for-self, or as self-consciousnesses. Each is indeed certain of its own self, but not of the other, and therefore its own self-certainty still has no truth. For it would have truth only if its own being-for-self had confronted it as an independent object, or, what is the same thing, if the object had presented itself as this pure self-certainty. But according to the Notion of recognition, this is possible only when each is for the other what the other is for it, only when each in its own self through its own action, and again through the action of the other, achieves this pure abstraction of being-for-self.

187. The presentation of itself, however, as the pure abstraction of self-consciousness consists in showing itself as the pure negation of its objective mode, or in showing that it is not attached to any specific *existence*, not to the individuality common to existence as such, that it is not attached to life. This presentation is a twofold action: action on the part of the other, and action on its own part. Insofar as it is the action of the *other*, each seeks the death of the other. But in doing so, the second kind of action, action on its own part, is also involved; for the former involves the staking of its own life. Thus the relation of the two self-conscious individuals is such that they prove themselves and each other

through a life-and-death struggle. They must engage in this struggle, for they must raise their certainty of being *for themselves* to truth, both in the case of the other and in their own case. And it is only through staking one's life that freedom is won; only thus is it proved that for self-consciousness, its essential being is not [just] being, not the *immediate* form in which it appears, not its submergence in the expanse of life, but rather that there is nothing present in it which could not be regarded as a vanishing moment, that it is only pure *being-for-self*. The individual who has not risked his life may well be recognized as a *person*, but he has not attained to the truth of this recognition as an independent self-consciousness. Similarly, just as each stakes his own life, so each must seek the other's death, for it values the other no more than itself; its essential being is present to it in the form of an "other," it is outside of itself and must rid itself of its self-externality. The other is an *immediate* consciousness entangled in a variety of relationships, and it must regard its otherness as a pure being-for-self or as an absolute negation.

188. This trial by death, however, does away with the truth which was supposed to issue from it, and so, too, with the certainty of self generally. For just as life is the *natural* setting of consciousness, independence without absolute negativity, so death is the *natural* negation of consciousness, negation without independence, which thus remains without the required significance of recognition. Death certainly shows that each staked his life and held it of no account, both in himself and in the other; but that is not for those who survived this struggle. They put an end to their consciousness in its alien setting of natural existence, that is to say, they put an end to themselves, and are done away with as *extremes* wanting to be *for themselves*, or to have an existence of their own. But with this there vanishes from their interplay the essential moment of splitting into extremes with opposite characteristics; and the middle term collapses into a lifeless unity which is split into lifeless, merely immediate, unopposed extremes; and the two do not reciprocally give and receive one another back from each other consciously, but leave each other free only indifferently, like things. Their act is an abstract negation, not the negation coming from consciousness, which supersedes in such a way as to preserve and maintain what is superseded, and consequently survives its own supersession.

189. In this experience, self-consciousness learns that life is as essential to it as pure self-consciousness. In immediate self-consciousness the simple "I" is the absolute object, which however for us or in itself is the absolute mediation, and has as its essential moment lasting independence. The dissolution of that simple unity is the result of the first experience; through this there is posited a pure self-consciousness, and a consciousness which is not purely for itself but for another, i.e., is a merely *immediate* consciousness, or consciousness in the form of *thinghood*. Both moments are essential. Since to begin with they are unequal and opposed, and their reflection into a unity has not yet been achieved, they exist as two opposed shapes of consciousness; one is the independent consciousness whose essential nature is to be for itself, the other is the dependent consciousness whose essential nature is simply to live or to be for another. The former is lord, the other is bondsman.

190. The lord is the consciousness that exists *for itself*, but no longer merely the Notion of such a consciousness. Rather, it is a consciousness existing *for itself* which is mediated with itself through another consciousness, i.e., through a consciousness whose nature it is to be bound up with an existence that is independent, or thinghood in general. The lord puts himself into relation with both of these moments, to a *thing* as such, the object of desire, and to the consciousness for which thinghood is the essential characteristic. And since he is (a) *qua* the Notion of self-consciousness an immediate relation of being-for-self, but (b) is now at the same time mediation, or a being-for-self which is for itself only through another, he is related (a) immediately to both, and (b) mediately to each through the other. The lord relates himself mediately to the bondsman through a being [a thing] that is independent, for it is

just this which holds the bondsman in bondage; it is his chain from which he could not break free in the struggle, thus proving himself to be dependent, to possess his independence in thinghood. But the lord is the power over this thing, for he proved in the struggle that it is something merely negative; since he is the power over this thing and this again is the power over the other [the bondsman], it follows that he holds the other in subjection. Equally, the lord relates himself mediately to the thing through the bondsman; the bondsman, *qua* self-consciousness in general, also relates himself negatively to the thing, and takes away its independence; but at the same time the thing is independent *vis-à-vis* the bondsman, whose negating of it, therefore, cannot go the length of being altogether done with it to the point of annihilation; in other words, he only works on it. For the lord, on the other hand, the *immediate* relation becomes through this mediation the sheer negation of the thing, or the enjoyment of it. What desire failed to achieve, he succeeds in doing, viz., to have done with the thing altogether, and to achieve satisfaction in the enjoyment of it. Desire failed to do this because of the thing's independence; but the lord, who has interposed the bondsman between it and himself, takes to himself only the dependent aspect of the thing and has the pure enjoyment of it. The aspect of its independence he leaves to the bondsman, who works on it.

191. In both of these moments the lord achieves his recognition through another consciousness; for in them, that other consciousness is expressly something unessential, both by its working on the thing, and by its dependence on a specific existence. In neither case can it be lord over the being of the thing and achieve absolute negation of it. Here, therefore, is present this moment of recognition, viz., that the other consciousness sets aside its own being-for-self, and in so doing itself does what the first does to it. Similarly, the other moment too is present, that this action of the second is the first's own action; for what the bondsman does is really the action of the lord. The latter's essential nature is to exist only for himself; he is the sheer negative power for whom the thing is nothing. Thus he is the pure, essential action in this relationship, while the action of the bondsman is impure and unessential. But for recognition proper the moment is lacking, that what the lord does to the other he also does to himself, and what the bondsman does to himself he should also do to the other. The outcome is a recognition that is one-sided and unequal.

192. In this recognition the unessential consciousness is for the lord the object, which constitutes the *truth* of his certainty of himself. But it is clear that this object does not correspond to its Notion, but rather that the object in which the lord has achieved his lordship has in reality turned out to be something quite different from an independent consciousness. What now really confronts him is not an independent consciousness, but a dependent one. He is, therefore, not certain of *being-for-self* as the truth of himself. On the contrary, his truth is in reality the unessential consciousness and its unessential action.

193. The *truth* of the independent consciousness is accordingly the servile consciousness of the bondsman. This, it is true, appears at first *outside* of itself and not as the truth of self-consciousness. But just as lordship showed that its essential nature is the reverse of what it wants to be, so too servitude in its consummation will really turn into the opposite of what it immediately is; as a consciousness forced back into itself, it will withdraw into itself and be transformed into a truly independent consciousness.

194. We have seen what servitude is only in relation to lordship. But it is a self-consciousness, and we have now to consider what as such it is in and for itself. To begin with, servitude has the lord for its essential reality; hence the *truth* for it is the independent consciousness that is *for itself*. However, servi-

tude is not yet aware that this truth is implicit in it. But it does in fact contain within itself this truth of pure negativity and being-for-self, for it has experienced this as its own essential nature. For this consciousness has been fearful, not of this or that particular thing or just at odd moments, but its whole being has been seized with dread; for it has experienced the fear of death, the absolute Lord. In that experience it has been quite unmanned, has trembled in every fiber of its being, and everything solid and stable has been shaken to its foundations. But this pure universal movement, the absolute melting away of everything stable, is the simple, essential nature of self-consciousness, absolute negativity, *pure being-for-self*, which consequently is *implicit* in this consciousness. This moment of pure being-for-self is also *explicit* for the bondsman, for in the lord it exists for him as his *object*. Furthermore, his consciousness is not this dissolution of everything stable merely in principle; in his service he *actually* brings this about. Through his service he rids himself of his attachment to natural existence in every single detail; and gets rid of it by working on it.

195. However, the feeling of absolute power both in general, and in the particular form of service, is only implicitly this dissolution, and although the fear of the lord is indeed the beginning of wisdom, consciousness is not therein aware that it is a being-for-self. Through work, however, the bondsman becomes conscious of what he truly is. In the moment which corresponds to desire in the lord's consciousness, it did seem that the aspect of unessential relation to the thing fell to the lot of the bondsman, since in that relation the thing retained its independence. Desire has reserved to itself the pure negating of the object and thereby its unalloyed feeling of self. But that is the reason why this satisfaction is itself only a fleeting one, for it lacks the side of objectivity and permanence. Work, on the other hand, is desire held in check, fleetingness staved off; in other words, work forms and shapes the thing. The negative relation to the object becomes its *form* and something permanent, because it is precisely for the worker that the object has independence. This *negative* middle term or the formative *activity* is at the same time the individuality or pure being-for-self of consciousness which now, in the work outside of it, acquires an element of permanence. It is in this way, therefore, that consciousness, *qua* worker, comes to see in the independent being [of the object] its *own* independence.

196. But the formative activity has not only this positive significance that in it the pure being-for-self of the servile consciousness acquires an existence; it also has, in contrast with its first moment, the negative significance of *fear*. For, in fashioning the thing, the bondsman's own negativity, his being-for-self, becomes an object for him only through his setting at nought the existing *shape* confronting him. But this objective *negative* moment is none other than the alien being before which it has trembled. Now, however, he destroys this alien negative moment, posits *himself* as a negative in the permanent order of things, and thereby becomes *for himself*, someone existing on his own account. In the lord, the being-for-self is an "other" for the bondsman, or is only *for* him [i.e., is not his own]; in fear, the being-for-self is present in the bondsman himself; in fashioning the thing, he becomes aware that being-for-self belongs to *him*, that he himself exists essentially and actually in his own right. The shape does not become something other than himself through being made external to him; for it is precisely this shape that is his pure being-for-self, which in this externality is seen by him to be the truth. Through this rediscovery of himself by himself, the bondsman realizes that it is precisely in his work wherein he seemed to have only an alienated sense that he acquires a mind of his own. For this reflection, the two moments of fear and service as such, as also that of formative activity, are necessary, both being at the same time in a universal mode. Without the discipline of service and obedience, fear remains at the formal stage, and does not extend to the known real world of existence. Without the formative activity, fear remains inward and mute, and consciousness does not become explicitly *for itself*. If consciousness fashions the thing without that initial absolute fear, it is only an empty self-centered

attitude; for its form or negativity is not negativity *per se*, and therefore its formative activity cannot give it a consciousness of itself as essential being. If it has not experienced absolute fear but only some lesser dread, the negative being has remained for it something external, its substance has not been infected by it through and through. Since the entire contents of its natural consciousness have not been jeopardized, determinate being still *in principle* attaches to it; having a "mind of one's own" is self-will, a freedom which is still enmeshed in servitude. Just as little as the pure form can become essential being for it, just as little is that form, regarded as extended to the particular, a universal formative activity, an absolute Notion; rather it is a skill which is master over some things, but not over the universal power and the whole of objective being.

2

EDMUND HUSSERL
(1859–1938)

The German philosopher Edmund Husserl is regarded as the father of modern phenomenology. He received his Ph.D. in mathematics from the University of Vienna in 1882, and in 1884 began attending the lectures of the Austrian philosophical psychologist, Franz Brentano. He taught philosophy at Halle and later at Göttingen and Freiburg, where he spent the remainder of his life. Husserl's Jewish ancestry meant that he was confronted in his final years with the growing anti-Semitism that plagued Germany, though he died before the worst of the atrocities.

Originally trained in mathematics and later in formal logic and psychology, Husserl sought to develop a rigorous philosophy on a par with the mathematical sciences. To this end, Husserl sounded a clarion call to philosophers to go "back to the things themselves" and describe "phenomena" (i.e., objects of conscious thought) in their own terms without presuppositions. Husserl dubbed this way of doing philosophy "phenomenology," elucidating its fundamental themes in his *Logical Investigations* (1900–1901). In his 1907 lectures "The Idea of a Phenomenology" and his book *Ideas: General Introduction to Phenomenology* (1913), he embarked upon a rigorous scientific program for philosophy that required suspending belief in the existence of the external world—the so-called natural attitude—in order to focus on the way things appear to consciousness. Husserl called such "bracketing" the "transcendental reduction" (*epoché*), which he described as a transition from the naïve realism of ordinary thinking to a scrupulous inspection of the contents of consciousness. Husserl's emphasis on the social, cultural, and historical aspects of the "life-world" (*Lebenswelt*) in his last major work, *The Crisis of the European Sciences and Transcendental Phenomenology* (1936), was to have a profound and lasting influence on subsequent generations of philosophers.

After suspending belief in the existence of the external world, Husserl was inevitably confronted with the perennial philosophical problem of solipsism. His solution was provided in the fifth of his *Cartesian Meditations* (1931), from which our selection is taken. In this work, Husserl argues that other human beings are not present to consciousness in the way that ordinary objects of perception are. I am indeed directly aware of the other's body, though I do not have access to the other's inner experience as such. How then does the other enter into my consciousness? Husserl's reply is that I perceive him or her as another ego that is *analogous* or similar to my own. This special act of consciousness is called "analogical appresentation," and is presupposed in every social encounter.

Select Bibliography of Husserl's Works in English

Cartesian Meditations: An Introduction to Phenomenology. Trans. Dorion Cairns. Dordrecht: Kluwer, 1991.
The Crisis of the European Sciences and Transcendental Phenomenology: An Introduction to Phenomenological Philosophy. Trans. David Carr. Evanston, IL: Northwestern University Press, 1970.
The Essential Husserl. Ed. Donn Welton. Bloomington, IN: Indiana University Press, 1999.

Experience and Judgment: Investigations in a Genealogy of Logic. Ed. Ludwig Landgrebe. Trans. James S. Churchill and Karl Ameriks. Evanston, IL: Northwestern University Press, 1973.

Formal and Transcendental Logic. Trans. Dorion Cairns. The Hague: Martinus Nijhoff, 1969.

Ideas: General Introduction to Pure Phenomenology. Trans. W.R. Boyce Gibson. London: Allen and Unwin, 1969.

Logical Investigations, 2 vols. Trans. J.N. Findlay. London: Routledge and Kegan Paul, 1970.

On the Phenomenology of Consciousness of Internal Time (1893–1917). Trans. John Barnett Brough. Dordrecht: Kluwer, 1991.

FIFTH MEDITATION

§43. The noematic-ontic mode of givenness of the Other, as transcendental clue for the constitutional theory of the experience of someone else.

First of all, my "transcendental clue" is the experienced Other, given to me in straightforward consciousness and as I immerse myself in examining the noematic-ontic content belonging to him (purely as correlate of my cogito, the particular structure of which is yet to be uncovered). By its remarkableness and multiplicity, that content already indicates the many-sidedness and difficulty of the phenomenological task. For example: in changeable harmonious multiplicities of experience I experience others as actually existing and, on the one hand, as world Objects—not as mere physical things belonging to Nature, though indeed as such things in respect of one side of them. They are in fact experienced also as *governing psychically* in their respective natural organisms. Thus peculiarly involved with animate organisms, as "psychophysical" Objects, they are *"in" the world*. On the other hand, I experience them at the same time as *subjects for this world*, as experiencing it (this same world that I experience) and, in so doing, experiencing me too, even as I experience the world and others in it. Continuing along this line, I can explicate a variety of other moments noematically.

In any case then, within myself, within the limits of my transcendentally reduced pure conscious life, I experience the world (including others)—and, according to its experiential sense, *not* as (so to speak) my *private* synthetic formation but as other than mine alone, as an *intersubjective* world, actually there for everyone, accessible in respect of its Objects to everyone. And yet each has his experiences, his appearances and appearance-unities, his world-phenomenon; whereas the experienced world exists in itself, over against all experiencing subjects and their world-phenomena.

What is the explanation of this? Imperturbably I must hold fast to the insight that every sense that any existent whatever has or can have for me—in respect of its "what" and its "it exists and actually is"—is a sense *in* and *arising from* my intentional life, becoming clarified and uncovered for me in consequence of my life's constitutive syntheses, in systems of harmonious verification. Therefore, in order to provide the basis for answering all imaginable questions that can have any sense—nay, in order that, step by step, these questions themselves may be propounded and solved—it is necessary to begin with a systematic explication of the overt and implicit intentionality in which the being of others for me becomes "made" and explicated in respect of its rightful content—that is, its fulfillment-content.

Thus the problem is stated at first as a special one, namely that of the "thereness-for-me" of others, and accordingly as the theme of a *transcendental theory of experiencing someone else*, a transcendental theory of so-called "empathy." But it soon becomes evident that the range of such a theory is much greater than at first it seems, that it contributes to the founding of a *transcendental theory of the Objective world* and, indeed, to the founding of such a theory in every respect, notably as regards Objective

Nature. The existence-sense of the world and of Nature in particular, as Objective Nature, includes, after all, as we have already mentioned, thereness-for-everyone. This is always cointended wherever we speak of Objective actuality. In addition, Objects with "spiritual" predicates belong to the experienced world. These Objects, in respect of their origin and sense, refer us to subjects, usually other subjects, and their actively constituting intentionality. Thus it is in the case of all cultural Objects (books, tools, works of any kind, and so forth), which moreover carry with them at the same time the experiential sense of thereness-for-everyone (that is, everyone belonging to the corresponding cultural community, such as the European or perhaps, more narrowly, the French cultural community, and so forth).

§44. Reduction of transcendental experience to the sphere of ownness.

If the transcendental constitution of other subjects and accordingly the transcendental sense, "other subjects," are in question, and consequently a universal sense-stratum that emanates from others and is indispensable to the possibility of an Objective world for me is also in question, then the sense, "other subjects," that is in question here cannot as yet be the sense: "Objective subjects, subjects existing in the world." As regards method, a prime requirement for proceeding correctly here is that first of all we carry out, *inside the universal transcendental sphere, a peculiar kind of epoché* with respect to our theme. For the present we exclude from the thematic field everything now in question: we *disregard all constitutional effects of intentionality relating immediately or mediately to other subjectivity* and delimit first of all the total nexus of that actual and potential intentionality in which the ego constitutes *within himself a peculiar ownness.*

This *reduction to my transcendental sphere of peculiar ownness* or to my transcendental concrete I-myself, by abstraction from everything that transcendental constitution gives me as Other, has an unusual sense. In the natural, the world-accepting attitude, I find differentiated and contrasted: myself and others. If I "abstract" (in the usual sense) from others, I "alone" remain. But such abstraction is not radical, such aloneness in no respect alters the natural world-sense, "experienceable by everyone," which attaches to the naturally understood Ego and would not be lost, even if a universal plague had left only me. Taken however in the transcendental attitude and at the same time with the constitutional abstraction that we have just characterized, my (the meditator's) ego in his transcendental ownness is not the usual I, this man, reduced to a mere correlate phenomenon and having his status within the total world-phenomenon. What concerns us is, on the contrary, *an essential structure, which is part of the all-embracing constitution* in which the transcendental ego, as constituting an Objective world, lives his life.

What is specifically peculiar to me as ego, my concrete being as a monad, purely in myself and for myself *with an exclusive ownness,* includes every intentionality and therefore, in particular, the intentionality directed to what is Other; but, for reasons of method, the synthetic effect of such intentionality (the actuality for me of what is Other) shall at first remain excluded from the theme. In this preeminent intentionality there becomes constituted for me the new existence-sense that goes beyond my monadic very-ownness; there becomes constituted an ego, not as "I-myself," but as mirrored in my own Ego, in my monad. The second ego, however, is not simply there and strictly presented; rather is he constituted as "alter ego"—the ego indicated as one moment by this expression being I myself in my ownness. The "Other," according to his own constituted sense, points to me myself; the other is a "mirroring" of my own self and yet not a mirroring proper, an analogue of my own self and yet again not an analogue in the usual sense. Accordingly if, as a first step, the ego in his peculiar ownness has been delimited, has been surveyed and articulated in respect of his constituents—not only in the way of life-processes but also in the way of accepted unities concretely inseparable from him—the question must then be asked: *How* can my ego, within his peculiar ownness, constitute under the name, "experience of something other," precisely something *other*—something, that is, with a sense that excludes the constituted from the concrete makeup of the sense-constituting I-myself, as somehow the latter's analogue? In the first place the question concerns no matter what alter egos; then however it concerns everything that acquires sense-determinations from them—in short, an Objective world in the proper and full signification of the phrase.

These problems will become more understandable if we proceed to characterize the ego's sphere of ownness, or, correlatively, to carry out explicitly the abstractive *epoché* that yields it. Thematic exclusion of the constitutional effects produced by experience of something other, together with the effects of all the further modes of consciousness relating to something other, does not signify merely phenomenological *epoché* with respect to naïve acceptance of the being of the other, as in the case of everything Objective existing for us in straightforward consciousness. After all, the transcendental attitude is and remains presupposed, the attitude according to which everything previously existing for us in straightforward consciousness is taken exclusively as "phenomenon," as a sense meant and undergoing verification, purely in the manner in which, as correlate of uncoverable constitutive systems, it has gained and is gaining existential sense. We are now preparing for just this uncovering and sense-clarification by the novel *epoché,* more particularly in the following manner.

As Ego in the transcendental attitude I attempt first of all to delimit, within my horizon of transcendental experience, *what is peculiarly my own*. First I say that it is *nonalien*. I begin by freeing that horizon abstractively from everything that is at all alien. A property of the transcendental phenomenon "world" is that of being given in harmonious straightforward experience; accordingly it is necessary to survey this world and pay attention to how something alien makes its appearance as jointly determining the sense of the world and, so far as it does so, to exclude it abstractively. Thus we abstract first of all from what gives men and brutes their specific sense as, so to speak, Ego-like living beings and consequently from all determinations of the phenomenal world that refer by their sense to "others" as Ego-subjects and, accordingly, presuppose these. For example, all cultural predicates. We can say also that we abstract from everything "*other-spiritual*," as that which makes possible, in the "alien" or "other" that is in question here, its specific sense. Furthermore the *characteristic of belonging to the surrounding world*, not merely for others who are also given at the particular time in actual experience, but also *for everyone*, the characteristic of being there for and accessible to everyone, of being capable of mattering or not mattering to each in his living and striving—a characteristic of all Objects belonging to the phenomenal world and the characteristic wherein their otherness consists—should not be overlooked, but rather excluded abstractively.

In this connection we note something important. When we thus abstract, *we retain a unitarily coherent stratum of the phenomenon world*, a stratum of the phenomenon that is the correlate of continuously harmonious, continuing world-experience. *Despite* our abstraction, we can *go on continuously in our experiencing intuition*, while remaining exclusively in the aforesaid stratum. This unitary stratum, furthermore, is distinguished by being essentially the *founding* stratum—that is to say: I obviously cannot have the "alien" or "other" as experience, and therefore cannot have the sense "Objective world" as an experiential sense, without having this stratum in actual experience; whereas the reverse is not the case. . . .

§48. The transcendency of the Objective world as belonging to a level higher than that of primordial transcendency.

That my own essence can be at all contrasted for me with something else, or that I (who am I) can become aware of someone else (who is not I but someone other than I), presupposes that *not all my own modes of consciousness are modes of my self-consciousness*. Since actual being is constituted originally by harmoniousness of experience, my own self must contain, in contrast to self-experience and the system of its harmoniousness (the system, therefore, of self-explication into components of my ownness), yet other experiences united in harmonious systems. And now the *problem* is how we are to understand the fact that the ego has, and can always go on forming, in himself such intentionalities of a different kind, intentionalities with an existence-sense whereby *he wholly transcends his own being*. How can something actually existent for me—and, as that, not just somehow meant but undergoing harmonious verification in me—be anything else than, so to speak, a point of intersection belonging to my constitutive synthesis? As concretely inseparable from my synthesis, is it peculiarly my own? But even the possibility of a vaguest, emptiest intending of something alien is problematic, if it is true that, essentially, every such mode of consciousness involves its possibilities of an uncovering of what is intended, its possibilities of becoming converted into either fulfilling or disillusioning experiences of what is meant, and moreover (as regards the genesis of the consciousness) points back to such experiences of the same intended object or a similar one.

The fact of experience of something alien (something that is not I), is present as experience of an Objective world and others in it (non-Ego in the form: other Ego); and an important result of the ownness-reduction performed on these experiences was that it brought out a substratum belonging to them, an intentional substratum in which a reduced "world" shows itself, as an "immanent transcendency." In the order pertaining to constitution of a world *alien to my Ego*—a world *"external" to my own concrete Ego* (but not at all in the natural spatial sense)—that reduced world is the intrinsically first, the *"primordial" transcendency* (or "world"); and, regardless of its *ideality* as a synthetic unity belonging to an infinite system of my potentialities, it is *still a determining part of my own concrete being*, the being that belongs to me as concrete ego.

It must now be made understandable *how*, at the founded higher level, the sense-bestowal pertaining to transcendency proper, to constitutionally secondary *Objective transcendency*, comes about—and does so as an experience. Here it is not a matter of uncovering a genesis going on in time, but a matter of *"static analysis."* The Objective world is constantly there before me as already finished, a datum of my livingly continuous Objective experience and, even in respect of what is no longer experienced, something I go on accepting habitually. It is a matter of examining this experience itself and uncovering intentionally the manner in which it bestows sense, the manner in which it can occur as experience and become verified as evidence relating to an actual existent with an explicatable essence of *its* own, which is not *my* own essence and has no place as a constituent part thereof, though it nevertheless can acquire sense and verification only in my essence.

§49. Predelineation of the course to be followed by intentional explication of experiencing what is other.

Constitution of the existence-sense, "Objective world," on the basis of my primordial "world," involves a number of levels. As the *first* of these, there is to be distinguished the constitutional level pertaining to the "other ego" or to any "other egos" whatever—that is: to egos *excluded* from my own concrete being (from me as the "primordial ego"). In connection with that and, indeed, motivated by it, there occurs a *universal superaddition of sense to my primordial world*, whereby the latter becomes the appearance *"of"* a determinate "Objective" world, as the identical world for everyone, myself included. Accordingly *the intrinsically first other* (the first "non-Ego") *is the other Ego*. And the other Ego makes constitutionally possible a new infinite domain of what is "other": an *Objective Nature* and a whole Objective world, to which all other Egos and I myself belong. This constitution, arising on the basis of the *"pure"* others (the other Egos who as yet have no worldly sense), is essentially such that the "others"-for-me do not remain isolated; on the contrary, an *Ego-community*, which includes me, becomes constituted (in my sphere of ownness, naturally) as a community of Egos existing with each other and for each other—*ultimately a community of monads*, which moreover (in its communalized intentionality) constitutes the *one identical world. In this world* all Egos again present themselves, but *in an Objectivating apperception* with the sense "*men*" or "psychophysical men as worldly Objects."

By virtue of the mentioned communalization, the transcendental intersubjectivity has an *intersubjective* sphere of ownness, in which it constitutes the Objective world; and thus, as the transcendental "We," it is a subjectivity for this world and also for the world of men, which is the form in which it has made itself Objectively actual. If, however, intersubjective sphere of ownness and Objective world are to be distinguished here, nevertheless, when I as ego take my stand on the basis of the intersubjectivity constituted from sources within my own essence, I can recognize that the Objective world does not, in the proper sense, *transcend* that sphere or that sphere's own intersubjective essence, but rather inheres in it as an "immanent" transcendency. Stated more precisely: the Objective world as an *idea*—the ideal correlate of an intersubjective (intersubjectively communalized) experience, which ideally can be and is carried on as constantly harmonious—is essentially related to intersubjectivity (itself constituted as having the ideality of endless openness), whose component particular subjects are equipped with mutually corresponding and harmonious constitutive systems. Consequently *the constitution of the world essentially involves a "harmony" of the monads*: precisely this harmony among particular constitutions in the particular monads; and accordingly it involves also a harmonious generation that goes on in each particular monad. That is not meant, however, as a "metaphysical" hypothesizing of monadic harmony, any more than the monads themselves are metaphysical inventions or hypotheses. On the contrary, it is itself part of the explication of the intentional components implicit in the fact of the experiential world that exists for us. Here again it is to be noted that, as has been repeatedly emphasized, the ideas referred to are not phantasies or modes of the "as if," but arise constitutionally in integral connection with all Objective experience and have their modes of legitimation and their development by scientific activity.

What we have just presented is a preliminary view of the course to be followed, level by level, in the intentional explication that we must carry out, if we are to solve the transcendental problem in the only conceivable way and actually execute the transcendental idealism of phenomenology.

§50. The mediate intentionality of experiencing someone else, as "appresentation" (analogical apperception).

After we have dealt with the prior stage, which is very important transcendentally—namely, definition and articulation of the primordial sphere—the genuine difficulties (and in fact they are not inconsiderable) are occasioned by the *first* of the above-indicated steps toward constitution of an Objective world: *the step taking us to the "other" ego*. They lie, accordingly, in the transcendental clarification of experiencing "someone else"—in the sense in which the other has not yet attained the senses "man."

Experience is original consciousness; and in fact we generally say, in the case of experiencing a man: the other is himself there before us "in person." On the other hand, this being there in person does not keep us from admitting forthwith that, properly speaking, neither the other Ego himself, nor his subjective processes or his appearances themselves, nor anything else belonging to his own essence, becomes given in our experience originally. If it were, if what belongs to the other's own essence were directly accessible, it would be merely a moment of my own essence, and ultimately he himself and I myself would be the same. The situation would be similar as regards his animate organism, if the latter were nothing else but the "body" that is a unity constituted purely in my actual and possible experiences, a unity belonging—as a product of my "sensuousness" exclusively—in my primordial sphere. *A certain mediacy of intentionality* must be present here, going out from the substratum, "primordial world," (which in any case is the incessantly underlying basis) and making present to consciousness a "there too," which nevertheless is not itself there and can never become an "itself-there." We have here, accordingly, a kind of *making "copresent,"* a kind of *"appresentation."*

An appresentation occurs even in external experience, since the strictly seen front of a physical thing always and necessarily appresents a rear aspect and prescribes for it a more or less determinate content. On the other hand, experiencing someone else cannot be a matter of just this kind of appresentation, which already plays a role in the constitution of primordial Nature: appresentation of this sort involves the possibility of verification by a corresponding fulfilling presentation (the back becomes the front); whereas, in the case of that appresentation which would lead over into the other original sphere, such verification must be excluded *a priori*. How can appresentation of another original sphere, and thereby the sense "someone else," be motivated in my original sphere and, in fact, motivated as experience—as the word "appresentation" (making intended as co-present) already indicates? Not every non-originary making-present can do that. A non-originary making-present can do it only in combination with an originary presentation, an itself-giving proper; and only as demanded by the originary presentation can it have the character of appresentation—somewhat as, in the case of experiencing a physical thing, what is there perceptually motivates something else being there too.

The perception proper that functions as the underlying basis is offered to us by our *perception of the primordially reduced world*, with its previously described articulation—a perception going on continually within the general bounds of the ego's *incessant self-perception*. The problem now is: In the perception of that reduced world, what in particular must be of account here? How does the motivation run? What becomes uncovered as involved in the very complicated intentional performance of the appresentation, which does in fact come about?

Initial guidance can be furnished by the verbal sense, *an Other*: an Other Ego. "Alter" signifies alter ego. And the ego involved here is I-myself, constituted within my primordial ownness, and uniquely, as the psychophysical unity (the primordial man): as "personal" Ego, governing immediately in my animate organism (the only animate organism) and producing effects mediately in the primordial surrounding world; the subject, moreover, of a concrete intentional life, of a psychic sphere relating to himself and the "world." All of that—with the grouping under types that arises in experiential life and the familiar forms of flow and combination—is at our disposal. As for the intentionalities by which it has become constituted (and they too are highly complicated)—admittedly we have not investigated them. They belong to a distinct stratum and are the theme of vast investigations into which we did not and could not enter.

Let us assume that another man enters our perceptual sphere. Primordially reduced, that signifies: in the perceptual sphere pertaining to my primordial Nature, a body is presented, which, as primordial, is of course only a determining part of myself: an "immanent transcendency." Since, in this Nature and this world, my animate organism is the only body that is or can be constituted originally as an animate organism (a functioning organ), the body over there, which is nevertheless apprehended as an animate organism, must have derived this sense by an *apperceptive transfer from my animate organism*, and done so in a manner that excludes an actually direct, and hence primordial, showing of the predicates belonging to an animate organism specifically, a showing of them in perception proper. It is clear from the very beginning that only a similarity connecting, within my primordial sphere, that body over there with my body can serve as the motivational basis for the *"analogizing" apprehension* of that body as another animate organism.

There would be, accordingly, a certain assimilative apperception; but it by no means follows that there would by an inference from analogy. Apperception is not inference, not a thinking act. *Every* apperception in which we apprehend at a glance, and noticingly grasp, objects given beforehand—for example, the already-given everyday world—every apperception in which we understand their sense and its horizons forthwith, points back to a *"primal instituting,"* in which an object with a similar sense became constituted for the first time. Even the physical things of this world that are unknown to us are, to speak generally, known in respect of their type. We have already seen like things before, though not precisely this thing here. Thus *each everyday experience* involves *an analogizing transfer* of an originally instituted objective sense to a new case, with its anticipative apprehension of the object as having a similar sense. To the extent that there is givenness beforehand, there is such a transfer. At the same time, that sense-component in further experience which proves to be actually new may function in turn as institutive and found a pregivenness that has a richer sense. The child who already sees physical things understands, let us say, for the first time the final sense of scissors; and from now on he sees scissors at the first glance *as* scissors—but naturally not in an explicit reproducing, comparing, and inferring. Yet the manner in which apperceptions arise—and consequently in themselves, by their sense and sense-horizon, point back to their genesis—varies greatly. There are different levels of apperception, corresponding to different layers of objective sense. Ultimately we always get back to the *radical differentiation of apperceptions* into those that, according to their genesis, belong purely to the *primordial sphere* and those that present themselves *with the sense "alter ego"* and, *upon* this sense, have built a new one—thanks to a genesis at a higher level.

§51. "Pairing" as an associatively constitutive component of my experience of someone else.

If we attempt to indicate the peculiar nature of that analogizing apprehension whereby a body within my primordial sphere, being similar to my own animate body, becomes *apprehended as likewise an animate organism*, we encounter: first, the circumstance that here the *primally institutive original* is *always livingly present*, and the primal instituting itself is therefore always going on in a livingly effective manner; secondly, the peculiarity we already know to be necessary, namely that what is *appresented* by virtue of the aforesaid analogizing can never attain actual presence, never become an object of perception proper. Closely connected with the first peculiarity is the circumstance that *ego* and *alter ego* are always and necessarily given *in an original "pairing."*

Pairing, occurrence in configuration as a pair and then as a group, a plurality, is a *universal* phenomenon of the transcendental sphere (and of the parallel sphere of intentional psychology); and, we may add forthwith, as far as a pairing is actually present, so far extends that remarkable kind of primal instituting of an analogizing apprehension—its continuous primal institution in living actuality—which we have already stressed as the first peculiarity of experiencing someone else. Hence it is not exclusively peculiar to this experience.

First of all, let us elucidate the essential nature of any "pairing" (or any forming of a plurality). Pairing is a *primal form of that passive synthesis* which we designate as *"association,"* in contrast to passive synthesis of "identification." In a *pairing association* the characteristic feature is that, in the most primitive case, two data are given intuitively, and with prominence, in the unity of a consciousness and that, on this basis—essentially, already in pure passivity (regardless therefore of whether they are noticed or unnoticed)—as data appearing with mutual distinctness, they *found phenomenologically a unity of similarity* and thus are always constituted precisely as a pair. If there are more than two such data, then a phenomenally unitary group, a plurality, becomes constituted. On more precise analysis we find essentially present here an intentional overreaching, coming about genetically (and by essential necessity) as soon as the data that undergo pairing have become prominent and simultaneously intended; we find, more particularly, a living mutual awakening and an overlaying of each with the objective sense of the other. This overlaying can bring a total or a partial coincidence, which in any particular instance has its degree, the limiting case being that of complete "likeness." As the result of this overlaying, there takes place in the paired data a mutual transfer of sense, that is to say: an apperception of each according to the sense of the other, so far as moments of sense actualized in what is experienced do not annul this transfer, with the consciousness of "different."

In that case of association and apperception which particularly interests us—namely apperception of the alter ego by the ego—pairing first comes about when the Other enters my field of perception. I, as the primordial psychophysical Ego, am always prominent in my primordial field of perception, regardless of whether I pay attention to myself and turn toward myself with some activity or other. In particular, my live body is always there and sensuously prominent; but, in addition to that and likewise with primordial originariness, it is equipped with the specific sense of an animate organism. Now in case there presents itself, as outstanding in my primordial sphere, a body "similar" to mine—that is to say, a body with determinations such that it must enter into a phenomenal *pairing* with mine—it *seems* clear without more ado that, with the transfer of sense, this body must forthwith appropriate from mine the sense: animate organism. But is the apperception actually so transparent? Is it a simple apperception by transfer, like any other? What makes this organism another's, rather than a second organism of my own? Obviously what we designated as the *second fundamental characteristic* of the apperception in question plays a part here: that none of the *appropriated* sense specific to an animate organism can become actualized originarily in my primordial sphere.

§52. Appresentation as a kind of experience with its own style of verification.

But now there arises for us the difficult problem of making it understandable *that such an apperception is possible* and need not be annulled forthwith. How does it happen that, as the fact tells us, the transferred sense is appropriated with existence-status, as a set of "psychic" determinations existing in combination with that body over there, even though they can never show themselves *as* themselves in the domain of originality, belonging to the primordial sphere (which alone is available)?

Let us look at the intentional situation more closely. The appresentation which gives that component of the Other which is not accessible originaliter is combined with an original presentation (of "his" body as part of the Nature given as included in my ownness). In this combination, moreover, the Other's animate body and his governing Ego are given in the manner that characterizes *a unitary transcending experience*. Every experience points to further experiences that would fulfill and verify the appresented horizons, which include, in the form of nonintuitive anticipations, potentially verifiable syntheses of harmonious further experience. Regarding experience of someone else, it is clear that its fulfillingly verifying continuation can ensue *only by means of new appresentations that proceed in a synthetically harmonious fashion*, and only by virtue of the manner in which *these appresentations owe their existence-value to their motivational connection with the changing presentations proper, within my ownness*, that continually appertain to them.

As a suggestive *clue* to the requisite clarification, this proposition may suffice: the experienced animate organism of another continues to prove itself as actually an animate organism, solely in its changing but incessantly *harmonious* "*behavior*." Such *harmonious* behavior (as having a physical side that indicates something psychic appresentatively) must present itself fulfillingly in original experience, and do so throughout the continuous change in behavior from phase to phase. The organism becomes experienced as a pseudo-organism, precisely if there is something discordant about its behavior.

The character of the existent "other" has its basis in this kind of verifiable accessibility of what is not originally accessible. Whatever can become presented, and evidently verified, *originally*—is something *I* am; or else it belongs to me as peculiarly my own. Whatever, by virtue thereof, is experienced in that founded manner which characterizes a primordially unfulfillable experience—an experience that does not give something itself originally but that consistently verifies something indicated is "other." It is therefore conceivable only as an analogue of something included in my peculiar ownness. Because of its sense-constitution it occurs necessarily as an *"intentional modification"* of that Ego of mine which is the first to be Objectivated, or as an intentional modification of my primordial "world": the Other as phenomenologically a "modification" of myself (which, for its part, gets this character of being "my" self by virtue of the contrastive pairing that necessarily takes place). It is clear that, with the other Ego, there is appresented, in an analogizing modification, everything that belongs to his concretion: first, *his* primordial world, and then his fully concrete ego. In other words, *another monad* becomes constituted appresentatively in mine.

Similarly (to draw an instructive comparison), within my ownness and moreover within the sphere of its living present, my past is given only by memory and is characterized in memory *as* my past, a past present—that is: an intentional modification. The experiential verification of it, as a modification, then goes on necessarily in harmonious syntheses of recollection; only thus does a past as such become verified. Somewhat as my memorial past, as a modification of my living present, "transcends" my present, the appresented other being "transcends" my own being (in the pure and most fundamental sense: what is included in my primordial ownness). In both cases the modification is inherent as a sense-component in the sense itself; it is a correlate of the intentionality constituting it. Just as, in my living present, in the domain of "internal perception," my past becomes constituted by virtue of the harmonious memories occurring in this present, so in my primordial sphere, by means of appresentations occurring in it and motivated by its contents, an ego other than mine can become constituted—accordingly, in non-originary presentations of a new type, which have a modificatum of a new kind as their correlate. To be sure, as long as I consider non-originary presentations within the sphere of my ownness, the Ego in whom they center is the one identical I-myself. On the other hand, to everything alien (as long as it remains within the appresented horizon of concreteness that necessarily goes with it) centers in an appresented Ego who is not I myself but, relative to me, a modificatum: an *other* Ego.

An actually sufficient explication of the noematic complexes involved in experience of what is alien—such an explanation as is absolutely necessary to a complete clarification of what this experience does constitutively, by constitutive association—is not yet completed with what has been shown up to now. There is need of a supplement, in order to reach the point where, on the basis of cognitions already acquired, the possibility and scope of a transcendental constitution of the Objective world can become evident and transcendental-phenomenological idealism can thus become entirely manifest.

3

MAX SCHELER
(1874–1928)

The German phenomenologist Max Scheler taught at the universities of Jena, Munich, Berlin, and Cologne. The first philosopher to offer a phenomenological account of ethics, he was also a university lecturer, independent writer, ardent nationalist, political diplomat, pacifist, convert to Catholicism, sociologist of knowledge, lapsed Catholic, and—in his final years—vitalist and quasi-pantheist. He accepted a position at the University of Frankfurt in 1928 and died the same year.

Under the influence of Franz Brentano and Edmund Husserl, Scheler sought to develop an "*a priori* phenomenology of values" in direct contrast to the formalistic ethics of Kant. In his main work, *Formalism in Ethics and Non-Formal Ethics of Values* (1913–1916; 2 vols.), Scheler argued that Kant's inflation of reason at the expense of feeling in ethics overlooks the important sense in which feelings are indispensable conditions for the moral "ought" (*Sollen*). Here Scheler followed Blaise Pascal's famous *logique du coeur* in which "the heart has its own reason which reason does not know," and attempted to show how every human comportment presupposes the experience of values rooted in feeling. These values are like any other phenomena in that they are given to particular acts of consciousness as objects of immediate intuition and belong to the nature of things themselves. His later writings offer rich phenomenological descriptions of various affective states, including resentment (*Ressentiment and Moral Value-Judgment* [1912]), sympathy and love (*The Nature of Sympathy* [1913]), and shame and repentance ("Shame and Feelings of Modesty" [1913] in *Person and Self-Value. Three Essays*). Scheler's conversion to Catholicism (1920) coincided with his extensive phenomenological treatment of religious values (*On the Eternal in Man* [1921]), which he regarded as inherent in every human being. In his final years, Scheler became preoccupied with the natural sciences and anthropology (*Man's Place in Nature* [1928]).

In *Formalism*, from which our selection is taken, Scheler contends that values are rooted in man's order of love ("*ordo amoris*"—Augustine) in which each rank corresponds to particular kinds of feelings. This hierarchical order of "rank among value modalities" is as follows: 1) agreeable values (including use or "technical" values); 2) vital values; 3) spiritual values; 4) holy values. Scheler calls "preferring" a special act that apprehends one value as "higher" than another. If a person prefers X-value (e.g., justice) to Y-value (e.g., sensual pleasure) it is because the difference in rank between the values is immediately evident to consciousness, i.e., prerationally intuitive. This remains the case even though the person might later come to revise his or her judgment in the light of further experience. For Scheler, morality is not included in the rank of values because morality has to do with how well one implements these values in a pure and spontaneous act of preferring.

Select Bibliography of Scheler's Works in English

On the Eternal in Man. Trans. Bernard Noble. Hamden, CT: Archon Books, 1972.

Formalism in Ethics and Non-Formal Ethics of Values. A New Attempt toward a Foundation of an Ethical Personalism. Trans. Manfred S. Frings and Roger L. Funk. Evanston, IL: Northwestern University Press, 1973.

Man's Place in Nature. Trans. Hans Meyerhoff. New York: Farrar, Straus and Giroux, 1981.

The Nature of Sympathy. Trans. Peter Heath. London: Routledge & Kegan Paul, 1954.

Selected Philosophical Essays. Trans. David Lachterman. Evanston, IL: Northwestern University Press, 1973.

Problems of a Sociology of Knowledge. Trans. Manfred S. Frings. London: Routledge & Kegan Paul, 1980.

Person and Self-Value. Three Essays. Trans. Manfred S. Frings. Dordrecht: Martinus Nijhoff, 1987.

Ressentiment. Trans. William W. Holdheim. Milwaukee, WI: Marquette University Press, 1994.

FORMALISM IN ETHICS
AND NONFORMAL ETHICS OF VALUES

In the *totality* of the realm of values there exists a singular order, an *"order of ranks"* that all values possess among themselves. It is because of this that a value is *"higher"* or *"lower"* than another one. This order lies in the *essence* of values themselves, as does the difference between "positive" and "negative" values. It does not belong simply to "values known" by us.[1]

The fact that one value is "higher" than another is apprehended in a special act of value cognition: the act of *preferring*. One must not assume that the height of a value is *"felt"* in the same manner as the value itself, and that the higher value is *subsequently* "preferred" or "placed after." Rather, the height of a value is "given" by virtue of its essence, only *in* the act of preferring. Whenever this is denied, one falsely equates this preferring with *"choosing"* in general, i.e., an act of conation. Without doubt, choosing must be grounded in the cognition of a higher value, for we choose that purpose among others which has its foundation in a higher value. But "preferring" occurs in the absence of all conation, choosing, and willing. For instance, we can say, "I prefer roses to carnations," *without* thinking of a choice. All "choosing" takes place between different deeds. By contrast, preferring also occurs with regard to any of the goods and values. This first kind of preferring (i.e., the preferring between different *goods*) may also be called *empirical* preferring.

On the other hand "preferring" is *a priori* if it occurs between different *values themselves*—independent of "goods." Such preferring always encompasses whole (and indefinitely wide) complexes of goods. He who "prefers" the noble to the agreeable will end up in an (inductive) experience of a *world of goods* very different from the one in which he who does not do so will find himself. The "height of a value" is "given" not "prior" to preferring, but *in* preferring. Hence, whenever we choose an end founded in a lower value, there must exist a *deception of preferring*. But this is not the place to discuss the possibility of such a deception. But one may not say that the "being-higher" of a value only "means" that it is the value "preferred." For if the height of a value is given "in" preferring, this height is nevertheless a relation in the *essence* of the values concerned. Therefore, the *"ordered ranks of values"* are themselves absolutely *invariable*, whereas the "rules of preferring" are, in principle, variable throughout history (a variation which is very different from the apprehension of new values.)

When an act of preferring takes place, it is not necessary that a multiplicity of values be given in feeling, nor is it necessary that such a multiplicity serve as a "foundation" for the act of preferring. . . .

Since all values stand essentially in an order of ranks—i.e., since all values are, in relation to each other, higher or lower—and since these relations are comprehensible only "in" preferring or rejecting them, the "feeling" of values has its foundation, by essential necessity, in "preferring" and "placing after." The feeling of values is by no means a "foundation" for the manner of preferring, as though preferring were "added" to the values comprehended in a primary intention of feeling as only a secondary act. Rather, all *widening* of the value range (e.g., of an individual) takes place only "in" preferring and placing after. Only those values which are originally "given" in these acts can *secondarily* be "felt." Hence, the *structure of preferring and placing after circumscribes* the value qualities that we feel.

Therefore, the order of the ranks of values can *never be deduced or derived*. Which value is "higher" can be comprehended only through the acts of preferring and placing after. There exists here an *intuitive "evidence of preference"* that cannot be replaced by logical deduction.

But we can and must ask whether or not there are *a priori essential interconnections* between the *higher* and *lower levels* of a value and its *other* essential properties.

We can find, in this respect, different characters of values—already to be found in everyday experiences—with which their "height" seems to grow. But these may be traced back to *one* factor.

It appears that values are "higher" the *more* they *endure* and the *less* they partake in "*extension*" and *divisibility*. They are higher the *less they are "founded"* through other values and the "*deeper*" the "*satisfaction*" connected with feeling them. Moreover, they are higher the *less* the feeling of them is *relative* to the *positing* of a specific bearer of "feeling" and "preferring."

1. Since time immemorial, the wisdom of life has been to prefer enduring goods to transient and changing ones. But for philosophy this "wisdom of life" is only a "problem." For if it is a matter of "*goods*," and one understands "*endurance*" in terms of the objective time in which they exist, this proposition makes little sense. "Fire" or "water" or any mechanical accident, for example, can destroy a work of art of the highest value. As Pascal states, a drop of "hot water" can destroy the health and life of the healthiest being; a "brick" can extinguish the light of a genius! . . .

The aforementioned proposition takes on a very different meaning if it is the higher *values* (and not goods) that, in their relation to lower values, are given in "*enduring*" by a phenomenal necessity. "*Endurance*" is, of course, basically an *absolute* and *qualitative phenomenon of time*. It has nothing to do with an absence of "succession." Endurance is, *eo ipso*, a positive mode, i.e., a mode of contents filling time as well as succession.[2] Whatever we may call "enduring" in this sense of the term may be relative (with respect to something else); however, endurance itself is not relative but a phenomenon absolutely different from "succession" (or change). A value is *enduring* through its quality of having the phenomenon of being "able" to exist through time, no matter how long its thing-bearer may exist. "Endurance" already belongs to something of value, in the particular sense of "being of value." This is the case, for instance, when we execute the act of loving a person (on the basis of his personal value)! *The phenomenon of endurance* is implicit in both the *value* to which we are directed and the experienced value of the *act of love*; hence there is also an implicit "*unceasing endurance*" of these values and this act. An inner attitude which would correspond to expressions like "I love you *now*" or "for a certain time" therefore contradicts the essential interconnection concerned. But there *is* this essential interconnection, no matter how long *in practice* love toward a real person may last in a span of objective time. If, on the other hand, this factual quality of the love for a person is in practical experience *not* filled in terms of endurance, so that we "do not any longer love" at a certain time, we tend to say, "I was mistaken; I never loved this person; there were only common interests that I held to be love," or "I was deceived by this person (and his value)." For there belongs to the *essence* of a genuine act of love a *sub specie quadam aeterni*. This shows us, too, that the mere *de facto* endurance of a partnership does not at all prove that love is the bond on which it rests. For a partnership or a bond of interests and habits can last for any length of time—as long as, or longer than, a factual "love between persons." Nevertheless, it lies in the *essence* of a *bond of interests*, as opposed to love and *its* implicit values, i.e., in the essence of such an intention and its own implicit value—namely, the value of usefulness—to be "*transient*." Something sensibly agreeable or its respective "good," which we enjoy, may last for any length of (objective) time. Likewise, the factual *feeling* of the agreeable. But it belongs to the *essence* of this value, as opposed to, say, the value of health, even more to the value of "cognition," to be given "as variable." This variableness is implicit in any act of apprehending the value of agreeableness.

All this becomes clear in considering the qualitatively and basically different *acts* in which we feel values and the very *values* of these experiences.[3] Thus, it lies in the *essence* of "blissfulness" and its opposite, "despair," to *persist* and "endure" throughout the vicissitudes of "happiness" and "unhappiness," no matter how long they may last in *objective* time. Likewise, it lies in the essence of "happiness" and "unhappiness," to persist and endure throughout the vicissitudes of "joy" and "suffering"[4] and in the essence of "joy" and "suffering," in turn, to persist and endure throughout the vicissitudes of (vital) "comfort" and "discomfort." And, again, it lies in the essence of "comfort" and "discomfort" to persist and endure throughout changes in sensible states of well-being and pain. In the very "quality" of these feeling experiences there also lies, by essential necessity, "*endurability*." Whenever, to whomever, and however long they are factually given, they are given as "enduring" or as "varying." Without having to wait for any experience of factual endurance, we experience in them a certain "endurability" and, with this, a certain measure of temporal "extendedness" in our souls, as well as a personal "permeation" by them as belonging to their *essence*.

No doubt, therefore, this "criterion" of the height of a value is of significance. For the lowest values are at the same time essentially the "*most transient*" ones; the highest values, at the same time "*eternal*" ones. And this is quite independent of any empirical "habitability" of mere sensible feeling or similar factors which belong only to psychophysical characteristics of special *bearers*.

But whether or not this "criterion" can also be considered an original criterion for the height of a value is another question.

2. There is also no question about the fact that values are "higher" *the less they are divisible*, that is, the *less* they must be *divided* in *participation by several*. The fact that the participation of several in "material" goods is possible only by dividing these goods (e.g., a piece of cloth, a loaf of bread) has this final *phenomenological* basis: the *values* of the *sensibly agreeable* are clearly *extensive in their essence*, and their felt experiences occur as localized and as extensive in the body.[5] For example, the agreeableness of sweet, etc., is spread over sugar, and the corresponding sensible feeling-state over the "tongue." From this simple phenomenological fact, based on the essence of this kind of value and this particular feeling-state that corresponds to it, it follows that material "*goods*" can only be distributed when they are *divided*, and that their value corresponds to their material extension—to the extent that they are still unformed, i.e., when they are "pure" material goods. Thus a piece of cloth is, more or less, double the *worth* of one half of it. The height of the value conforms in this case to the extension of its bearer. In strict contrast to this there stands a "work of art," for example, which is "indivisible" and of which there is no "piece." It is therefore essentially impossible for one and the same value of the value series of the "sensibly agreeable" to be enjoyed by several beings *without* the division of its bearer and of the value itself. For this reason there are also, in the *essence* of this value modality, "conflicts of interest" relative to the striving for a realization of these values, and relative, to their enjoyment—quite independent of the amount of goods (amount being important only for the socioeconomic value of material goods). This, however, also implies that it belongs to the *essence* of these values to *divide*, not to unite, the individuals who feel them.[6]

The most extreme opposites of these values, the values of the "*holy*," of "*cognition*," and of the "*beautiful*," etc., as well as their corresponding spiritual feeling-states, have a totally different character. There is no participation in extension and divisibility with these values; nor is there any need to divide their bearers if they are to be felt and experienced by any *number* of beings. A work of spiritual culture can be simultaneously apprehended by any number of beings and can be felt and enjoyed in its value. It lies in the essence of values of this kind to be *communicable without limit* and without any division and diminution (even though this proposition seemingly becomes relative by reason of the existence of their bearers and their materiality, by the limits of possible access to these bearers, e.g., in buying books, or the inaccessibility of material bearers of a work of art). Nothing unites beings more immediately and intimately, however, than the common worship and adoration of the "*holy*," which by its nature excludes a "material" bearer, though not a symbolic one. This pertains, first, to the "absolute" and "infinitely holy," the infinitely holy person—the "*divine*." This value, the "divine," is in principle "proper" to any being just because it is the *most indivisible* value. No matter how men have been *divided* by what came to be considered "holy" in history (e.g., wars of religion, denominational quarrels), it lies in the *essence* of the *intention toward the holy* to *unite and join together*. All possible divisions are based solely on *symbols and techniques*, not on the holy *itself*.

Although we are concerned here, as these examples show, with essential interconnections, the question remains whether the criteria of extension and divisibility reveal the basic nature of "higher" and "lower" values.

3. I maintain that a value B is the "*foundation*" of a value A if a certain value A can only be given on the condition of the givenness of a certain value B, and this by virtue of an essential lawful necessity. If this is so, the "founding" value, i.e., the value B, is in each case the "*higher*" value. Thus the value of what is "*useful*" is "founded" in the value of what is "*agreeable*." For the "useful" is the value of something that reveals itself as a "means" to something agreeable, not in terms of a conclusion, but in terms of immediate intuition. . . .

No matter how independent of *spiritual* values (e.g., values of cognition, beauty, etc.) the value series of the *noble* and *vulgar* may be, it remains "founded" in these values. Life *has* these values in fact only insofar as *life* itself (in all its forms) *is* a bearer of values that take on certain heights in an absolutely objective scale. But such an "order of value ranks" is comprehensible only through *spiritual* acts that are not vitally conditioned. For instance, it would be an "anthropomorphism" to consider man the most valuable living being if the value of this value cognition, with *all* its values (including the value of the cognition that "man is the most valuable living being"), were "relative to man." But this proposition is "true," independent of man, "for" man ("for" in the objective sense of the word). *Life simpliciter* has a value, apart from the differentiations among vital value qualities, only insofar as there are spiritual values and spiritual acts through which they are grasped. If values were "relative" to life alone, *life itself would have no value*. It would be a value-indifferent being.

However, *all* possible values are "founded" in the *value of an infinitely personified spirit* and its correlative "*world of values*." Acts which comprehend values comprehend absolutely objective values only if they are executed "*in*" this world of values, and values are absolute values only if they appear in this realm.

4. The "*depth of contentment*," too, is a criterion of the heights of values. This depth accompanies the feeling of a value height. But the height does not *consist* in this depth. Yet it is an essential interconnection that a "*higher* value" yields a "*deeper* contentment."[7] "Contentment" here has nothing to do with *pleasure*, much as "pleasure" may result from it. "Contentment" is an *experience of fulfillment*; it sets in only if an intention toward a value is fulfilled through the appearance of this value. There is no "contentment" *without* the *acceptance* of objective values. . . . But we must distinguish again between the "degree" of contentment and its "*depth*," which alone concerns us here. The contentment in feeling one value is deeper than the contentment in feeling another value if the former proves to be *independent* of the latter while the latter remains dependent on the former. For instance, it is a quite peculiar phenomenon that sensuous enjoyment or a harmlessly trivial delight (e.g., attending a party or going for a walk) will bring us full "contentment" *only* when we feel "content" in the more central sphere of our life, where everything is "serious." It is only against this background of a deeper contentment that a fully content laughter can resound about the most trivial joys. Conversely, if the more central sphere is not content, there arises a "discontentment" and a restless search for *pleasure values* that at once replace a full contentment in feeling the lower values concerned. One can draw a conclusion from this: the many forms of hedonism always reveal a token of "discontentment" with

regard to higher values. There exists a reciprocal relation, then, between the degrees of *searching* for pleasure and the depth of contentment in a value of the value series in question.

Nevertheless, on whatever essential interconnections the above four criteria of value heights may rest, they do not give us the *ultimate* meaning of value heights. Is there another such . . . principle, then, one that can bring us nearer to the meaning of "being-higher," and from which the above criteria may be derived?

5. Whatever "objectivity" and "factual nature" are attributable to all "values," and however *independent* their interrelations may be of the reality and the real connections of goods in which they are real, there is yet another distinguishing element among values that has nothing to do with apriority or aposteriority: this is the *level* of the "*relativity* of values," or their *relationship* to "absolute values."[8]

The basic mutual interconnection between the act and its correlate implies that we must not presuppose any objective existence of values and their types (let alone of real goods that bear values of a certain kind) unless we can find types of acts and functions *belonging* to the experience of such types of values. For instance, for a non-sensible being there are no values of the agreeable. Indeed, such a being may know that "there are sensibly feeling beings," and that "they feel values of the agreeable"; and it may also know the *value* of this fact and its exemplifications. But the *value* of the *agreeable* itself does not exist for such an imaginary creature. We cannot assume that God, like men and animals, has a *lived experience* of all values of the agreeable. In this particular sense I maintain that the values of the agreeable and disagreeable are "*relative*" to a "sensibly feeling being," just as the values of "noble and vulgar" are relative to "living beings" in general. In strict contrast to this, however, I maintain that *absolute values* are those that exist in "pure" feeling (and preferring and loving), i.e., they exist in a type of feeling that is *independent* of the *nature* of sensibility and of life as such. This feeling possesses its own functional characteristics and laws. Among the values belonging to this feeling are *moral* values. In *pure* feeling we may be able to "understand" the feeling of sensible values (i.e., in a feeling manner) without performing sensible feeling-functions through which we (or others) enjoy the agreeable, but we cannot feel them in this manner. From this we infer that God can "understand" pain, for instance, but that he does so without feeling pain.

Such relativity of the being of *kinds* of values has, of course, *nothing* to do with another relativity: that of the *kinds of goods* that are the *bearers* of such values. For kinds of goods are, *in addition*, relative to the special factual psychophysical constitution of the real being that has such goods. The fact that the same object can be poisonous for one species and nutritious for another, for instance, or that something may be agreeable to the perverted drives of one living being and "disagreeable" or "harmful" to the normal drives of another being of the same species, determines only a relativity of values *in relation to* the *goods* in question. But this relativity in no way represents an ontic relativity of the values themselves. It is one of a "second order" only, which has nothing to do with the relativity of the above-mentioned "first order." One cannot reduce this relativity of *kinds* of values to that of goods (*in relation* to kinds of values). Both orders are essentially different. . . .

Taking the words *relative* and *absolute* in *this* sense, I assert it to be an essential interconnection that values given in immediate intuition "*as higher*" are values that are given as *nearer* to *absolute* values *in* feeling and preferring (and not by way of deliberation). Entirely outside the sphere of "judgment" or "deliberation" there is an *immediate* feeling of the "relativity" of a value. And for this feeling the variability of a relative value in comparison with the concomitant constancy of a less "relative" value (no matter if variability and constancy pertain to "endurance," "divisibility," "depth of contentment") is a *confirmation*, but not a *proof*. Thus the value of the cognition of a truth, or the value of the silent beauty of a work of art, has a *phenomenal detachment* from the concomitant feeling of our *life*—above all, from our sensible feeling-states. Such a value is also quite independent of an estimative deliberation about the permanence of such beauty or truth with regard to the "experiences of life," which tend more to detract us from true absolute values than to bring us nearer to them. In living an act of pure love toward a person, the *value* of this person is detached from all simultaneously felt value levels of our own personal world of values when we experience these as connected with our sense and feeling of life. Again, this value is also quite independent of any estimative deliberation about the permanence that an act of pure loving may have through happiness and sorrow, the inherent or accidental fate of life. *Implicit* in the very kind of the given value experience there is a *guarantee* (and not a "conclusion") that there is here an absolute value. This *evidence* of an absolute value stems neither from an estimative deliberation about the permanence it may have in practical life nor from the universality of a judgment which holds that "this value is absolute in *all* moments of our lives." Rather, it is the *felt absoluteness* of this value that makes us feel that a defection from it in favor of other values constitutes "*possible* guilt" as well as a "falling away" from the height of value experience which we had just reached. . . .

A *Priori* Relations of Rank among Value Modalities

The most important and most fundamental *a priori* relations obtain as an *order of ranks* among the systems of qualities of nonformal values which we call *value modalities*. They constitute the *nonformal a priori* proper in the intuition of values and the intuition of preferences. . . . The ultimate divisions of value qualities that are presupposed for these essential interconnections must be as independent of all factual goods and the special organizations of living beings that feel values as is the order of the ranks of the value modalities.

Rather than giving a full development and establishment of these systems of qualities and their implicit laws of preferring, the following presents an explanation through examples of the kinds of *a priori* orders of ranks among values.

1. The values ranging from *the agreeable to the disagreeable* represent a sharply delineated value modality. The function of *sensible feeling* (with its modes of enjoying and suffering) is correlative to this modality. The respective feeling-states, the so-called feelings of sensation, are pleasure and pain. As in all value modalities, there are values of things, . . . values of *feeling-functions*, and values of *feeling-states*.

This modality is "*relative*" to beings endowed with sensibility in general. But it is relative *neither* to a specific species, e.g., man, *nor* to specific things or events of the real world that are "agreeable" or "disagreeable" to a being of a particular species. Although one type of event may be agreeable to one man and disagreeable to another (or agreeable and disagreeable to different animals), the difference between the values of agreeable and disagreeable as such is an *absolute* difference, clearly given prior to any cognition of things.

The proposition that the agreeable is preferable to the disagreeable (*ceteris paribus*) is not based on observation and induction. The preference lies in the essential contents of these values as well as in the nature of sensible feelings. If a traveler or a historian or a zoologist were to tell us that this preference is reversed in a certain kind of animal, we would "*a priori*" disbelieve his story. We would say that this is impossible unless it is only *things* different from ours that this animal feels are disagreeable and agreeable, or unless its preferring the disagreeable to the agreeable is based on a value of a *modality* (perhaps unknown to us) that is "higher" than that of the agreeable and the disagreeable. In the latter case the animal would only "put up with" the disagreeable in preferring the value for the extra modality. There may also be cases of perverted drives in this animal, allowing it to experience as agreeable those things that are *detrimental* to life. The state of affairs in all of these examples, as well as that which our proposition expresses, namely, that the agreeable is preferable to the disagreeable, also serves as a *law of understanding* external expressions of life and concrete (e.g., historical) valuation (even one's *own*, e.g., in remembering); our proposition is a *presupposition* of all observation and induction, and it is "*a priori*" to all ethnological experience.

Nor can this proposition and its respective facts be "explained" by way of evolutionary theories. It is nonsense to say that values (and their laws of preference) "developed" as *signs* of kinetic combinations that proved purposeful for the individual or its species. Such a theory can explain only the accompanying feeling-*states* that are connected with impulsive actions directed toward things. But the *values themselves* and their *laws* of *preferring* could *never* be thus explained. For the latter are independent of all specific organizations of living beings.

Certain groups of consecutive values (technical values[9] and symbolic values) correspond to these self values of the modality of the agreeable and the disagreeable. But they do not concern us here.

2. The essence of values correlated to *vital feeling* differs sharply from the above modality. Its thing values, insofar as they are self values, are such qualities as those encompassed by the "*noble*" and the "*vulgar*" (and by the "good" in the pregnant sense of "excellent" as opposed to "bad" rather than "evil").[10] All corresponding consecutive values (technical and symbolic) belong to the sphere denoted by "*weal*," or "*well-being*."[11] They are *subordinated* to the noble and its opposite. The feeling-states of this modality include all modes of the feelings of life (e.g., the feelings of "quickening" and "declining" life, the feelings of health and illness, the feeling of aging and oncoming death, the feelings of "weakness," "strength," etc.). Certain emotional reactions also belong to this modality—(a certain kind of) "being glad about" or "being sad about," drive reactions such as "courage," "anxiety," revengeful impulses, ire, etc. Here we cannot even indicate the tremendous richness of these value qualities and their correlates.

Vital values form an entirely *original* modality. They cannot be "reduced" to the values of the agreeable and the useful, nor can they be reduced to spiritual values. Previous ethical theories made a *basic* mistake in ignoring this fact. . . .

The particular character of this modality lies in the fact that "*life*" is a *genuine essence* and not an "empirical generic conception" that contains only "common properties" of all living organisms. When this fact is misconceived, the uniqueness of vital values is overlooked. We will not go into this in further detail here.

3. The realm of *spiritual values* is distinct from that of vital values as an original modal unity. In the kind of their *givenness*, spiritual values have a peculiar detachment from and independence of the spheres of the lived body and the environment. Their unity reveals itself in the clear evidence that vital values "ought" to be sacrificed for them. The functions and acts in which they are apprehended are functions of *spiritual* feeling and acts of *spiritual* preferring, loving, and hating. They are set off from like-named *vital* functions and acts by pure phenomenological evidence as well as by their *own proper lawfulness* (which *cannot be reduced* to any "biological" lawfulness).

The main types of spiritual values are the following: (1) the values of "*beautiful*" and "*ugly*," together with the whole range of purely aesthetic values; (2) the values of "*right*" and "*wrong*," . . . objects that are "values" and wholly different from what is "correct" and "incorrect" according to a law, which form the ultimate phenomenal basis of the idea of the objective *order of right*, . . . an order that is independent of the idea of "law," the idea of the state, and the idea of the life-community on which the state rests (it is especially independent of all positive legislation);[12] (3) the values of the "*pure cognition of truth*," whose realization is sought in *philosophy* (in contrast to positive "science," which is guided by the aim of controlling natural appearances).[13] Hence "*values of science*" are consecutive values of the values of the cognition of truth. So-called *cultural values* in general are the consecutive (technical and symbolic) values of *spiritual* values and belong to the value sphere of *goods* (e.g., art treasures, scientific institutions, positive legislation, etc.). The correlative feeling-states of spiritual values—for instance, the feeling-states of spiritual joy and sorrow (as opposed to the vital "being gay" and "not being gay")—possess the phenomenal quality of appearing *without mediation*. That is to say, they do not appear on an "ego" as its states, nor does an antecedent givenness of the lived body of a person serve as a condition of their appearance. Spiritual feeling-states vary *independent* of changes in vital feeling-states (and, of course, sensible feeling-states). Their variations are directly dependent upon the variations of the values of the *objects themselves* and occur according to their own proper laws.

Finally, there are the reactions belonging to this modality, including "pleasing" and "displeasing," "approving" and "disapproving," "respect" and "disrespect," "retributive conation" (as opposed to the vital impulses of revenge) and "spiritual sympathy" (which is the foundation of friendship, for instance).

4. Values of the last modality are those of the *holy* and the *unholy*. This modality differs sharply from the above modalities. It forms a unit of value qualities not subject to further definition. Nevertheless, these values have *one* very definite condition of intention as "absolute objects." This expression, however, refers *not* to a specific or definable *class* of objects, but (in principle) to *any* object given in the "absolute sphere." Again, this modality is quite independent of all that has been considered "holy" by different peoples at various times, such as holy things, powers, persons, institutions, and the like (i.e., from ideas of fetishism to the purest conceptions of God). These latter problems do not belong to an *a priori phenomenology of values* . . . and the theory of ordered ranks of values.[14] They concern the *positive representations of goods* within this value sphere. With regard to the values of the holy, however, *all* other values are at the same time given as symbols for these values.

The feeling-states belonging to this modality range from "blissfulness" to "despair"; they are independent of "happiness" and "unhappiness," whether it be in occurrence, duration, or change. In a certain sense these feeling-states indicate the "nearness" or the "remoteness" of the divine in experience.

"Faith" and "lack of faith," "awe," "adoration," and analogous attitudes are specific reactions in this modality.

However, the act through which we *originally* apprehend the value of the holy is an act of a specific kind of *love* (whose value direction *precedes* and *determines* all pictorial representations and concepts of holy objects); that is to say, in essence the act is directed toward persons, or toward something of the *form of a personal being, no matter what* content or what "*conception*" of a personhood is implied. The self value in the sphere of the values of the "holy" is therefore, by essential necessity, a "*value of the person.*"

The values of things and forms of worship implicit in cults and sacraments are consecutive values (technical and symbolic) of all holy values of the person. They represent genuine "symbolic values," not mere "symbols of values."

Notes

1. On the other hand, one cannot reduce this division to one of positive and negative values or to one of "greater" and "smaller" values. Brentano's axiom that a value which is the sum of the values W1 and W2 must be a higher value (a value to be preferred, according to his definition), than W1 or W2 is not an autonomous value proposition but only the application of an arithmetic proposition to values, indeed, only to symbols of values. It cannot be that a value is "higher" than another simply because it is a sum of values. For it is characteristic of the contrast between "higher" and "lower" values that an infinite magnitude of a value, say, the agreeable (or the disagreeable), never yields any magnitude of, say, the noble (or the base) or of a spiritual value (of cognition, for instance). The *sum* of values is to be preferred to single values; but it is an error on Brentano's part to assume that the higher value is in this case to be identified with the one to be "preferred." For preferring is (essentially) the *access* to the "higher value," but in individual cases it is subject to "deception." Besides, the "greater value" in this case pertains only to the act of "choosing," not to the act of "preferring." For the act of preferring always takes place in the sphere of a value series that has a specific "position" in the order of values. Finally, I cannot

agree with Brentano when he leaves it up to *historical relativity* to determine what the nonformal ranks of values actually are, when, for instance, he does not wish to decide (see the notes to his *Vom Ursprung sittlicher Erkenntnis*) whether an "act of cognition" is of higher value than an "act of noble love" (as Aristotle and the Greeks held) or whether the opposite is the case (as the Christians held), in other words, when he does not make a decision on the basis of the nonformal values themselves.

2. It is false to maintain, as, e.g., David Hume does, that time belongs only to a "succession" of different contents, i.e., to assume that if the world consisted of only one and the same content, there would be no *time*, and that "duration" therefore consists only in the relation of two successions of different speeds. "Duration" is no mere difference of succession but a positive quality that can be intuited without any appearance of succession.

3. The experience of values and the value of this experience are, of course, to be distinguished.

4. Taken as phenomenological unities.

5. Extensive does not mean "in a spatial order" or "measurable." A pain in the leg or a sensible feeling is, according to its nature, localized and extensive, but is in no way ordered spatially or "in" space.

6. "Cofeeling" is least possible in feeling these values. It is not possible to cofeel a sensible pleasure as one can a joy, or to cofeel a pain (in the strict sense) as one can a sorrow. See *The Nature of Sympathy*, trans. Peter Heath (London: Routledge & Kegan Paul, 1954).

7. H. Cornelius, *Einleitung in die Philosophie* (Leipzig: Teubner, 1911), has attempted a subtle reduction of the higher value to the value of deeper contentment.

8. Because a "relative" value is relative does not mean that it is a "subjective" value. For instance, a hallucinated body-thing is "relative" to an individual, yet this object is not "subjective" in the way that feeling is. An emotive hallucination, for example, is *both* "subjective" and "relative" to the individual. And a "real" feeling is "subjective," but not "relative," to an individual even when only the individual concerned has access to the cognition of its reality. On the other hand a mirror image, as a physical phenomenon, is "relative" to the mirror and the mirrored object, but is not relative to the individual.

9. They are in part technical values concerning the *production* of agreeable things and are unified in the concept of the "useful" (*values of civilization*), and in part values concerning the enjoyment of agreeable things (*luxury values*).

10. One also uses "noble" and its opposite with respect to vital values ("noble horse," "noble tree," "noble race," "nobility," etc.).

11. "Weal" and "well-being" therefore do not coincide with vital values in general; the value of well-being is determined by the extent to which the individual or the community, which can be in a good or a bad state, is *noble* or *base*. On the other hand, "weal" is superior as a vital value to mere "usefulness" (and "agreeableness"), and the well-being of a community is superior to the sum of its interests (as a society).

12. "Law" is only a consecutive value for the self value of the "order of right"; positive law (of a state) is the consecutive value for the (objective) "order of right" which is valid in the state and which lawmakers *and* judges must realize.

13. We speak of the value of "cognition," not of the value of "truth." Truth does *not* belong among the values.

14. Thus, e.g., an oath is an affirmation and a promise with reference to the value of the holy, no matter what is holy to the man concerned, no matter by what he swears.

4

MARTIN HEIDEGGER
(1889–1976)

The German philosopher Martin Heidegger studied theology, mathematics, and philosophy at the University of Freiburg, where he obtained his Ph.D. in 1914. Seven years earlier, when he was only a seventeen-year-old high school student, Heidegger was presented with Brentano's dissertation "On the Manifold Meaning of Being according to Aristotle." The work had a decisive impact on Heidegger and stimulated his first foray into the question that would constitute his lifelong preoccupation: "the question of Being" (*Seinsfrage*). Heidegger was also heavily influenced by the phenomenological method of his mentor, Husserl, to whose chair at the University of Freiburg he succeeded in 1928. In 1933, Heidegger became the first Nazi rector of the university, a political compromise that was to impede the reception of his work and embarrass his followers to this day. In 1945, he was barred from university teaching by the Allies for his support of the Nazis. He was reinstated as an ordinary emeritus professor at Freiburg in 1951, and spent the rest of his life in relative seclusion working on his *Seinsfrage*. He died in his birth town of Messkirch in 1976.

Heidegger's monumental work *Being and Time* (1927) is widely regarded as one of the most important philosophical treatises of the twentieth century. It sets out to raise anew the question of the meaning of Being—a question Heidegger claimed was the guiding question for the ancient Greeks, but which, since Plato and Aristotle, "has been forgotten." For Heidegger such an inquiry is called "fundamental ontology" and gains its urgency from the crises in the basic concepts of the sciences (e.g., biology and its inability to define "life"). Part Two of *Being and Time* was never completed as Heidegger found himself constrained by metaphysical language, which was not adequate to the task at hand. This led in the mid-thirties to the famous "turning" (*Kehre*) to the question of language and the limits of ontological conceptuality in an effort to think beyond the tradition. Heidegger thus embarked on what he called a "*Destruktion*" of the history of ontology, which had failed to attend to the difference between beings (*Seiendes*) and Being (*Sein*). For Heidegger, this history comprised several epochs: early Greek thinking, Platonic-Aristotelian philosophy, medieval philosophy, and modernity inaugurated by Descartes and culminating in the age of technological nihilism in which Being is reduced to pure objectivity and presence. The fruits of this labor were harvested in various publications and lecture courses, among the most important of which are *Kant and the Problem of Metaphysics* (1929), "The Origin of the Work of Art" (1935), *Introduction to Metaphysics* (1935), "Letter on 'Humanism'" (1947; see Chapter 10 below), "The Question Concerning Technology" (1954), *On the Way to Language* (1959), and Heidegger's last major essay, "The End of Philosophy and the Task of Thinking" (1966).

Our selection from *Being and Time* on "Being-with" belongs to Heidegger's preliminary project of elaborating an "existential analytic of *Dasein*." *Dasein*, which in German literally means "there-being," is the term that Heidegger reserves for the unique mode of existence characteristic of human beings. Human beings are distinctive inasmuch as they live in an understanding of Being. The interpretive structures that apply to them are thus not "categories," which pertain to mere things, but rather are what Heidegger calls "existentialia," which includes Being-with (*Mitsein*). Accordingly, *Dasein* is never an isolated Cartesian "subject" which has to build an "ontological bridge" to relate to others (the so-called problem of other minds). Even when physically alone, *Dasein* encounters things environmentally in a "world" or meaningful context that is shared with other *Daseins*. The significance of this fact of original sociality cannot be overestimated for understanding Heidegger's famous description of the Being of Dasein as "care"—which includes a concern for human beings that he calls "solicitude" (*Fürsorge*).

Select Bibliography of Heidegger's Works in English

An Introduction to Metaphysics. Trans. Ralph Manheim. Garland City, NY: Doubleday, 1961.
Being and Time. Trans. John Macquarrie and Edward Robinson. Oxford: Blackwell, 1987.
Discourse on Thinking. Trans. John M. Anderson and E. Hans Freund. New York: Harper and Row, 1966.
Identity and Difference. Trans. Joan Stambaugh. New York: Harper and Row, 1969.
Martin Heidegger: Basic Writings. Ed. David Farrell Krell. New York: Harper San Francisco, 1993.
On the Way to Language. Trans. Peter D. Hertz. San Francisco: Harper and Row, 1982.
Pathmarks. Ed. William McNeill. Cambridge: Cambridge University Press, 1998.
Poetry, Language, Thought. Trans. Albert Hofstadter. New York: Harper and Row, 1975.
The Question Concerning Technology, and Other Essays. Trans. William Lovitt. New York: Harper and Row, 1975.
What Is Called Thinking? Trans. J. Glenn Gray. New York: Harper and Row, 1972.

BEING AND TIME

§26. The Dasein-with of Others and everyday Being-with.

The answer to the question of the "who" of everyday Dasein is to be obtained by analyzing that kind of Being in which Dasein maintains itself proximally and for the most part. Our investigation takes its orientation from Being-in-the-world—that basic state of Dasein by which every mode of its Being gets co-determined. If we are correct in saying that by the foregoing explication of the world, the remaining structural items of Being-in-the-world have become visible, then this must also have prepared us, in a way, for answering the question of the "who."

In our "description" of that environment which is closest to us—the work-world of the craftsman, for example—the outcome was that along with the equipment to be found when one is at work, those Others for whom the "work" is destined are "encountered too." If this is ready-to-hand, then there lies in the kind of Being which belongs to it (that is, in its involvement) an essential assignment or reference to possible wearers, for instance, for whom it should be "cut to the figure." Similarly, when material is put to use, we encounter its producer or "supplier" as one who "serves" well or badly. When, for example, we walk along the edge of a field but "outside it," the field shows itself as belonging to such-and-such a person, and decently kept up by him; the book we have used was bought at So-and-so's shop and given by such-and-such a person, and so forth.

The boat anchored at the shore is assigned in its Being-in-itself to an acquaintance who undertakes voyages with it; but even if it is a "boat which is strange to us," it still is indicative of Others. The Others who are thus "encountered" in a ready-to-hand, environmental context of equipment, are not somehow added on in thought to some Thing which is proximally just present-at-hand; such "Things" are encountered from out of the world in which they are ready-to-hand for Others—a world which is always mine too in advance. In our previous analysis, the range of what is encountered within-the-world was, in the first instance, narrowed down to equipment ready-to-hand or Nature present-at-hand, and thus to entities with a character other than that of Dasein. This restriction was necessary not only for the purpose of simplifying our explication but above all because the kind of Being which belongs to the Dasein of Others, as we encounter it within-the-world, differs from readiness-to-hand and presence-at-hand. Thus Dasein's world frees entities which not only are quite distinct from equipment and Things, but which also—in accordance with their kind of Being *as Dasein* themselves—are "in" the world in which they are at the same time encountered within-the-world, and are "in" it by way of Being-in-the-world. These entities are neither present-at-hand nor ready-to-hand; on the contrary, they are *like* the very Dasein which frees them, in that *they are there too, and there with it*. So if one should want to identify the world in general with entities within-the-world, one would have to say that Dasein too is "world."

Thus in characterizing the encountering of Others, one is again still oriented by that Dasein which is in each case one's *own*. But even in this characterization does one not start by marking out and isolating the "I" so that one must then seek some way of getting over to the Others from this isolated subject? To avoid this misunderstanding we must notice in what sense we are talking about "the Others." By "Others" we do not mean everyone else but me—those over against whom the "I" stands out. They are rather those from whom, for the most part, one does *not* distinguish oneself—those among whom one is too. This Being-there-too with them does not have the ontological character of a Being-present at-hand-along-"with" them within a world. This "with" is something of the character of Dasein; the "too" means a sameness of Being as circumspectively concernful Being-in-the-world. "With" and "too" are to be understood *existentially*, not categorially. By reason of this *with-like* Being-in-the-world, the world is always the one that I share with Others. The world of Dasein is a *with-world* [*Mitwelt*]. Being-in is *Being-with* [*Mitsein*] Others. Their Being-in-themselves within-the-world is Dasein-with [*Mitdasein*].

When Others are encountered, it is not the case that one's own subject is *proximally* present-at-hand and that the rest of the subjects, which are likewise occurrents, get discriminated beforehand and then apprehended; nor are they encountered by a primary act of looking at oneself in such a way that the opposite pole of a distinction first gets ascertained. They are encountered from out of the *world*, in which concernfully circumspective Dasein essentially dwells. Theoretically concocted "explanations" of the Being-present-at-hand of Others urge themselves upon us all too easily; but over against such explanations we must hold fast to the phenomenal facts of the case which we have pointed out, namely, that Others are encountered *environmentally*. This elemental worldly kind of encountering, which belongs to Dasein and is closest to it, goes so far that even one's *own* Dasein becomes something that it can itself proximally "come across" only when it *looks away* from "Experiences" and the "center of its actions," or does not as yet "see" them at all. Dasein finds "itself" proximally in *what* it does, uses, expects, avoids—in those things environmentally ready-to-hand with which it is proximally *concerned*.

And even when Dasein explicitly addresses itself as "I here," this locative personal designation must be understood in terms of Dasein's existential spatiality. In Interpreting this we have already intimated that this "I-here" does not mean a certain privileged point—that of an I-Thing—but is to be understood as Being-in in terms of the "yonder" of the world that is ready-to-hand—the "yonder" which is the dwelling-place of Dasein as *concern*.

W. von Humboldt[1] has alluded to certain languages which express the "I" by "here," the "thou" by "there," the "he" by "yonder," thus rendering the personal pronouns by locative adverbs, to put it grammatically. It is controversial whether indeed the primordial signification of locative expressions is adverbial or pronominal. But this dispute loses its basis if one notes that locative adverbs have a relationship to the "I" *qua* Dasein. The "here" and the "there" and the "yonder" are primarily not mere ways of designating the location of entities present-at-hand within-the-world at positions in space; they are rather characteristics of Dasein's primordial spatiality. These supposedly locative adverbs are Dasein-designations; they have a signification which is primarily existential, not categorial. But they are not pronouns either; their signification is prior to the differentiation of locative adverbs and personal pronouns: these expressions have a Dasein-signification which is authentically spatial, and which serves as evidence that when we interpret Dasein without any theoretical distortions we can see it immediately as "Being-alongside" the world with which it concerns itself, and as Being-alongside it spatially—that is to say, as desevering and giving directionality. In the "here," the Dasein which is absorbed in its world speaks not towards itself but away from itself towards the "yonder" of something circumspectively ready-to-hand; yet it still has *itself* in view in its existential spatiality. Dasein understands itself proximally and for the most part in terms of its world; and the Dasein-with of Others is often encountered in terms of what is ready-to-hand within-the-world. But even if Others become themes for study, as it were, in their own Dasein, they are not encountered as person-Things present-at-hand: we meet them "at work," that is, primarily in their Being-in-the-world. Even if we see the Other "just standing around," he is never apprehended as a human-Thing present-at-hand, but his "standing-around" is an existential mode of Being—an unconcerned, uncircumspective tarrying alongside everything and nothing. The Other is encountered in his Dasein-with in the world.

The expression "Dasein," however, shows plainly that "in the first instance" this entity is unrelated to Others, and that of course it can still be "with" Others afterwards. Yet one must not fail to notice that we use the term "Dasein-with" to designate that Being for which the Others who are [*die seienden Anderen*] are freed within-the-world. This Dasein-with of the Others is disclosed within-the-world for a Dasein, and so too for those who are Daseins with us, only because Dasein in itself is essentially Being-with. The phenomenological assertion that "Dasein is essentially Being-with" has an existential-ontological meaning. It does not seek to establish ontically that factically I am not present-at-hand alone, and that Others of my kind occur. If this were what is meant by the proposition that Dasein's Being-in-the-world is essentially constituted by Being-with, then Being-with would not be an existential attribute which Dasein, of its own accord, has coming to it from its own kind of Being. It would rather be something which turns up in every case by reason of the occurrence of Others. Being-with is an existential characteristic of Dasein even when factically no Other is present-at-hand or perceived. Even Dasein's Being-alone is Being-with in the world. The Other can *be missing* only *in* and *for* a Being-with. Being-alone is a deficient mode of Being-with; its very possibility is the proof of this. On the other hand, factical Being-alone is not obviated by the occurrence of a second example of a human being "beside" me, or by ten such examples. Even if these and more are present-at-hand, Dasein can still be alone. So Being-with and the facticity of Being with one another are not based on the occurrence together of several "subjects." Yet Being-alone "among" many does not mean that with regard to their Being they are merely present-at-hand there alongside us. Even in our Being "among them" they are *there with* us; their Dasein-with is encountered in a mode in which they are indifferent and alien. Being missing and "Being away" are modes of Dasein-with, and are possible only because Dasein as Being-with lets the Dasein of Others be encountered in its world. Being-with is in every case a characteristic of one's own Dasein; Dasein-with characterizes the Dasein of Others to the extent that it is freed by its world for a Being-with. Only so far as one's own Dasein has the essential structure of Being-with, is it Dasein-with as encounterable for Others.

If Dasein-with remains existentially constitutive for Being-in-the-world, then, like our circumspective dealings with the ready-to-hand within-the-world (which, by way of anticipation, we have called "concern"), it must be Interpreted in terms of the phenomenon of *care*; for as "care" the Being of Dasein in general is to be defined. Concern is a character-of-Being which Being-with cannot have as its own, even though Being-with, like concern, is a *Being towards* entities encountered within-the-world. But those entities towards which Dasein as Being-with comports itself do not have the kind of Being which belongs to equipment ready-to-hand; they are themselves Dasein. These entities are not objects of concern, but rather of *solicitude*.

Even "concern" with food and clothing, and the nursing of the sick body, are forms of solicitude. But we understand the expression "solicitude" in a way which corresponds to our use of "concern" as a term for an *existentiale*. For example, "welfare work," as a factical social arrangement, is grounded in Dasein's state of Being as Being-with. Its factical urgency gets its motivation in that Dasein maintains itself proximally and for the most part in the deficient modes of solicitude. Being for, against, or without one another, passing one another by, not "mattering" to one another—these are possible ways of solicitude. And it is precisely these last-named deficient and Indifferent modes that characterize everyday, average Being-with-one-another. These modes of Being show again the characteristics of inconspicuousness and obviousness which belong just as much to the everyday Dasein-with of Others within-the-world as to the readiness-to-hand of the equipment with which one is daily concerned.

These Indifferent modes of Being-with-one-another may easily mislead ontological Interpretation into interpreting this kind of Being, in the first instance, as the mere Being-present-at-hand of several subjects. It seems as if only negligible variations of the same kind of Being lie before us; yet ontologically there is an essential distinction between the "indifferent" way in which Things at random occur together and the way in which entities who are with one another do not "matter" to one another.

With regard to its positive modes, solicitude has two extreme possibilities. It can, as it were, take away "care" from the Other and put itself in his position in concern: it can *leap in* for him. This kind of solicitude takes over for the Other that with which he is to concern himself. The Other is thus thrown out of his own position; he steps back so that afterwards, when the matter has been attended to, he can either take it over as something finished and at his disposal, or disburden himself of it completely. In such solicitude the Other can become one who is dominated and dependent, even if this domination is a tacit one and remains hidden from him. This kind of solicitude, which leaps in and takes away "care," is to a large extent determinative for Being with one another, and pertains for the most part to our concern with the ready-to-hand.

In contrast to this, there is also the possibility of a kind of solicitude which does not so much leap in for the Other as *leap ahead* of him in his existentiell potentiality-for-Being, not in order to take away his "care" but rather to give it back to him authentically as such for the first time. This kind of solicitude pertains essentially to authentic care—that is, to the existence of the Other, not to a "*what*" with which he is concerned; it helps the Other to become transparent to himself *in* his care and to become *free for* it.

Solicitude proves to be a state of Dasein's Being—one which, in accordance with its different possibilities, is bound up with its Being towards the world of its concern, and likewise with its authentic Being towards itself. Being with one another is based proximally and often exclusively upon what is a matter of common concern in such Being. A Being-with-one-another which arises from one's doing the same thing as someone else, not only keeps for the most part within the outer limits, but enters the mode of distance and reserve. The Being-with-one-another of those who are hired for the same affair often thrives only on mistrust. On the other hand, when they devote themselves to the same affair in common, their doing so is determined by the manner in which their Dasein, each in its own way, has been taken hold of. They thus become *authentically* bound together, and this makes possible the right kind of objectivity, which frees the Other in his freedom for himself.

Everyday Being-with-one-another maintains itself between the two extremes of positive solicitude—that which leaps in and dominates, and that which leaps forth and liberates. It brings numerous mixed forms to maturity; to describe these and classify them would take us beyond the limits of this investigation.

Just as *circumspection* belongs to concern as a way of discovering what is ready-to-hand, solicitude is guided by *considerateness* and *forbearance*. Like solicitude, these can range through their respective deficient and Indifferent modes up to the point of *inconsiderateness* or the perfunctoriness for which indifference leads the way.

The world not only frees the ready-to-hand as entities encountered within-the-world; it also frees Dasein, and the Others in their Dasein with. But Dasein's ownmost meaning of Being is such that this entity (which has been freed environmentally) is Being-in in the same world in which, as encounterable for Others, it is there with them. We have interpreted worldhood as that referential totality which constitutes significance. In Being-familiar with this significance and previously understanding it, Dasein lets what is ready-to-hand be encountered as discovered in its involvement. In Dasein's Being, the context of references or assignments which significance implies is tied up with Dasein's ownmost Being—a Being which essentially can have no involvement, but which is rather that Being *for the sake of which* Dasein itself is as it is.

According to the analysis which we have now completed, Being with Others belongs to the Being of Dasein, which is an issue for Dasein in its very Being. Thus as Being-with, Dasein "is" essentially for the sake of Others. This must be understood as an existential statement as to its essence. Even if the particular factical Dasein does *not* turn to Others, and supposes that it has no need of them or manages to get along without them, it *is* in the way of Being-with. In Being-with, as the existential "for-the-sake-of" of Others, these have already been disclosed in their Dasein. With their Being-with, their disclosedness has been constituted beforehand; accordingly, this disclosedness also goes to make up significance—that is to say, worldhood. And, significance, as worldhood, is tied up with the existential "for-the-sake-of-which." Since the worldhood of that world in which every Dasein essentially is already, is thus constituted, it accordingly lets us encounter what is environmentally ready-to-hand as something with which we are circumspectively concerned, and it does so in such a way that together with it we encounter the Dasein-with of Others. The structure of the world's worldhood is such that Others are not proximally present-at-hand as free-floating subjects along with other Things, but show themselves in the world in their special environmental Being, and do so in terms of what is ready-to-hand in that world.

Being-with is such that the disclosedness of the Dasein-with of Others belongs to it; this means that because Dasein's Being is Being-with, its understanding of Being already implies the understanding of Others. This understanding, like any understanding, is not an acquaintance derived from knowledge about them, but a primordially existential kind of Being, which, more than anything else, makes such knowledge and acquaintance possible. Knowing oneself is grounded in Being-with, which understands primordially. It operates proximally in accordance with the kind of Being which is closest to us—Being-in-the-world as Being-with; and it does so by an acquaintance with that which Dasein, along with the Others, comes across in its environmental circumspection and concerns itself with—an acquaintance in which Dasein understands. Solicitous concern is understood in terms of what we are concerned with, and along with our understanding of it. Thus in concernful solicitude the Other is proximally disclosed.

But because solicitude dwells proximally and for the most part in the deficient or at least the Indifferent modes (in the indifference of passing one another by), the kind of knowing-oneself which is essential and closest, demands that one become acquainted with oneself. And when, indeed, one's knowing-oneself gets lost in such ways as aloofness, hiding oneself away, or putting on a disguise, Being-with-one-another must follow special routes of its own in order to come close to Others, or even to "see through them."

But just as opening oneself up or closing oneself off is grounded in one's having Being-with-one-another as one's kind of Being at the time, and indeed *is* nothing else but this, even the explicit disclosure of the Other in solicitude grows only out of one's primarily Being with him in each case. Such a disclosure of the Other (which is indeed thematic, but not in the manner of theoretical psychology) easily becomes the phenomenon which proximally comes to view when one considers the theoretical problematic of understanding the "psychical life of Others." In this phenomenally "proximal" manner it thus presents a way of Being with one another understandingly; but at the same time it gets taken as that which, primordially and "in the beginning," constitutes Being towards Others and makes it possible at all. This phenomenon, which is none too happily designated as *"empathy"* (*"Einfühlung"*), is then supposed, as it were, to provide the first ontological bridge from one's own subject, which is given proximally as alone, to the other subject, which is proximally quite closed off.

Of course Being towards Others is ontologically different from Being towards Things which are present-at-hand. The entity which is "other" has itself the same kind of Being as Dasein. In Being with and towards Others, there is thus a relationship of Being from Dasein to Dasein. But it might be said that this relationship is already constitutive for one's own Dasein, which, in its own right, has an understanding of Being, and which thus relates itself towards Dasein. The relationship-of-Being which one has towards Others would then become a Projection of one's own Being-towards-oneself "into something else." The Other would be a duplicate of the Self.

But while these deliberations seem obvious enough, it is easy to see that they have little ground to stand on. The presupposition which this argument demands—that Dasein's Being towards an Other is its Being toward itself—fails to hold. As long as the legitimacy of this presupposition has not turned out to be evident, one may still be puzzled as to how Dasein's relationship to itself is thus to be disclosed to the Other as Other.

Not only is Being towards Others an autonomous, irreducible relationship of Being: this relationship, as Being-with, is one which, with Dasein's Being, already is. Of course it is indisputable that a lively mutual acquaintanceship on the basis of Being-with often depends upon how far one's own Dasein has understood itself at the time; but this means that it depends only upon how far one's essential Being with Others has made itself transparent and has not disguised itself. And that is possible only if Dasein, as Being-in-the-world, already is with Others. "Empathy" does not first constitute Being-with; only on the basis of Being-with does "empathy" become possible: it gets its motivation from the unsociability of the dominant modes of Being-with.

But the fact that "empathy" is not a primordial existential phenomenon, any more than is knowing in general, does not mean that there is nothing problematical about it. The special hermeneutic of empathy will have to show how Being-with-one-another and Dasein's knowing of itself are led astray and obstructed by the various possibilities of Being which Dasein itself possesses, so that a genuine "understanding" gets suppressed, and Dasein takes refuge in substitutes; the possibility of understanding the stranger correctly presupposes such a hermeneutic as its positive existential condition. Our analysis has shown that Being-with is an existential constituent of Being-in-the-world. Dasein-with has proved to be a kind of Being which entities encountered within-the-world have as their own. So far as Dasein *is* at all, it has Being-with-one-another as its kind of Being. This cannot be conceived as a summative result of the occurrence of several "subjects." Even to come across a number of "subjects" becomes possible only if the Others who are concerned proximally in their Dasein-with are treated merely as numerals. Such a number of "subjects" gets discovered only by a definite Being-with-and-towards-one-another. This "inconsiderate" Being-with "reckons" with the Others without seriously "counting on them," or without even wanting to "have anything to do" with them.

One's own Dasein, like the Dasein-with of Others, is encountered proximally and for the most part in terms of the with-world with which we are environmentally concerned. When Dasein is absorbed in the world of its concern—that is, at the same time, in its Being-with towards Others—it is not itself. *Who* is it, then, who has taken over Being as everyday Being-with-one-another?

Notes

1. Wilhelm von Humboldt, "Über die Verwandtschaft der Ortsadverbien mit dem Pronomen in einigen Sprachen," *Gesammelte Schriften: Ausgabe Der Preussischen Akademie Der Wissenschaften* (Berlin: Prussian Academy of Sciences), Vol. VI, Part I, 304–30.

5

EMMANUEL LEVINAS
(1906–1995)

Emmanuel Levinas is arguably the most important ethical thinker in twentieth-century Continental philosophy. He was born in 1906 into a Jewish family living in Lithuania, and from a young age was immersed in the Hebrew Bible and the great Russian novelists. The influence of Russian literature in particular prompted Levinas to undertake the study of philosophy in 1923 at the University of Strasbourg, where he began a lifelong friendship with Maurice Blanchot. In 1928 to 1929, he moved to the University of Freiburg, and studied under Husserl and Heidegger. Levinas's dissertation *The Theory of Intuition in Husserl's Phenomenology* (1930) and his subsequent writings on Husserl and Heidegger almost single-handedly introduced phenomenology to a generation of postwar French thinkers, including Jean-Paul Sartre. In the thirties, Levinas became a nationalized French citizen and at the outbreak of World War II was drafted into the French army. In 1940, he became a prisoner of war in Germany and lived out the rest of the war in captivity. In his short autobiography entitled "Signature" (see *Difficult Freedom* [1963]), Levinas described his life as "dominated by the presentiment and the memory of the Nazi horror"—a regime that led to the murder of his birth family. Returning to civilian life in France after the war, Levinas became director of the Ecole Normale Israélite Orientale, and later taught at Paris-Nanterre and the Sorbonne. He died in 1995.

It was mainly during the fifties that Levinas began to work out a highly original ethics with the aim of going beyond the ethically neutral tradition of ontology. Levinas's first major work, *Totality and Infinity* (1961), influenced in part by the Jewish philosophies of Franz Rosenzweig and Martin Buber, sought to make this departure through an analysis of the "face" of the Other. The face, which is not a phenomenon in the strict Husserlian sense, resists thematization and knowledge while challenging the complacency of the I through Desire, language, and the concern for justice. This analysis was extended in Levinas's second magnum opus, *Otherwise Than Being or Beyond Essence* (1974), an immensely sophisticated work that sought to push philosophical intelligibility to the limit in an effort to reduce its dependence on the ontological tradition. In addition to Levinas's strictly philosophical works, mention should also be made of his "confessional" writings on contemporary Jewish issues (*Difficult Freedom*) and his numerous original readings of the Talmud. Levinas's work has had an inestimable impact on many prominent Continental philosophers, including Jean-François Lyotard (see Chapter 17 below), Jacques Derrida (see Chapter 19 below), and Luce Irigaray (see Chapter 24 below).

Our selection, "Philosophy and the Idea of Infinity" (1957), serves as an ideal introduction to Levinas's ethics. Here the reader will encounter in outline many of the motifs of *Totality and Infinity*, including the critique of freedom, the critique of Heidegger's ontology, the otherness of the Other, the Cartesian "idea of infinity," Desire, conscience, and the face-to-face.

Select Bibliography of Levinas's Works in English

Beyond the Verse. Trans. Gary D. Mole. Bloomington, IN: Indiana University Press, 1994.

Collected Philosophical Papers. Trans. Alphonso Lingis. The Hague: Martinus Nijhoff, 1987.

Discovering Existence with Husserl. Trans. and Ed. Richard A. Cohen and Michael B. Smith. Evanston, IL: Northwestern University Press, 1998.

Difficult Freedom. Trans. Seán Hand. Baltimore, MD: Johns Hopkins University Press, 1990.

Emmanuel Levinas: Basic Philosophical Writings. Eds. Adriaan T. Peperzak, Simon Critchley, and Robert Bernasconi. Bloomington, IN: Indiana University Press, 1995.

Ethics and Infinity. Trans. Richard Cohen. Pittsburgh, PA: Duquesne University Press, 1985.

Existence and Existents. Trans. Alphonso Lingis. Pittsburgh, PA: Duquesne University Press, 2001.

The Levinas Reader. Ed. Seán Hand. Oxford: Blackwell, 1989.

Otherwise Than Being or Beyond Essence. Trans. Alphonso Lingis. The Hague: Martinus Nijhoff, 1981.

Totality and Infinity: An Essay on Exteriority. Trans. Alphonso Lingis. The Hague: Martinus Nijhoff, 1969.

The Theory of Intuition in Husserl's Phenomenology. Trans. A. Orianne. Evanston, IL: Northwestern University Press, 1973.

Time and the Other. Trans. Richard Cohen. Pittsburgh, PA: Duquesne University Press, 1985.

PHILOSOPHY AND THE IDEA OF INFINITY

1. Autonomy and Heteronomy

Every philosophy seeks truth. Sciences too can be defined by this search, for from the philosophic *eros,* alive or dormant in them, they derive their noble passion. If this definition seems too general and rather empty, it will, however, permit us to distinguish two directions the philosophical spirit takes, and this will clarify its physiognomy. These directions interact in the idea of truth.

1. Truth implies experience. In the truth a thinker maintains a relationship with a reality distinct from him, other than him—"absolutely other," according to the expression taken up again by Jankélévitch. For experience deserves its name only if it transports us beyond what constitutes our nature. Genuine experience must even lead us beyond the nature that surrounds us, which is not jealous for the marvelous secrets it harbors, and, in complicity with men, submits to their reasons and inventions; in it men also feel themselves to be at home. Truth would thus designate the outcome of a movement that leaves a world that is intimate and familiar, even if we have not yet explored it completely, and goes toward the stranger, toward a *beyond*, as Plato puts it. Truth would imply more than exteriority: transcendence. Philosophy would be concerned with the absolutely other; it would be heteronomy itself. Let us go yet further. Distance alone does not suffice to distinguish transcendence from exteriority. Truth, the daughter of experience, has very lofty pretensions; it opens upon the very dimension of the ideal. In this way philosophy means metaphysics, and metaphysics inquires about the divine.

2. But truth also means the free adherence to a proposition, the outcome of a free research. The freedom of the investigator, the thinker on whom no constraint weighs, is expressed in truth. What else is this freedom but the thinking being's refusal to be alienated in the adherence, the preserving of his nature, his identity, the feat of remaining the same despite the unknown lands into which thought seems to lead? Perceived in this way, philosophy would be engaged in reducing to the same all that is opposed to it as *other*. It would be moving toward *auto-nomy*, a stage in which nothing irreducible would limit thought any longer, in which, consequently, thought, nonlimited, would be free. Philosophy would thus be tantamount to the conquest of being by man over the course of history.

Freedom, autonomy, the *reduction of the other to the same,* lead to this formula: the conquest of being by man over the course of history. This reduction does not represent some abstract schema; it is man's ego. The existence of an ego takes place as an identification of the diverse. So many events happen to it, so many years age it, and yet the ego remains the same! The ego, the oneself, the ipseity (as it is called in our time), does not remain invariable in the midst of change like a rock assailed by the waves (which is anything but invariable); the ego remains the same by making of disparate and diverse events a history—its history. And this is the original event of the identification of the same, prior to the identity of a rock, and a condition of that identity.

Autonomy or heteronomy? The choice of Western philosophy has most often been on the side of freedom and the same. Was not philosophy born, on Greek soil, to dethrone opinion, in which all tyrannies lurk and threaten? With opinion the most subtle and treacherous poison seeps into the soul, altering it in its depths, making of it an other. The soul "eaten up by the others," as M. Teste would say, does not feel its alteration, and is hence exposed to all violences. But this penetration and this prestige of opinion presuppose a mythical stage of being in which souls participate in one another, in the sense Levy-Bruhl has given to the term. Against the turbid and disturbing participation opinion presupposes, philosophy willed souls that are separate and in a sense impenetrable. The idea of the same, the idea of freedom, seemed to offer the most firm guarantee of such a separation.

Thus Western thought very often seemed to exclude the transcendent, encompass every other in the same, and proclaim the philosophical birthright of autonomy.

2. Narcissism, or the Primacy of the Same

Autonomy, the philosophy which aims to ensure the freedom, or the identity, of beings, presupposes that freedom itself is sure of its right, is justified without recourse to anything further, is complacent in itself, like Narcissus. When, in the philosophical life that realizes this freedom, there arises a term foreign to the philosophical life, other—the land that supports us and disappoints our efforts, the sky that elevates us and ignores us, the forces of nature that aid us and kill us, things that encumber us or serve us, men who love us and enslave us—it becomes an obstacle; it has to be surmounted and integrated into this life. But truth is just this victory and this integration. In evidence the violence of the encounter with the non-I is deadened. The commerce with exterior truth as enacted in true cognition is thus not opposed to freedom, but coincides with it. The search for truth becomes the very respiration of a free being, exposed to exterior realities that shelter, but also threaten, its freedom. Thanks to truth these realities, whose plaything I am in danger of becoming, are understood by me.

The "I think," thought in the first person, the soul conversing with itself, or, *qua* reminiscence, rediscovering the teachings it receives, thus promotes freedom. Freedom will triumph when the soul's monologues will have reached universality, will have encompassed the totality of being, encompassing even the animal individual which lodged this thought. Every experience of the world, of the elements and objects, lends itself to this dialectic of the soul conversing with itself, enters into it, belongs to it. The things will be ideas, and will be conquered, dominated, possessed in the course of an economic and political history in which this thought will be unfolded. It is doubtless for this reason that Descartes will say that the soul might be the origin of the ideas that relate to exterior things, and thus account for the real.

The essence of truth, therefore, would not be in the heteronomous relation with an unknown God, but in the already-known which has to be uncovered or freely invented in oneself, and in which everything unknown is comprised. It is fundamentally opposed to a God that reveals. Philosophy is atheism, or rather unreligion, negation of a God that reveals himself and puts truths into us. This is Socrates' teaching, when he leaves to the master only the exercise of maieutics: every lesson introduced into the soul was already in it. The I's identification, its marvelous autarchy, is the natural crucible of this transmutation of the other into the same. Every philosophy is—to use Husserl's neologism—an egology. And when Descartes comes to discern an acquiescence of the will in even the most rational truth, he not only explains the possibility of error, but sets up reason as an ego and truth as dependent on a movement that is free, and thus sovereign and justified.

This identification requires mediation. Whence a second characteristic of the philosophy of the same: its recourse to neuters. To understand the non-I, access must be found through an entity, an abstract essence which is and is not. In it is dissolved the other's *alterity*. The foreign being, instead of maintaining itself in the inexpugnable fortress of its singularity, instead of facing, becomes a theme and an object. It fits under a concept already, or dissolves into relations. It falls into the network of *a priori* ideas, which I bring to bear, so as to capture it. To know is to surprise in the individual confronted, in this wounding stone, this upward plunging pine, this roaring lion, that by which it is not this very individual, this foreigner, that by which it is already betrayed and by which it gives the free will, vibrant in all certainty, hold over it, is grasped and conceived, enters into a concept. Cognition consists in grasping the individual, which alone exists, not in its singularity which does not count, but in its generality, of which alone there is science.

And here every power begins. The surrender of exterior things to human freedom through their generality does not only mean, in all innocence, their comprehension, but also their being taken in hand, their domestication, their possession. Only in possession does the I complete the identification of the diverse. To possess is, to be sure, to maintain the reality of this other one possessed, but to do so while suspending its independence. In a civilization which the philosophy of the same reflects, freedom is realized as a wealth. Reason, which reduces the other, is appropriation and power.

But if things do not resist the ruses of thought, and confirm the philosophy of the same, without ever putting into question the freedom of the I, is this also true of men? Are they given to me as the things are? Do they not put into question my freedom?

They can, to begin with, block it by opposing it with more than their force—their freedoms. They wage war. War is not a pure confrontation of forces; it can perhaps be defined as a relationship in which force does not alone enter into account, for the unforeseeable contingencies of freedom—skill, courage, and invention—count too. But in war the free will may fail without being put into question, without renouncing its rights and its revenge. Freedom is put into question by the other, and is revealed to be unjustified, only when it knows itself to be unjust. Its knowing itself to be unjust is not something added on to spontaneous and free consciousness, which would be present to itself and know itself to be, *in addition*, guilty. A new situation is created; consciousness's presence to itself acquires a different modality; its positions collapse. To put it just in formal terms, the same does not find again its priority over the other, it does not rest peaceably on itself, is no longer the principle. We shall endeavor to make these formulas more clear. And if the same does not peaceably rest on itself, philosophy does not seem to be indissolubly bound up with the adventure that includes every other in the same.

We shall return to this shortly; let us first observe that this supremacy of the same over the other seems to be integrally maintained in the philosophy of Heidegger, the most renowned of our time. When Heidegger traces the way of access to each real singularity through Being, which is not a particular being nor a genus in which all the particulars would enter, but is rather the very act of being which the verb to be, and not the substantive, expresses (and which, with M. De Waelhens, we write with a capital "B"), he leads us to the singularity across a neuter which illuminates and commands thought, and renders intelligible. When he sees man possessed by freedom rather than possessing freedom, he puts over man a neuter term which illuminates freedom without putting it in question. And thus he is not destroying, but summing up a whole current of Western philosophy.

The Dasein Heidegger puts in place of the soul, consciousness, or the ego, retains the structure of the same. Independence—autarchy—came to the Platonic soul (and to all its counterfeit versions) from its homeland, the world of Ideas; according to the *Phaedo*, the soul is related to that world, and consequently cannot encounter anything really foreign in it. Reason, the power to maintain oneself identical above the variations of becoming, formed the soul of this soul. Heidegger contests this dominant position for man, but leaves Dasein in the same, *qua* mortal. The possibility of being annihilated is in fact constitutive of Dasein, and thus maintains its ipseity. This nothingness is a death, is my death, my possibility (of impossibility), my power. No one can substitute himself for me to die. The supreme moment of resoluteness is solitary and personal.

To be sure, for Heidegger man's freedom depends on the light of Being, and thus does not seem to be a principle. But that was also the case in classical idealism, where free will was considered the lowest form of freedom, and true freedom obeyed universal reason. The Heideggerian freedom is obedient, but obedience makes it arise and does not put it into question, does not reveal its injustice. Being, equivalent to the independence and extraneousness of realities, is equivalent to phosphorescence, light. It converts into intelligibility. The "mystery" essential to this "dark light" is a modality of this conversion. Independence ends in radiation. *Being and Time*, Heidegger's first and principal work, perhaps always maintained but one thesis: Being is inseparable from the comprehension of Being; Being already invokes subjectivity. But Being *is not* a being. It is a neuter which orders thought and beings, but which hardens the will instead of making it ashamed. The consciousness of his finitude does not come to man from the idea of infinity, that is, is not revealed as an imperfection, does not refer to the Good, does not know itself to be wicked. Heideggerian philosophy precisely marks the apogee of a thought in which the finite does not refer to the infinite (prolonging certain tendencies of Kantian philosophy: the separation between the understanding and reason, diverse themes of the transcendental dialectic), in which every deficiency is but weakness and every fault, committed against oneself—the outcome of a long tradition of pride, heroism, domination, and cruelty.

Heideggerian ontology subordinates the relation with the other to the relation with the neuter, Being, and it thus continues to exalt the will to power, whose legitimacy the other alone can unsettle, troubling good conscience. When Heidegger calls attention to the forgetting of Being, veiled by the diverse realities it illuminates, a forgetting for which the philosophy developed from Socrates on would be guilty, when he deplores the orientation of the intellect toward technology, he maintains a regime of power more inhuman than mechanism and which perhaps does not have the same source as it. (It is not sure that National Socialism arises from the mechanist reification of men, and that it does not rest on peasant enrootedness and a feudal adoration of subjugated men for the masters and lords who command them). This is an existence which takes itself to be natural, for whom its place in the sun, its ground, its *site*, orient all signification—a pagan *existing*. Being directs it building and cultivating, in the midst of a familiar landscape, on a maternal earth. Anonymous, neuter, it directs it, ethically indifferent, as a heroic freedom, foreign to all guilt with regard to the other.

Indeed this earth-maternity determines the whole Western civilization of property, exploitation, political tyranny, and war. Heidegger does not discuss the pretechnological power of possession effected in the enrootedness of perception (which no one has described so brilliantly as he), in which the most abstract geometrical space is in the last analysis embedded, but which cannot find any place in the whole infinity of mathematical extension. The Heideggerian analyses of the world which in *Being and Time* were based on gear or fabricated things are in this philosophy borne by the vision of the lofty landscapes of nature, an impersonal fecundity, matrix of particular beings, inexhaustible matter of things.

Heidegger does not only sum up a whole evolution of Western philosophy. He exalts it by showing in the most pathetic way its antireligious essence become a religion in reverse. The lucid sobriety of those who call themselves friends of truth and enemies of opinion would then have a mysterious prolongation! In Heidegger atheism is a paganism, the pre-Socratic texts anti-Scriptures. Heidegger shows in what intoxication the lucid sobriety of philosophers is steeped. To conclude, the well-known theses of Heideggerian philosophy—the preeminence of Being over beings, of ontology over metaphysics—end up affirming a tradition in which the same dominates the other, in which freedom, even the freedom that is identical with reason, precedes justice. Does not justice consist in putting the obligation with regard to the other before obligations to oneself, in putting the other before the same?

3. The Idea of Infinity

By reversing the terms we believe we are following a tradition at least as ancient, that which does not read right in might and does not reduce *every other* to the same. Against the Heideggerians and neo-Hegelians for whom philosophy begins with atheism, we have to say that the tradition of the other is not necessarily religious, that it is philosophical. Plato stands in this tradition when he situates the good above Being, and, in the *Phaedrus*, defines true discourse as a discourse with gods. But what we find most distinctive is the Cartesian analysis of the idea of infinity, although we shall retain only the *formal* design of the structure it outlines.

In Descartes the I that thinks maintains a relationship with the infinite. This relationship is not that which connects a container to a content, since the I cannot contain the infinite, nor that which binds a content to a container, since the I is separated from the infinite. The relationship which is thus described negatively is the idea of infinity in us.

We have of course also ideas of things; the idea of infinity is exceptional in that its ideatum surpasses its idea. In it the distance between idea and ideatum is not equivalent to the distance that separates a mental act from its object in other representations. The abyss that separates a mental act from its object is not deep enough for Descartes not to say that the soul can account for the ideas of finite things by itself. The intentionality that animates the idea of infinity is not comparable with any other; it aims at what it cannot embrace and is in this sense the infinite. To take the converse of the formulas we used above, we can say that the alterity of the infinite is not cancelled, is not extinguished in the thought that thinks it. In thinking infinity, the I from the first *thinks more than it thinks*. Infinity does not enter into the *idea* of infinity, is not grasped; this idea is not a concept. The infinite is the radically, absolutely other. The transcendence of infinity with respect to the ego that is separated from it and thinks it constitutes the first mark of its infinitude.

The idea of infinity is then not the only one that teaches what we are ignorant of. It has been *put* into us. It is not a reminiscence. It is experience in the sole radical sense of the term: a relationship with the exterior, with the other, without this exteriority being able to be integrated into the same. The thinker who has the idea of infinity is *more than himself*, and this inflating, this surplus, does not come from within, as in the celebrated *project* of modern philosophers, in which the subject surpasses himself by creating.

How can such a structure be still philosophical? What is the relationship which, while remaining one of *the more in the less*, is not transformed into the relationship in which, according to the mystics, the butterfly drawn by the fire is consumed in the fire? How can separate beings be maintained, and not sink into participation, against which the philosophy of the same will have the immortal merit to have protested?

4. The Idea of Infinity and the Face of the Other

Experience, the idea of infinity, occurs in the relationship with the other. The idea of infinity is the social relationship.

This relationship consists in approaching an absolutely exterior being. The infinity of this being, which one can therefore not contain, guarantees and constitutes this exteriority. It is not equivalent to the distance between a subject and an object. An object, we know, is integrated into the identity of the same; the I makes of it its theme, and then its property, its booty, its prey or its victim. The exteriority of the infinite being is manifested in the absolute resistance which by its apparition, its epiphany, it opposes to *all* my powers. Its epiphany is not simply the apparition of a form in the light, sensible or intelligible, but already this *no* cast to powers; its logos is: "You shall not kill."

To be sure, the other is exposed to all my powers, succumbs to all my ruses, all my crimes. Or he resists me with all his force and all the unpredictable resources of his own freedom. I measure *myself* against him. But he can also—and here is where he presents me his face—oppose himself to me beyond all measure, with the total uncoveredness and nakedness of his defenseless eyes, the straightforwardness, the absolute frankness of his gaze. The solipsist disquietude of consciousness, seeing itself, in all its adventures, a captive of itself, comes to an end here: true exteriority is in this gaze which forbids me my conquest. Not that conquest is beyond my too weak powers, but I *am no longer able to have power*: the structure of my freedom is, we shall see further, completely reversed. Here is established a relationship not with a very great resistance, but with the absolutely other, with the resistance of what has no resistance, with ethical resistance. It opens the very dimension of infinity, of what puts a stop to the irresistible imperialism of the same and the I. We call a *face* the epiphany of what can thus present itself directly, and therefore also exteriorly, to an I.

A face is not like a plastic form, which is always already deserted, betrayed, by the being it reveals, such as marble from which the gods it manifests already absent themselves. It differs from an animal's head in which a being, in its brutish dumbness, is not yet in touch with itself. In a face the expressed attends its expression, expresses its very expression, always remains master of the meaning it delivers. A "pure act" in its own way, it resists identification, does not enter into the already known, brings aid to itself, as Plato puts it, speaks. The epiphany of a face is wholly language.

Ethical resistance is the presence of infinity. If the resistance to murder, inscribed on a face, were not ethical, but real, we would have access to a reality that is very weak or very strong. It perhaps would block our will. The will would be judged unreasonable and arbitrary. But we would not have access to an exterior being, to what one absolutely can neither take in nor possess, where our freedom renounces its imperialism proper to the ego, where it is found to be not only arbitrary, but unjust. But then the other is not simply another freedom; to give me knowledge of injustice, his gaze must come to me from a dimension of the ideal. The other must be closer to God than I. This is certainly not a philosopher's invention, but the first given of conscience (*la conscience morale*), which could be defined as the consciousness (*conscience*) of the privilege the other has relative to me. Justice well ordered begins with the other.

5. The Idea of Infinity as Desire

The ethical relationship is not grafted on to an antecedent relationship of cognition; it is a foundation and not a superstructure. To distinguish it from cognition is not to reduce it to a subjective sentiment. The idea of infinity, in which being overflows the idea, in which the other overflows the same, breaks with the inward play of the soul and alone deserves the name experience, a relationship with the exterior. It is then more *cognitive* than cognition itself, and all objectivity must participate in it.

Malebranche's vision in God (cf. the Second *Metaphysical Discourse*) expresses both this reference of all cognition to the idea of infinity and the fact that the idea of infinity is not like the cognition that refers to it. For one cannot maintain that this idea itself is a thematization or an objectification without reducing it to the presence of the other in the same, a presence with which it in fact contrasts. In Descartes, a certain ambiguity concerning this point remains, since the *cogito* which rests on God elsewhere founds the existence of God: the priority of the infinite is subordinated to the free adhesion of the will, which initially is master of itself.

We separate ourselves from the letter of Cartesianism in affirming that the movement of the soul that is more cognitive than cognition could have a structure different from contemplation. Infinity is not the object of a contemplation, that is, is not proportionate to the thought that thinks it. The idea of infinity is a thought which at every moment thinks more than it thinks. A thought that thinks more than it thinks is Desire. Desire "measures" the infinity of the infinite.

The term we have chosen to mark the propulsion, the inflation, of this going beyond is opposed to the affectivity of love and the indigence of need. Outside of the hunger one satisfies, the thirst one quenches, and the senses one allays, exists the other, absolutely other, desired beyond these satisfactions, when the body knows no gesture to slake the desire, where it is not possible to invent any new caress. This desire is unquenchable, not because it answers to an infinite hunger, but because it does not call for food. This desire without satisfaction hence takes cognizance of the alterity of the other. It situates it in the dimension of height and of the ideal, which it opens up in being.

The desires one can satisfy resemble this Desire only intermittently, in the deceptions of satisfaction or in the increases of emptiness which mark their voluptuousness. They wrongly pass for the essence of desire. The true Desire is that which the Desired does not satisfy, but hollows out. It is goodness. It does not refer to a lost fatherland or plenitude; it is not homesickness, is not nostalgia. It is the lack in a being which *is* completely, and lacks nothing. Can the Platonic myth of love, son of abundance and of poverty, be interpreted as bearing witness to the indigence of a wealth in Desire, the insufficiency of what is self-sufficient? Has not Plato, in the *Symposium*, with the myth of an androgynous being, affirmed the nonnostalgic nature of Desire, the plenitude and joy of the being who experiences it?

6. The Idea of Infinity and Conscience

How does a face escape the discretionary power of the will which deals with evidence? Is not knowing a face *acquiring* a consciousness of it, and is not to acquire consciousness to adhere *freely*? Does not the idea of infinity, *qua idea*, inevitably refer back to the schema of the same encompassing the other?—Unless the idea of infinity means the collapse of the good conscience of the same. For everything comes to pass as though the presence of a face, the idea of infinity in the I, were the putting of my freedom into question.

That the free will is arbitrary, and that one must leave this elementary stage, is an old certainty of philosophers. But for all of them the arbitrariness refers to a rational foundation, a justification of freedom by itself. The rational foundation of freedom is still preeminence of the same.

Moreover, the necessity of justifying the arbitrary is due only to the failure suffered by an arbitrary power. *The very spontaneity of freedom is not put into question*—such seems to be the dominant tradition of Western philosophy. Only the limitation of freedom would be tragic or scandalous. Freedom poses a problem only because it has not chosen itself. The failure of my spontaneity is said to awaken reason and theory; a pain is said to be the mother of wisdom. Failure would lead me to put brakes on my violence and introduce order into human relations, for everything is permitted but the impossible. In particular, modern political theories since Hobbes deduce the social order from the legitimacy, the incontestable right, of freedom.

The other's face is the revelation not of the arbitrariness of the will, but its injustice. Consciousness of my injustice is produced when I incline myself not before facts, but before the other. In his face the other appears to me not as an obstacle, nor as a menace I evaluate, but as what measures me. For me to feel myself to be unjust I must measure myself against infinity. One must have the idea of infinity, which, as Descartes knows, is also the idea of the perfect, to know my own imperfection. The infinite does not stop me like a force blocking my force; it puts into question the naïve right of my powers, my glorious spontaneity as a living being, a "force on the move."

This way of measuring oneself against the perfection of the infinite is not a theoretical consideration in its turn, in which freedom would spontaneously take up its rights again. It is a *shame* freedom has of itself, discovering itself to be murderous and usurpatory in its very exercise. A second-century exegete, more concerned with what he had to do than with what he had to hope for, did not understand why the Bible begins with the account of creation instead of putting us from the first before the first command-ments of Exodus. Only with great difficulty did he come to concede that the account of creation was all the same necessary for the life of the just man: for if the earth had not been given to man but simply taken by him, he would have possessed it only as an outlaw. Spontaneous and naïve possession cannot be justified by virtue of its own spontaneity.

Existence is not condemned to freedom, but judged and invested as a freedom. Freedom could not present itself completely naked. This investiture of freedom constitutes moral life itself, which is through and through a heteronomy.

The will that in the meeting with the other is judged does not assume the judgment it welcomes. That would still be a return of the same deciding for the other in the final analysis, heteronomy absorbed in autonomy. The structure of the free will becoming *goodness* is not like the glorious and self-sufficient spontaneity of the I and of happiness, which would be the ultimate movement of being; it is, as it were, its converse. The life of freedom discovering itself to be unjust, the life of freedom in heteronomy, con-sists in an infinite movement of freedom putting itself ever more into question. This is how the very depth of inwardness is hollowed out. The augmentation of exigency I have in regard to myself aggra-vates the judgment that is borne on me, that is, my responsibility. And the aggravation of my responsi-bility increases these exigencies. In this movement my freedom does not have the last word; I never find my solitude again—or, one might say, moral consciousness is essentially unsatisfied, or again, is always Desire.

The unsatisfiedness of science is not simply a suffering of delicate and scrupulous souls, but is the very contraction, the hollow, the withdrawal into itself, and the systole of consciousness as such. Ethi-cal consciousness itself is not invoked in this exposition as a "particularly recommendable" variety of consciousness, but as the concrete form of a movement more fundamental than freedom, the idea of in-finity. It is the concrete form of what precedes freedom, but does not lead us back to violence, the con-fusion of what is separated, necessity, or fatality.

Here above all is the situation in which one is not alone. But if this situation does not yield proof of the existence of the other, this is because proof already presupposes the movement and adherence of a free will, a certainty. Thus the situation in which the free will is invested precedes proof. For every cer-tainty is the work of a solitary freedom. As a welcome of the real into my *a priori* ideas, an adhesion of my free will, the last gesture of cognition is freedom. The face-to-face situation in which this freedom is put into question as unjust, in which it finds it has a master and a judge, is realized prior to certainty, but also prior to uncertainty.

This situation is an experience in the strongest sense of the term: a contact with a reality that does not fit into any *a priori* idea, which overflows all of them—and it is just for this reason that we have been able to speak of infinity. No movement of freedom could appropriate a face to itself or seem to "constitute" it. The face has already been there when it was anticipated or constituted; it collaborated in that work, it spoke. A face is pure experience, conceptless experience. The conception according to which the data of our senses are put together in the ego ends—before the other—with the de-ception by the dispossession which characterizes all our attempts to encompass this real. But the purely negative incomprehension of the other, which depends on our bad will, must be distinguished from the essential incomprehension of the infinite, which has a positive side, is conscience and Desire.

The unsatisfiedness of conscience, the de-ception before the other, coincides with Desire—this is one of the essential points of this exposition. The Desire for infinity does not have the sentimental complacency of love, but the rigor of moral exigency. And the rigor of moral exigency is not bluntly imposed, but is a Desire, due to the attraction and infinite height of being itself, for the benefit of which goodness is exercised. God commands only through the men for whom one must act.

Consciousness, the presence of self to self, passes for the ultimate theme of reflection. Conscience, a variation on this theme, a species of consciousness, is taken to add to it the concern for values and norms. We have raised several questions concerning this: Can the self present itself to itself with so much natural complacency? Can it appear, shamelessly, in its own eyes? Is narcissism possible?[1] Is not conscience the critique of and the principle of the presence of self to self? Then if the essence of philosophy consists in going back from all certainties toward a principle, if it lives from critique, the face of the other would be the starting point of philosophy. This is a thesis of heteronomy which breaks with a very venerable tradition. But, on the other hand, the situation in which one is not alone is not reducible to the fortunate meeting of fraternal souls that greet one another and converse. This situation is the moral conscience, the exposedness of my freedom to the judgment of the other. It is a disalignment which has authorized us to catch sight of the dimension of height and the ideal in the gaze of him to whom justice is due.

Notes

1. We have dealt with the different themes relevant to this matter in three articles published in the *Revue de Métaphysique et de Morale*: "L'ontologie est-elle fondamentale?" (1951), "Liberté et Commandement" (1953), and "Le Moi et la totalité" (1954). [Editors' note: These essays have subsequently appeared in English as "Is Ontology Fundamental?" trans. Peter Atterton, *Emmanuel Levinas: Basic Philosophical Writings*, eds. Adriaan T. Peperzak, Simon Critchley, and Robert Bernasconi (Bloomington, IN: Indiana University Press, 1995), 2–10; "Freedom and Command," in *Collected Philosophical Papers*, trans. Alphonso Lingis (The Hague: Martinus Nijhoff, 1987), 15–23; and "The Ego and Totality," in *Collected Philosophical Papers*, 25–45.]

Part 2

EXISTENTIALISM

6

SØREN KIERKEGAARD
(1813–1855)

The Danish philosopher and religious writer, Søren Kierkegaard, is frequently referred to as the first existentialist. In 1830, he enrolled in the University of Copenhagen to study theology, though he spent much of his time reading psychological, literary, and philosophical works. In many ways, Kierkegaard's life mirrored his famous "three stages." His young adult years were spent in the pursuit of pleasure, leading to his engagement in 1840 to Regine Olsen. Kierkegaard, however, ended the relationship the following year, claiming that "God had vetoed the marriage." It was a decision he would regret for the rest of his life. From this point on, Kierkegaard lived a life of relative solitude, and published a large body of works, many of which attacked the hypocrisy of the Danish Church and what he called "Christendom." He died in 1855. In keeping with his solitary manner of existing, Kierkegaard requested that his epitaph read simply "That Individual"—a request that was not granted.

Much of Kierkegaard's thinking can be read as a defense of the "single individual" against the totalizing tendencies of the Hegelian "system," the dominant philosophy of the time. Within the anonymity of the system, Kierkegaard argues, persons lose their status as uniquely existing individuals and become bearers of universal concepts that they share with other individuals. He went on to develop this critique in various "pseudonymous works," including *Either/Or* (1843), *Repetition* (1843), and *Concluding Unscientific Postscript* (1846). Kierkegaard preferred the use of pseudonyms in order to communicate "indirectly" with his readers, allowing them to detach themselves from the authority of the author (Kierkegaard) and adopt an individual stance toward the existential issues raised in these works. For Kierkegaard, the more *subjectively* truth is felt, the more impassioned is the individual's relationship with existence and the less the individual is mired in the anonymity of "the crowd." Toward the end of his life, Kierkegaard also published a large number of "edifying" works on Christians themes dedicated to "that solitary individual." Among the most important of these are *Purity of Heart Is to Will One Thing* (1846), *The Sickness unto Death* (1849), and *Training in Christianity* (1850).

Kierkegaard maintained that human life comprises three stages: *the aesthetic*, which is governed by the pursuit of pleasure, *the ethical*, where one acts in accord with universal laws and duty, and *the religious*, which consists in a "paradoxical" relationship with a personal God who is infinitely unknowable. The religious life is examined at length in *Fear and Trembling* (1843), which includes Kierkegaard's famous retelling of the story of Abraham and Isaac (Gen. 22:1–19), excerpted below. For Kierkegaard, Abraham personifies the "knight of faith," the man whose religious faith is so strong that he is prepared to sacrifice everything he loves—including his son—should God require it. At the same time, Abraham believes "by virtue of the absurd" that God will not require such a sacrifice. The irresolvable tension between the universal demands of the ethical life and the purely subjective requirements of faith leads Kierkegaard to ask: "Is there a teleological suspension of the ethical?"—a question he answers in the affirmative.

Select Bibliography of Kierkegaard's Works in English

The Concept of Anxiety. Trans. Reidar Thomte and Albert B. Anderson. Princeton, NJ: Princeton University Press, 1980.

The Concept of Irony, with Continual Reference to Socrates. Trans. Howard V. Hong and Edna H. Hong. Princeton, NJ: Princeton University Press, 1989.

Concluding Unscientific Postscript to Philosophical Fragments, 2 vols. Trans. Howard V. Hong and Edna H. Hong. Princeton, NJ: Princeton University Press, 1992.

Either/Or, 2 vols. Trans. Howard V. Hong and Edna H. Hong. Princeton, NJ: Princeton University Press, 1987.

Fear and Trembling, and Repetition. Trans. Howard V. Hong and Edna H. Hong. Princeton, NJ: Princeton University Press, 1983.

Kierkegaard's Writings. Trans. Howard V. Hong and Edna H. Hong. Princeton, NJ: Princeton University Press, 1978.

Practice in Christianity. Trans. Howard V. Hong and Edna H. Hong. Princeton, NJ: Princeton University Press, 1991.

Purity of Heart Is to Will One Thing. Trans. Douglas V. Steere. New York: Harper Torchbooks, 1956.

The Sickness unto Death. Trans. Howard V. Hong and Edna H. Hong. Princeton, NJ: Princeton University Press, 1980.

Stages on Life's Way. Trans. Howard V. Hong and Edna H. Hong. Princeton, NJ: Princeton University Press, 1988.

Upbuilding Discourses in Various Spirits. Trans. Howard V. Hong and Edna H. Hong. Princeton, NJ: Princeton University Press, 1993.

Works of Love. Trans. Howard V. Hong and Edna H. Hong. Princeton, NJ: Princeton University Press, 1995.

IS THERE A TELEOLOGICAL
SUSPENSION OF THE ETHICAL?

The ethical as such is the universal, and as the universal it applies to everyone, which from another angle means that it applies at all times. It rests immanent in itself, has nothing outside itself that is its *telos* [end, purpose] but is itself the *telos* for everything outside itself, and when the ethical has absorbed this into itself, it goes not further. The single individual, sensately and psychically qualified in immediacy, is the individual who has his *telos* in the universal, and it is his ethical task continually to express himself in this, to annul his singularity in order to become the universal. As soon as the single individual asserts himself in his singularity before the universal, he sins, and only by acknowledging this can he be reconciled again with the universal. Every time the single individual, after having entered the universal, feels an impulse to assert himself as the single individual, he is in a spiritual trial, from which he can work himself only by repentantly surrendering as the single individual in the universal. If this is the highest that can be said of man and his existence, then the ethical is of the same nature as a person's eternal salvation, which is his *telos* forevermore and at all times, since it would be a contradiction for this to be capable of being surrendered (that is, teleologically suspended), because as soon as this is suspended it is relinquished, whereas that which is suspended is not relinquished but is preserved in the higher, which is its *telos*.

If this is the case, then Hegel is right in "The Good and Conscience," where he qualifies man only as the individual and considers this qualification as a "moral form of evil" (see especially *The Philosophy of Right*), which must be annulled in the teleology of the moral in such a way that the single individual who remains in that stage either sins or is immersed in spiritual trial. But Hegel is wrong in speaking about faith; he is wrong in not protesting loudly and clearly against Abraham's enjoying honor and glory as a father of faith when he ought to be sent back to a lower court and shown up as a murderer.

Faith is namely this paradox that the single individual is higher than the universal—yet, please note, in such a way that the movement repeats itself, so that after having been in the universal he as the single individual isolates himself as higher than the universal. If this is not faith, then Abraham is lost, then faith has never existed in the world precisely because it has always existed. For if the ethical— that is, social morality—is the highest and if there is in a person no residual incommensurability in some way such that this incommensurability is not evil (i.e., the single individual, who is to be expressed in the universal), then no categories are needed other than what Greek philosophy had or what can be deduced from them by consistent thought. Hegel should not have concealed this, for, after all, he had studied Greek philosophy.

People who are profoundly lacking in learning and are given to clichés are frequently heard to say that a light shines over the Christian world, whereas a darkness enshrouds paganism. This kind of talk has always struck me as strange, inasmuch as every more thorough thinker, every more earnest artist still regenerates himself in the eternal youth of the Greeks. The explanation for such a statement is that one does not know what one should say but only that one must say something. It is quite right to say that paganism did not have faith, but if something is supposed to have been said thereby, then one must have a clearer understanding of what faith is, for otherwise one falls into such clichés. It is easy to explain all existence, faith along with it, without having a conception of what faith is, and the one who counts on being admired for such an explanation is not such a bad calculator, for it is as Boileau says: "One fool always finds a bigger fool who admires him."

Faith is precisely the paradox that the single individual as the single individual is higher than the universal, is justified before it, not as inferior to it but as superior—yet in such a way, please note, that it is the single individual who, after being subordinate as the single individual to the universal, now by means of the universal becomes the single individual who as the single individual is superior, that the single individual as the single individual stands in an absolute relation to the absolute. This position cannot be mediated, for all mediation takes place only by virtue of the universal; it is and remains for all eternity a paradox, impervious to thought. And yet faith is this paradox, or else (and I ask the reader to bear these consequences *in mente* [in mind] even though it would be too prolix for me to write them all down) or else faith has never existed simply because it has always existed, or else Abraham is lost.

It is certainly true that the single individual can easily confuse this paradox with spiritual trial, but it ought not to be concealed for that reason. It is certainly true that many persons may be so constituted that they are repulsed by it, but faith ought not therefore to be made into something else to enable one to have it, but one ought rather to admit to not having it, while those who have faith ought to be prepared to set forth some characteristics whereby the paradox can be distinguished from a spiritual trial.

The story of Abraham contains just such a teleological suspension of the ethical. There is no dearth of keen minds and careful scholars who have found analogies to it. What their wisdom amounts to is the beautiful proposition that basically everything is the same. If one looks more closely, I doubt very much that anyone in the whole wide world will find one single analogy, except for a later one, which proves nothing if it is certain that Abraham represents faith and that it is manifested normatively in him, whose life not only is the most paradoxical that can be thought but is also so paradoxical that it simply cannot be thought. He acts by virtue of the absurd, for it is precisely the absurd that he as the single individual is higher than the universal. This paradox cannot be mediated, for as soon as Abraham begins to do so, he has to confess that he was in a spiritual trial, and if that is the case, he will never sacrifice Isaac, or if he did sacrifice Isaac, then in repentance he must come back to the universal. He gets Isaac back again by virtue of the absurd. Therefore, Abraham is at no time a tragic hero but is something entirely different, either a murderer or a man of faith. Abraham does not have the middle term that saves the tragic hero. This is why I can understand a tragic hero but cannot understand Abraham, even though in a certain demented sense I admire him more than all others.

In ethical terms, Abraham's relation to Isaac is quite simply this: the father shall love the son more than himself. But within its own confines the ethical has various gradations. We shall see whether this story contains any higher expression for the ethical that can ethically explain his behavior, can ethically justify his suspending the ethical obligation to the son, but without moving beyond the teleology of the ethical.

When an enterprise of concern to a whole nation is impeded, when such a project is halted by divine displeasure, when the angry deity sends a dead calm that mocks every effort, when the soothsayer carries out his sad task and announces that the deity demands a young girl as sacrifice—then the father must heroically bring this sacrifice. He must nobly conceal his agony, even though he could wish he were "the lowly man who dares to weep" [Euripides, *Iphigenia in Aulis*] and not the king who must behave in a kingly manner. Although the lonely agony penetrates his breast and there are only three persons in the whole nation who know his agony, soon the whole nation will be initiated into his agony and also into his deed, that for the welfare of all he will sacrifice her, his daughter, this lovely young girl. O bosom! O fair cheeks, flaxen hair (v. 687). And the daughter's tears will agitate him, and the father will turn away his face, but the hero must raise the knife. And when the news of it reaches the father's house, the beautiful Greek maidens will blush with enthusiasm, and if the daughter was engaged, her betrothed will not be angry but will be proud to share in the father's deed, for the girl belonged more tenderly to him than to the father.

When the valiant judge [Judges 11:30–40] who in the hour of need saved Israel binds God and himself in one breath by the same promise, he will heroically transform the young maiden's jubilation, the beloved daughter's joy to sorrow, and all Israel will sorrow with her over her virginal youth. But every freeborn man will understand, every resolute woman will admire Jephthah, and every virgin in Israel will wish to behave as his daughter did, because what good would it be for Jephthah to win the victory by means of a promise if he did not keep it—would not the victory be taken away from the people again?

When a son forgets his duty, when the state entrusts the sword of judgment to the father, when the laws demand punishment from the father's hand, then the father must heroically forget that the guilty one is his son, he must nobly hide his agony, but no one in the nation, not even the son, will fail to admire the father, and every time the Roman laws are interpreted, it will be remembered that many interpreted them more learnedly but no one more magnificently than Brutus.

But if Agamemnon, while a favorable wind was taking the fleet under full sail to its destination, had dispatched that messenger who fetched Iphigenia to be sacrificed; if Jephthah, without being bound by any promise that decided the fate of the nation, had said to his daughter: Grieve now for two months over your brief youth, and then I will sacrifice you; if Brutus had had a righteous son and yet had summoned the lictors to put him to death—who would have understood them? If, on being asked why they did this, these three men had answered: It is an ordeal in which we are being tried—would they have been better understood?

When in the crucial moment Agamemnon, Jephthah, and Brutus heroically have overcome the agony, heroically have lost the beloved, and have only to complete the task externally, there will never be a noble soul in the world without tears of compassion for their agony, of admiration for their deed. But if in the crucial moment these three men were to append to the heroic courage with which they bore the agony the little phrase: But it will not happen anyway—who then would understand them? If they went on to explain: This we believe by virtue of the absurd—who would understand them any better, for who would not readily understand that it was absurd, but who would understand that one could then believe it?

The difference between the tragic hero and Abraham is very obvious. The tragic hero is still within the ethical. He allows an expression of the ethical to have its *telos* in a higher expression of the ethical; he scales down the ethical relation between father and son or daughter and father to a feeling that has its dialectic in its relation to the idea of moral conduct. Here there can be no question of a teleological suspension of the ethical itself.

Abraham's situation is different. By his act he transgressed the ethical altogether and had a higher *telos* outside it, in relation to which he suspended it. For I certainly would like to know how Abraham's act can be related to the universal, whether any point of contact between what Abraham did and the universal can be found other than that Abraham transgressed it. It is not to save a nation, not to uphold the idea of the state that Abraham does it; it is not to appease the angry gods. If it were a matter of the deity's being angry, then he was, after all, angry only with Abraham, and Abraham's act is totally unrelated to the universal, is a purely private endeavor. Therefore, while the tragic hero is great because of his moral virtue, Abraham is great because of a purely personal virtue. There is no higher expression for the ethical in Abraham's life than that the father shall love the son. The ethical in the sense of the moral is entirely beside the point. Insofar as the universal was present, it was cryptically in Isaac, hidden, so to speak, in Isaac's loins, and must cry out with Isaac's mouth: Do not do this, you are destroying everything.

Why, then, does Abraham do it? For God's sake and—the two are wholly identical—for his own sake. He does it for God's sake because God demands this proof of his faith; he does it for his own sake so that he can prove it. The unity of the two is altogether correctly expressed in the word already used to describe this relationship. It is an ordeal, a temptation. A temptation—but what does that mean? As a rule, what tempts a person is something that will hold him back from doing his duty, but here the temptation is the ethical itself: which would hold him back from doing God's will. But what is duty? Duty is simply the expression for God's will.

Here the necessity of a new category for the understanding of Abraham becomes apparent. Paganism does not know such a relationship to the divine. The tragic hero does not enter into any private relationship to the divine, but the ethical is the divine, and thus the paradox therein can be mediated in the universal.

Abraham cannot be mediated; in other words, he cannot speak. As soon as I speak, I express the universal, and if I do not do so, no one can understand me. As soon as Abraham wants to express himself in the universal, he must declare that his situation is a spiritual trial, for he has no higher expression of the universal that ranks above the universal he violates.

Therefore, although Abraham arouses my admiration, he also appalls me. The person who denies himself and sacrifices himself because of duty gives up the finite in order to grasp the infinite and is adequately assured; the tragic hero gives up the certain for the even more certain, and the observer's eye views him with confidence. But the person who gives up the universal in order to grasp something even higher that is not the universal—what does he do? Is it possible that this can be anything other than a spiritual trial? And if it is possible, but the individual makes a mistake, what salvation is there for him? He suffers all the agony of the tragic hero, he shatters his joy in the world, he renounces everything, and perhaps at the same time he barricades himself from the sublime joy that was so precious to him that he would buy it at any price. The observer cannot understand him at all; nor can his eye rest upon him with confidence. Perhaps the believer's intention cannot be carried out at all, because it is inconceivable. Or if it could be done but the individual has misunderstood the deity—what salvation would there be for him? The tragic hero needs and demands tears, and where is the envious eye so arid that it could not weep with Agamemnon, but where is the soul so gone astray that it has the audacity to weep for Abraham? The tragic hero finishes his task at a specific moment in time, but as time passes he does what is no less significant: he visits the person encompassed by sorrow, who cannot breathe because of his anguished sighs, whose thoughts oppress him, heavy with tears. He appears to him, breaks the witchcraft of sorrow, loosens the bonds, evokes the tears, and the suffering one forgets his own sufferings in those of the tragic hero. One cannot weep over Abraham. One approaches him with a *horror religiosus* as Israel approached Mount Sinai. What if he himself is distraught, what if he had made a mistake, this lonely man who climbs Mount Moriah, whose peak towers sky-high over the flatlands of Aulis, what if he is not a sleepwalker safely crossing the abyss while the one standing at the foot of the mountain looks up, shakes with anxiety, and then in his deference and horror does not even dare to call to him?—Thanks, once again thanks, to a man who, to a person overwhelmed by life's sorrows and left behind naked, reaches out the words, the leafage of language by which he can conceal his misery. Thanks to you, great Shakespeare, you who can say everything, everything, everything just as it is—and yet, why did you never articulate this torment? Did you perhaps reserve it for yourself, like the beloved's name that one cannot bear to have the world utter, for with his little secret that he cannot divulge the poet buys this power of the word to tell everybody else's dark secrets. A poet is not an apostle; he drives out devils only by the power of the devil.

But if the ethical is teleologically suspended in this manner, how does the single individual in whom it is suspended exist? He exists as the single individual in contrast to the universal. Does he sin, then, for from the point of view of the idea, this is the form of sin. Thus, even though the child does not sin, because it is not conscious of its existence as such, its existence, from the point of view of the idea, is nevertheless sin, and the ethical makes its claim upon it at all times. If it is denied that this form can be repeated in such a way that it is not sin, then judgment has fallen upon Abraham. How did Abraham exist? He had faith. This is the paradox by which he remains at the apex, the paradox that he cannot explain to anyone else, for the paradox is that he as the single individual places himself in an absolute relation to the absolute. Is he justified? Again, his justification is the paradoxical, for if he is, then he is justified not by virtue of being something universal but by virtue of being the single individual.

How does the single individual reassure himself that he is legitimate? It is a simple matter to level all existence to the idea of the state or the idea of a society. If this is done, it is also simple to mediate, for one never comes to the paradox that the single individual as the single individual is higher than the universal, something I can also express symbolically in a statement by Pythagoras to the effect that the odd number is more perfect than the even number. If occasionally there is any response at all these days with regard to the paradox, it is likely to be: One judges it by the result. Aware that he is a paradox who cannot be understood, a hero who has become a *skandalon* [offense] to his age will shout confidently to his contemporaries: The result will indeed prove that I was justified. This cry is rarely heard in our age, inasmuch as it does not produce heroes—this is its defect—and it likewise has the advantage that it produces few caricatures. When in our age we hear these words: It will be judged by the result—then we know at once with whom we have the honor of speaking. Those who talk this way are a numerous type whom I shall designate under the common name of assistant professors. With security in life, they live in their thoughts: they have a *permanent* position and a *secure* future in a well-organized state. They have hundreds, yes, even thousands of years between them and the earthquakes of existence; they are not afraid that such things can be repeated, for then what would the police and the newspapers say? Their life task is to judge the great men, judge them according to the result. Such behavior toward greatness betrays a strange mixture of arrogance and wretchedness—arrogance because they feel called to pass judgment, wretchedness because they feel that their lives are in no way allied with the lives of the great. Anyone with even a smattering *erectioris ingenii* [of nobility of nature] never becomes an utterly cold and clammy worm, and when he approaches greatness, he is never devoid of the thought that since the creation of the world it has been customary for the result to come last and that if one is truly going to learn something from greatness one must be particularly aware of the beginning. If the one who is to act wants to judge himself by the result, he will never begin. Although the result may give joy to the entire world, it cannot help the hero, for he would not know the result until the whole thing was over, and he would not become a hero by that but by making a beginning.

Moreover, in its dialectic the result (insofar as it is finitude's response to the infinite question) is altogether incongruous with the hero's existence. Or should Abraham's receiving Isaac by a *marvel* be able to prove that Abraham was justified in relating himself as the single individual to the universal? If Abraham actually had sacrificed Isaac, would he therefore have been less justified?

But we are curious about the result, just as we are curious about the way a book turns out. We do not want to know anything about the anxiety, the distress, the paradox. We carry on an esthetic flirtation with the result. It arrives just as unexpectedly but also just as effortlessly as a prize in a lottery, and when we have heard the result, we have built ourselves up. And yet no manacled robber of churches is so despicable a criminal as the one who plunders holiness in this way, and not even Judas, who sold his Lord for thirty pieces of silver, is more contemptible than someone who peddles greatness in this way.

It is against my very being to speak inhumanly about greatness, to make it a dim and *nebulous* far-distant shape or to let it be great but devoid of the emergence of the humanness without which it ceases to be great, for it is not what happens to me that makes me great but what I do, and certainly there is no one who believes that someone became great by winning the big lottery prize. A person might have been born in lowly circumstances, but I would still require him not to be so inhuman toward himself that he could imagine the king's castle only at a distance and ambiguously dream of its greatness, and destroy it at the same time he elevates it because he elevated it so basely. I require him to be man enough to tread confidently and with dignity there as well. He must not be so inhuman that he insolently violates everything by barging right off the street into the king's hall—he loses more thereby than the king. On the contrary, he should find a joy in observing every bidding of propriety with a happy and confident enthusiasm, which is precisely what makes him a free spirit. This is merely a metaphor, for that distinction is only a very imperfect expression of the distance of spirit. I require every person not to think so inhumanly of himself that he does not dare to enter those palaces where the memory of the chosen ones lives or even those where they themselves live. He is not to enter rudely and foist his affinity upon them. He is to be happy for every time he bows before them, but he is to be confident, free of spirit, and always more than a charwoman, for if he wants to be no more than that, he will never get in. And the very thing that is going to help him is the anxiety and distress in which the great were tried, for otherwise, if he has any backbone, they will only arouse his righteous envy. And anything that can be great only at a distance, that someone wants to make great with empty and hollow phrases—is destroyed by that very person.

Who was as great in the world as that favored woman, the mother of God, the Virgin Mary? And yet how do we speak of her? That she was the favored one among women does not make her great, and if it would not be so very odd for those who listen to be able to think just as inhumanly as those who speak, then every young girl might ask: Why am I not so favored? And if I had nothing else to say, I certainly would not dismiss such a question as stupid, because, viewed abstractly, vis-à-vis a favor, every person is just as entitled to it as the other. We leave out the distress, the anxiety, the paradox. My thoughts are as pure as anybody's, and he who can think this way surely has pure thoughts, and, if not, he can expect something horrible, for anyone who has once experienced these images cannot get rid of them again, and if he sins against them, they take a terrible revenge in a silent rage, which is more terrifying than the stridency of ten ravenous critics. To be sure, Mary bore the child wondrously, but she nevertheless did it "after the manner of women" [Gen 18:1], and such a time is one of anxiety, distress, and paradox. The angel was indeed a ministering spirit, but he was not a meddlesome spirit who went to the other young maidens in Israel and said: Do not scorn Mary, the extraordinary is happening to her. The angel went only to Mary, and no one could understand her. Has any woman been as infringed upon as was Mary, and is it not true here also that the one whom God blesses he curses in the same breath? This is the spirit's view of Mary, and she is by no means—it is revolting to me to say it but even more so that people have inanely and unctuously made her out to be thus—she is by no means a lady idling in her finery and playing with a divine child. When, despite this, she said: Behold, I am the handmaid of the Lord—then she is great, and I believe it should not be difficult to explain why she became the mother of God. She needs worldly admiration as little as Abraham needs tears, for she was no heroine and he was no hero, but both of them became greater than these, not by being exempted in any way from the distress and the agony and the paradox, but became greater by means of these.

It is great when the poet in presenting his tragic hero for public admiration dares to say: Weep for him, for he deserves it. It is great to deserve the tears of those who deserve to shed tears. It is great that the poet dares to keep the crowd under restraint, dares to discipline men to examine themselves individually to see if they are worthy to weep for the hero, for the slop water of the snivelers is a debasement of the sacred. But even greater than all this is the knight of faith's daring to say to the noble one who wants to weep for him: Do not weep for me, but weep for yourself.

We are touched, we look back to those beautiful times. Sweet sentimental longing leads us to the goal of our desire, to see Christ walking about in the promised land. We forget the anxiety, the distress, the paradox. Was it such a simple matter not to make a mistake? Was it not terrifying that this man walking around among the others was God? Was it not terrifying to sit down to eat with him? Was it such an easy matter to become an apostle? But the result, the eighteen centuries—that helps, that contributes to this mean deception whereby we deceive ourselves and others. I do not feel brave enough to wish to be contemporary with events like that, but I do not for that reason severely condemn those who made a mistake, nor do I depreciate those who saw what was right.

But I come back to Abraham. During the time before the result, either Abraham was a murderer every minute or we stand before a paradox that is higher than all mediations.

The story of Abraham contains, then, a teleological suspension of the ethical. As the single individual he became higher than the universal. This is the paradox, which cannot be mediated. How he entered into it is just as inexplicable as how he remains in it. If this is not Abraham's situation, then Abraham is not even a tragic hero but a murderer. It is thoughtless to want to go on calling him the father of faith, to speak of it to men who have an interest only in words. A person can become a tragic hero through his own strength—but not the knight of faith. When a person walks what is in one sense the hard road of the tragic hero, there are many who can give him advice, but he who walks the narrow road of faith has no one to advise him—no one understands him. Faith is a marvel, and yet no human being is excluded from it; for that which unites all human life is passion,[1] and faith is a passion.

Notes

1. Lessing has somewhere said something similar from a purely esthetic point of view. He actually wants to show in this passage that grief, too, can yield a witty remark. With that in mind, he quotes the words spoken on a particular occasion by the unhappy king of England, Edward II. In contrast he quotes from Diderot a story about a peasant woman and a remark she made. He goes on to say:

   That also was wit, and the wit of a peasant woman, besides; but the situation made it inevitable. And consequently one must not seek the excuse for the witty expressions of pain and sorrow in the fact that the person who said them was a distinguished, well-educated, intelligent, and also witty person; *for the passions make all men equal again*: but in this, that in the same situation probably every person, without exception, would have said the same thing. A queen could have had and must have had the thought of a peasant woman, just as a peasant could have said and no doubt would have said what the king said there.

   See *Sämmtliche Werke*, XXX, 223.

7

FRIEDRICH NIETZSCHE
(1844–1900)

The German philosopher Friedrich Nietzsche was born into a deeply religious family in 1844. His father and two grandfathers were Lutheran pastors, and as a result Nietzsche was also expected to enter the priesthood. In 1864, he studied theology and classical philology at the University of Bonn, but the next year he gave up theology in order to concentrate on philology at the University of Leipzig. He was an extraordinarily gifted student and at the young age of twenty-four was appointed to the chair of classical philology at the University of Basel, Switzerland. Due to ill-health, however, he was forced to resign his post in 1879, and for the next ten years he traveled throughout Europe while writing books and trying to regain his health. In January 1889, as he left his hotel in Turin, Nietzsche was overcome with grief at the sight of a horse being flogged by a coachman. He ran up to the animal, threw his arms around its neck, and suffered a complete mental collapse. He was never to recover his sanity. He died eleven years later in 1900.

Nietzsche's first book, *The Birth of Tragedy* (1872), introduces his famous distinction between the opposing forces of the "Apollinian" (restraint, harmony, reason) and the "Dionysian" (excess, intoxication, frenzy), which attain synthesis in Greek tragedy and music. This synthesis—which he went on to simply call "the Dionysian"—is later opposed to the crucified Christ, which for Nietzsche symbolizes all that is life-denying, unnatural, and uncreative in human existence. Nietzsche's scathing attack on Christianity, the hallmark of his thinking, is summed up in his most famous pronouncement, "God is dead" (*The Gay Science* [1882]), by which he means that the belief in the Judeo-Christian God has become untenable. In place of a religious explanation for things, Nietzsche offers a materialist philosophy, one that places becoming above being, instinct above reason, art above truth, and the *Übermensch* above man. These ideas were expressed in a rich outpouring of works written from 1886 to 1889, including *Beyond Good and Evil* (1886), *On the Genealogy of Morals* (1887), *Twilight of the Idols* (1889), *Ecce Homo* (written 1888, published 1908), and culminating in *The Antichrist* (written 1888, published 1895).

Nietzsche's most philosophically rigorous treatment of morality is presented in *On the Genealogy of Morals*, from which our selection is taken. In offering a genealogy of morality, Nietzsche seeks to provide us with a naturalistic (as opposed to supernatural) and historical account of the origins of our moral values. He claims that the notion of "good" did not originally apply to altruistic actions, but was used by the Greek masters to denote the "noble, powerful, high-stationed and high-minded." Bad was something of an "afterthought"—merely the opposite of good, i.e., "the low, low-minded, common and plebeian." With the appearance of Judaism and Christianity, however, another morality came into being, one that "dared to invert the aristocratic value equation." Nietzsche calls this the "slave revolt in morality." Slaves construct their value scheme purely in response to their suffering and frustration at the hands of their "evil" masters. Their value scheme is thus wholly reactive and negative.

Select Bibliography of Nietzsche's Works in English

Beyond Good and Evil. Trans. Walter Kaufmann. New York: Vintage, 1966.

The Birth of Tragedy. Trans. Walter Kaufmann. New York: Vintage, 1966.

Daybreak: Thoughts on the Prejudices of Morality. Trans. R.J. Hollingdale. Cambridge: Cambridge University Press, 1982.

Ecce Homo. Trans. Walter Kaufmann. New York: Vintage, 1967.

The Gay Science. Trans. Walter Kaufmann. New York: Vintage, 1974.

On the Genealogy of Morals. Trans. Walter Kaufmann and R.J. Hollingdale. New York: Vintage, 1967.

Thus Spoke Zarathustra. Trans. R.J. Hollingdale. Harmondsworth, UK: Penguin, 1973.

Twilight of the Idols. Trans. Walter Kaufmann. In *The Portable Nietzsche.* New York: Viking, 1954.

The Will to Power. Trans. Walter Kaufmann and R.J. Hollingdale. New York: Vintage, 1967.

ON THE GENEALOGY OF MORALS

"Good and Evil," "Good and Bad"

1

These English psychologists, whom one has also to thank for the only attempts hitherto to arrive at a history of the origin of morality—they themselves are no easy riddle; I confess that, as living riddles, they even possess one essential advantage over their books—*they are interesting*! These English psychologists—what do they really want? One always discovers them voluntarily or involuntarily at the same task, namely at dragging the *partie honteuse* of our inner world into the foreground and seeking the truly effective and directing agent, that which has been decisive in its evolution, in just that place where the intellectual pride of man would least *desire* to find it (in the *vis inertiae* of habit, for example, or in forgetfulness, or in a blind and chance mechanistic hooking-together of ideas, or in something purely passive, automatic, reflexive, molecular, and thoroughly stupid)—what is it really that always drives these psychologists in just *this* direction? Is it a secret, malicious, vulgar, perhaps self-deceiving instinct for belittling man? Or possibly a pessimistic suspicion, the mistrustfulness of disappointed idealists grown spiteful and gloomy? Or a petty subterranean hostility and rancor toward Christianity (and Plato) that has perhaps not even crossed the threshold of consciousness? Or even a lascivious taste for the grotesque, the painfully paradoxical, the questionable and absurd in existence? Or finally—something of each of them, a little vulgarity, a little gloominess, a little anti-Christianity, a little itching and need for spice?

But I am told they are simply old, cold, and tedious frogs, creeping around men and into men as if in their own proper element, that is, in a *swamp*. I rebel at that idea; more, I do not believe it; and if one may be allowed to hope where one does not know, then I hope from my heart they may be the reverse of this—that these investigators and microscopists of the soul may be fundamentally brave, proud, and magnanimous animals, who know how to keep their hearts as well as their sufferings in bounds and have trained themselves to sacrifice all desirability to truth, *every* truth, even plain, harsh, ugly, repellent, unchristian, immoral truth.—For such truths do exist.—

2

All respect them for the good spirits that may rule in these historians of morality! But it is, unhappily, certain that the *historical spirit* itself is lacking in them, that precisely all the good spirits of history itself have left them in the lurch! As is the hallowed custom with philosophers, the thinking of all of them is *by nature* unhistorical; there is no doubt about that. The way they have bungled their moral genealogy comes to light at the very beginning, where the task is to investigate the origin of the concept and judgment "good." "Originally"—so they decree—"one approved unegoistic actions and called them good from the point of view of those to whom they were done, that is to say, those to whom they were *useful*; later one *forgot* how this approval originated and, simply because unegoistic actions were always *habitually* praised as good, one also felt them to be good—as if they were something good in themselves." One sees straightaway that this primary derivation already contains all the typical traits of the idiosyncrasy of the English psychologists—we have "utility," "forgetting," "habit," and finally "error," all as the basis of an evaluation of which the higher man has hitherto been proud as though it were a kind of prerogative of man as such. This pride *has* to be humbled, this evaluation disvalued: has that end been achieved?

Now it is plain to me, first of all, that in this theory the source of the concept "good" has been sought and established in the wrong place: the judgment "good" did *not* originate with those to whom "goodness" was shown! Rather it was "the good" themselves, that is to say, the noble, powerful, high-stationed and high-minded, who felt and established themselves and their actions as good, that is, of the first rank, in contradistinction to all the low, low-minded, common and plebeian. It was out of this *pathos of distance* that they first seized the right to create values and to coin names for these values: what had they to do with utility! The viewpoint of utility is as remote and inappropriate as it possibly could be in face of such a burning eruption of the highest rank-ordering, rank-defining value judgments: for here feeling has attained the antithesis of that low degree of warmth which any calculating prudence, any calculus of utility, presupposes—and not for once only, not for an exceptional hour, but for good. The pathos of nobility and distance, as aforesaid, the protracted and domineering fundamental total feeling on the part of a higher ruling order in relation to a lower order, to a "below"—*that* is the origin of the antithesis "good" and "bad." (The lordly right of giving names extends so far that one should allow oneself to conceive the origin of language itself as an expression of power on the part of the rulers: they say "this *is* this and this," they seal every thing and event with a sound and, as it were, take possession of it.) It follows from this origin that the word "good" was definitely *not* linked from the first and by necessity to "unegoistic" actions, as the superstition of these genealogists of morality would have it. Rather it was only when aristocratic value judgments *declined* that the whole antithesis "egoistic" "unegoistic" obtruded itself more and more on the human conscience—it is, to speak in my own language, the *herd instinct* that through this antithesis at last gets its word (and its *words*) in. And even then it was a long time before that instinct attained such dominion that moral evaluation was actually stuck and halted at this antithesis (as, for example, is the case in contemporary Europe: the prejudice that takes "moral," "unegoistic," "*désintéressé*" as concepts of equivalent value already rules today with the force of a "fixed idea" and brain-sickness).

3

In the second place, however: quite apart from the historical untenability of this hypothesis regarding the origin of the value judgment "good," it suffers from an inherent psychological absurdity. The utility of the unegoistic action is supposed to be the source of the approval accorded it, and this source is supposed to have been *forgotten*—but how is this forgetting *possible*? Has the utility of such actions come to an end at some time or other? The opposite is the case: this utility has rather been an everyday experience at all times, therefore something that has been underlined again and again: consequently, instead of fading from consciousness, instead of becoming easily forgotten, it must have been impressed on the consciousness more and more clearly. How much more reasonable is that opposing theory (it is not for that reason more true—) which Herbert Spencer, for example, espoused: that the concept "good" is essentially identical with the concept "useful," "practical," so that in the judgments "good" and "bad" mankind has summed up and sanctioned precisely its *unforgotten* and *unforgettable* experiences regarding what is useful-practical and what is harmful-practical. According to this theory, that which has always proved itself useful is good: therefore it may claim to be "valuable in the highest degree," "valuable in itself." This road to an explanation is, as aforesaid, also a wrong one, but at least the explanation is in itself reasonable and psychologically tenable.

4

The signpost to the *right* road was for me the question: What was the real etymological significance of the designations for "good" coined in the various languages? I found they all led back to the *same conceptual transformation*—that everywhere "noble," "aristocratic" in the social sense, is the basic concept from which "good" in the sense of "with aristocratic soul," "noble," "with a soul of a high order," "with a privileged soul" necessarily developed: a development which always runs parallel with that other in which "common," "plebeian," "low" are finally transformed into the concept "bad." The most convincing example of the latter is the German word *schlecht* [bad] itself: which is identical with *schlicht* [plain, simple]—compare *schlechtweg* [plainly], *schlechterdings* [simply]—and originally designated the plain, the common man, as yet with no inculpatory implication and simply in contradistinction to the nobility. About the time of the Thirty Years' War, late enough therefore, this meaning changed into the one now customary.

With regard to a moral genealogy this seems to me a *fundamental* insight; that it has been arrived at so late is the fault of the retarding influence exercised by the democratic prejudice in the modern world toward all questions of origin. And this is so even in the apparently quite objective domain of natural science and physiology, as I shall merely hint here. But what mischief this prejudice is capable of doing, especially to morality and history, once it has been unbridled to the point of hatred is shown by the notorious case of Buckle [Henry Thomas Buckle (1821–1862), English historian]; here the *plebeianism* of the modern spirit, which is of English origin, erupted once again on its native soil, as violently as a mud volcano and with that salty, noisy, vulgar eloquence with which all volcanos have spoken hitherto.—

5

With regard to *our* problem, which may on good grounds be called a *quiet* problem and one which fastidiously directs itself to few ears, it is of no small interest to ascertain that through those words and roots which designate "good" there frequently still shines the most important nuance by virtue of which the noble felt themselves to be men of a higher rank. Granted that, in the majority of cases, they designate themselves simply by their superiority in power (as "the powerful," "the masters," "the commanders") or by the most clearly visible signs of this superiority, for example, as "the rich," "the possessors" (this is the meaning of *arya*; and of corresponding words in Iranian and Slavic). But they also do it by a *typical character trait*: and this is the case that concerns us here. They call themselves, for instance, "the truthful"; this is so above all of the Greek nobility, whose mouthpiece is the Megarian poet Theognis [Theognis of Megara, sixth century B.C.]. The root of the word coined for this, *esthlos* [Greek: good, brave], signifies one who *is*, who possesses reality, who is actual, who is true; then, with a subjective turn, the true as the truthful: in this phase of conceptual transformation it becomes a slogan and catchword of the nobility and passes over entirely into the sense of "noble," as distinct from the *lying* common man, which is what Theognis takes him to be and how he describes him—until finally, after the decline of the nobility, the word is left to designate nobility of soul and becomes as it were ripe and sweet. In the word *kakos* [Greek: bad, ugly, ill-born, mean, craven], as in *deilos* [Greek: cowardly, worthless, vile, wretched] (the plebeian in contradistinction to the *agathos* [Greek: good, well-born, gentle, brave, capable]), cowardice is emphasized: this perhaps gives an indication in which direction one should seek the etymological origin of *agathos*, which is susceptible of several interpretations. The Latin *malus* [bad] (beside which I set *melas* [Greek: black, dark]) may designate the common man as the dark-colored, above all as the black-haired man ("*hic niger est—*" [From Horace's *Satires*]), as the pre-Aryan occupant of the soil of Italy who was distinguished most obviously from the blond, that is Aryan, conqueror race by his color; Gaelic, at any rate, offers us a precisely similar case—*fin* (for example in the name *Fin-Gal*), the distinguishing word for nobility, finally for the good, noble, pure, originally meant the blond-headed, in contradistinction to the dark, black-haired aboriginal inhabitants.

The Celts, by the way, were definitely a blond race; it is wrong to associate traces of an essentially dark-haired people which appear on the more careful ethnographical maps of Germany with any sort of Celtic origin or blood-mixture, as Virchow [Rudolf Virchow (1821–1902), German pathologist and liberal politician] still does: it is rather the *pre-Aryan* people of Germany who emerge in these places. (The same is true of virtually all Europe: the suppressed race has gradually recovered the upper hand again, in coloring, shortness of skull, perhaps even in the intellectual and social instincts: who can say whether modern democracy, even more modern anarchism and especially that inclination for "*commune,*" for the most primitive form of society, which is now shared by all the socialists of Europe, does not signify in the main a tremendous *counterattack*—and that the conqueror and *master race*, the Aryan, is not succumbing physiologically, too?

I believe I may venture to interpret the Latin *bonus* [Good] as "the warrior," provided I am right in tracing *bonus* back to an earlier *duonus* [old form of *bonus; duellum* old form of *bellum* (war)] (compare *bellum = duellum = duen-lum*, which seems to me to contain *duonus*). Therefore *bonus* as the man of strife, of dissension (*duo*), as the man of war: one sees what constituted the "goodness" of man in ancient Rome. Our German *gut* [good] even: does it not signify "the godlike," the man of "godlike race"? And is it not identical with the popular (originally noble) name of the Goths? The grounds for this conjecture cannot be dealt with here.—

6

To this rule that a concept denoting political superiority always resolves itself into a concept denoting superiority of soul it is not necessarily an exception (although it provides occasions for exceptions) when the highest caste is at the same time the *priestly* caste and therefore emphasizes in its total description of itself a predicate that calls to mind its priestly function. It is then, for example, that "pure" and "impure" confront one another for the first time as designations of station; and here too there evolves a "good" and a "bad" in a sense no longer referring to station. One should be warned, moreover, against taking these concepts "pure" and "impure" too ponderously or broadly, not to say symbolically: all the concepts of ancient man were rather at first incredibly uncouth, coarse, external, narrow, straightforward, and altogether *unsymbolical* in meaning to a degree that we can scarcely conceive. The "pure one" is from the beginning merely a man who washes himself, who forbids himself certain foods that produce skin ailments, who does not sleep with the dirty women of the lower strata, who has an aversion to blood—no more, hardly more! On the other hand, to be sure, it is clear from the whole nature of an essentially priestly aristocracy why antithetical valuations could in precisely this instance soon become dangerously deepened, sharpened, and internalized; and indeed they finally tore chasms between man and man that a very Achilles of a free spirit would not venture to leap without a shudder. There is from the first something *unhealthy* in such priestly aristocracies and in the habits ruling in them which turn them away from action and alternate between brooding and emotional explosions, habits which seem to have as their almost invariable consequences that intestinal morbidity and neurasthenia which has afflicted priests at all times; but as to that which they themselves devised as a remedy for this morbidity—must one not assert that it has ultimately proved itself a hundred times more dangerous in its effects than the sickness it was supposed to cure? Mankind itself is still ill with the effects of this priestly naïveté in medicine! Think, for example, of certain forms of diet (abstinence from meat), of fasting, of sexual continence, of flight "into the wilderness" (the Weir Mitchell isolation cure—without, to be sure, the subsequent fattening and overfeeding which constitute the most effective remedy for the hysteria induced by the ascetic ideal): add to these the entire antisensualistic metaphysics of the priests that makes men indolent and overrefined, their autohypnosis in the manner of fakirs and Brahmins—Brahma used in the shape of a glass knob and a fixed idea—and finally the only-too-comprehensible satiety with all this, together with the radical cure for it, *nothingness* (or God—the desire for a *unio mystica* with God is the desire of the Buddhist for nothingness, Nirvana—and no more!). For with the priests *everything* becomes more dangerous, not only cures and remedies, but also arrogance, revenge, acuteness, profligacy, love, lust to rule, virtue, disease—but it is only fair to add that it was on the soil of this *essentially dangerous* form of human existence, the priestly form, that man first became *an interesting animal*, that only here did the human soul in a higher sense acquire *depth* and become *evil*—and these are the two basic respects in which man has hitherto been superior to other beasts!

7

One will have divined already how easily the priestly mode of valuation can branch off from the knightly-aristocratic and then develop into its opposite; this is particularly likely when the priestly caste and the warrior caste are in jealous opposition to one another and are unwilling to come to terms. The knightly-aristocratic value judgments presupposed a powerful physicality, a flourishing, abundant, even overflowing health, together with that which serves to preserve it: war, adventure, hunting, dancing, war games, and in general all that involves vigorous, free, joyful activity. The priestly-noble mode of valuation presupposes, as we have seen, other things: it is disadvantageous for when it comes to war! As is well known, the priests are the *most evil enemies*—but why? Because they are the most impotent. It is because of their impotence that in them hatred grows to monstrous and uncanny proportions, to the most spiritual and poisonous kind of hatred. The truly great haters in world history have always been priests; likewise the most ingenious [*Geistreich*] haters: other kinds of spirit [*Geist*] hardly come into consideration when compared with the spirit of priestly vengefulness. Human history would be altogether too stupid a thing without the spirit that the impotent have introduced into it—let us take at once the most notable example. All that has been done on earth against "the noble," "the powerful," "the masters," "the rulers," fades into nothing compared with what the *Jews* have done against them; the Jews, that priestly people, who in opposing their enemies and conquerors were ultimately satisfied with nothing less than a radical revaluation of their enemies' values, that is to say, an act of the *most spiritual revenge*. For this alone was appropriate to a priestly people, the people embodying the most deeply repressed [*Zurückgetretensten*] priestly vengefulness. It was the Jews who, with awe-inspiring consistency, dared to invert the aristocratic value-equation (good = noble = powerful = beautiful = happy = beloved of God) and to hang on to this inversion with their teeth, the teeth of the most abysmal hatred (the hatred of impotence), saying "the wretched alone are the good; the poor, impotent, lowly alone are the good; the suffering, deprived, sick, ugly alone are pious, alone are blessed by God, blessedness is for them alone—and you, the powerful and noble, are on the contrary the evil, the cruel, the lustful, the insatiable, the godless to all eternity; and you shall be in all eternity the unblessed, accursed, and damned!". . . One knows *who* inherited this Jewish revaluation. . . . In connection with the tremendous and immeasurably fateful initiative provided by the Jews through this most fundamental of all declarations of war, I recall the proposition I arrived at on a previous occasion (*Beyond Good and*

Evil, section 195)—that with the Jews there began *the slave revolt in morality*: that revolt which has a history of two thousand years behind it and which we no longer see because it—has been victorious.

8

But you do not comprehend this? You are incapable of seeing something that required two thousand years to achieve victory?—There is nothing to wonder at in that: all *protracted* things are hard to see, to see whole. *That*, however, is what has happened: from the trunk of that tree of vengefulness and hatred, Jewish hatred—the profoundest and sublimest kind of hatred, capable of creating ideals and reversing values, the like of which has never existed on earth before—there grew something equally incomparable, a *new love*, the profoundest and sublimest kind of love—and from what other trunk could it have grown?

One should not imagine it grew up as the denial of that thirst for revenge, as the opposite of Jewish hatred! No, the reverse is true! That love grew out of it as its crown, as its triumphant crown spreading itself farther and farther into the purest brightness and sunlight, driven as it were into the domain of light and the heights in pursuit of the goals of that hatred—victory, spoil, and seduction—by the same impulse that drove the roots of that hatred deeper and deeper and more and more covetously into all that was profound and evil. This Jesus of Nazareth, the incarnate gospel of love, this "Redeemer" who brought blessedness and victory to the poor, the sick, and the sinners—was he not this seduction in its most uncanny and irresistible form, a seduction and bypath to precisely those *Jewish* values and new ideals? Did Israel not attain the ultimate goal of its sublime vengefulness precisely through the bypath of this "Redeemer," this ostensible opponent and disintegrator of Israel? Was it not part of the secret black art of truly *grand* politics of revenge, of a farseeing, subterranean, slowly advancing, and premeditated revenge, that Israel must itself deny the real instrument of its revenge before all the world as a mortal enemy and nail it to the cross, so that "all the world," namely all the opponents of Israel, could unhesitatingly swallow just this bait? And could spiritual subtlety imagine any *more dangerous* bait than this? Anything to equal the enticing, intoxicating, overwhelming, and undermining power of that symbol of the "holy cross," that ghastly paradox of a "God on the cross," that mystery of an unimaginable ultimate cruelty and self-crucifixion of God *for the salvation of man*?

What is certain, at least, is that *sub hoc signo* [under this sign] Israel, with its vengefulness and revaluation of all values, has hitherto triumphed again and again over all other ideals, over all *nobler* ideals.—

9

"But why are you talking about *nobler* ideals! Let us stick to the facts: the people have won—or 'the slaves' or 'the mob' or 'the herd' or whatever you like to call them—if this has happened through the Jews, very well! In that case no people ever had a more world-historic mission. 'The masters' have been disposed of; the morality of the common man has won. One may conceive of this victory as at the same time a blood-poisoning (it has mixed the races together)—I shan't contradict; but this intoxication has undoubtedly been *successful*. The 'redemption' of the human race (from 'the masters,' that is) is going forward; everything is visibly becoming Judaized, Christianized, mob-ized (what do the words matter!). The progress of this poison through the entire body of mankind seems irresistible, its pace and tempo may from now on even grow slower, subtler, less audible, more cautious—there is plenty of time.—To this end, does the Church today still have any *necessary* role to play? Does it still have the right to exist? Or could one do without it? *Quaeritur* [One asks]. It seems to hinder rather than hasten this progress. But perhaps that is its usefulness.—Certainly it has, over the years, become something crude and boorish, something repellent to a more delicate intellect, to a truly modern taste. Ought it not to become at least a little more refined?—Today it alienates rather than seduces.—Which of us would be a free spirit if the Church did not exist? It is the Church, and not its poison, that repels us.— Apart from the Church, we, too, love the poison.—"

This is the epilogue of a "free spirit" to my speech; an honest animal, as he has abundantly revealed, and a democrat, moreover; he had been listening to me till then and could not endure to listen to my silence. For at this point I have much to be silent about.

10

The slave revolt in morality begins when *ressentiment* itself becomes creative and gives birth to values: the *ressentiment* of natures that are denied the true reaction, that of deeds, and compensate themselves with an imaginary revenge. While every noble morality develops from a triumphant affirmation of itself, slave morality from the outset says No to what is "outside," what is "different," what is "not itself"; and *this* No is its creative deed. This inversion of the value-positing eye—this *need* to direct one's view outward instead of back to oneself—is of the essence of *ressentiment*; in order to exist, slave morality always first needs a hostile external world; it needs, physiologically speaking, external stimuli in order to act at all—its action is fundamentally reaction.

The reverse is the case with the noble mode of valuation: it acts and grows spontaneously, it seeks its opposite only so as to affirm itself more gratefully and triumphantly—its negative concept "low," "common," "bad" is only a subsequently invented pale, contrasting image in relation to its positive basic concept—filled with life and passion through and through—"we noble ones, we good, beautiful, happy ones!" When the noble mode of valuation blunders and sins against reality, it does so in respect to the sphere with which it is *not* sufficiently familiar, against a real knowledge of which it has indeed inflexibly guarded itself: in some circumstances it misunderstands the sphere it despises, that of the common man, of the lower orders; on the other hand, one should remember that, even supposing that the affect of contempt, of looking down from a superior height, *falsifies* the image of that which it despises, it will at any rate still be a much less serious falsification than that perpetrated on its opponent—in *effigie* of course—by the submerged hatred, the vengefulness of the impotent. There is indeed too much carelessness, too much taking lightly, too much looking away and impatience involved in contempt, even too much joyfulness, for it to be able to transform its object into a real caricature and monster.

One should not overlook the almost benevolent nuances that the Greek nobility, for example, bestows on all the words it employs to distinguish the lower orders from itself; how they are continuously mingled and sweetened with a kind of pity, consideration, and forbearance, so that finally almost all the words referring to the common man have remained as expressions signifying "unhappy," "pitiable" (campore *deilos*, *deilaios*, *poneros*, *mochtheros*, the last two of which properly designate the common man as work-slave and beast of burden) [Greek: the first four mean *wretched*; and also, *deilos*: cowardly, worthless, vile; *deilaios*: paltry; *poneros*: oppressed by toils, good for nothing, worthless, knavish, base, cowardly; *mochtheros*: suffering hardship, knavish]—and how on the other hand "bad," "low," "unhappy" have never ceased to sound to the Greek ear as one note with a tone-color in which "unhappy" preponderates: this as an inheritance from the ancient nobler aristocratic mode of evaluation, which does not belie itself even in its contempt (—philologists should recall the sense in which *oïzyros* [woeful, miserable, toilsome; wretch], *anolbos* [unblest, wretched, luckless, poor], *tlemon* [wretched, miserable], *dystychein* [to be unlucky, unfortunate], *xymphora* [misfortune] are employed). The "well-born" *felt* themselves to be the "happy"; they did not have to establish their happiness artificially by examining their enemies, or to persuade themselves, *deceive* themselves, that they were happy (as all men of *ressentiment* are in the habit of doing); and they likewise knew, as rounded men replete with energy and therefore *necessarily* active, that happiness should not be sundered from action—being active was with them necessarily a part of happiness (whence *eu prattein* [to do well in the sense of faring well] takes its origin)—all very much the opposite of "happiness" at the level of the impotent, the oppressed, and those in whom poisonous and inimical feelings are festering, with whom it appears as essentially narcotic, drug, rest, peace, "sabbath," slackening of tension and relaxing of limbs, in short *passively*.

While the noble man lives in trust and openness with himself (*gennaios* [high-born, noble, high-minded] "of noble descent" underlines the nuance "upright" and probably also "naïve"), the man of *ressentiment* is neither upright nor naïve nor honest and straightforward with himself. His soul *squints*; his spirit loves hiding places, secret paths and back doors, everything covert entices him as *his* world, *his* security, *his* refreshment; he understands how to keep silent, how not to forget, how to wait, how to be provisionally self-deprecating and humble. A race of such men of *ressentiment* is bound to become eventually *cleverer* than any noble race; it will also honor cleverness to a far greater degree: namely, as a condition of existence of the first importance; while with nobler men cleverness can easily acquire a subtle flavor of luxury and subtlety—for here it is far less essential than the perfect functioning of the regulating *unconscious* instincts or even that a certain imprudence, perhaps a bold recklessness whether in the face of danger or of the enemy, or that enthusiastic impulsiveness in anger, love, reverence, gratitude, and revenge by which noble souls have at all times recognized one another. *Ressentiment* itself, if it should appear in the noble man, consummates and exhausts itself in an immediate reaction, and therefore does not *poison*: on the other hand, it fails to appear at all on countless occasions on which it inevitably appears in the weak and impotent.

To be incapable of taking one's enemies, one's accidents, even one's misdeeds seriously for very long—that is the sign of strong, full natures in whom there is an excess of the power to form, to mold, to recuperate and to forget (a good example of this in modern times is Mirabeau [Honoré Gabriel Riqueti, Comte de Mirabeau (1749–1791), a French Revolutionary statesman and writer], who had no memory for insults and vile actions done him and was unable to forgive simply because he—forgot). Such a man shakes off with a single *shrug* many vermin that eat deep into others; here alone genuine "love of one's enemies" is possible—supposing it to be possible at all on earth. How much reverence has a noble man for his enemies!—and such reverence is a bridge to love.— For he desires his enemy for himself, as his mark of distinction; he can endure no other enemy than one in whom there is nothing to despise and *very much* to honor! In contrast to this, picture "the enemy" as the man of *ressentiment* conceives him—and here precisely is his deed, his creation: he has conceived "the evil enemy," "*the Evil One*," and this in fact is his basic concept, from which he then evolves, as an afterthought and pendant, a "good one"—himself!

8

MARTIN BUBER
(1878–1965)

The German-Jewish philosopher and theologian Martin Buber was born in Vienna in 1878. He studied philosophy and art history at the universities of Vienna, Leipzig, Berlin, and Zurich, and later became professor of Jewish Religion and Ethics at the University of Frankfurt-am-Main. After the Nazis prohibited Buber from teaching in 1933, he became head of the Freies Jüdisches Lehrhaus, an institute for Jewish adult education, where he took on the role of a courageous spokesman for Jewish spiritual resistance against Nazi oppression. He eventually settled in Palestine in 1938, and became professor at the Hebrew University, a position he held until his retirement in 1951. During the remaining years of his life, Buber lectured extensively throughout Europe and the United States, and made strenuous efforts to improve Arab-Israeli relations. He died in Jerusalem in 1965.

Buber's philosophy falls roughly into three periods. The first (1897–1923) marks his early encounter with Jewish mysticism (*Daniel* [1913]); the second (1923–1938), influenced in part by the philosophy of Ludwig Feuerbach, coincides with his philosophy of dialogue (*I and Thou* [1923]); and the third (1938–1965) concentrates on the social and political implications of dialogue, especially as they concern the then–newly formed State of Israel (*Paths in Utopia* [1949]). A polyglot, Buber also translated Nietzsche into Polish and, with Franz Rosenzweig, he painstakingly translated the Hebrew Bible into German.

Our reading is taken from Buber's most influential work *I and Thou*. The central claim of this work is that human experience can be described in terms of two "basic words": "I-It" and "I-You." The I-It relation designates the impersonal relation between the I and the world of things, known objectively and scientifically. By contrast, the I-You relation is one of genuine dialogue and "meeting," where the other is recognized in his or her "spiritual reality" as radically distinct from the I. While Buber privileges the interhuman relation, governed by what he calls "reciprocity," he acknowledges the possibility of a You-saying with respect to the rest of nature, including trees and animals. Buber also points out that "in every You we address the eternal You," or God. The relation with the "eternal You" is the only relation that is incapable of becoming an I-It.

Select Bibliography of Buber's Works in English

Between Man and Man. Trans. Ronald Gregor Smith. New York: Collier, 1965.
Daniel: Dialogues on Realization. Trans. Maurice Friedman. New York: Holt, Rinehart, & Winston, 1964.
Eclipse of God: Studies in the Relation between Religion and Philosophy. Trans. Maurice Friedman et al. New York: Harper, 1957.
I and Thou. Trans. Walter Kaufmann. New York: Scribner's, 1970.
The Knowledge of Man: A Philosophy of the Interhuman. New York: Harper and Row, 1965.

Philosophical Interrogations. Ed. Sydney Rome and Beatrice Rome. New York: Holt, Rinehart & Winston.
The Philosophy of Martin Buber. Ed. Paul Arthur Schilpp and Maurice Friedman. La Salle, IL: Open Court, 1967.
Paths and Utopias. Trans. R.F.C. Hull. New York: Macmillan, 1988.

I AND THOU

The world is twofold for man in accordance with his twofold attitude.

The attitude of man is twofold in accordance with the two basic words he can speak.

The basic words are not single words but word pairs.

One basic word is the word pair I-You.

The other basic word is the word pair I-It; but this basic word is not changed when He or She takes the place of It.

Thus the I of man is also twofold.

For the I of the basic word I-You is different from that in the basic word I-It.

*

Basic words do not state something that might exist outside them; by being spoken they establish a mode of existence.

Basic words are spoken with one's being.

When one says You, the I of the word pair I-You is said, too.

When one says It, the I of the word pair I-It is said, too.

The basic word I-You can only be spoken with one's whole being.

The basic word I-It can never be spoken with one's whole being.

*

There is no I as such but only the I of the basic word I-You and the I of the basic word I-It.

When a man says I, he means one or the other. The I he means is present when he says I. And when he says You or It, the I of one or the other basic word is also present.

Being I and saying I are the same. Saying I and saying one of the two basic words are the same.

Whoever speaks one of the basic words enters into the word and stands in it.

*

The life of a human being does not exist merely in the sphere of goal-directed verbs. It does not consist merely of activities that have something for their object.

I perceive something. I feel something. I imagine something. I want something. I sense something. I think something. The life of a human being does not consist merely of all this and its like.

All this and its like is the basis of the realm of It.

But the realm of You has another basis.

*

Whoever says You does not have something for his object. For wherever there is something there is also another something; every It borders on other Its; It is only by virtue of bordering on others. But where You is said there is no something. You has no borders.

Whoever says You does not have something; he has nothing. But he stands in relation.

*

We are told that man experiences his world. What does this mean?

Man goes over the surfaces of things and experiences them. He brings back from them some knowledge of their condition—an experience. He experiences what there is to things.

But it is not experiences alone that bring the world to man.

For what they bring to him is only a world that consists of It and It and It, of He and He and She and She and It.

I experience something.

All this is not changed by adding "inner" experiences to the "external" ones, in line with the noneternal distinction that is born of mankind's craving to take the edge off the mystery of death. Inner things like external things, things among things!

I experience something.

And all this is not changed by adding "mysterious" experiences to "manifest" ones, self-confident in the wisdom that recognizes a secret compartment in things, reserved for the initiated, and holds the key. O mysteriousness without mystery, O piling up of information! It, It, It!

*

Those who experience do not participate in the world. For the experience is "in them" and not between them and the world.

The world does not participate in experience. It allows itself to be experienced, but it is not concerned, for it contributes nothing, and nothing happens to it.

*

The world as experience belongs to the basic word I-It.

The basic word I-You establishes the world of relation.

*

Three are the spheres in which the world of relation arises.

The first: life with nature. Here the relation vibrates in the dark and remains below language. The creatures stir across from us, but they are unable to come to us, and the You we say to them sticks to the threshold of language.

The second: life with men. Here the relation is manifest and enters language. We can give and receive the You.

The third: life with spiritual beings. Here the relation is wrapped in a cloud but reveals itself, it lacks but creates language. We hear no You and yet feel addressed; we answer—creating, thinking, acting: with our being we speak the basic word, unable to say You with our mouth.

But how can we incorporate into the world of the basic word what lies outside language?

In every sphere, through everything that becomes present to us, we gaze toward the train of the eternal You; in each we perceive a breath of it; in every You we address the eternal You, in every sphere according to its manner.

*

I contemplate a tree.

I can accept it as a picture: a rigid pillar in a flood of light, or splashes of green traversed by the gentleness of the blue silver ground.

I can feel it as movement: the flowing veins around the sturdy, striving core, the sucking of the roots, the breathing of the leaves, the infinite commerce with earth and air—and the growing itself in its darkness.

I can assign it to a species and observe it as an instance, with an eye to its construction and its way of life.

I can overcome its uniqueness and form so rigorously that I recognize it only as an expression of the law—those laws according to which a constant opposition of forces is continually adjusted, or those laws according to which the elements mix and separate.

I can dissolve it into a number, into a pure relation between numbers, and eternalize it.

Throughout all of this the tree remains my object and has its place and its time span, its kind and condition.

But it can also happen, if will and grace are joined, that as I contemplate the tree I am drawn into a relation, and the tree ceases to be an It. The power of exclusiveness has seized me.

This does not require me to forego any of the modes of contemplation. There is nothing that I must not see in order to see, and there is no knowledge that I must forget. Rather is everything, picture and movement, species and instance, law and number included and inseparably fused.

Whatever belongs to the tree is included: its form and its mechanics, its colors and its chemistry, its conversation with the elements and its conversation with the stars—all this in its entirety.

The tree is no impression, no play of my imagination, no aspect of a mood; it confronts me bodily and has to deal with me as I must deal with it—only differently.

One should not try to dilute the meaning of the relation: relation is reciprocity.

Does the tree then have consciousness, similar to our own? I have no experience of that. But thinking that you have brought this off in your own case, must you again divide the indivisible? What I encounter is neither the soul of a tree nor a dryad, but the tree itself.

*

When I confront a human being as my You and speak the basic word I-You to him, then he is no thing among things nor does he consist of things.

He is no longer He or She, limited by other Hes and Shes, a dot in the world grid of space and time, nor a condition that can be experienced and described, a loose bundle of named qualities. Neighborless and seamless, he is You and fills the firmament. Not as if there were nothing but he; but everything else lives in *his* light.

Even as a melody is not composed of tones, nor a verse of words, nor a statue of lines—one must pull and tear to turn a unity into a multiplicity—so it is with the human being to whom I say You. I can abstract from him the color of his hair or the color of his speech or the color of his graciousness; I have to do this again and again; but immediately he is no longer You.

And even as prayer is not in time but time in prayer, the sacrifice not in space but space in the sacrifice—and whoever reverses the relation annuls the reality—I do not find the human being to whom I say You in any Sometime and Somewhere. I can place him there and have to do this again and again, but immediately he becomes a He or a She, an It, and no longer remains my You.

As long as the firmament of the You is spread over me, the tempests of causality cower at my heels, and the whirl of doom congeals.

The human being to whom I say You I do not experience. But I stand in relation to him, in the sacred basic word. Only when I step out of this do I experience him again. Experience is remoteness from You.

The relation can obtain even if the human being to whom I say You does not hear it in his experience. For You is more than It knows. You does more, and more happens to it, than It knows. No deception reaches this far: here is the cradle of actual life.

*

This is the eternal origin of art, that a human being confronts a form that wants to become a work through him. Not a figment of his soul but something that appears to the soul and demands the soul's creative power. What is required is a deed that a man does with his whole being: if he commits it and speaks with his being the basic word to the form that appears, then the creative power is released and the work comes into being.

The deed involves a sacrifice and a risk. The sacrifice: infinite possibility is surrendered on the altar of the form; all that but a moment ago floated playfully through one's perspective has to be exterminated; none of it may penetrate into the work; the exclusiveness of such a confrontation demands this. The risk: the basic word can only be spoken with one's whole being; whoever commits himself may not hold back part of himself; and the work does not permit me, as a tree or man might, to seek relaxation in the It-world; it is imperious: if I do not serve it properly, it breaks, or it breaks me.

The form that confronts me I cannot experience nor describe; I can only actualize it. And yet I see it, radiant in the splendor of the confrontation, far more clearly than all clarity of the experienced world. Not as a thing among the "internal" things, not as a figment of the "imagination," but as what is present. Tested for its objectivity, the form is not "there" at all; but what can equal its presence? And it is an actual relation: it acts on me as I act on it.

Such work is creation, inventing is finding. Forming is discovery. As I actualize, I uncover. I lead the form across—into the world of It. The created work is a thing among things and can be experienced and described as an aggregate of qualities. But the receptive beholder may be bodily confronted now and again.

*

——What, then, does one experience of the You?

——Nothing at all. For one does not experience it.

——What, then, does one know of the You?

——Only everything. For one no longer knows particulars.

*

The You encounters me by grace—it cannot be found by seeking. But that I speak the basic word to it is a deed of my whole being, is my essential deed.

The You encounters me. But I enter into a direct relationship to it. Thus the relationship is election and electing, passive and active at once: an action of the whole being must approach passivity, for it does away with all partial actions and thus with any sense of action, which always depends on limited exertions.

The basic word I-You can be spoken only with one's whole being. The concentration and fusion into a whole being can never be accomplished by me, can never be accomplished without me. I require a You to become; becoming I, I say You.

All actual life is encounter.

*

The relation to the You is unmediated. Nothing conceptual intervenes between I and You, no prior knowledge and no imagination; and memory itself is changed as it plunges from particularity into wholeness. No purpose intervenes between I and You, no greed and no anticipation; and longing itself is changed as it plunges from the dream into appearance. Every means is an obstacle. Only where all means have disintegrated encounters occur.

*

Before the immediacy of the relationship everything mediate becomes negligible. It is also trifling whether my You is the It of other Is ("object of general experience") or can only become that as a result of my essential deed. For the real boundary, albeit one that floats and fluctuates, runs not between experience and nonexperience, nor between the given and the not-given, nor between the world of being and the world of value, but across all the regions between You and It: between presence and object.

*

The present—not that which is like a point and merely designates whatever our thoughts may posit as the end of "elapsed" time, the fiction of the fixed lapse, but the actual and fulfilled present—exists only insofar as presentness, encounter, and relation exist. Only as the You becomes present does presence come into being.

The I of the basic word I-It, the I that is not bodily confronted by a You but surrounded by a multitude of "contents," has only a past and no present. In other words: insofar as a human being makes do with the things that he experiences and uses, he lives in the past, and his moment has no presence. He has nothing but objects; but objects consist in having been.

Presence is not what is evanescent and passes but what confronts us, waiting and enduring. And the object is not duration but standing still, ceasing, breaking off, becoming rigid, standing out, the lack of relation, the lack of presence.

What is essential is lived in the present, objects in the past.

*

This essential twofoldness cannot be overcome by invoking a "world of ideas" as a third element that might transcend this opposition. For I speak only of the actual human being, of you and me, of our life and our world, not of any I-in-itself and not of any Being-in-itself. But for an actual human being the real boundary also runs across the world of ideas.

To be sure, some men who in the world of things make do with experiencing and using have constructed for themselves an idea annex or superstructure in which they find refuge and reassurance in the face of intimations of nothingness. At the threshold they take off the clothes of the ugly weekday, shroud themselves in clean garments, and feel restored as they contemplate primal being or what ought to be—something in which their life has no share. It may also make them feel good to proclaim it.

But the It-humanity that some imagine, postulate, and advertise has nothing in common with the bodily humanity to which a human being can truly say You. The noblest fiction is a fetish, the most sublime fictitious sentiment is a vice. The ideas are just as little enthroned above our heads as they reside inside them; they walk among us and step up to us. Pitiful are those who leave the basic word unspoken, but wretched are those who instead of that address the ideas with a concept or a slogan as if that were their name!

*

That direct relationships involve some action on what confronts us becomes clear in one of three examples. The essential deed of art determines the process whereby the form becomes a work. That which confronts me is fulfilled through the encounter through which it enters into the world of things in order to remain incessantly effective, incessantly It—but also infinitely able to become again a You, enchanting and inspiring. It becomes "incarnate": out of the flood of spaceless and timeless presence it rises to the shore of continued existence.

Less clear is the element of action in the relation to a human You. The essential act that here establishes directness is usually understood as a feeling, and thus misunderstood. Feelings accompany the metaphysical and metapsychical fact of love, but they do not constitute it; and the feelings that accompany it can be very different. Jesus' feeling for the possessed man is different from his feeling for the beloved disciple; but the love is one. Feelings one "has"; love occurs. Feelings dwell in man, but man dwells in his love. This is no metaphor but actuality: love does not cling to an I, as if the You were merely its "content" or object; it is between I and You. Whoever does not know this, know this with his being, does not know love, even if he should ascribe to it the feelings that he lives through, experiences, enjoys, and expresses. Love is a cosmic force. For those who stand in it and behold in it, men emerge from their entanglement in busyness; and the good and the evil, the clever and the foolish, the beautiful and the ugly, one after another become actual and a You for them; that is, liberated, emerging into a unique confrontation. Exclusiveness comes into being miraculously again and again—and now one can act, help, heal, educate, raise, redeem. Love is responsibility of an I for a You: in this consists what cannot consist in any feeling—the equality of all lovers, from the smallest to the greatest and from the blissfully secure whose life is circumscribed by the life of one beloved human being to him that is nailed his lifelong to the cross of the world, capable of what is immense and bold enough to risk it: to love *man*.

Let the meaning of action in the third example, that of the creature and its contemplation, remain mysterious. Believe in the simple magic of life, in service in the universe, and it will dawn on you what this waiting, peering, "stretching of the neck" of the creature means. Every word must falsify; but look, these beings live around you, and no matter which one you approach you always reach Being.

*

Relation is reciprocity. My You acts on me as I act on it. Our students teach us, our works form us. The "wicked" become a revelation when they are touched by the sacred basic word. How are we educated by children, by animals! Inscrutably involved, we live in the currents of universal reciprocity.

*

——You speak of love as if it were the only relationship between men; but are you even justified in choosing it as an example, seeing that there is also hatred?

——As long as love is "blind"—that is, as long as it does not see a *whole* being—it does not yet truly stand under the basic word of relation. Hatred remains blind by its very nature; one can hate only part of a being. Whoever sees a whole being and must reject it, is no longer in the dominion of hatred but in the human limitation of the capacity to say You. It does happen to men that a human being confronts them and they are unable to address him with the basic word that always involves an affirmation of the being one addresses, and then they have to reject either the other person or themselves: when entering-into-relationship comes to this barrier, it recognizes its own relativity which disappears only when this barrier is removed.

Yet whoever hates directly is closer to a relation than those who are without love and hate.

*

This, however, is the sublime melancholy of our lot, that every You must become an It in our world. However exclusively present it may have been in the direct relationship—as soon as the relationship has run its course or is permeated by *means*, the You becomes an object among objects, possibly the noblest one and yet one of them, assigned its measure and boundary. The actualization of the work

83

involves a loss of actuality. Genuine contemplation never lasts long; the natural being that only now revealed itself to me in the mystery of reciprocity has again become describable, analyzable, classifiable—the point at which manifold systems of laws intersect. And even love cannot persist in direct relation; it endures, but only in the alternation of actuality and latency. The human being who but now was unique and devoid of qualities, not at hand but only present, not experienceable, only touchable, has again become a He or She, an aggregate of qualities, a quantum with a shape. Now I can again abstract from him the color of his hair, of his speech, of his graciousness; but as long as I can do that he is my You no longer and not yet again.

Every You in the world is doomed by its nature to become a thing or at least to enter into thinghood again and again. In the language of objects: every thing in the world can—either before or after it becomes a thing—appear to some I as its You. But the language of objects catches only one corner of actual life.

The It is the chrysalis, the You the butterfly. Only it is not always as if these states took turns so neatly; often it is an intricately entangled series of events that is tortuously dual.

*

In the beginning is the relation.

Consider the language of "primitive" peoples, meaning those who have remained poor in objects and whose life develops in a small sphere of acts that have a strong presence. The nuclei of this language, their sentence-words—primal pregrammatical forms that eventually split into the multiplicity of different kinds of words—generally designate the wholeness of a relation. We say, "far away"; the Zulu has a sentence-word instead that means: "where one cries, 'mother, I am lost.'" And the Fuegian surpasses our analytical wisdom with a sentence-word of seven syllables that literally means: "they look at each other, each waiting for the other to offer to do that which both desire but neither wishes to do." In this wholeness persons are still embedded like reliefs without achieving the fully rounded independence of nouns or pronouns. What counts is not these products of analysis and reflection but the genuine original unity, the lived relationship. . . .

*

In the history of the primitive mind the fundamental difference between the two basic words appears in this: even in the original relational event, the primitive man speaks the basic word I-You in a natural, as it were still unformed manner, not yet having recognized himself as an I; but the basic word I-It is made possible only by this recognition, by the detachment of the I.

The former word splits into I and You, but it did not originate as their aggregate, it antedates any I. The latter originated as an aggregate of I and It, it postdates the I.

Owing to its exclusiveness, the primitive relational event includes the I. For by its nature this event contains only two partners, man and what confronts him, both in their full actuality, and the world becomes a dual system; and thus man begins to have some sense of that cosmic pathos of the I without as yet realizing this.

In the natural fact, on the other hand, that will give way to the basic word I-It and I-elated experience, the I is not yet included. This fact is the discreteness of the human body as the carrier of its sensations, from its environment. In this particularity the body learns to know and discriminate itself, but this discrimination remains on the plane where things are next to each other, and therefore it cannot assume the character of implicit I-likeness.

But once the I of the relation has emerged and has become existent in its detachment, it somehow etherializes and functionalizes itself and enters into the natural fact of the discreteness of the body from its environment, awakening I-likeness in it. Only now can the conscious I-act, the first form of the basic word I-It, of experience by an I, come into being. The I that has emerged proclaims itself as the carrier of sensations and the environment as their object. Of course, this happens in a "primitive" and not in an "epistemological" manner; yet once the sentence "I see the tree" has been pronounced in such a way that it no longer relates a relation between a human I and a tree You but the perception of the tree object by the human consciousness, it has erected the crucial barrier between subject and object; the basic word I-It, the word of separation, has been spoken.

*

——Then our melancholy lot took shape in primal history?

——Indeed, it developed—insofar as man's conscious life developed—in primal history. But in conscious life cosmic being recurs as human becoming. Spirit appears in time as a product, even a by-product, of nature, and yet it is spirit that envelops nature timelessly.

The opposition of the two basic words has many names in the ages and worlds; but in its nameless truth it inheres in the creation.

*

——Then you believe after all in some paradise in the primal age of humanity?

——Even if it was a hell—and the age to which we can go back in historical thought was certainly full of wrath and dread and torment and cruelty—unreal it was not.

Primal man's experiences of encounter were scarcely a matter of tame delight; but even violence against a being one really confronts is better than ghostly solicitude for faceless digits! From the former a path leads to God, from the latter only to nothingness.

*

Even if we could fully understand the life of the primitive, it would be no more than a metaphor for that of the truly primal man. Hence the primitive affords us only brief glimpses into the temporal sequence of the two basic words. More complete information we receive from the child.

Here it becomes unmistakably clear how the spiritual reality of the basic words emerges from a natural reality: that of the basic word I-You from a natural association, that of the basic word I-It from a natural discreteness.

85

The prenatal life of the child is a pure natural association, a flowing toward each other, a bodily reciprocity; and the life horizon of the developing being appears uniquely inscribed, and yet also not inscribed, in that of the being that carries it; for the womb in which it dwells is not solely that of the human mother. This association is so cosmic that it seems like the imperfect deciphering of a primeval inscription when we are told in the language of Jewish myth that in his mother's womb man knows the universe and forgets it at birth. And as the secret image of a wish, this association remains to us. But this longing ought not to be taken for a craving to go back, as those suppose who consider the spirit, which they confound with their own intellect, a parasite of nature. For the spirit is nature's blossom, albeit exposed to many diseases. What this longing aims for is the cosmic association of the being that has burst into spirit with its true You.

Every developing human child rests, like all developing beings, in the womb of the great mother—the undifferentiated, not-yet-formed primal world. From this it detaches itself to enter a personal life, and it is only in dark hours when we slip out of this again (as happens even to the healthy, night after night) that we are close to her again. But this detachment is not sudden and catastrophic like that from the bodily mother. The human child is granted some time to exchange the natural association with the world that is slipping away for a spiritual association—a relationship. From the glowing darkness of the chaos he has stepped into the cool and light creation without immediately possessing it: he has to get it up, as it were, and make it a reality for himself; he gains his world by seeing, listening, feeling, forming. It is in encounter that the creation reveals its formhood; it does not pour itself into senses that are waiting but deigns to meet those that are reaching out. What is to surround the finished human being as an object, has to be acquired and wooed strenuously by him while he is still developing. No thing is a component of experience or reveals itself except through the reciprocal force of confrontation. Like primitives, the child lives between sleep and sleep (and a large part of waking is still sleep), in the lightning and counterlightning of encounter.

The innateness of the longing for relation is apparent even in the earliest and dimmest stage. Before any particulars can be perceived, dull glances push into the unclear space toward the indefinite; and at times when there is obviously no desire for nourishment, soft projections of the hands reach, aimlessly to all appearances, into the empty air toward the indefinite. Let anyone call this animalic: that does not help our comprehension. For precisely these glances will eventually, after many trials, come to rest upon a red wallpaper arabesque and not leave it until the soul of red has opened up to them. Precisely this motion will gain its sensuous form and definiteness in contact with a shaggy toy bear and eventually apprehend lovingly and unforgettably a complete body: in both cases not experience of an object but coming to grips with a living, active being that confronts us, if only in our "imagination." (But this "imagination" is by no means a form of "panpsychism"; it is the drive to turn everything into a You, the drive to panrelation—and where it does not find a living, active being that confronts it but only an image or symbol of that, it supplies the living activity from its own fullness.) Little inarticulate sounds still ring out senselessly and persistently into the nothing; but one day they will have turned imperceptibly into a conversation—with what? Perhaps with a bubbling teakettle, but into a conversation. Many a motion that is called a reflex is a sturdy trowel for the person building up his world. It is not as if a child first saw an object and then entered into some relationship with that. Rather, the longing for relation is primary, the cupped hand into which the being that confronts us nestles; and the relation to that, which is a wordless anticipation of saying You, comes second. But the genesis of the thing is a late product that develops out of the split of the primal encounters, out of the separation of the associated partners—as does the genesis of the I. In the beginning is the relation—as the category of being, as readiness, as a form that reaches out to be filled, as a model of the soul; the *a priori* of relation; *the innate You.*

9

JEAN-PAUL SARTRE
(1905–1980)

The most famous of the French existentialists, Jean-Paul Sartre made important contributions not only in philosophy but also in literature and in drama. He was born into a middle-class family in Paris in 1905, and mostly taught in the French *lycée* system until World War II. In 1941, he joined the French Resistance and began editing the left-wing newspaper *Combat* with his close friend Albert Camus. Three years later, Sartre founded *Les Temps modernes* with Simone de Beauvoir and Maurice Merleau-Ponty, which became the most prestigious intellectual journal in France until the 1960s. Sartre was the consummate *philosophe engagé*. Although a fierce critic of the French Communist Party and Stalinism, he was a staunch Marxist and indefatigable defender of human rights. He was a leading figure in the May 1968 student-worker uprising, and, along with Bertrand Russell, sat on a committee to judge American politicians as war criminals for their involvement in Vietnam. In 1964, he was offered the Nobel Prize for Literature, but refused it, claiming that he did not want to become an "institution." When he died in 1980, some fifty thousand people attended his funeral.

Having been introduced to phenomenology in the early 1930s through his reading of Emmanuel Levinas's *Theory of Intuition in Husserl's Phenomenology*, Sartre resolved in 1933 to go to Berlin to study with Husserl firsthand. It was during this period that he wrote *The Transcendence of the Ego* (1936) and *Nausea* (1938), and began to lay the philosophical foundations of his monumental work *Being and Nothingness* (1943). This work was to have an enormous impact on postwar French philosophy. In it, Sartre introduced his fundamental distinction between two types of being: being-for-itself, which is the being of consciousness, and being-in-itself, or the being of things. For Sartre, human consciousness is literally "no-thing." It does not have a determinate character but is fundamentally free inasmuch as it is open to various possibilities of being. Sartre's commitment to a philosophy of freedom, summed up in his famous phrase, "Man is condemned to be free," is evident in nearly everything he wrote, including his important later works *Critique of Dialectical Reason* (1960) and the posthumously published *Notebooks for an Ethics* (1992).

Sartre's most popular and accessible presentation of his thought is a lecture he delivered in Paris in 1945, translated as *Existentialism and Humanism*. In our selection from this lecture, Sartre is responding to the charges of quietism, pessimism, and nihilism that have been leveled against existentialism. He begins with the assumption that God does not exist. If God does not exist, then human beings are not created in "the image of God" and thus have no pregiven nature. This idea is encapsulated in the classic existentialist motto that "existence precedes essence." By this Sartre means we are all in an absolute position of freedom to choose ourselves. In choosing ourselves, we also choose certain values to live by. Sartre recognizes along with the bulk of moral philosophers that to value something is to set it up as a value for everybody. Values prescribe or recommend a certain way of life, a certain ideal for living. Thus when one chooses for oneself one chooses for all humanity.

Select Bibliography of Sartre's Works in English

Being and Nothingness. Trans. Hazel E. Barnes. New York: Washington Square Press, 1992.

Between Existentialism and Marxism: Sartre on Philosophy, Politics, Psychology, and the Arts. Trans. John Mathews. New York: Pantheon Books, 1983.

Critique of Dialectical Reason: Theory of Practical Ensembles. Trans. Alan Sheridan-Smith. London: NLB, 1976.

Existentialism and Humanism. Trans. Philip Mairet. London: Methuen, 1982.

Imagination: A Psychological Critique. Trans. Forrest Williams. Ann Arbor, MI: University of Michigan Press, 1962.

Life/Situations: Essays Written and Spoken. Trans. Paul Auster and Lydia Davis. New York: Pantheon Books, 1977.

Nausea. Trans. Lloyd Alexander. New York: New Directions Publishing, 1969.

Notebooks for an Ethics. Trans. David Pellauer. Chicago: University of Chicago Press, 1992.

Search for a Method. Trans. Hazel E. Barnes. New York: Vintage, 1968.

Transcendence of the Ego. Trans. Forrest Williams and Robert Kirkpatrick. New York: Noonday Press, 1957.

EXISTENTIALISM
IS A HUMANISM

My purpose here is to offer a defense of existentialism against several reproaches that have been laid against it.

First, it has been reproached as an invitation to people to dwell in quietism of despair. For if every way to a solution is barred, one would have to regard any action in this world as entirely ineffective, and one would arrive finally at a contemplative philosophy. Moreover, since contemplation is a luxury, this would be only another bourgeois philosophy. This is, especially, the reproach made by the Communists.

From another quarter we are reproached for having underlined all that is ignominious in the human situation, for depicting what is mean, sordid, or base to the neglect of certain things that possess charm and beauty and belong to the brighter side of human nature: for example, according to the Catholic critic, Mlle. Mercier, we forget how an infant smiles. Both from this side and from the other we are also reproached for leaving out of account the solidarity of mankind and considering man in isolation. And this, say the Communists, is because we base our doctrine upon pure subjectivity—upon the Cartesian "I think": which is the moment in which solitary man attains to himself; a position from which it is impossible to regain solidarity with other men who exist outside of the self. The *ego* cannot reach them through the *cogito*.

From the Christian side, we are reproached as people who deny the reality and seriousness of human affairs. For since we ignore the commandments of God and all values prescribed as eternal, nothing remains but what is strictly voluntary. Everyone can do what he likes, and will be incapable, from such a point of view, of condemning either the point of view or the action of anyone else.

It is to these various reproaches that I shall endeavor to reply today; that is why I have entitled this brief exposition "Existentialism Is a Humanism." Many may be surprised at the mention of humanism in this connection, but we shall try to see in what sense we understand it. In any case, we can begin by saying that existentialism, in our sense of the word, is a doctrine that does render human life possible; a doctrine, also, which affirms that every truth and every action imply both an environment and a human subjectivity. The essential charge laid against us is, of course, that of overemphasis upon the evil side of human life. I have lately been told of a lady who, whenever she lets slip a vulgar expression in a moment of nervousness, excuses herself by exclaiming, "I believe I am becoming an existentialist." So it appears that ugliness is being identified with existentialism. That is why some people say we are "naturalistic," and if we are, it is strange to see how much we scandalize and horrify them, for no one seems to be much frightened or humiliated nowadays by what is properly called naturalism. Those who can quite well keep down a novel by Zola such as *La Terre* are sickened as soon as they read an existentialist novel. Those who appeal to the wisdom of the people—which is a sad wisdom—find ours sadder still. And yet, what could be more disillusioned than such sayings as "Charity begins at home" or "Promote a rogue and he'll sue you for damage, knock him down and he'll do you homage"? We all know how many common sayings can be quoted to this effect, and they all mean much the same—that you must not oppose the powers that be; that you must not fight against superior force; must not meddle in matters that are above your station. Or that any action not in accordance with some tradition is mere romanticism; or that any undertaking which has not the support of proven experience is foredoomed to frustration; and that since experience has shown men to be invariably inclined to evil, there must be firm rules to restrain them, otherwise we shall have anarchy. It is, however, the people who are forever mouthing these dismal proverbs and, whenever they are told of some more or less repulsive action, say "How like human nature!"—it is these very people, always harping upon realism, who complain that existentialism is too gloomy a view of things. Indeed their excessive protests make me suspect that what is annoying them is not so much our pessimism, but, much more likely, our optimism. For at bottom, what is alarming in the doctrine that I am about to try to explain to you is—is it not?—that it confronts man with a possibility of choice. To verify this, let us review the whole question upon the strictly philosophic level. What, then, is this that we call existentialism?

Most of those who are making use of this word would be highly confused if required to explain its meaning. For since it has become fashionable, people cheerfully declare that this musician or that painter is "existentialist." A columnist in *Clartés* signs himself "The Existentialist," and, indeed, the word is now so loosely applied to so many things that it no longer means anything at all. It would appear that, for the lack of any novel doctrine such as that of surrealism, all those who are eager to join in the latest scandal or movement now seize upon this philosophy in which, however, they can find nothing to their purpose. For in truth this is of all teachings the least scandalous and the most austere: it is intended strictly for technicians and philosophers. All the same, it can easily be defined.

The question is only complicated because there are two kinds of existentialists. There are, on the one hand, the Christians, amongst whom I shall name Karl Jaspers and Gabriel Marcel, both professed Catholics; and on the other the existential atheists, amongst whom we must place Heidegger as well as the French existentialists and myself. What they have in common is simply the fact that they believe that *existence* comes before *essence*—or, if you will, that we must begin from the subjective. What exactly do we mean by that?

If one considers an article of manufacture as, for example, a book or a paper-knife—one sees that it has been made by an artisan who had a conception of it; and he has paid attention, equally, to the conception of a paper-knife and to the preexistent technique of production which is a part of that conception and is, at bottom, a formula. Thus the paper-knife is at the same time an article producible in a certain manner and one which, on the other hand, serve a definite purpose, for one cannot suppose that a man would produce a paper-knife without knowing what it was for. Let us say, then, of the paper-knife that its essence—that is to say the sum of the formulae and the qualities which made its production and its definition possible—precedes its existence. The presence of such-and-such a paper-knife or book is thus determined before my eyes. Here, then, we are viewing the world from a technical standpoint, and we can say that production precedes existence.

When we think of God as the creator, we are thinking of him, most of the time, as a supernal artisan. Whatever doctrine we may be considering, whether it be a doctrine like that of Descartes, or of Leibnitz himself, we always imply that the will follows, more or less, from the understanding or at least accompanies it, so that when God creates he knows precisely what he is creating. Thus, the conception of man in the mind of God is comparable to that of the paper-knife in the mind of the artisan: God makes man according to a procedure and a conception, exactly as the artisan manufactures a paper-knife, following a definition and a formula. Thus each individual man is the realization of a certain conception which dwells in the divine understanding. In the philosophic atheism of the eighteenth century, the notion of God is suppressed, but not, for all that, the idea that essence is prior to existence; something of that idea we still find everywhere, in Diderot, in Voltaire, and even in Kant. Man possesses a human nature; that "human nature," which is the conception of human being, is found in every man; which means that each man is a particular example of a universal conception, the conception of Man. In Kant, this universality goes so far that the wild man of the woods, man in the state of nature, and the bourgeois are all contained in the same definition and have the same fundamental qualities. Here again, the essence of man precedes that historic existence which we confront in experience.

Atheistic existentialism, of which I am a representative, declares with greater consistency that if God does not exist there is at least one being whose existence comes before its essence, a being which exists before it can be defined by any conception of it. That being is man or, as Heidegger has it, the human reality. What do we mean by saying that existence precedes essence? We mean that man first of all exists, encounters himself, surges up in the world—and defines himself afterwards. If man as the existentialist sees him is not definable, it is because to begin with he is nothing. He will not be anything until later, and then he will be what he makes of himself. Thus, there is no human nature, because there is no God to have a conception of it. Man simply is. Not that he is simply what he conceives himself to be, but he is what he wills, and as he conceives himself after already existing—as he wills to be after that leap towards existence. Man is nothing else but that which he makes of himself. That is the first principle of existentialism. And this is what people call its "subjectivity," using the word as a reproach against us. But what do we mean to say by this, but that man is of a greater dignity than a stone or a table? For we mean to say that man primarily exists—that man is, before all else, something which propels itself towards a future and is aware that it is doing so. Man is, indeed, a project which possesses a subjective life, instead of being a kind of moss, or a fungus, or a cauliflower. Before that projection of the self nothing exists; not even in the heaven of intelligence: man will only attain existence when he is what he purposes to be. Not, however, what he may wish to be. For what we usually understand by wishing or willing is a conscious decision taken—much more often than not—after we have made ourselves what we are. I may wish to join a party, to write a book or to marry—but in such a case what is usually called my will is probably a manifestation of a prior and more spontaneous decision. If, however, it is true that existence is prior to essence, man is responsible for what he is. Thus, the first effect of existentialism is that it puts every man in possession of himself as he is, and places the entire responsibility for his existence squarely upon his own shoulders. And, when we say that man is responsible for himself, we do not mean that he is responsible only for his own individuality, but that he is responsible for all men. The word "subjectivism" is to be understood in two senses, and our adversaries play upon only one of them. Subjectivism means, on the one hand, the freedom of the individual subject and, on the other, that man cannot pass beyond human subjectivity. It is the latter which is the deeper meaning of existentialism. When we say that man chooses himself, we do mean that every one of us must choose himself; but by that we also mean that in choosing for himself he chooses for all men. For in effect, of all the actions a man may take in order to create himself as he wills to be, there is not one which is not creative, at the same time, of an image of man such as he believes he ought to be. To choose between this or that is at the same time to affirm the value of that which is chosen; for we are unable ever to choose the worse. What we choose is always the better; and nothing can be better for us unless it is better for all. If, moreover, existence precedes essence and we will to exist at the same time as we fashion our image, that image is valid for all and for the entire epoch in which we find ourselves. Our responsibility is thus much greater than we had supposed, for it concerns mankind as a whole. If I am a worker, for instance, I may choose to join a Christian rather than a communist trade union. And if, by that membership, I choose to signify that resignation is, after all, the attitude that best becomes a man, that man's kingdom is not upon this earth, I do not commit myself alone to that view. Resignation is my will for everyone, and my action is, in consequence, a commitment on behalf of all mankind. Or if, to take a more personal case, I decide to marry and to have children, even though this decision proceeds simply from my situation, from my passion or my desire, I am thereby committing not only myself, but humanity as a whole, to the practice of monogamy. I am thus responsible for myself and for all men, and I am creating a certain image of man as I would have him to be. In fashioning myself I fashion man.

This may enable us to understand what is meant by such terms—perhaps a little grandiloquent—as anguish, abandonment, and despair. As you will soon see, it is very simple. First, what do we mean by anguish?—The existentialist frankly states that man is in anguish. His meaning is as follows: when a man commits himself to anything, fully realizing that he is not only choosing what he will be, but is thereby at the same time a legislator deciding for the whole of mankind—in such a moment a man cannot escape from the sense of complete and profound responsibility. There are many, indeed, who show no such anxiety. But we affirm that they are merely disguising their anguish or are in flight from it. Certainly, many people think that in what they are doing they commit no one but themselves to anything: and if you ask them, "What would happen if everyone did so?" they shrug their shoulders and reply, "Everyone does not do so." But in truth, one ought always to ask oneself what would happen if everyone did as one is doing; nor can one escape from that disturbing thought except by a kind of self-deception. The man who lies in self-excuse, by saying "Everyone will not do it" must be ill at ease in his conscience, for the act of lying implies the universal value which it denies. By its very disguise his anguish reveals itself. This is the anguish that Kierkegaard called "the anguish of Abraham." You know the story: an angel commanded Abraham to sacrifice his son; and obedience was obligatory, if it really was an angel who had appeared and said, "Thou, Abraham, shalt sacrifice thy son." But anyone in such a case would wonder, first, whether it was indeed an angel, and second, whether I am really Abraham. Where are the proofs? A certain mad woman who suffered from hallucinations said that people were telephoning to her, and giving her orders. The doctor asked, "But who is it that speaks to you?" She replied: "He says it is God." And what, indeed, could prove to her that it was God? If an angel appears to me, what is the proof that it is an angel; or, if I hear voices, who can prove that they proceed from Heaven and not from Hell, or from my own subconsciousness or some pathological condition? Who can prove that they are really addressed to me?

Who, then, can prove that I am the proper person to impose, by my own choice, my conception of man upon mankind? I shall never find any proof whatever; there will be no sign to convince me of it. If a voice speaks to me, it is still I myself who must decide whether the voice is or is not that of an angel. If I regard a certain course of action as good, it is only I who choose to say that it is good and not bad. There is nothing to show that I am Abraham: nevertheless I also am obliged at every instant to perform actions which are examples. Everything happens to every man as though the whole human race had its eyes fixed upon what he is doing and regulated its conduct accordingly. So every man ought to say, "Am I really a man who has the right to act in such a manner that humanity regulates itself by what I do." If a man does not say that, he is dissembling his anguish. Clearly, the anguish with which we are concerned here is not one that could lead to quietism or inaction. It is anguish pure and simple, of the kind well known to all those who have borne responsibilities. When, for instance, a military leader takes upon himself the responsibility for an attack and sends a number of men to their death, he chooses to do it and at bottom he alone chooses. No doubt under a higher command, but its orders, which are more general, require interpretation by him and upon that interpretation depends the life of ten, fourteen, or twenty men. In making the decision, he cannot but feel a certain anguish. All leaders know that anguish. It does not prevent their acting, on the contrary it is the very condition of their action, for the action presupposes that there is a plurality of possibilities, and in choosing one of these, they realize that it has value only because it is chosen. Now it is anguish of that kind which existentialism describes, and moreover, as we shall see, makes explicit through direct responsibility towards other men who are concerned. Far from being a screen which could separate us from action, it is a condition of action itself.

And when we speak of "abandonment"—a favorite word of Heidegger—we only mean to say that God does not exist, and that it is necessary to draw the consequences of his absence right to the end. The existentialist is strongly opposed to a certain type of secular moralism which seeks to suppress God at the least possible expense. Towards 1880, when the French professors endeavored to formulate a secular morality, they said something like this: God is a useless and costly hypothesis, so we will do without it. However, if we are to have morality, a society, and a law-abiding world, it is essential that certain values should be taken seriously; they must have an *a priori* existence ascribed to them. It must be considered obligatory *a priori* to be honest, not to lie, not to beat one's wife, to bring up children, and so forth; so we are going to do a little work on this subject, which will enable us to show that these values exist all the same, inscribed in an intelligible heaven although, of course, there is no God. In other words—and this is, I believe, the purport of all that we in France call radicalism—nothing will be changed if God does not exist; we shall rediscover the same norms of honesty, progress, and humanity, and we shall have disposed of God as an out-of-date hypothesis which will die away quietly of itself. The existentialist, on the contrary, finds it extremely embarrassing that God does not exist, for there disappears with Him all possibility of finding values in an intelligible heaven. There can no longer be any good *a priori*, since there is no infinite and perfect consciousness to think it. It is nowhere written that "the good" exists, that one must be honest or must not lie, since we are now upon the plane where there are only men. Dostoyevsky once wrote: "If God did not exist, everything would be permitted"; and that, for existentialism, is the starting point. Everything is indeed permitted if God does not exist, and man is in consequence forlorn, for he cannot find anything to depend upon either within or outside himself. He discovers forthwith that he is without excuse. For if indeed existence precedes essence, one will never be able to explain one's action by reference to a given and specific human nature; in other words, there is no determinism—man is free, man *is* freedom. Nor, on the other hand, if God does not exist, are we provided with any values or commands that could legitimize our behavior. Thus we have neither behind us, nor before us in a luminous realm of values, any means of justification or excuse. We are left alone, without excuse. That is what I mean when I say that man is condemned to be free. Condemned, because he did not create himself, yet is nevertheless at liberty, and from the moment that he is thrown into this world he is responsible for everything he does. The existentialist does not believe in the power of passion. He will never regard a grand passion as a destructive torrent upon which a man is swept into certain actions as by fate, and which, therefore, is an excuse for them. He thinks that man is responsible for his passion. Neither will an existentialist think that a man can find help through some sign being vouchsafed upon earth for his orientation: for he thinks that the man himself interprets the sign as he chooses. He thinks that every man, without any support or help whatever, is condemned at every instant to invent man. As Ponge has written in a very fine article, "Man is the future of man." That is exactly true. Only, if one took this to mean that the future is laid up in Heaven, that God knows what it is, it would be false, for then it would no longer even be a future. If, however, it means that, whatever man may now appear to be, there is a future to be fashioned, a virgin future that awaits him—then it is a true saying. But in the present one is forsaken.

As an example by which you may the better understand this state of abandonment, I will refer to the case of a pupil of mine, who sought me out in the following circumstances. His father was quarrelling with his mother and was also inclined to be a "collaborator"; his elder brother had been killed in the German offensive of 1940 and this young man, with a sentiment somewhat primitive but generous, burned to avenge him. His mother was living alone with him, deeply afflicted by the semi-treason of his father and by the death of her eldest son, and her one consolation was in this young man. But he, at this moment, had the choice between going to England to join the Free French Forces or of staying near his mother and helping her to live. He fully realized that this woman lived only for him and that his disappearance—or perhaps his death—would plunge her into despair. He also realized that, concretely and in fact, every action he performed on his mother's behalf would be sure of effect in the sense of aiding her to live, whereas anything he did in order to go and fight would be an ambiguous action which might vanish like water into sand and serve no purpose. For instance, to set out for England he would have to wait indefinitely in a Spanish camp on the way through Spain; or, on arriving in England or in Algiers he might be put into an office to fill up forms. Consequently, he found himself confronted by two very different modes of action; the one concrete, immediate, but directed towards only one individual; and the other an action addressed to an end infinitely greater, a national collectivity, but for that very reason ambiguous—and it might be frustrated on the way. At the same time, he was hesitating between two kinds of morality; on the one side the morality of sympathy, of personal devotion, and, on the other side, a morality of wider scope but of more debatable validity. He had to choose between those two. What could help him to choose? Could the Christian doctrine? No. Christian doctrine says: act with charity, love your neighbor, deny yourself for others, choose the way which is hardest, and so forth. But which is the harder road? To whom does one owe the more brotherly love, the patriot or the mother? Which is the more useful aim, the general one of fighting in and for the whole community, or the precise aim of helping one particular person to live? Who can give an answer to that *a priori*? No one. Nor is it given in any ethical scripture. The Kantian ethic says: never regard another as a means, but always as an end. Very well; if I remain with my mother, I shall be regarding her as the end and not as a means: but by the same token I am in danger of treating as means those who are fighting on my behalf; and the converse is also true, that if I go to the aid of the combatants I shall be treating them as the end at the risk of treating my mother as a means.

If values are uncertain, if they are still too abstract to determine the particular, concrete case under consideration, nothing remains but to trust in our instincts. That is what this young man tried to do; and when I saw him he said: "In the end, it is feeling that counts; the direction in which it is really pushing me is the one I ought to choose. If I feel that I love my mother enough to sacrifice everything else for her—my will to be avenged, all my longings for action and adventure—then I stay with her. If, on the contrary, I feel that my love for her is not enough, I go." But how does one estimate the strength of a feeling? The value of his feeling for his mother was determined precisely by the fact that he was standing by her. I may say that I love a certain friend enough to sacrifice such or such a sum of money for him, but I cannot prove that unless I have done it. I may say, "I love my mother enough to remain with her," if actually I have remained with her. I can only estimate the strength of this affection if I have performed an action by which it is defined and ratified. But if I then appeal to this affection to justify my action, I find myself drawn into a vicious circle.

Moreover, as Gide has very well said, a sentiment which is playacting and one which is vital are two things that are hardly distinguishable one from another. To decide that I love my mother by staying beside her, and to play a comedy the upshot of which is that I do so—these are nearly the same thing. In other words, feeling is formed by the deeds that one does; therefore I cannot consult it as a guide to action. And that is to say that I can neither seek within myself for an authentic impulse to action, nor can I expect, from some ethic, formulae that will enable me to act. You may say that the youth did, at least, go to a professor to ask for advice. But if you seek counsel—from a priest, for example—you have selected that priest; and at bottom you already knew, more or less, what he would advise. In other words, to choose an adviser is nevertheless to commit oneself by that choice. If you are a Christian, you will say: consult a priest; but there are collaborationists, priests who are resisters, and priests who wait for the tide to turn: Which will you choose? Had this young man chosen a priest of the Resistance, or one of the collaboration, he would have decided beforehand the kind of advice he was to receive. Similarly, in coming to me, he knew what advice I should give him, and I had but one reply to make. You are free, therefore choose—that is to say, invent. No rule of general morality can show you what you ought to do: no signs are vouchsafed in this world.

10

MARTIN HEIDEGGER
(1889–1976)

(See Chapter 4 for a biographical sketch and bibliography of Heidegger.) Our second reading from Martin Heidegger is an excerpt from his influential postwar publication entitled "Letter on 'Humanism'" (1947). Heidegger's letter was written in response to a set of questions presented to him by a French disciple named Jean Beaufret. The questions were prompted by Beaufret's reading of Jean-Paul Sartre's "Existentialism Is a Humanism" (see Chapter 9), which had been delivered the previous year. Specifically Beaufret wanted to know whether we can restore a meaning to the word "humanism," and whether humanism has a place in Heidegger's thought.

In his response, Heidegger seeks to distance his thinking from Sartre's existentialism while also calling into question any uncritical reliance on the concept of "humanism." According to Heidegger, humanism has traditionally defined man as *animal rationale*—the animal with reason. While this definition is not false, it nevertheless fails to address the more fundamental question concerning the ground of human existence itself, which he calls "ek-sistence." Heidegger's position, then, is not so much a rejection of humanism as a call for a radical rethinking of the very essence of human beings.

In the closing portion of the essay, Heidegger turns to the question of the place of ethics in his work. Much like "humanism," the concept of "ethics" belongs to the metaphysical tradition and as a result blocks access to the type of thinking Heidegger is interested in pursuing. This is not to say that Heidegger is opposed to ethics as such. Indeed, he claims that "if the name 'ethics,' in keeping with the basic meaning of the word *ēthos*, should now say that 'ethics' ponders the abode of man," then his thinking has been "ethical" all along.

LETTER ON "HUMANISM"

We are still far from pondering the essence of action decisively enough. We view action only as causing an effect. The actuality of the effect is valued according to its utility. But the essence of action is accomplishment. To accomplish means to unfold something into the fullness of its essence, to lead it forth into this fullness—*producere*. Therefore only what already is can really be accomplished. But what "is" above all is Being. Thinking accomplishes the relation of Being to the essence of man. It does not make or cause the relation. Thinking brings this relation to Being solely as something handed over to it from Being. Such offering consists in the fact that in thinking Being comes to language. Language is the house of Being. In its home man dwells. Those who think and those who create with words are the guardians of this home. Their guardianship accomplishes the manifestation of Being insofar as they bring the manifestation to language and maintain it in language through their speech. Thinking does not become action only because some effect issues from it or because it is applied. Thinking acts insofar as it thinks. Such action is presumably the simplest and at the same time the highest, because it concerns the relation of Being to man. But all working or effecting lies in Being and is directed toward beings. Thinking, in contrast, lets itself be claimed by Being so that it can say the truth of Being. Thinking accomplishes this letting. Thinking is *l'engagement par l'Être pour l'Être* [engagement by Being for Being]. I do not know whether it is linguistically possible to say both of these ("*par*" and "*pour*") at once, in this way: *penser, c'est l'engagement de l'Être* [thinking is the engagement of Being]. Here the possessive form "*de l'*. . ." is supposed to express both subjective and objective genitives. In this regard "subject" and "object" are inappropriate terms of metaphysics, which very early on in the form of Occidental "logic" and "grammar" seized control of the interpretation of language. We today can only begin to descry what is concealed in that occurrence; the liberation of language from grammar into a more original essential framework is reserved for thought and poetic creation. Thinking is not merely *l'engagement dans l'action* for and by beings, in the sense of the actuality of the present situation. Thinking is *l'engagement* by and for the truth of Being. The history of Being is never past but stands ever before; it sustains and defines every *condition et situation humaine*. In order to learn how to experience the aforementioned essence of thinking purely, and that means at the same time to carry it through, we must free ourselves from the technical interpretation of thinking. The beginnings of that interpretation reach back to Plato and Aristotle. They take thinking itself to be a *technē*, a process of reflection in service to doing and making. But here reflection is already seen from the perspective of *praxis* and *poēisis*. For this reason thinking, when taken for itself, is not "practical." The characterization of thinking as *theōria* and the determination of knowing as "theoretical" behavior occur already within the "technical" interpretation of thinking. Such characterization is a reactive attempt to rescue thinking and preserve its autonomy over against acting and doing. Since then "philosophy" has been in the constant predicament of having to justify its existence before the "sciences." It believes it can do that most effectively by elevating itself to the rank of a science. But such an effort is the abandonment of the essence of thinking. Philosophy is hounded by the fear that it loses prestige and validity if it is not a science. Not to be a science is taken as a failing that is equivalent to being unscientific. Being, as the element of thinking, is abandoned by the technical interpretation of thinking. "Logic," beginning with the Sophists and Plato, sanctions this explanation. Thinking is judged by a standard that does not measure up to it. Such judgment may be compared to the procedure of trying to evaluate the essence and powers of a fish by seeing how long it can live on dry land. For a long time now, all too long, thinking has been stranded on dry land. Can then the effort to return thinking to its element be called "irrationalism"?

Surely the questions raised in your letter would have been better answered in direct conversation. In written form thinking easily loses its flexibility. But in writing it is difficult above all to retain the multidimensionality of the realm peculiar to thinking. The rigor of thinking, in contrast to that of the sciences, does not consist merely in an artificial, that is, technical-theoretical exactness of concepts. It lies in the fact that speaking remains purely in the element of Being and lets the simplicity of its manifold dimensions rule. On the other hand, written composition exerts a wholesome pressure toward deliberate linguistic formulation. Today I would like to grapple with only one of your questions. Perhaps its discussion will also shed some light on the others.

You ask: *Comment redonner un sens au mot "Humanisme"?* [How can we restore meaning to the word "humanism"?] This question proceeds from your intention to retain the word "humanism." I wonder whether that is necessary. Or is the damage caused by all such terms still not sufficiently obvious? True, "-isms" have for a long time now been suspect. But the market of public opinion continually demands new ones. We are always prepared to supply the demand. Even such names as "logic," "ethics," and "physics" begin to flourish only when original thinking comes to an end. During the time of their greatness the Greeks thought without such headings. They did not even call thinking "philosophy." Thinking comes to an end when it slips out of its element. The element is what enables thinking to be a thinking. The element is what properly enables: it is the enabling. It embraces thinking and so brings it into its essence. Said plainly, thinking is the thinking of Being. The genitive says something twofold. Thinking is of Being inasmuch as thinking, propriated by Being, belongs to Being. At the same time thinking is of Being insofar as thinking, belonging to Being, listens to Being. As the belonging to Being that listens, thinking is what it is according to its essential origin. Thinking *is*—this says: Being has fatefully embraced its essence. To embrace a "thing" or a "person" in its essence means to love it, to favor it. Thought in a more original way, such favoring means to bestow essence as a gift. Such favoring is the proper essence of enabling, which not only can achieve this or that but also can let something essentially unfold in its provenance, that is, let it be. It is on the "strength" of such enabling by favoring that something is properly able to be. This enabling is what is properly "possible," whose essence resides in favoring. From this favoring Being enables thinking. The former makes the latter possible. Being is the enabling-favoring, the "may be." As the element, Being is the "quiet power" of the favoring-enabling, that is, of the possible. Of course, our words *möglich* [possible] and *Möglichkeit* [possibility], under the dominance of "logic" and "metaphysics," are thought solely in contrast to "actuality"; that is, they are thought on the basis of a definite—the metaphysical—interpretation of Being as *actus* and *potentia*, a distinction identified with the one between *existentia* and *essentia*. When I speak of the "quiet power of the possible" I do not mean the *possibile* of a merely represented *possibilitas*, nor *potentia* as the *essentia* of an *actus* of *existentia*; rather, I mean Being itself, which in its favoring presides over thinking and hence over the essence of humanity, and that means over its relation to Being. To enable something here means to preserve it in its essence, to maintain it in its element.

When thinking comes to an end by slipping out of its element, it replaces this loss by procuring a validity for itself as *technē*, as an instrument of education and therefore as a classroom matter and later a cultural concern. By and by, philosophy becomes a technique for explaining from highest causes. One no longer thinks; one occupies oneself with "philosophy." In competition with one another, such occupations publicly offer themselves as "-isms" and try to offer more than the others. The dominance of such terms is not accidental. It rests above all in the modern age upon the peculiar dictatorship of the public realm. However, so-called "private existence" is not really essential, that is to say free, human being. It simply insists on negating the public realm. It remains an offshoot that depends upon the public and nourishes itself by a mere withdrawal from it. Hence it testifies, against its own will, to its subservience to the public realm. But because it stems from the dominance of subjectivity, the public realm itself is the metaphysically conditioned establishment and authorization of the openness of individual beings in their unconditional objectification. Language thereby falls into the service of expediting communication along routes where objectification—the uniform accessibility of everything to everyone—branches out and disregards all limits. In this way language comes under the dictatorship of the public realm, which decides in advance what is intelligible and what must be rejected as unintelligible. What is said in *Being and Time* (1927), sections 27 and 35, about the "they" in no way means to furnish an incidental contribution to sociology. Just as little does the "they" mean merely the opposite, understood in an ethical-existentiell way, of the selfhood of persons. Rather, what is said there contains a reference, thought in terms of the question of the truth of Being, to the word's primordial belongingness to Being. This relation remains concealed beneath the dominance of subjectivity that presents itself as the public realm. But if the truth of Being has become thought-provoking for thinking, then reflection on the essence of language must also attain a different rank. It can no longer be a mere philosophy of language. That is the only reason *Being and Time* (section 34) contains a reference to the essential dimension of language and touches upon the simple question as to what mode of Being language as language in any given case has. The widely and rapidly spreading devastation of language not only undermines aesthetic and moral responsibility in every use of language; it arises from a threat to the essence of humanity. A merely cultivated use of language is still no proof that we have as yet escaped the danger to our essence. These days, in fact, such usage might sooner testify that we have not yet seen and cannot see the danger because we have never yet placed ourselves in view of it. Much bemoaned of late, and much too lately, the downfall of language is, however, not the grounds for, but already a consequence of, the state of affairs in which language under the dominance of the modern metaphysics of subjectivity almost irremediably falls out of its element. Language still denies us its essence: that it is the house of the truth of Being. Instead, language surrenders itself to our mere willing and trafficking as an instrument of domination over beings. Beings themselves appear as actualities in the interaction of cause and effect. We encounter beings as actualities in a calculative businesslike way, but also scientifically and by way of philosophy, with explanations and proofs. Even the assurance that something is inexplicable belongs to these explanations and proofs. With such statements we believe that we confront the mystery. As if it were already decided that the truth of Being lets itself at all be established in causes and explanatory grounds or, what comes to the same, in their incomprehensibility.

But if man is to find his way once again into the nearness of Being, he must first learn to exist in the nameless. In the same way he must recognize the seductions of the public realm as well as the impotence of the private. Before he speaks man must first let himself be claimed again by Being, taking the risk that under this claim he will seldom have much to say. Only thus will the pricelessness of its essence be once more bestowed upon the word, and upon man a home for dwelling in the truth of Being.

But in the claim upon man, in the attempt to make man ready for this claim, is there not implied a concern about man? Where else does "care" tend but in the direction of bringing man back to his essence? What else does that in turn betoken but that man (*homo*) become human (*humanus*)? Thus *humanitas* really does remain the concern of such thinking. For this is humanism: meditating and caring, that man be human and not inhumane, "inhuman," that is, outside his essence. But in what does the humanity of man consist? It lies in his essence.

But whence and how is the essence of man determined? Marx demands that "man's humanity" be recognized and acknowledged. He finds it in "society." "Social" man is for him "natural" man. In "society" the "nature" of man, that is, the totality of "natural needs" (food, clothing, reproduction, economic sufficiency) is equably secured. The Christian sees the humanity of man, the *humanitas* of *homo*, in contradistinction to *Deitas*. He is the man of the history of redemption who as a "child of God" hears and accepts the call of the Father in Christ. Man is not of this world, since the "world," thought in terms of Platonic theory, is only a temporary passage to the beyond.

Humanitas, explicitly so called, was first considered and striven for in the age of the Roman Republic. *Homo humanus* was opposed to *homo barbarus*. *Homo humanus* here means the Romans, who exalted and honored Roman *virtus* through the "embodiment" of the *paideia* [education] taken over from the Greeks. These were the Greeks of the Hellenistic age, whose culture was acquired in the schools of philosophy. It was concerned with *eruditio et institutio in bonas artes* [scholarship and training in good conduct]. *Paideia* thus understood was translated as *humanitas*. The genuine *romanitas* of *homo romanus* consisted in such *humanitas*. We encounter the first humanism in Rome: it therefore remains in essence a specifically Roman phenomenon, which emerges from the encounter of Roman civilization with the culture of late Greek civilization. The so-called Renaissance of the fourteenth and fifteenth centuries in Italy is a *renascentia romanitatis*. Because *romanitas* is what matters, it is concerned with *humanitas* and therefore with Greek *paideia*. But Greek civilization is always seen in its later form, and this itself is seen from a Roman point of view. The *homo romanus* of the Renaissance also stands in opposition to *homo barbarus*. But now the in-humane is the supposed barbarism of Gothic Scholasticism in the Middle Ages. Therefore a *studium humanitatis*, which in a certain way reaches back to the ancients and thus also becomes a revival of Greek civilization, always adheres to historically understood humanism. For Germans this is apparent in the humanism of the eighteenth century supported by Winckelmann, Goethe, and Schiller. On the other hand, Hölderlin does not belong to "humanism," precisely because he thought the destiny of man's essence in a more original way than "humanism" could.

But if one understands humanism in general as a concern that man become free for his humanity and find his worth in it, then humanism differs according to one's conception of the "freedom" and "nature" of man. So too are there various paths toward the realization of such conceptions. The humanism of Marx does not need to return to antiquity any more than the humanism which Sartre conceives existentialism to be. In this broad sense Christianity too is a humanism, in that according to its teaching everything depends on man's salvation (*salus aeterna*); the history of man appears in the context of the history of redemption. However different these forms of humanism may be in purpose and in principle, in the mode and means of their respective realizations, and in the form of their teaching, they nonetheless all agree in this, that the *humanitas* of *homo humanus* is determined with regard to an already established interpretation of nature, history, world, and the ground of the world, that is, of beings as a whole.

Every humanism is either grounded in a metaphysics or is itself made to be the ground of one. Every determination of the essence of man that already presupposes an interpretation of beings without asking about the truth of Being, whether knowingly or not, is metaphysical. The result is that what is peculiar to all metaphysics, specifically with respect to the way the essence of man is determined, is that it is "humanistic." Accordingly, every humanism remains metaphysical. In defining the humanity of man, humanism not only does not ask about the relation of Being to the essence of man; because of its metaphysical origin, humanism even impedes the question by neither recognizing nor understanding it. On the contrary, the necessity and proper form of the question concerning the truth of Being, forgotten in and through metaphysics, can come to light only if the question "What is metaphysics?" is posed in the midst of metaphysics's domination. Indeed every inquiry into Being, even the one into the truth of Being, must at first introduce its inquiry as a "metaphysical" one.

The first humanism, Roman humanism, and every kind that has emerged from that time to the present has presupposed the most universal "essence" of man to be obvious. Man is considered to be an *animal rationale*. This definition is not simply the Latin translation of the Greek *zōon logon echon* but rather a metaphysical interpretation of it. This essential definition of man is not false. But it is conditioned by metaphysics. The essential provenance of metaphysics, and not just its limits, became questionable in *Being and Time*. What is questionable is above all commended to thinking as what is to be thought, but not at all left to the gnawing doubts of an empty skepticism.

Metaphysics does indeed represent beings in their Being, and so it thinks the Being of beings. But it does not think the difference of both.[1] Metaphysics does not ask about the truth of Being itself. Nor does it therefore ask in what way the essence of man belongs to the truth of Being. Metaphysics has not only failed up to now to ask this question, the question is inaccessible to metaphysics as such. Being is still waiting for the time when it will become thought-provoking to man. With regard to the definition of man's essence, however one may determine the *ratio* of the *animal* and the reason of the living being, whether as a "faculty of principles" or a "faculty of categories" or in some other way, the essence of reason is always and in each case grounded in this: for every apprehending of beings in their Being, Being itself is already illumined and propriated in its truth. So too with *animal*, *zōon*, an interpretation of "life" is already posited that necessarily lies in an interpretation of beings as *zōē* and *physis*, within which what is living appears. Above and beyond everything else, however, it finally remains to ask whether the essence of man primordially and most decisively lies in the dimension of *animalitas* at all. Are we really on the right track toward the essence of man as long as we set him off as one living creature among others in contrast to plants, beasts, and God? We can proceed in that way; we can in such fashion locate man within being as one being among others. We will thereby always be able to state something correct about man. But we must be clear on this point, that when we do this, we abandon man to the essential realm of *animalitas* even if we do not equate him with beasts but attribute a specific difference to him. In principle we are still thinking of *homo animalis*—even when *anima* [soul] is posited as *animus sive mens* [spirit or mind], and this in turn is later posited as subject, person, or spirit [*Geist*]. Such positing is the manner of metaphysics. But then the essence of man is too little heeded and not thought in its origin, the essential provenance that is always the essential future for historical mankind. Metaphysics thinks of man on the basis of *animalitas* and does not think in the direction of his *humanitas*.

Metaphysics closes itself to the simple essential fact that man essentially occurs only in his essence, where he is claimed by Being. Only from that claim "has" he found that wherein his essence dwells. Only from this dwelling "has" he "language" as the home that preserves the ecstatic for his essence. Such standing in the clearing of Being I call the ek-sistence of man. This way of Being is proper only to man. Ek-sistence so understood is not only the ground of the possibility of reason, *ratio*, but is also that in which the essence of man preserves the source that determines him.

Ek-sistence can be said only of the essence of man, that is, only of the human way "to be." For as far as our experience shows, only man is admitted to the destiny of ek-sistence. Therefore ek-sistence can also never be thought of as a specific kind of living creature among others—granted that man is destined to think the essence of his Being and not merely to give accounts of the nature and history of his constitution and activities. Thus even what we attribute to man as *animalitas* on the basis of the comparison with "beasts" is itself grounded in the essence of ek-sistence. The human body is something essentially other than an animal organism. Nor is the error of biologism overcome by adjoining a soul to the human body, a mind to the soul, and the existentiell to the mind, and then louder than before singing the praises of the mind—only to let everything relapse into "life experience," with a warning that thinking by its inflexible concepts disrupts the flow of life and that thought of Being distorts existence. The fact that physiology and physiological chemistry can scientifically investigate man as an organism is no proof that in this "organic" thing, that is, in the body scientifically explained, the essence of man consists. That has as little validity as the notion that the essence of nature has been discovered in atomic energy. It could even be that nature, in the face it turns toward man's technical mastery, is simply concealing its essence. Just as little as the essence of man consists in being an animal organism can this insufficient definition of man's essence be overcome or offset by outfitting man with an immortal soul, the power of reason, or the character of a person. In each instance essence is passed over, and passed over on the basis of the same metaphysical projection.

What man is—or, as it is called in the traditional language of metaphysics, the "essence" of man—lies in his ek-sistence. But ek-sistence thought in this way is not identical with the traditional concept of *existentia*, which means actuality in contrast to the meaning of *essentia* as possibility. In *Being and Time* (p. 42) this sentence is italicized: "The 'essence' of Dasein lies in its existence." However, here the opposition between *existentia* and *essentia* is not under consideration, because neither of these metaphysical determinations of Being, let alone their relationship, is yet in question. Still less does the sentence contain a universal statement about *Dasein*, since the word came into fashion in the eighteenth century as a name for "object," intending to express the metaphysical concept of the actuality of the actual. On the contrary, the sentence says: man occurs essentially in such a way that he is the "there" [*das "Da"*], that is, the clearing of Being. The "Being" of the *Da*, and only it, has the fundamental character of ek-sistence, that is, of an ecstatic inherence in the truth of Being. The ecstatic essence of man consists in ek-sistence, which is different from the metaphysically conceived *existentia*. Medieval philosophy conceives the latter as *actualitas*. Kant represents *existentia* as actuality in the sense of the objectivity of experience. Hegel defines *existentia* as the self-knowing Idea of absolute subjectivity. Nietzsche grasps *existentia* as the eternal recurrence of the same. Here it remains an open question whether through *existentia*—in these explanations of it as actuality, which at first seem quite different—the Being of a stone or even life as the Being of plants and animals is adequately thought. In any case living creatures are as they are without standing outside their Being as such and within the truth of Being, preserving in such standing the essential nature of their Being. Of all the beings that are, presumably the most difficult to think about are living creatures, because on the one hand they are in a certain way most closely akin to us, and on the other are at the same time separated from our ek-sistent essence by an abyss. However, it might also seem as though the essence of divinity is closer to us than what is so alien in other living creatures, closer, namely, in an essential distance which, however distant, is nonetheless more familiar to our ek-sistent essence than is our scarcely conceivable, abysmal bodily kinship with the beast. Such reflections cast a strange light upon the current and therefore always still premature designation of man as *animal rationale*. Because plants and animals are lodged in their respective environments but are never placed freely in the clearing of Being which alone is "world," they lack language. But in being denied language they are not thereby suspended worldlessly in their environment. Still, in this word "environment" converges all that is puzzling about living creatures. In its essence, language is not the utterance of an organism; nor is it the expression of a living thing. Nor can it ever be thought in an essentially correct way in terms of its symbolic character, perhaps not even in terms of the character of signification. Language is the clearing-concealing advent of Being itself.

Ek-sistence, thought in terms of *ecstasis*, does not coincide with *existentia* in either form or content. In terms of content, ek-sistence means standing out into the truth of Being. *Existentia* (existence) means in contrast *actualitas*, actuality as opposed to mere possibility as Idea. Ek-sistence identifies the determination of what man is in the destiny of truth. *Existentia* is the name for the realization of something that is as it appears in its Idea. The sentence "Man ek-sists" is not an answer to the question of whether man actually is or not; rather, it responds to the question concerning man's "essence." We are accustomed to posing this question with equal impropriety whether we ask what man is or who he is.

For in the *Who?* or the *What?* we are already on the lookout for something like a person or an object. But the personal no less than the objective misses and misconstrues the essential unfolding of ek-sistence in the history of Being. That is why the sentence cited from *Being and Time* (p. 42) is careful to enclose the word "essence" in quotation marks. This indicates that "essence" is now being defined from neither *esse essentiae* nor *esse existentiae* but rather from the ek-static character of Dasein. As ek-sisting, man sustains Da-sein in that he takes the *Da*, the clearing of Being, into "care." But Da-sein itself occurs essentially as "thrown." It unfolds essentially in the throw of Being as the fateful sending.

But it would be the ultimate error if one wished to explain the sentence about man's ek-sistent essence as if it were the secularized transference to human beings of a thought that Christian theology expresses about God (*Deus est suum esse* [God is His Being]); for ek-sistence is not the realization of an essence, nor does ek-sistence itself even effect and posit what is essential. If we understand what *Being and Time* calls "projection" as a representational positing, we take it to be an achievement of subjectivity and do not think it in the only way the "understanding of Being" in the context of the "existential analysis" of "being-in-the-world" can be thought—namely, as the ecstatic relation to the clearing of Being. The adequate execution and completion of this other thinking that abandons subjectivity is surely made more difficult by the fact that in the publication of *Being and Time,* the third division of the first part, "Time and Being," was held back. Here everything is reversed. The division in question was held back because thinking failed in the adequate saying of this turning [*Kehre*] and did not succeed with the help of the language of metaphysics. The lecture "On the Essence of Truth," thought out and delivered in 1930 but not printed until 1943, provides a certain insight into the thinking of the turning from "Being and Time" to "Time and Being." This turning is not a change of standpoint from *Being and Time*, but in it the thinking that was sought first arrives at the location of that dimension out of which *Being and Time* is experienced, that is to say, experienced from the fundamental experience of the oblivion of Being.

By way of contrast, Sartre expresses the basic tenet of existentialism in this way: existence precedes essence. In this statement he is taking *existentia* and *essentia* according to their metaphysical meaning, which from Plato's time on has said that *essentia* precedes *existentia*. Sartre reverses this statement. But the reversal of a metaphysical statement remains a metaphysical statement. With it he stays with metaphysics in oblivion of the truth of Being. For even if philosophy wishes to determine the relation of *essentia* and *existentia* in the sense it had in medieval controversies, in Leibniz's sense, or in some other way, it still remains to ask first of all from what destiny of Being this differentiation in Being as *esse essentiae* and *esse existentiae* comes to appear to thinking. We have yet to consider why the question about the destiny of Being was never asked and why it could never be thought. Or is the fact that this is how it is with the differentiation of *essentia* and *existentia* not at all a sign of forgetfulness of Being? We must presume that this destiny does not rest upon a mere failure of human thinking, let alone upon a lesser capacity of early Western thinking. Concealed in its essential provenance, the differentiation of *essentia* (essentiality) and *existentia* (actuality) completely dominates the destiny of Western history and of all history determined by Europe.

Sartre's key proposition about the priority of *existentia* over *essentia* does, however, justify using the name "existentialism" as an appropriate title for a philosophy of this sort. But the basic tenet of "existentialism" has nothing at all in common with the statement from *Being and Time*—apart from the fact that in *Being and Time* no statement about the relation of *essentia* and *existentia* can yet be expressed, since there it is still a question of preparing something precursory. As is obvious from what we have just said, that happens clumsily enough. What still today remains to be said could perhaps become an impetus for guiding the essence of man to the point where it thoughtfully attends to that dimension of the truth of Being which thoroughly governs it. But even this could take place only to the honor of Being and for the benefit of Da-sein, which man ek-sistingly sustains; not, however, for the sake of man, so that civilization and culture through man's doings might be vindicated.

But in order that we today may attain to the dimension of the truth of Being in order to ponder it, we should first of all make clear how Being concerns man and how it claims him. Such an essential experience happens to us when it dawns on us that man is in that he ek-sists. Were we now to say this in the language of the tradition, it would run: the ek-sistence of man is his substance. That is why in *Being and Time* the sentence often recurs, "The 'substance' of man is existence." But "substance," thought in terms of the history of Being, is already a blanket translation of *ousia*, a word that designates the presence of what is present and at the same time, with puzzling ambiguity, usually means what is present itself. If we think the metaphysical term "substance" in the sense already suggested in accordance with the "phenomenological destructuring" carried out in *Being and Time*, then the statement "The 'substance' of man is ek-sistence" says nothing else but that the way that man in his proper essence becomes present to Being is ecstatic inherence in the truth of Being. Through this determination of the essence of man the humanistic interpretations of man as *animal rationale*, as "person," as spiritual-ensouled-bodily being, are not declared false and thrust aside. Rather, the sole implication is that the highest determinations of the essence of man in humanism still do not realize the proper dignity of man. To that extent the thinking in *Being and Time* is against humanism. But this opposition does not mean that such thinking aligns itself against the humane and advocates the inhuman, that it promotes the inhumane and deprecates the dignity of man. Humanism is opposed because it does not set the *humanitas* of man high enough. Of course the essential worth of man does not consist in his being the substance of beings, as the "Subject" among them, so that as the tyrant of Being he may deign to release the beingness of beings into an all-too-loudly bruited "objectivity.". . .

Should we still keep the name "humanism" for a "humanism" that contradicts all previous humanism—although it in no way advocates the inhuman? And keep it just so that by sharing in the use of the name we might perhaps swim in the predominant currents, stifled in metaphysical subjectivism and submerged in oblivion of Being? Or should thinking, by means of open resistance to "humanism," risk a shock that could for the first time cause perplexity concerning the *humanitas* of *homo humanus* and its basis? In this way it could awaken a reflection—if the world-historical moment did not itself already compel such a reflection—that thinks not only about man but also about the "nature" of man, not only about his nature but even more primordially about the dimension in which the essence of man, determined by Being itself, is at home. Should we not rather suffer a little while longer those inevitable misinterpretations to which the path of thinking in the element of Being and time has hitherto been exposed and let them slowly dissipate? These misinterpretations are natural reinterpretations of what was read, or simply mirrorings of what one believes he knows already before he reads. They all betray "the same structure and the same foundation."

Because we are speaking against "humanism," people fear a defense of the inhuman and a glorification of barbaric brutality. For what is more "logical" than that for somebody who negates humanism nothing remains but the affirmation of inhumanity?

Because we are speaking against "logic," people believe we are demanding that the rigor of thinking be renounced and in its place the arbitrariness of drives and feelings be installed and thus that "irrationalism" be proclaimed as true. For what is more "logical" than that whoever speaks against the logical is defending the alogical?

Because we are speaking against "values" people are horrified at a philosophy that ostensibly dares to despise humanity's best qualities. For what is more "logical" than that a thinking that denies values must necessarily pronounce everything valueless?

Because we say that the Being of man consists in "being-in-the-world" people find that man is downgraded to a merely terrestrial being, whereupon philosophy sinks into positivism. For what is more "logical" than that whoever asserts the worldliness of human being holds only this life as valid, denies the beyond, and renounces all "Transcendence"?

Because we refer to the word of Nietzsche on the "death of God" people regard such a gesture as atheism. For what is more "logical" than that whoever has experienced the death of God is godless?

Because in all the respects mentioned we everywhere speak against all that humanity deems high and holy our philosophy teaches an irresponsible and destructive "nihilism." For what is more "logical" than that whoever roundly denies what is truly in being puts himself on the side of nonbeing and thus professes the pure nothing as the meaning of reality?

What is going on here? People hear talk about "humanism," "logic," "values," "world," and "God." They hear something about opposition to these. They recognize and accept these things as positive. But with hearsay—in a way that is not strictly deliberate—they immediately assume that what speaks against something is automatically its negation and that this is "negative" in the sense of destructive. And somewhere in *Being and Time* there is explicit talk of "the phenomenological destructuring." With the assistance of logic and *ratio*—so often invoked—people come to believe that whatever is not positive is negative and thus that it seeks to degrade reason—and therefore deserves to be branded as depravity. We are so filled with "logic" that anything that disturbs the habitual somnolence of prevailing opinion is automatically registered as a despicable contradiction. We pitch everything that does not stay close to the familiar and beloved positive into the previously excavated pit of pure negation, which negates everything, ends in nothing, and so consummates nihilism. Following this logical course, we let everything expire in a nihilism we invented for ourselves with the aid of logic.

But does the "against" which a thinking advances against ordinary opinion necessarily point toward pure negation and the negative? This happens—and then, to be sure, happens inevitably and conclusively, that is, without a clear prospect of anything else—only when one posits in advance what is meant by the "positive" and on this basis makes an absolute and absolutely negative decision about the range of possible opposition to it. Concealed in such a procedure is the refusal to subject to reflection this presupposed "positive" in which one believes oneself saved, together with its position and opposition. By continually appealing to the logical, one conjures up the illusion that one is entering straightforwardly into thinking when in fact one has disavowed it. It ought to be somewhat clearer now that opposition to "humanism" in no way implies a defense of the inhuman but rather opens other vistas.

"Logic" understands thinking to be the representation of beings in their Being, which representation proposes to itself in the generality of the concept. But how is it with meditation on Being itself, that is, with the thinking that thinks the truth of Being? This thinking alone reaches the primordial essence of *logos*, which was already obfuscated and lost in Plato and in Aristotle, the founder of "logic." To think against "logic" does not mean to break a lance for the illogical but simply to trace in thought the *logos* and its essence, which appeared in the dawn of thinking, that is, to exert ourselves for the first time in preparing for such reflection. Of what value are even far-reaching systems of logic to us if, without really knowing what they are doing, they recoil before the task of simply inquiring into the essence of *logos*? If we wished to bandy about objections, which is of course fruitless, we could say with more right: irrationalism, as a denial of *ratio*, rules unnoticed and uncontested in the defense of "logic," which believes it can eschew meditation on *logos* and on the essence of *ratio*, which has its ground in *logos*.

To think against "values" is not to maintain that everything interpreted as "a value"—"culture," "art," "science," "human dignity," "world," and "God"—is valueless. Rather, it is important finally to realize that precisely through the characterization of something as "a value," what is so valued is robbed of its worth. That is to say, by the assessment of something as a value, what is valued is admitted only as an object for man's estimation. But what a thing is in its Being is not exhausted by its being an object, particularly when objectivity takes the form of value. Every valuing, even where it values positively, is a subjectivizing. It does not let beings: be. Rather, valuing lets beings: be valid—solely as the objects of its doing. The bizarre effort to prove the objectivity of values does not know what it is doing. When one proclaims "God" the altogether "highest value," this is a degradation of God's essence. Here, as elsewhere, thinking in values is the greatest blasphemy imaginable against Being. To think against values therefore does not mean to beat the drum for the valuelessness and nullity of beings. It means rather to bring the clearing of the truth of Being before thinking, as against subjectivizing beings into mere objects.

The reference to "being-in-the-world" as the basic trait of the *humanitas* of *homo humanus* does not assert that man is merely "worldly" creature understood in a Christian sense, thus a creature turned away from God and so cut loose from "Transcendence." What is really meant by this word would be more clearly called "the transcendent." The transcendent is supersensible being. This is considered the highest being in the sense of the first cause of all beings. God is thought as this first cause. However, in the name "being-in-the-world," "world" does not in any way imply earthly as opposed to heavenly being, nor the "worldly" as opposed to the "spiritual." For us "world" does not at all signify beings or any realm of beings but the openness of Being. Man is, and is man, insofar as he is the ek-sisting one. He stands out into the openness of Being. Being itself, which as the throw has projected the essence of man into "care," is as this openness. Thrown in such fashion, man stands "in" the openness of Being. "World" is the clearing of Being into which man stands out on the basis of his thrown essence. "Being-in-the-world" designates the essence of ek-sistence with regard to the cleared dimension out of which the "ek-" of ek-sistence essentially unfolds. Thought in terms of ek-sistence, "world" is in a certain sense precisely "the beyond" within existence and for it. Man is never first and foremost man on the hither side of the world, as a "subject," whether this is taken as "I" or "We." Nor is he ever simply a mere subject which always simultaneously is related to objects, so that his essence lies in the subject-object relation. Rather, before all this, man in his essence is ek-sistent into the openness of Being, into the open region that clears the "between" within which a "relation" of subject to object can "be."

The statement that the essence of man consists in being-in-the-world likewise contains no decision about whether man in a theologico-metaphysical sense is merely a this-worldly or an otherworldly creature.

With the existential determination of the essence of man, therefore, nothing is decided about the "existence of God" or his "nonbeing," no more than about the possibility or impossibility of gods. Thus it is not only rash but also an error in procedure to maintain that the interpretation of the essence of man from the relation of his essence to the truth of Being is atheism. And what is more, this arbitrary classification betrays a lack of careful reading. No one bothers to notice that in my essay "On the Essence of Ground" the following appears: "Through the ontological interpretation of Dasein as being-in-the-world no decision, whether positive or negative, is made concerning a possible being toward God. It is, however, the case that through an illumination of transcendence we first achieve an *adequate concept of Dasein*, with respect to which it can now be asked how the relationship of Dasein to God is ontologically ordered."[2] If we think about this remark too quickly, as is usually the case, we will declare that such a philosophy does not decide either for or against the existence of God. It remains stalled in indifference. Thus it is unconcerned with the religious question. Such indifferentism ultimately falls prey to nihilism.

But does the foregoing observation teach indifferentism? Why then are particular words in the note italicized—and not just random ones? For no other reason than to indicate that the thinking that thinks from the question concerning the truth of Being questions more primordially than metaphysics can.

Only from the truth of Being can the essence of the holy be thought. Only from the essence of the holy is the essence of divinity to be thought. Only in the light of the essence of divinity can it be thought or said what the word "God" is to signify. Or should we not first be able to hear and understand all these words carefully if we are to be permitted as men, that is, as ek-sistent creatures, to experience a relation of God to man? How can man at the present stage of world history ask at all seriously and rigorously whether the god nears or withdraws, when he has above all neglected to think into the dimension in which alone that question can be asked? But this is the dimension of the holy, which indeed remains closed as a dimension if the open region of Being is not cleared and in its clearing is near man. Perhaps what is distinctive about this world-epoch consists in the closure of the dimension of the hale [*des Heilen*]. Perhaps that is the sole malignancy [*Unheil*].

But with this reference the thinking that points toward the truth of Being as what is to be thought has in no way decided in favor of theism. It can be theistic as little as atheistic. Not, however, because of an indifferent attitude, but out of respect for the boundaries that have been set for thinking as such, indeed set by what gives itself to thinking as what is to be thought, by the truth of Being. Insofar as thinking limits itself to its task, it directs man at the present moment of the world's destiny into the primordial dimension of his historical abode. When thinking of this kind speaks the truth of Being, it has entrusted itself to what is more essential than all values and all types of beings. Thinking does not overcome metaphysics by climbing still higher, surmounting it, transcending it somehow or other; thinking overcomes metaphysics by climbing back down into the nearness of the nearest. The descent, particularly where man has strayed into subjectivity, is more arduous and more dangerous than the ascent. The descent leads to the poverty of the ek-sistence of *homo humanus*. In ek-sistence the region of *homo animalis*, of metaphysics, is abandoned. The dominance of that region is the mediate and deeply rooted basis for the blindness and arbitrariness of what is called "biologism," but also of what is known under the heading "pragmatism." To think the truth of Being at the same time means to think the humanity of *homo humanus*. What counts is *humanitas* in the service of the truth of Being, but without humanism in the metaphysical sense.

But if *humanitas* must be viewed as so essential to the thinking of Being, must not "ontology" therefore be supplemented by "ethics"? Is not that effort entirely essential which you express in the sentence, "*Ce que je cherche à faire, depuis longtemps déjà, c'est préciser le rapport de l'ontologie avec une éthique possible*" ["What I have been trying to do for a long time now is to determine precisely the relation of ontology to a possible ethics"]?

Soon after *Being and Time* appeared, a young friend asked me, "When are you going to write an ethics?" Where the essence of man is thought so essentially, i.e., solely from the question concerning the truth of Being, but still without elevating man to the center of beings, a longing necessarily awakens for a peremptory directive and for rules that say how man, experienced from ek-sistence toward Being, ought to live in a fitting manner. The desire for an ethics presses ever more ardently for fulfillment as the obvious no less than the hidden perplexity of man soars to immeasurable heights. The greatest care must be fostered upon the ethical bond at a time when technological man, delivered over to mass society, can be kept reliably on call only by gathering and ordering all his plans and activities in a way that corresponds to technology.

Who can disregard our predicament? Should we not safeguard and secure the existing bonds even if they hold human beings together ever so tenuously and merely for the present? Certainly. But does this need ever release thought from the task of thinking what still remains principally to be thought and, as Being, prior to all beings, is their guarantor and their truth? Even further, can thinking refuse to think Being after the latter has lain hidden so long in oblivion but at the same time has made itself known in the present moment of world history by the uprooting of all beings?

Before we attempt to determine more precisely the relationship between "ontology" and "ethics," we must ask what "ontology" and " ethics" themselves are. It becomes necessary to ponder whether what can be designated by both terms still remains near and proper to what is assigned to thinking, which as such has to think above all the truth of Being.

Of course if both "ontology" and "ethics," along with all thinking in terms of disciplines, become untenable, and if our thinking therewith becomes more disciplined, how then do matters stand with the question about the relation between these two philosophical disciplines?

Along with "logic" and "physics," "ethics" appeared for the first time in the school of Plato. These disciplines arose at a time when thinking was becoming "philosophy," philosophy *epistēmē* (science), and science itself a matter for schools and academic pursuits. In the course of a philosophy so understood, science waxed and thinking waned. Thinkers prior to this period knew neither a "logic" nor an "ethics" nor "physics." Yet their thinking was neither illogical nor immoral. But they did think *physis* in a depth and breadth that no subsequent "physics" was ever again able to attain. The tragedies of Sophocles—provided such a comparison is at all permissible—preserve the *ēthos* in their sagas more primordially than Aristotle's lectures on "ethics." A saying of Heraclitus which consists of only three words says something so simply that from it the essence of the *ēthos* immediately comes to light.

The saying of Heraclitus (Fragment 119) goes: *ēthos anthrōpōi daimōn*. This is usually translated, "A man's character is his daimon." This translation thinks in a modern way, not a Greek one. *Ethos* means abode, dwelling-place. The word names the open region in which man dwells. The open region of his abode allows what pertains to man's essence, and what in thus arriving resides in nearness to him, to appear. The abode of man contains and preserves the advent of what belongs to man in his essence. According to Heraclitus's phrase, this is *daimōn*, the god. The fragment says: Man dwells, insofar as he is man, in the nearness of god. A story that Aristotle reports (*De partibus animalium*, 1, 5, 645a 17ff.) agrees with this fragment of Heraclitus.

> The story is told of something Heraclitus said to some strangers who wanted to come visit him. Having arrived, they saw him warming himself at a stove. Surprised, they stood there in consternation—above all because he encouraged them, the astounded ones, and called for them to come in, with the words: "For here too the gods are present."

The story certainly speaks for itself, but we may stress a few aspects.

The group of foreign visitors, in their importunate curiosity about the thinker, are disappointed and perplexed by their first glimpse of his abode. They believe they should meet the thinker in circumstances which, contrary to the ordinary round of human life, everywhere bear traces of the exceptional and rare and so of the exciting. The group hopes that in their visit to the thinker they will find things that will provide material for entertaining conversation—at least for a while. The foreigners who wish to visit the thinker expect to catch sight of him perchance at that very moment when, sunk in profound meditation, he is thinking. The visitors want this "experience" not in order to be overwhelmed by thinking but simply so they can say they saw and heard someone everybody says is a thinker.

Instead of this, the sightseers find Heraclitus by a stove. That is surely a common and insignificant place. True enough, bread is baked here. But Heraclitus is not even busy baking at the stove. He stands there merely to warm himself. In this altogether everyday place he betrays the whole poverty of his life. The vision of a shivering thinker offers little of interest. At this disappointing spectacle even the curious lose their desire to come any closer. What are they supposed to do here? Such an everyday and unexciting occurrence—somebody who is chilled warming himself at a stove—anyone can find any time at home. So why look up a thinker? The visitors are on the verge of going away again. Heraclitus reads the frustrated curiosity in their faces. He knows that for the crowd the failure of an expected sensation to materialize is enough to make those who have just arrived leave. He therefore encourages them. He invites them explicitly to come in with the words, *Einai gar kai entautha theous*, "Here too the gods come to presence."

This phrase places the abode (*ēthos*) of the thinker and his deed in another light. Whether the visitors understood this phrase at once—or at all—and then saw everything differently in this other light the story does not say. But the story was told and has come down to us today because what it reports derives from and characterizes the atmosphere surrounding this thinker. *Kai entautha*, "even here," at the stove, in that ordinary place where every thing and every condition, each deed and thought, is intimate and commonplace, that is, familiar, "even there" in the sphere of the familiar, *einai theous*, it is the case that "the gods come to presence."

Heraclitus himself says, *ēthos anthrōpōi daimōn*, "The (familiar) abode for man is the open region for the presencing of god (the unfamiliar one)."

If the name "ethics," in keeping with the basic meaning of the word *ēthos*, should now say that "ethics" ponders the abode of man, then that thinking which thinks the truth of Being as the primordial element of man, as one who ek-sists, is in itself the original ethics. However, this thinking is not ethics in the first instance, because it is ontology. For ontology always thinks solely the being (*on*) in its Being. But as long as the truth of Being is not thought, all ontology remains without its foundation. Therefore the thinking that in *Being and Time* tries to advance thought in a preliminary way into the truth of Being characterizes itself as "fundamental ontology." [See *Being and Time*, sections 3 and 4.] It strives to reach back into the essential ground from which thought concerning the truth of Being emerges. By initiating another inquiry, this thinking is already removed from the "ontology" of metaphysics (even that of Kant). "Ontology" itself, however, whether transcendental or precritical, is subject to criticism, not because it thinks the Being of beings and thereby reduces Being to a concept, but because it does not think the truth of Being and so fails to recognize that there is a thinking more rigorous than the conceptual. In the poverty of its first breakthrough, the thinking that tries to advance thought into the truth of Being brings only a small part of that wholly other dimension to language. This language even falsifies itself, for it does not yet succeed in retaining the essential help of phenomenological seeing while dispensing with the inappropriate concern with "science" and "research." But in order to make the attempt at thinking recognizable and at the same time understandable for existing philosophy, it could at first be expressed only within the horizon of that existing philosophy and its use of current terms.

In the meantime I have learned to see that these very terms were bound to lead immediately and inevitably into error. For the terms and the conceptual language corresponding to them were not rethought by readers from the matter particularly to be thought; rather, the matter was conceived according to the established terminology in its customary meaning. The thinking that inquires into the truth of Being and so defines man's essential abode from Being and toward Being is neither ethics nor ontology. Thus the question about the relation of each to the other no longer has any basis in this sphere. Nonetheless, your question, thought in a more original way, retains a meaning and an essential importance.

For it must be asked: If the thinking that ponders the truth of Being defines the essence of *humanitas* as ek-sistence from the latter's belongingness to Being, then does thinking remain only a theoretical representation of Being and of man; or can we obtain from such knowledge directives that can be readily applied to our active lives?

The answer is that such thinking is neither theoretical nor practical. It comes to pass before this distinction. Such thinking is, insofar as it is, recollection of Being and nothing else. Belonging to Being, because thrown by Being into the preservation of its truth and claimed for such preservation, it thinks

Being. Such thinking has no result. It has no effect. It satisfies its essence in that it is. But it is by say-ing its matter. Historically, only one saying [*Sage*] belongs to the matter of thinking, the one that is in each case appropriate to its matter. Its material relevance is essentially higher than the validity of the sciences, because it is freer. For it lets Being—be.

Notes

1. Cf. Martin Heidegger, *Vom Wesen des Grundes* (1929), 8; *Kant and the Problem of Metaphysics*, trans. Richard Taft (Bloomington, IN: Indiana University Press, 1990), section 43; *Being and Time*, section 44, 230.
2. Martin Heidegger, *Vom Wesen des Grundes*, 28 n.1.

Part 3

CRITICAL THEORY

11

WALTER BENJAMIN
(1892–1940)

Walter Benjamin, an influential German literary critic, aesthetician, and Marxist thinker, was born into a Jewish family in 1892. He studied philosophy in Berlin and then later at Freiburg, Munich, and Bern before returning to Berlin in 1920. Benjamin was never able to secure a long-term teaching position and worked as a literary critic and translator. When the Nazis rose to power in 1933, Benjamin moved to Paris, where he continued to write essays and reviews for literary journals. When France capitulated to the Germans in 1940, he tried to flee to the United States. His journey took him southward to the Franco-Spanish border, where he was informed that he would be turned over to the Gestapo. Upon hearing the news, Benjamin committed suicide by taking a lethal dose of morphine.

Benjamin (along with Max Horkheimer, Theodor Adorno, and Herbert Marcuse) was a leading member of the Frankfurt School. This school combined psychoanalysis, existentialism, and cultural analysis to form a new philosophy called "critical theory." Critical theorists, including Benjamin, sought to address the problems of modernity, aesthetics, and culture from a Hegelian-Marxist standpoint while maintaining a certain critical distance from Soviet Marxism and dialectical materialism. In his "Theses on the Philosophy of History" (1940), Benjamin criticized the idea of history as a progressive, uninterrupted continuum. Such an idea, according to Benjamin, reinforces the hegemony of the oppressors within history while muting the anonymous voices of the oppressed. To this reductionist account of history, Benjamin opposed his "angel of history," whose "face is turned toward the past. Where we perceive a chain of events, he sees one single catastrophe which keeps piling wreckage upon wreckage." The redemptive angel seeks to "fight for the oppressed past" by interrupting continuous history and bearing witness to the victims of the triumphs within history in the hope of unleashing a new potential for a utopian ("messianic") future.

In the "Critique of Violence" (1921), reprinted here, Benjamin seeks to separate the legitimate exercise of power from sheer force. The former is associated with proletarian violence represented by Marxism and the workers' struggle; the latter takes the form of "lawmaking" and "law-preserving" violence of the state (e.g., militarism, conscription, death penalty, the police). Revolutionary counterviolence—from strikes to a general class war—is vehemently opposed to state violence grounded in "mythical" lawmaking. Perhaps the most interesting feature of Benjamin's enigmatic—and somewhat question-begging—account of the dialectic of violence is his appeal at the end of his essay to an "expiatory" or "pure divine violence." Such violence manages to put a stop to the cycle of violence, and, according to Benjamin, ushers in "a new historical epoch" of universal justice.

Select Bibliography of Benjamin's Works in English

The Arcades Project. Trans. Howard Eiland and Kevin McLaughlin. Cambridge, MA: Harvard University Press, 1999.

Charles Baudelaire: A Lyric Poet in the Era of High Capitalism. Trans. H. Zohn. London: New Left Books, 1983.

Illuminations. Trans. H. Zohn. New York: Schocken Books, 1969.

Moscow Diary. Trans. R. Sieburth. Cambridge, MA: Harvard University Press, 1986.

The Origin of German Tragic Drama. Trans. J. Osborne. London: New Left Books, 1977.

Reflections. Trans. Edmund Jephcott. New York: Schocken Books, 1978.

Selected Writings. Eds. Marcus Bollock and Michael W. Jennings. Cambridge, MA: Harvard University Press, 1996–1999.

Understanding Brecht. Trans. A. Bostock. London: New Left Books, 1983.

CRITIQUE OF VIOLENCE

The task of a critique of violence can be summarized as that of expounding its relation to law and justice. For a cause, however effective, becomes violent, in the precise sense of the word, only when it bears on moral issues. The sphere of these issues is defined by the concepts of law and justice. With regard to the first of these, it is clear that the most elementary relationship within any legal system is that of ends to means and, further, that violence can first be sought only in the realm of means, not of ends. These observations provide a critique of violence with more—and certainly different—premises than perhaps appears. For if violence is a means, a criterion for criticizing it might seem immediately available. It imposes itself in the question whether violence, in a given case, is a means to a just or an unjust end. A critique of it would then be implied in a system of just ends. This, however, is not so. For what such a system, assuming it to be secure against all doubt, would contain is not a criterion for violence itself as a principle but, rather, the criterion for cases of its use. The question would remain open whether violence, as a principle could be a moral means even to just ends. To resolve this question a more exact criterion is needed, which would discriminate within the sphere of means themselves, without regard for the ends they serve.

The exclusion of this more precise critical approach is perhaps the predominant feature of a main current of legal philosophy: natural law. It perceives in the use of violent means to just ends no greater problem than a man sees in his "right" to move his body in the direction of a desired goal. According to this view (for which the terrorism in the French Revolution provided an ideological foundation), violence is a product of nature, as it were a raw material, the use of which is in no way problematical, unless force is misused for unjust ends. If, according to the theory of state of natural law, people give up all their violence for the sake of the state, this is done on the assumption (which Spinoza, for example, states explicitly in his *Tractatus Theologico-Politicus*) that the individual, before the conclusion of this rational contract, has *de jure* the right to use at will the violence that is *de facto* at his disposal. Perhaps these views have been recently rekindled by Darwin's biology, which, in a thoroughly dogmatic manner, regards violence as the only original means, besides natural selection, appropriate to all the vital ends of nature. Popular Darwinistic philosophy has often shown how short a step it is from this dogma of natural history to the still cruder one of legal philosophy, which holds that the violence that is, almost alone, appropriate to natural ends is thereby also legal.

This thesis of natural law that regards violence as a natural datum is diametrically opposed to that of positive law, which sees violence as a product of history. If natural law can judge all existing law only in criticizing its ends, so positive law can judge all evolving law only in criticizing its means. If justice is the criterion of ends, legality is that of means. Notwithstanding this antithesis, however, both schools meet in their common basic dogma: just ends can be attained by justified means, justified means used for just ends. Natural law attempts, by the justness of the ends, to "justify" the means, positive law to "guarantee" the justness of the ends through the justification of the means. This antinomy would prove insoluble if the common dogmatic assumption were false, if justified means on the one hand and just ends on the other were in irreconcilable conflict. No insight into this problem could be gained, however, until the circular argument had been broken, and mutually independent criteria both of just ends and of justified means were established.

The realm of ends, and therefore also the question of a criterion of justness, is excluded for the time being from this study. Instead, the central place is given to the question of the justification of certain means that constitute violence. Principles of natural law cannot decide this question, but can only lead to bottomless casuistry. For if positive law is blind to the absoluteness of ends, natural law is equally so to the contingency of means. On the other hand, the positive theory of law is acceptable as a hypothetical basis at the outset of this study, because it undertakes a fundamental distinction between kinds of violence independently of cases of their application. This distinction is between historically acknowledged, so-called sanctioned violence, and unsanctioned violence. If the following considerations proceed from this it cannot, of course, mean that given forms of violence are classified in terms of whether they are sanctioned or not. For in a critique of violence, a criterion for the latter in positive law cannot concern its uses but only its evaluation. The question that concerns us is: What light is thrown on the nature of violence by the fact that such a criterion or distinction can be applied to it at all, or, in other words, what is the meaning of this distinction? That this distinction supplied by positive law is meaningful, based on the nature of violence, and irreplaceable by any other, will soon enough be shown, but at the same time light will be shed on the sphere in which alone such a distinction can be made. To sum up: if the criterion established by positive law to assess the legality of violence can be analyzed with regard to its meaning, then the sphere of its application must be criticized with regard to its value. For this critique a standpoint outside positive legal philosophy but also outside natural law must be found. The extent to which it can only be furnished by a historico-philosophical view of law will emerge.

The meaning of the distinction between legitimate and illegitimate violence is not immediately obvious. The misunderstanding in natural law by which a distinction is drawn between violence used for just and unjust ends must be emphatically rejected. Rather, it has already been indicated that positive law demands of all violence a proof of its historical origin, which under certain conditions is declared legal, sanctioned. Since the acknowledgment of legal violence is most tangibly evident in a deliberate submission to its ends, a hypothetical distinction between kinds of violence must be based on the presence or absence of a general historical acknowledgment of its ends. Ends that lack such acknowledgment may be called natural ends, the other, legal ends. The differing function of violence, depending on whether it serves natural or legal ends, can be most clearly traced against a background of specific legal conditions. For the sake of simplicity, the following discussion will relate to contemporary European conditions.

Characteristic of these, as far as the individual as legal subject is concerned, is the tendency not to admit the natural ends of such individuals in all those cases in which such ends could, in a given situation, be usefully pursued by violence. This means: this legal system tries to erect, in all areas where individual ends could be usefully pursued by violence, legal ends that can only be realized by legal power. Indeed, it strives to limit by legal ends even those areas in which natural ends are admitted in principle within wide boundaries, like that of education, as soon as these natural ends are pursued with an excessive measure of violence, as in the laws relating to the limits of educational authority to punish. It can be formulated as a general maxim of present-day European legislation that all the natural ends of individuals must collide with legal ends if pursued with a greater or lesser degree of violence. (The contradiction between this and the right of self-defense will be resolved in what follows.) From this maxim it follows that law sees violence in the hands of individuals as a danger undermining the legal system. As a danger nullifying legal ends and the legal executive? Certainly not; for then violence as such would not be condemned, but only that directed to illegal ends. It will be argued that a system of legal ends cannot be maintained if natural ends are anywhere still pursued violently. In the first place, however, this is a mere dogma. To counter it one might perhaps consider the surprising possibility that the law's interest in a monopoly of violence *vis-à-vis* individuals is not explained by the intention of preserving legal ends but, rather, by that of preserving the law itself; that violence, when not in the hands of the law, threatens it not by the ends that it may pursue but by its mere existence outside the law. The same may be more drastically suggested if one reflects how often the figure of the "great" criminal, however repellent his ends may have been, has aroused the secret admiration of the public. This cannot result from his deed, but only from the violence to which it bears witness. In this case, therefore, the violence of which present-day law is seeking in all areas of activity to deprive the individual appears really threatening, and arouses even in defeat the sympathy of the mass against law. By what function violence can with reason seem so threatening to law, and be so feared by it, must be especially evident where its application, even in the present legal system, is still permissible.

This is above all the case in the class struggle, in the form of the workers' guaranteed right to strike. Organized labor is, apart from the state, probably today the only legal subject entitled to exercise violence. Against this view there is certainly the objection that an omission of actions, a nonaction, which a strike really is, cannot be described as violence. Such a consideration doubtless made it easier for a state power to conceive the right to strike, once this was no longer avoidable. But its truth is not unconditional, and therefore not unrestricted. It is true that the omission of an action, or service, where it amounts simply to a "severing of relations," can be an entirely nonviolent, pure means. And as in the view of the state or the law, the right to strike conceded to labor is certainly not a right to exercise violence but, rather, to escape from a violence indirectly exercised by the employer, strikes conforming to this may undoubtedly occur from time to time and involve only a "withdrawal" or "estrangement" from the employer. The moment of violence, however, is necessarily introduced, in the form of extortion, into such an omission, if it takes place in the context of a conscious readiness to resume the suspended action under certain circumstances that either have nothing whatever to do with this action or only superficially modify it. Understood in this way, the right to strike constitutes in the view of labor, which is opposed to that of the state, the right to use force in attaining certain ends. The antithesis between the two conceptions emerges in all its bitterness in the face of a revolutionary general strike. In this, labor will always appeal to its right to strike, and the state will call this appeal an abuse, since the right to strike was not "so intended," and take emergency measures. For the state retains the right to declare that a simultaneous use of strike in all industries is illegal, since the specific reasons for strike admitted by legislation cannot be prevalent in every workshop. In this difference of interpretation is expressed the objective contradiction in the legal situation, whereby the state acknowledges a violence whose ends, as natural ends, it sometimes regards with indifference, but in a crisis (the revolutionary general strike) confronts inimically. For, however paradoxical this may appear at first sight, even conduct involving the exercise of a right can nevertheless, under certain circumstances, be described as violent. More specifically, such conduct, when active, may be called violent if it exercises a right in order to overthrow the legal system that has conferred it; when passive, it is nevertheless to be so described if it constitutes extortion in the sense explained above. It therefore reveals an objective contradiction in the legal situation, but not a logical contradiction in the law, if under certain circumstances the law meets the strikers, as perpetrators of violence, with violence. For in a strike the state fears above all else that function of violence which it is the object of this study to identify as the only secure foundation of its critique. For if violence were, as first appears, merely the means to secure directly whatever happens to be sought, it could fulfill its end as predatory violence. It would be entirely unsuitable as a basis for, or a modification to, relatively stable conditions. The strike shows, however, that it can be so, that it is able to found and modify legal conditions, however offended the sense of justice may find itself thereby. It will be objected that such a function of violence is fortuitous and isolated. This can be rebutted by a consideration of military violence.

The possibility of military law rests on exactly the same objective contradiction in the legal situation as does that of strike law, that is to say, on the fact that legal subjects sanction violence whose ends remain for the sanctioners natural ends, and can therefore in a crisis come into conflict with their own legal or natural ends. Admittedly, military violence is in the first place used quite directly, as predatory violence, toward its ends. Yet it is very striking that even—or, rather, precisely—in primitive conditions that know hardly the beginnings of constitutional relations, and even in cases where the victor has established himself in invulnerable possession, a peace ceremony is entirely necessary. Indeed, the word "peace," in the sense in which it is the correlative to the word "war" (for there is also a quite different meaning, similarly unmetaphorical and political, the one used by Kant in talking of "Eternal Peace"), denotes this *a priori,* necessary sanctioning, regardless of all other legal conditions, of every victory. This sanction consists precisely in recognizing the new conditions as a new "law," quite regardless of whether they need *de facto* any guarantee of their continuation. If, therefore, conclusions can be drawn from military violence, as being primordial and paradigmatic of all violence used for natural ends, there is inherent in all such violence a lawmaking character. We shall return later to the implications of this insight. It explains the abovementioned tendency of modern law to divest the individual, at least as a legal subject, of all violence, even that directed only to natural ends. In the great criminal this violence confronts the law with the threat of declaring a new law, a threat that even today, despite its impotence, in important instances horrifies the public as it did in primeval times. The state, however, fears this violence simply for its lawmaking character, being obliged to acknowledge it as lawmaking whenever external powers force it to concede them the right to conduct warfare, and classes the right to strike.

If in the last war the critique of military violence was the starting point for a passionate critique of violence in general—which taught at least one thing, that violence is no longer exercised and tolerated naïvely—nevertheless, violence was not only subject to criticism for its lawmaking character, but was also judged, perhaps more annihilatingly, for another of its functions. For a duality in the function of violence is characteristic of militarism, which could only come into being through general conscription. Militarism is the compulsory, universal use of violence as a means to the ends of the state. This compulsory use of violence has recently been scrutinized as closely as, or still more closely than, the use of violence itself. In it violence shows itself in a function quite different from its simple application for natural ends. It consists in the use of violence as a means of legal ends. For the subordination of citizens to laws—in the present case, to the law of general conscription—is a legal end. If that first function of violence is called the lawmaking function, this second will be called the law-preserving function. Since conscription is a case of law-preserving violence that is not in principle distinguished from others, a really effective critique of it is far less easy than the declamations of pacifists and activists suggest. Rather, such a critique coincides with the critique of all legal violence—that is, with the critique of legal or executive force—and cannot be performed by any lesser program. Nor, of course— unless one is prepared to proclaim a quite childish anarchism—is it achieved by refusing to acknowledge any constraint toward persons and declaring: "What pleases is permitted." Such a maxim merely excludes reflection on the moral and historical spheres, and thereby on any meaning in action, and beyond this on any meaning in reality itself, which cannot be constituted if "action" is removed from its sphere. More important is the fact that even the appeal, so frequently attempted, to the categorical imperative, with its doubtless incontestable minimum program—act in such a way that at all times you use humanity both in your person and in the person of all others as an end, and never merely as a means—is in itself inadequate for such a critique.[1] For positive law, if conscious of its roots, will certainly claim to acknowledge and promote the interest of mankind in the person of each individual. It sees this interest in the representation and preservation of an order imposed by fate. While this view, which claims to preserve law in its very basis, cannot escape criticism, nevertheless all attacks that are made merely in the name of a formless "freedom," without being able to specify this higher order of freedom, remain impotent against it. And most impotent of all when, instead of attacking the legal system root and branch, they impugn particular laws or legal practices that the law, of course, takes under the protection of its power, which resides in the fact that there is only one fate and that what exists, and in particular what threatens, belongs inviolably to its order. For law-preserving violence is a threatening violence. And its threat is not intended as the deterrent that uninformed liberal theorists interpret it to be. A deterrent in the exact sense would require a certainty that contradicts the nature of a threat and is not attained by any law, since there is always hope of eluding its arm. This makes it all the more threatening, like fate, on which depends whether the criminal is apprehended. The deepest purpose of the uncertainty of the legal threat will emerge from the later consideration of the sphere of fate in which it originates. There is a useful pointer to it in the sphere of punishments. Among them, since the validity of positive law has been called into question, capital punishment has provoked more criticism than all others. However superficial most cases have been, their motives were and are rooted in principle. The opponents of these critics felt, perhaps without knowing why and probably involuntarily, that an attack on capital punishment assails, not legal measure, not laws, but law itself in its origin. For if violence, violence crowned by fate, is the origin of law, then it may be readily supposed that where the highest violence, that over life and death, occurs in the legal system, the origins of law jut manifestly and fearsomely into existence. In agreement with this is the fact that the death penalty in primitive legal systems is imposed even for such crimes as offenses against property, to which it seems quite out of "proportion." Its purpose is not to punish the infringement of law but to establish new law. For in the exercise of violence over life and death more than in any other legal act, law reaffirms itself. But in this very violence something rotten in law is revealed, above all to a finer sensibility, because the latter knows itself to be infinitely remote from conditions in which fate might imperiously have shown itself in such a sentence. Reason must, however, attempt to approach such conditions all the more resolutely, if it is to bring to a conclusion its critique of both lawmaking and law-preserving violence.

In a far more unnatural combination than in the death penalty, in a kind of spectral mixture, these two forms of violence are present in another institution of the modern state, the police. True, this is violence for legal ends (in the right of disposition), but with the simultaneous authority to decide these ends itself within wide limits (in the right of decree). The ignominy of such an authority, which is felt by few simply because its ordinances suffice only seldom for the crudest acts, but are therefore allowed to rampage all the more blindly in the most vulnerable areas and against thinkers, from whom the state is not protected by law—this ignominy lies in the fact that in this authority the separation of lawmaking and law-preserving violence is suspended. If the first is required to prove its worth in victory, the second is subject to the restriction that it may not set itself new ends. Police violence is emancipated from both conditions. It is lawmaking, for its characteristic function is not the promulgation of laws but the assertion of legal claims for any decree, and law-preserving, because it is at the disposal of these ends. The assertion that the ends of police violence are always identical or even connected to those of general law is entirely untrue. Rather, the "law" of the police really marks the point at which the state, whether from impotence or because of the immanent connections within any legal system, can no longer guarantee through the legal system the empirical ends that it desires at any price to attain. Therefore the police intervene "for security reasons" in countless cases where no clear legal situation exists, when they are not merely, without the slightest relation to legal ends, accompanying the citizen as a brutal encumbrance through a life regulated by ordinances, or simply supervising him.

Unlike law, which acknowledges in the "decision" determined by place and time a metaphysical category that gives it a claim to critical evaluation, a consideration of the police institution encounters nothing essential at all. Its power is formless, like its nowhere tangible, all-pervasive, ghostly presence in the life of civilized states. And though the police may, in particulars, everywhere appear the same, it cannot finally be denied that their spirit is less devastating where they represent, in absolute monarchy, the power of a ruler in which legislative and executive supremacy are united, than in democracies where their existence, elevated by no such relation, bears witness to the greatest conceivable degeneration of violence.

All violence as a means is either lawmaking or law-preserving. If it lays claim to neither of these predicates, it forfeits all validity. It follows, however, that all violence as a means, even in the most favorable case, is implicated in the problematic nature of law itself. And if the importance of these problems cannot be assessed with certainty at this stage of the investigation, law nevertheless appears, from what has been said, in so ambiguous a moral light that the question poses itself whether there are no other than violent means for regulating conflicting human interests. We are above all obligated to note that a totally nonviolent resolution of conflicts can never lead to a legal contract. For the latter, however peacefully it may have been entered into by the parties, leads finally to possible violence. It confers on both parties the right to take recourse to violence in some form against the other, should he break the agreement. Not only that; like the outcome, the origin of every contract also points toward violence. It need not be directly present in it as lawmaking violence, but is represented in it insofar as the power that guarantees a legal contract is in turn of violent origin even if violence is not introduced into the contract itself. When the consciousness of the latent presence of violence in a legal institution disappears, the institution falls into decay. In our time, parliaments provide an example of this. They offer the familiar, woeful spectacle because they have not remained conscious of the revolutionary forces to which they owe their existence. Accordingly, in Germany in particular, the last manifestation of such forces bore no fruit for parliaments. They lack the sense that a lawmaking violence is represented by themselves; no wonder that they cannot achieve decrees worthy of this violence, but cultivate in compromise a supposedly nonviolent manner of dealing with political affairs. This remains, however, a "product situated within the mentality of violence, no matter how it may disdain all open violence, because the effort toward compromise is motivated not internally but from outside, by the opposing effort, because no compromise, however freely accepted, is conceivable without a compulsive character. 'It would be better otherwise' is the underlying feeling in every compromise."[2] Significantly, the decay of parliaments has perhaps alienated as many minds from the ideal of a nonviolent resolution of political conflicts as were attracted to it by the war. The pacifists are confronted by the Bolsheviks and Syndicalists. These have effected an annihilating and on the whole apt critique of present-day parliaments. Nevertheless, however desirable and gratifying a flourishing parliament might be by comparison, a discussion of means of political agreement that are in principle nonviolent cannot be concerned with parliamentarianism. For what parliament achieves in vital affairs can only be those legal decrees that in their origin and outcome are attended by violence.

Is any nonviolent resolution of conflict possible? Without doubt. The relationships of private persons are full of examples of this. Nonviolent agreement is possible wherever a civilized outlook allows the use of unalloyed means of agreement. Legal and illegal means of every kind that are all the same violent may be confronted with nonviolent ones as unalloyed means. Courtesy, sympathy, peaceableness, trust, and whatever else might here be mentioned, are their subjective preconditions. Their objective manifestation, however, is determined by the law (the enormous scope of which cannot be discussed here) that unalloyed means are never those of direct, but always those of indirect solutions. They therefore never apply directly to the resolution of conflict between man and man, but only to matters concerning objects. The sphere of nonviolent means opens up in the realm of human conflicts relating to goods. For this reason technique in the broadest sense of the word is their most particular area. Its profoundest example is perhaps the conference, considered as a technique of civil agreement. For in it not only is nonviolent agreement possible, but also the exclusion of violence in principle is quite explicitly demonstrable by one significant factor: there is no sanction for lying. Probably no legislation on earth originally stipulated such a sanction. This makes clear that there is a sphere of human agreement that is nonviolent to the extent that it is wholly inaccessible to violence: the proper sphere of "understanding," language. Only late and in a peculiar process of decay has it been penetrated by legal violence in the penalty placed on fraud. For whereas the legal system at its origin, trusting to its victorious power, is content to defeat lawbreaking wherever it happens to show itself, and deception, having itself no trace of power about it, was, on the principle *ius civile vigilantibus scriptum est*, exempt from punishment in Roman and ancient Germanic law, the law of a later period, lacking confidence in its own violence, no longer felt itself a match for that of all others. Rather, fear of the latter and mistrust of itself indicate its declining vitality. It begins to set itself ends, with the intention of sparing law-preserving violence more taxing manifestations. It turns to fraud, therefore, not out of moral considerations, but for fear of the violence that it might unleash in the defrauded party. Since such fear conflicts with the violent nature of law derived from its origins, such ends are inappropriate to the justified means of law. They reflect not only the decay of its own sphere, but also a diminution of pure means. For, in prohibiting fraud, law restricts the use of wholly nonviolent means because they could produce reactive violence. This tendency of law has also played a part in the concession of the right to strike, which contradicts the interests of the state. It grants this right because it forestalls violent actions the state is afraid to oppose. Did not workers previously resort at once to sabotage and set fire to factories? To induce men to reconcile their interests peacefully without involving the legal system, there is, in the end, apart from all virtues, one effective motive that often enough puts into the most reluctant hands pure instead of violent means; it is the fear of mutual disadvantages that threaten to arise from violent confrontation, whatever the outcome might be. Such motives are clearly visible in countless cases of conflict of interests between private persons. It is different when classes and nations are in conflict, since the higher orders that threaten to overwhelm equally victor and vanquished are hidden from the feelings of most, and from the intelligence of almost all. Space does not here permit me to trace such higher orders and the common interests corresponding to them, which constitute the most enduring motive for a policy of pure means.[3] We can therefore only point to pure means in politics as analogous to those which govern peaceful intercourse between private persons.

As regards class struggles, in them strike must under certain conditions be seen as a pure means. Two essentially different kinds of strike, the possibilities of which have already been considered, must now be more fully characterized. Sorel has the credit—from political, rather than purely theoretical, considerations—of having first distinguished them. He contrasts them as the political and the proletarian general strike. They are also antithetical in their relation to violence. Of the partisans of the former he says: "The strengthening of state power is the basis of their conceptions; in their present organizations the politicians (viz. the moderate socialists) are already preparing the ground for a strong centralized and disciplined power that will be impervious to criticism from the opposition, capable of imposing silence, and of issuing its mendacious decrees."[4] "The political general strike demonstrates how the state will lose none of its strength, how power is transferred from the privileged to the privileged, how the mass of producers will change their masters." In contrast to this political general strike (which incidentally seems to have been summed up by the abortive German revolution), the proletarian general strike sets itself the sole task of destroying state power. It "nullifies all the ideological consequences of every possible social policy; its partisans see even the most popular reforms as bourgeois." "This general strike clearly announces its indifference toward material gain through conquest by declaring its intention to abolish the state; the state was really . . . the basis of the existence of the ruling group, who in all their enterprises benefit from the burdens borne by the public." While the first form of interruption of work is violent since it causes only an external modification of labor conditions, the second, as a pure means, is nonviolent. For it takes place not in readiness to resume work following external concessions and this or that modification to working conditions, but in the determination to resume only a wholly transformed work, no longer enforced by the state, an upheaval that this kind of strike not so much causes as consummates. For this reason, the first of these undertakings is lawmaking but the second, anarchistic. Taking up occasional statements by Marx, Sorel rejects every kind of program, of utopia—in a word, of lawmaking—for the revolutionary movement: "With the general strike all these fine things disappear; the revolution appears as a clear, simple revolt, and no place is reserved either for the sociologists or for the elegant amateurs of social reforms or for the intellectuals who have made it their profession to think for the proletariat." Against this deep, moral, and genuinely revolutionary conception, no objection can stand that seeks, on grounds of its possibly catastrophic consequences, to brand such a general strike as violent. Even if it can rightly be said that the modern economy, seen as a whole, resembles much less a machine that stands idle when abandoned by its stoker than a beast that goes berserk as soon as its tamer turns his back, nevertheless the violence of an action can be assessed no more from its effects than from its ends, but only from the law of its means. State power, of course, which has eyes only for effects, opposes precisely this kind of strike for its alleged violence, as distinct from partial strikes which are for the most part actually extortionate. The extent to which such a rigorous conception of the general strike as such is capable of diminishing the incidence of actual violence in revolutions, Sorel has explained with highly ingenious arguments. By contrast, an outstanding example of violent omission, more immoral and cruder than the political general strike, akin to a blockade, is the strike by doctors, such as several German cities have seen. In this is revealed at its most repellent an unscrupulous use of violence that is positively depraved in a professional class that for years, without the slightest attempts at resistance, "secured death its prey," and then at the first opportunity abandoned life of its own free will. More clearly than in recent class struggles, the means of nonviolent agreement have developed in thousands of years of the history of states. Only occasionally does the task of diplomats in their transactions consist of modifications to legal systems. Fundamentally they have, entirely on the analogy of agreement between private persons, to resolve conflicts case by case, in the names of their states, peacefully and without contracts. A delicate task that is more robustly performed by referees, but a method of solution that in principle is above that of the referee because it is beyond all legal systems, and therefore beyond violence. Accordingly, like the intercourse of private persons, that of diplomats has engendered its own forms and virtues, which were not always mere formalities, even though they have become so.

Among all the forms of violence permitted by both natural law and positive law there is not one that is free of the gravely problematic nature, already indicated, of all legal violence. Since, however, every conceivable solution to human problems, not to speak of deliverance from the confines of all the world-historical conditions of existence obtaining hitherto, remains impossible if violence is totally excluded in principle, the question necessarily arises as to other kinds of violence than all those envisaged by legal theory. It is at the same time the question of the truth of the basic dogma common to both theories: just ends can be attained by justified means, justified means used for just ends. How would it be, therefore, if all the violence imposed by fate, using justified means, were of itself in irreconcilable conflict with just ends, and if at the same time a different kind of violence came into view that certainly could be either the justified or the unjustified means to those ends, but was not related to them as means at all but in some different way? This would throw light on the curious and at first discouraging discovery of the ultimate insolubility of all legal problems (which in its hopelessness is perhaps comparable only to the possibility of conclusive pronouncements on "right" and "wrong" in evolving languages). For it is never reason that decides on the justification of means and the justness of ends, but fate-imposed violence on the former and God on the latter. And insight that is uncommon only because of the stubborn prevailing habit of conceiving those just ends as ends of a possible law, that is, not only as generally valid (which follows analytically from the nature of justice), but also as capable of generalization, which, as could be shown, contradicts the nature of justice. For ends that for one situation are just, universally acceptable, and valid, are so for no other situation, no matter how similar it may be in other respects. The nonmediate function of violence at issue here is illustrated by everyday experience. As regards man, he is impelled by anger, for example, to the most visible outbursts of a violence that is not related as a means to a preconceived end. It is not a means but a manifestation. Moreover, this violence has thoroughly objective manifestations in which it can be subjected to criticism. These are to be found, most significantly, above all in myth.

Mythical violence in its archetypal form is a mere manifestation of the gods. Not a means to their ends, scarcely a manifestation of their will, but first of all a manifestation of their existence. The legend of Niobe contains an outstanding example of this. True, it might appear that the action of Apollo and Artemis is only a punishment. But their violence establishes a law far more than it punishes for the infringement of one already existing. Niobe's arrogance calls down fate upon itself not because her arrogance offends against the law but because it challenges fate—to a fight in which fate must triumph, and can bring to light a law only in its triumph. How little such divine violence was to the ancients the law-preserving violence of punishment is shown by the heroic legends in which the hero—for example, Prometheus—challenges fate with dignified courage, fights it with varying fortunes, and is not left by the legend without hope of one day bringing a new law to men. It is really this hero and the legal violence of the myth native to him that the public tries to picture even now in admiring the miscreant. Violence therefore bursts upon Niobe from the uncertain, ambiguous sphere of fate. It is not actually destructive. Although it brings a cruel death to Niobe's children, it stops short of the life of their mother, whom it leaves behind, more guilty than before through the death of the children, both as an eternally mute bearer of guilt and as a boundary stone on the frontier between men and gods. If this immediate violence in mythical manifestations proves closely related, indeed identical to lawmaking violence, it reflects a problematic light on lawmaking violence, insofar as the latter was characterized above, in the account of military violence, as merely a mediate violence. At the same time this connection promises further to illuminate fate, which in all cases underlies legal violence, and to conclude in broad outline the critique of the latter. For the function of violence in lawmaking is twofold, in the sense that lawmaking pursues as its end, with violence as the means, *what* is to be established as law, but at the moment of instatement does not dismiss violence; rather, at this very moment of lawmaking, it specifically establishes as law not an end unalloyed by violence, but one necessarily and intimately bound to it, under the title of power. Lawmaking is power-making, and, to that extent, an immediate manifestation of violence. Justice is the principle of all divine end–making, power the principle of all mythical lawmaking.

An application of the latter that has immense consequences is to be found in constitutional law. For in this sphere the establishing of frontiers, the task of "peace" after all the wars of the mythical age, is the primal phenomenon of all lawmaking violence. Here we see most clearly that power, more than the most extravagant gain in property, is what is guaranteed by all lawmaking violence. Where frontiers are decided the adversary is not simply annihilated; indeed, he is accorded rights even when the victor's superiority in power is complete. And these are, in a demonically ambiguous way, "equal" rights: for both parties to the treaty it is the same line that may not be crossed. Here appears, in a terribly primitive form, the same mythical ambiguity of laws that may not be "infringed" to which Anatole France refers satirically when he says: "Poor and rich are equally forbidden to spend the night under the bridges." It also appears that Sorel touches not merely on a cultural-historical but also on a metaphysical truth in surmising that in the beginning all right was the prerogative of the kings or the nobles—in short, of the mighty; and that, *mutatis mutandis,* it will remain so as long as it exists. For from the point of view of violence, which alone can guarantee law, there is no equality, but at the most equally great violence. The act of fixing frontiers, however, is also significant for an understanding of law in another respect. Laws and unmarked frontiers remain, at least in primeval times, unwritten laws. A man can unwittingly infringe upon them and thus incur retribution. For each intervention of law that is provoked by an offense against the unwritten and unknown law is called, in contradistinction to punishment, retribution. But however unluckily it may befall its unsuspecting victim, its occurrence is, in the understanding of the law, not chance, but fate showing itself once again in its deliberate ambiguity. Hermann Cohen, in a brief reflection on the ancients' conception of fate, has spoken of the "inescapable realization" that it is "fate's orders themselves that seem to cause and bring about this infringement, this offense."[5] To this spirit of law even the modern principle that ignorance of a law is not protection against punishment testifies, just as the struggle over written law in the early period of the ancient Greek communities is to be understood as a rebellion against the spirit of mythical statutes.

Far from inaugurating a purer sphere, the mythical manifestation of immediate violence shows itself fundamentally identical with all legal violence, and turns suspicion concerning the latter into certainty of the perniciousness of its historical function, the destruction of which thus becomes obligatory. This very task of destruction poses again, in the last resort, the question of a pure immediate violence that might be able to call a halt to mythical violence. Just as in all spheres God opposes myth, mythical violence is confronted by the divine. And the latter constitutes its antithesis in all respects. If mythical violence is lawmaking, divine violence is law-destroying; if the former sets boundaries, the latter boundlessly destroys them; if mythical violence brings at once guilt and retribution, divine power only expiates; if the former threatens, the latter strikes; if the former is bloody, the latter is lethal without spilling blood. The legend of Niobe may be confronted, as an example of this violence, with God's judgment on the company of Korah. It strikes privileged Levites, strikes them without warning, without threat, and does not stop short of annihilation. But in annihilating it also expiates, and a deep connection between the lack of bloodshed and the expiatory character of this violence is unmistakable. For blood is the symbol of mere life. The dissolution of legal violence stems, as cannot be shown in detail here, from the guilt of more natural life, which consigns the living, innocent and unhappy, to a retribution that "expiates" the guilt of mere life—and doubtless also purifies the guilty, not of guilt, however, but of law. For with mere life the rule of law over the living ceases. Mythical violence is bloody power over mere life for its own sake, divine violence, pure power over all life for the sake of the living. The first demands sacrifice, the second accepts it.

This divine power is not only attested by religious tradition but is also found in present-day life in at least one sanctioned manifestation. The educative power, which in its perfected form stands outside the law, is one of its manifestations. These are defined, therefore, not by miracles directly performed by God, but by the expiating moment in them that strikes without bloodshed and, finally, by the absence of all lawmaking. To this extent it is justifiable to call this violence, too, annihilating; but it is so only relatively, with regard to goods, right, life, and suchlike, never absolutely, with regard to the soul of the living. The premise of such an extension of pure or divine power is sure to provoke, particularly today, the most violent reactions, and to be countered by the argument that taken to its logical conclusion it confers on men even lethal power against one another. This, however, cannot be conceded. For the question "May I kill?" meets its irreducible answer in the commandment "Thou shalt not kill." This commandment precedes the deed, just as God was "preventing" the deed. But just as it may not be fear of punishment that enforces obedience, the injunction becomes inapplicable, incommensurable once the deed is accomplished. No judgment of the deed can be derived from the commandment. And so neither the divine judgment, nor the grounds for this judgment, can be known in advance. Those who base a condemnation of all violent killing of one person by another on the commandment are therefore mistaken. It exists not as a criterion of judgment, but as a guideline for the actions of persons or communities who have to wrestle with it in solitude and, in exceptional cases, to take on themselves the responsibility of ignoring it. Thus it was understood by Judaism, which expressly rejected the condemnation of killing in self-defense. But those thinkers who take the opposed view refer to a more distant theorem, on which they possibly propose to base even the commandment itself. This is the doctrine of the sanctity of life, which they either apply to all animal or even vegetable life, or limit to human life. Their argumentation, exemplified in an extreme case by the revolutionary killing of the oppressor, runs as follows: "If I do not kill I shall never establish the world dominion of justice . . . that is the argument of the intelligent terrorist. . . . We, however, profess that higher even than the happiness and justice of existence stands existence itself."[6] As certainly as this last proposition is false, indeed ignoble, it shows the necessity of seeking the reason for the commandment no longer in what the deed does to the victim, but in what it does to God and the doer. The proposition that existence stands higher than a just existence is false and ignominious, if existence is to mean nothing other than mere life—and it has this meaning in the argument referred to. It contains a mighty truth, however, if existence, or, better, life (words whose ambiguity is readily dispelled, analogously to that of freedom, when they are referred to two distinct spheres), means the irreducible, total condition that is "man"; if the proposition is intended to mean that the nonexistence of man is something more terrible than the (admittedly subordinate) not-yet-attained condition of the just man. To this ambiguity the proposition quoted above owes its plausibility. Man cannot, at any price, be said to coincide with the mere life in him, no more than with any other of his conditions and qualities, not even with the uniqueness of his bodily person. However sacred man is (or that life in him that is identically present in earthly life, death, and afterlife), there is no sacredness in his condition, in his bodily life vulnerable to injury by his fellow men. What, then, distinguishes it essentially from the life of animals and plants? And even if these were sacred, they could not be so by virtue only of being alive, of being in life. It might be well worthwhile to track down the origin of the dogma of the sacredness of life. Perhaps, indeed probably, it is relatively recent, the last mistaken attempt of the weakened Western tradition to seek the saint it has lost in cosmological impenetrability. (The antiquity of all religious commandments against murder is no counterargument, because these are based on other ideas than the modern theorem.) Finally, this idea of man's sacredness gives grounds for reflection that what is here pronounced sacred was according to ancient mythical thought the marked bearer of guilt: life itself.

The critique of violence is the philosophy of its history—the "philosophy" of this history, because only the idea of its development makes possible a critical, discriminating, and decisive approach to its temporal data. A gaze directed only at what is close at hand can at most perceive a dialectical rising and falling in the lawmaking and law-preserving formations of violence. The law governing their oscillation rests on the circumstance that all law-preserving violence, in its duration, indirectly weakens the lawmaking violence represented by it, through the suppression of hostile counterviolence. (Various symptoms of this have been referred to in the course of this study.) This lasts until either new forces or those earlier suppressed triumph over the hitherto lawmaking violence and thus found a new law, destined in its turn to decay. On the breaking of this cycle maintained by mythical forms of law, on the suspension of law with all the forces on which it depends as they depend on it, finally therefore on the abolition of state power, a new historical epoch is founded. If the rule of myth is broken occasionally in the present age, the coming age is not so unimaginably remote that an attack on law is altogether futile. But if the existence of violence outside the law, as pure immediate violence, is assured, this furnishes the proof that revolutionary violence, the highest manifestation of unalloyed violence by man, is possible, and by what means. Less possible and also less urgent for humankind, however, is to decide when unalloyed violence has been realized in particular cases. For only mythical violence, not divine, will be recognizable as such with certainty, unless it be in incomparable effects, because the expiatory power of violence is not visible to men. Once again all the eternal forms are open to pure divine violence, which myth bastardized with law. It may manifest itself in a true war exactly as in the divine judgment of the multitude on a criminal. But all mythical, lawmaking violence, which we may call executive, is pernicious. Pernicious, too, is the law-preserving, administrative violence that serves it. Divine violence, which is the sign and seal but never the means of sacred execution, may be called sovereign violence.

Notes

1. One might, rather, doubt whether this famous demand does not contain too little, that is, whether it is permissible to use, or allow to be used, oneself or another in any respect as a means. Very good grounds for such doubt could be adduced.
2. Unger, *Politik und Metaphysik* (Berlin, 1921), 8.
3. But see Unger, 18ff.
4. Sorel, *Réflexions sur la violence*, 5th ed. (Paris, 1919), 250.
5. Hermann Cohen, *Ethik des reinen Willens*, 2nd ed. (Berlin, 1907), 362.
6. Kurt Hiller in a yearbook of *Das Ziel*.

12

MAX HORKHEIMER
(1895–1971)

THEODOR ADORNO
(1903–1969)

Born in Stuttgart, Germany, Max Horkheimer, along with Theodor Adorno, was one of the principal architects of the Frankfurt School. (See Benjamin, Chapter 11.) He became director of the Institute of Social Research in Frankfurt in 1930, during which time he expounded the central tenets of critical theory in the school's journal, *Zeitschrift für Sozialforschung* (1932–1939). Theodor Adorno, who was born in Frankfurt, became involved in the Institute of Social Research while teaching at the university. After the rise of the Nazis, Horkheimer and Adorno, who were both Jewish, emigrated to the United States, where they reestablished the institute in New York as the New School for Social Research. Horkheimer and Adorno, along with the institute, returned to Frankfurt in the early 1950s. Horkheimer remained director of the institute until his retirement in 1959, whereupon Adorno took over the role until his death 1969. Horkheimer died two years later.

Horkheimer is best known for his collection of essays on critical theory written during the 1930s (see *Critical Theory: Selected Essays* [1968]), as well as the *Dialectic of Enlightenment* (1944), which he coauthored with Adorno. Horkheimer's later writings include *Eclipse of Reason* (1947) and *Critique of Reason* (1967). Adorno published widely in music (*Philosophy of Modern Music* [1949]), cultural criticism (*Prisms* [1955]), philosophy (*Negative Dialectics* [1966]); *The Jargon of Authenticity* [1964]), and art (*Aesthetic Theory* [1970]).

In the *Dialectic of Enlightenment* (1947), from which our reading is taken, Horkheimer and Adorno seek to show how the project of the Enlightenment contains within it the seeds of its own destruction. The central aim of the Enlightenment is to give reason (*ratio*) free reign in order to liberate humanity from the fetters of myth and superstition. Horkheimer and Adorno, however, show that reason and myth are not mutually exclusive, but rather that reason reverts to myth. The more Enlightenment rationality strives to free itself from unreason and myth through science and technology, the more it resembles myth in its attempt to master and control nature. Horkheimer and Adorno illustrate this idea when they argue that Kantian ethics culminates in the writings of Sade and Nietzsche. Sade in particular is said to have revealed the dark underbelly of instrumental reason in his novel *Juliette*. The eponymous heroine, who engages in the most merciless and ruthless acts, is the quintessence of the bourgeois individual freed from "tutelage," the Kantian subject who is self-sufficient, expedient, calculative, and impassible. Enlightenment reason or morality is thus understood by Horkheimer and Adorno pessimistically in terms of unreason and immorality.

Select Bibliography of Horkheimer's Works in English

Critical Theory: Selected Essays. Trans. Matthew J. O'Connell et al. New York: Continuum, 1992.
Critique of Instrumental Reason: Lectures and Essays since the End of World War II. Trans. Matthew J. O'Connell et al. New York: Continuum, 1992.

Dialectic of Enlightenment (with Adorno). Trans. John Cumming. New York: Continuum, 1995.
Eclipse of Reason. Trans. New York: Continuum, 1995.

Select Bibliography of Adorno's Works in English

Aesthetic Theory. London: Routledge and Kegan Paul, 1984.
Against Epistemology: A Metacritique: Studies in Husserl and the Phenomenological Antinomies. Trans. Willis Domingo. Cambridge, MA: MIT Press, 1983.
Minima Moralia: Reflections on a Damaged Life. Trans. Edmund Jephcott. London: New Left Books, 1978.
Negative Dialectics. Trans. E.B. Ashton. New York: Continuum, 1983.
The Jargon of Authenticity. Trans. Knut Tarnowski and Frederic Will. London: Routledge and Kegan Paul, 1973.
Prisms. Trans. Samuel Weber and Shierry Weber. Cambridge, MA: MIT Press, 1981.

ENLIGHTENMENT AND MORALITY

Enlightenment, according to Kant, is "man's emergence from his self-incurred immaturity. Immaturity is the inability to use one's understanding without the guidance of another person."[1] "Understanding without the guidance of another person" is understanding guided by reason. This means no more than that, by virtue of its own consistency, it organizes the individual data of cognition into a system. "Reason has . . . for its object only the understanding and its purposive employment."[2] It makes "a certain collective unity the aim of the operations of the understanding,"[3] and this unity is the system. Its rules are the indications for a hierarchical construction of concepts. For Kant, as for Leibniz and Descartes, rationality consists of "completing the systematical connection, both in ascending to higher genera, and in descending to lower species."[4] The "systematizing" of knowledge is "its coherence according to one principle."[5] In the Enlightenment's interpretation, thinking is the creation of unified, scientific order and the derivation of factual knowledge from principles, whether the latter are elucidated as arbitrarily postulated axioms, innate ideas, or higher abstractions. Logical laws produce the most general relations within the arrangement, and define them. Unity resides in agreement. The resolution of contradiction is the stem *in nuce*. Knowledge consists of subsumption under principles. Any other than systematically directed thinking is unoriented or authoritarian. Reason contributes only the idea of systematic unity, the formal elements of fixed conceptual coherence. Every substantial goal which men might adduce as an alleged rational insight is, in the strict Enlightenment sense, delusion, lies, or "rationalization," even though individual philosophers try to advance from this conclusion toward the postulate of philanthropic emotion. Reason is the "faculty . . . of deducing the particular from the general."[6] According to Kant, the homogeneity of the general and the particular is guaranteed by the "schematism of pure understanding," or the unconscious operation of the intellectual mechanism which structures perception in accordance with the understanding. The understanding impresses the intelligibility of the matter (which subjective judgment discovers there) on it as an objective quality, before it enters into the ego. Without such a schematism—in short, without intellectual perception—no impression would harmonize with a concept, and no category with an example; and the unity of thought (let alone of system) toward which everything is directed would not prevail. To produce this unity is the conscious task of science. If "all empirical laws . . . are only special determinations of the pure laws of the understanding,"[7] research must always ensure that the principles are always properly linked with factual judgments. "This concurrence of nature with our cognitive faculty is an *a priori* assumption . . . of judgment."[8] " It is the "guideline"[9] for organized experience.

The system must be kept in harmony with nature; just as the facts are predicted from the system, so they must confirm it. Facts, however, belong to practice; they always characterize the individual's contact with nature as a social object: experience is always real action and suffering. In physics, of course, perception—by means of which a theory may be proved—is usually reduced to the electric sparks visible in the experimental apparatus. Its absence is as a rule without practical consequence, for it destroys no more than a theory—or possibly the career of the assistant responsible for setting up the experiment. But laboratory conditions constitute the exception. Thinking that does not make system and perception accord conflicts with more than isolated visual impressions; it conflicts with practice. The expected event fails to occur, yes, but the unexpected event does occur: the bridge collapses, the crops wither, or the drug kills. The spark which most surely indicates the lack of systematic thinking, the violation of logic, is no transient percept, but sudden death. The system the Enlightenment has in mind is the form of knowledge which copes most proficiently with the facts and supports the individual most effectively in the mastery of nature. Its principles are the principles of self-preservation. Immaturity is then the inability to survive. The burgher, in the successive forms of slave owner, free entrepreneur, and administrator, is the logical subject of the Enlightenment.

The difficulties in the concept of reason caused by the fact that its subjects, the possessors of that very reason, contradict one another are concealed by the apparent clarity of the judgments of the Western Enlightenment. In the *Critique of Pure Reason*, however, they are expressed in the unclear relation of the transcendental to the empirical ego, and in the other unresolved contradictions. Kant's concepts are ambiguous. As the transcendental, supraindividual self, reason comprises the idea of a free, human social life in which men organize themselves as the universal subject and overcome the conflict between pure and empirical reason in the conscious solidarity of the whole. This represents the idea of true universality: utopia. At the same time, however, reason constitutes the court of judgment of calculation, which adjusts the world for the ends of self-preservation and recognizes no function other than the preparation of the object from mere sensory material in order to make it the material of subjugation. The true nature of schematism, of the general and the particular, of concept and individual case reconciled from without, is ultimately revealed in contemporary science as the interest of industrial society. Being is apprehended under the aspect of manufacture and administration. Everything—even the human individual, not to speak of the animal—is converted into the repeatable, replaceable process, into a mere example for the conceptual models of the system. Conflict between administrative, reifying science, between the public mind and the experience of the individual, is precluded by circumstances. The conceptual apparatus determines the senses, even before perception occurs; *a priori*, the citizen sees the world as the matter from which he himself manufactures it. Intuitively, Kant foretold what Hollywood consciously put into practice: in the very process of production, images are precensored according to the norm of the understanding which will later govern their apprehension. Even before its occurrence, the perception which serves to confirm the public judgment is adjusted by that judgment. Even if the secret utopia in the concept of reason pointed, despite fortuitous distinctions between individuals, to their common interest, reason—functioning, in compliance with ends, as a mere systematic science—serves to level down that same identical interest. It allows no determination other than the classifications of the societal process to operate. No one is other than what he has come to be: a useful, successful, or frustrated member of vocational and national groups. He is one among many representatives of his geographical, psychological, and sociological type. Logic is democratic; in this respect the great have no advantage over the insignificant. The great are classed as the important, and the insignificant as prospective objects for social relief. Science in general relates to nature and man only as the insurance company in particular relates to life and death. Whoever dies is unimportant: it is a question of ratio between accidents and the company's liabilities. Not the individuality but the law of the majority recurs in the formula. The concurrence of the general and the particular is no longer hidden in the one intellect which perceives the particular only as one case of the general, and the general only as the aspect of the particular by which it can be grasped and manipulated. Science itself is not conscious of itself; it is only a tool. Enlightenment, however, is the philosophy which equates the truth with scientific systematization. The attempt to establish this identity, which Kant was still able to undertake with a philosophic intention, led to concepts which have no meaning in a scientific sense, because they are not mere indications for manipulation according to the rules of the game. The notion of the self-understanding of science contradicts the notion of science itself. Kant's work transcends experience as mere operation, and for that reason—in accordance with its own principles—is now condemned by the Enlightenment as dogmatic. With Kant's consequent, full confirmation of the scientific system as the form of truth, thought seals its own nullity, for science is technical practice, as far removed from reflective consideration of its own goal as are other forms of labor under the pressure of the system.

The moral teachings of the Enlightenment bear witness to a hopeless attempt to replace enfeebled religion with some reason for persisting in society when interest is absent. As genuine burghers, the philosophers come to terms with the powers who, in theory, are to be condemned. The theories are firm and consistent, whereas the moral doctrines are propagandist and sentimental (even when they seem rigorous), or else they are mere *coups de main* by reason of the consciousness that morality itself is underivable—as in the case of Kant's recourse to ethical forces as a fact. His attempt (even though more careful than Western philosophy as a whole) to derive the duty of mutual respect from a law of reason finds no support in the *Critique*. It is the conventional attempt of bourgeois thought to ground respect, without which civilization cannot exist, upon something other than material interest and force; it is more sublime and paradoxical than, yet as ephemeral as, any previous attempt. The citizen who would forego profit only on the Kantian motive of respect for the mere form of law would not be enlightened, but superstitious—a fool. The root of Kantian optimism, according to which moral behavior is rational even if the mean and wretched would prevail, is actually an expression of horror at the thought of reversion to barbarism. If (so Kant wrote to Haller) one of these great moral forces of mutual love and respect were to founder, "then nothingness (immorality) would open wide its maw and swallow the whole realm of (moral) virtue as if it were a drop of water."[10] But, according to Kant, in the face of scientific reason moral forces are no less neutral impulses and modes of behavior than the immoral forces into which they suddenly change when directed not to that hidden possibility but to reconciliation with power. Enlightenment expels the distinction from the theory. It treats emotions *"ac si quaestio de lineis, planis aut de corporibus esset."*[11] The totalitarian order has carried this out with all seriousness. Liberated from the control of the same class which tied the nineteenth-century businessman to Kantian respect and mutual love, fascism (which by its iron discipline saves its subject peoples the trouble of moral feelings) no longer needs to uphold any disciplines. In contradistinction to the categorical imperative and all the more in accordance with pure reason, it treats men as things—as the loci of modes of behavior. The rulers were anxious to protect the bourgeois world against the ocean of open force (which has now really broken into Europe), only so long as the economic concentration had made inadequate progress. Previously, only the poor and savages were exposed to the fury of the capitalist elements. But the totalitarian order gives full rein to calculation and abides by science as such. Its canon is its own brutal efficiency. It was the hand of philosophy that wrote it on the wall—from Kant's *Critique* to Nietzsche's *Genealogy of Morals*; but one man made out the detailed account. The work of the Marquis de Sade portrays "understanding without the guidance of another person": that is, the bourgeois individual freed from tutelage.

Self-preservation is the constitutive principle of science, the soul of the table of categories, even when it is to be deduced idealistically, as with Kant. Even the ego, the synthetic unity of apperception, the instance which Kant calls the highest point, on which the possibility of the logical form of all knowledge necessarily depends,[12] is in fact the product of, as well as the condition for, material existence. Individuals, who have to look after themselves, develop the ego as the instance of the reflective preliminary and general view; it is extended and contracted as the prospects of economic self-sufficiency and productive ownership extend and contract from generation to generation. Finally it passes from the dispossessed bourgeoisie to the totalitarian cartel-lords, whose science has become the inclusive concept of the methods of reproduction of the subjugated mass society. Sade erected an early monument to their sense of planning. The conspiracy of the power-holders against the people by means of undeviating organization is as close as the bourgeois republic to the unenlightened spirit since Machiavelli and Hobbes. It is inimical to authority only when authority does not have power enough to compel obedience—the force which is no fact. So long as the identity of the user of reason is disregarded, the affinity of reason is as much to force as the mediation; according to the individual or group situation, it permits peace or war, tolerance or repression. Since it exposes substantial goals as the power of nature over mind, as the erosion of its self-legislation, reason is—by virtue, too, of its very formality—at the service of any natural interest. Thinking becomes an organic medium pure and simple, and reverts to nature. But for the rulers, men become material, just as nature as a whole is material for society. After the short intermezzo of liberalism, in which the bourgeois kept one another in check, domination appears as archaic terror in a fascistically rationalized form. As Francavilla says at the court of King Ferdinand of Naples:

> Religious chimeras must be replaced by the most extreme forms of terror. If the people are freed from fear of a future hell, as soon as it has vanished they will abandon themselves to anything. But if this chimerical fear is replaced by utterly relentless penal laws, which of course apply only to the people, then they alone will provoke unrest in the State; the discontented will be born only into the lowest class. What does the idea of a curb which they never experience themselves mean to the rich, if with this empty semblance they are able to preserve a justice that allows them to crush all those who live under their yoke? You will find no one in that class who would not submit to the worst tyranny so long as all others must suffer it.[13]

Reason is the organ of calculation, of planning; it is neutral in regard to ends; its element is coordination. What Kant grounded transcendentally, the affinity of knowledge and planning, which impressed the stamp of inescapable expediency on every aspect of a bourgeois existence that was wholly rationalized, even in every breathing-space, Sade realized empirically more than a century before sport was conceived. The teams of modern sport, whose interaction is so precisely regulated that no member has any doubt about his role, and which provide a reserve for every player, have their exact counterpart in the sexual teams of *Juliette*, which employ every moment usefully, neglect no human orifice, and carry out every function. Intensive, purposeful activity prevails in spirit as in all branches of mass culture, while the inadequately initiated spectator cannot divine the difference in the combinations, or the meaning of variations, by the arbitrarily determined rules. The architectonic structure of the Kantian system, like the gymnastic pyramids of Sade's orgies and the schematized principles of the early bourgeois freemasonry—which has its cynical mirror image in the strict regimentation of the libertine society of the *120 Journées*—reveals an organization of life as a whole which is deprived of any substantial goal. These arrangements amount not so much to pleasure as to its regimented pursuit—organization—just as in other demythologized epochs (Imperial Rome and the Renaissance, as well as the Baroque) the schema of an activity was more important than its content. In the modern era, Enlightenment separated the notions of harmony and fulfillment from their hypostatization in the religious Beyond, and, in the form of systematization, transferred them as criteria to human aspiration. When utopia, which provided the French Revolution with its content of hope, entered German music and philosophy (effectively and ineffectively), the established civil order wholly functionalized reason, which became a purposeless purposiveness which might thus be attached to all ends. In this sense, reason is planning considered solely as planning. The totalitarian state manipulates the people. Or, as Sade's Francavilla puts it:

The government must control the population, and must possess all the means necessary to exterminate them when afraid of them, or to increase their numbers when that seems desirable. There should never be any counterweight to the justice of government other than that of the interests or passions of those who govern, together with the passions and interests of those who, as we have said, have received from it only so much power as is requisite to reproduce their own.[14]

Francavilla indicates the road that imperialism, the most terrible form of the *ratio*, has always taken: "Take its god from the people that you wish to subjugate, and then demoralize it; so long as it worships no other god than you, and has no other morals than your morals, you will always be its master . . . allow it in return the most extreme criminal license; punish it only when it turns upon you."[15]

Since reason posits no substantial goals, all affects are equally removed from its governance, and are purely natural. The principle by which reason is merely set over against all that is unreasonable, is the basis of the true antithesis of Enlightenment and mythology. Mythology recognizes spirit only as immersed in nature, as natural power. Like the powers without, inward impulses appear as living powers of divine or demonic origin. Enlightenment, on the other hand, puts back coherence, meaning, and life into subjectivity, which is properly constituted only in this process. For subjectivity, reason is the chemical agent which absorbs the individual substance of things and volatilizes them in the mere autonomy of reason. In order to escape the superstitious fear of nature, it wholly transformed objective effective entities and forms into the mere veils of a chaotic matter, and anathematized their influence on humanity as slavery, until the ideal form of the subject was no more than unique, unrestricted, though vacuous authority.

All the power of nature was reduced to mere indiscriminate resistance to the abstract power of the subject. The particular mythology which the Western Enlightenment, even in the form of Calvinism, had to get rid of was the Catholic doctrine of the *ordo* and the popular pagan religion which still flourished under it. The goal of bourgeois philosophy was the liberate men from all this. But the liberation went further than its humane progenitors had conceived. The unleashed market economy was both the actual form of reason and the power which destroyed reason. The Romantic reactionaries only expressed what the bourgeois themselves experienced: that in their world freedom tended toward organized anarchy. The Catholic counterrevolution proved itself right as against the Enlightenment, just as the Enlightenment had shown itself to be right in regard to Catholicism. The Enlightenment committed itself to liberalism. If all affects are of equal value, then survival—which anyway governs the form of the system—seems also to be the most probable source of maxims for human conduct. Self-preservation, in fact, was given full rein in the free-market economy. Those somber writers of the bourgeois dawn—Machiavelli, Hobbes, Mandeville, and so on—who decried the egotism of the self, acknowledged in so doing that society was the destructive principle, and denounced harmony before it was elevated as the official doctrine by the serene and classical authors. The latter boosted the totality of the bourgeois order as the misery that finally fused both general and particular, society and self, into one. With the development of the economic system in which control of the economic apparatus by private groups divides men, survival as affirmed by reason—the reified drive of the individual bourgeois—was revealed as destructive natural power, no longer to be distinguished from self-destruction. The two were now indissolubly blended. Pure reason became unreason, a faultless and insubstantial mode of procedure. But the utopia which proclaimed reconciliation between nature and the individual emerged together with the revolutionary avant-garde from its concealment in German philosophy, simultaneously irrational and rational, as the idea of the combination of free men, and called down on itself all the wrath of the *ratio*. In society as it is, despite all the wretched moralistic attempts to propagate humanity as the most rational of means, survival remains free from utopia, which is denounced as myth. Among the rulers, cunning self-preservation takes the form of struggle for fascist power; among individuals, it is expressed as adaptation to injustice at any price. Enlightened reason is as little capable of finding a standard by which to measure any drive in itself, and in comparison with all other drives, as of arranging the universe in spheres. It established natural hierarchy as a reflex of medieval society, and later enterprises are branded as lies in order to indicate a new, objective value ranking. Irrationalism, as it appears in such empty reconstructions, is far from being able to withstand the *ratio*. With Leibniz and Hegel, mainstream philosophy—even in those subjective and objective assertions which only approximate to thought—discovered the claim to truth in emotions, institutions, and works of art, but irrationalism (close in this as in other respects to modern positivism, that last remnant of the Enlightenment) demarcates emotion, like religion and art, from everything deserving of the title of knowledge or cognition. It limits cold reason in favor of immediate living, yet makes this no more than a principle inimical to thought. Under the cover of this enmity, emotion and finally all human expression, even culture as a whole, are withdrawn from thought; thereby, however, they are transformed into a neutralized element of the comprehensive *ratio* of the economic system—itself irrationalized long ago. From the start, it was unable to rely on its own pull, which it enhanced with the cult of feeling. But wherever it has recourse to the emotions, it militates against their very medium, thought, which was always suspicious of this self-alienated reason. The exuberantly tender affection of the lover in the movie strikes a blow against the unmoved theory—a blow continued in that sentimental polemic against thought which presents itself as an attack upon injustice. Though feelings are raised in this way to the level of an ideology, they continue to be despised in reality. When set against the firmament to which ideology transfers them, they still seem rather too vulgar; the effect is to exile them all the more. As a natural impulse, self-preservation has, like all other impulses, a bad conscience; but efficiency and the institutions which meant to serve it—that is, independent mediation, the apparatus, the organization, systematization—like to appear reasonable, both in theory and in practice; and the emotions are made to share in this apparent rationality.

The Enlightenment of modern times advanced from the very beginning under the banner of radicalism; this distinguishes it from any of the earlier stages of demythologization. When a new mode of social life allowed room for a new religion and a new way of thinking, the overthrow of the old classes, tribes, and nations was usually accompanied by that of the old gods. But especially where a nation (the Jews, for example) was brought by its own destiny to change to a new form of social life, the time-honored customs, sacred activities, and objects of worship were magically transformed into heinous crimes and phantoms. Present-day fears and idiosyncrasies, derided and execrated character traits, may be deciphered as the marks of the violent onset of this or that stage of progress in human development. From the reflex of disgust at excrement or human flesh to the suspicion of fanaticism, laziness, and poverty, whether intellectual or material, there is a long line of modes of behavior which were metamorphosed from the adequate and necessary into abominations. This is the line both of destruction and of civilization. Each step forward on it represents some progress, a stage of Enlightenment. But whereas all earlier changes, from preanimism to magic, from the matriarchal to a patriarchal culture, from the polytheism of the slave owners to the Catholic hierarchy, replaced the older mythologies with new—though enlightened—ones, and substituted the god of legions for the Great Mother, the adoration of the Lamb for that of the totem, the brilliance of enlightened reason banished as mythological any form of devotion which claimed to be objective and grounded in actuality. All previous obligations therefore succumbed to the verdict which pronounced them taboo—not excluding those which were necessary for the existence of the bourgeois order itself. The instrument by means of which the bourgeoisie came to power, the liberation of forces, universal freedom, self-determination—in short,

ENLIGHTENMENT AND MORALITY

the Enlightenment itself turned against the bourgeoisie once, as a system of domination, it had recourse to suppression. In accordance with its principle, Enlightenment does not stop at the minimum of belief, without which the bourgeois world cannot exist. It does not give domination the reliable service which the old ideologies always allowed it. Its antiauthoritarian tendency, which (though of course only in a subterranean form) still relates to the utopia in the concept of reason, ultimately makes it as inimical to the bourgeoisie as it was to the aristocracy—with which the bourgeoisie is then very soon allied. Finally, the antiauthoritarian principle has to change into its very antithesis—into opposition to reason; the abrogation of everything inherently binding, which it brings about, allows domination to ordain as sovereign and to manipulate whatever bonds and obligations prove appropriate to it. After civil virtue and love of humanity (for which it already had no adequate grounds), philosophy proceeded to proclaim authority and hierarchy as virtues, when the Enlightenment had long posited them as lies. But the Enlightenment possesses no argument against even such a perversion of its proper nature, for the plain truth had no advantage over distortion, and rationalization none over the *ratio*, if they could prove no practical benefit in themselves. With the formalization of reason, to the extent that its preferred function is that of a symbol for neutral procedures, theory itself becomes an incomprehensible concept, and thought appears meaningful only when meaning has been discarded. Once it is harnessed to the dominant mode of production, the Enlightenment—which strives to undermine any order which has become repressive—abrogates itself. This was obvious even in the early attacks of the contemporary Enlightenment on Kant, the universal reducer. Just as Kant's moral philosophy restricted his enlightened critique, in order to preserve the possibility of reason, so—conversely—unreflective enlightened thinking based on the notion of survival always tends to convert into skepticism, in order to make enough room for the existing order.

On the other hand, the work of the Marquis de Sade, like that of Nietzsche, constitutes the intransigent critique of practical reason, in contradistinction to which Kant's critique itself seems a revocation of his own thought. It makes the scientistic the destructive principle. Of course Kant had so far cleansed the moral law within me of all heteronomous belief that respect for Kant's assurances was a mere natural psychological fact, just as the starry heavens above me were a natural physical fact. Kant himself called it a "fact of reason,"[16] and Leibniz's term for it was *un instinct général de société.*[17] But facts have no validity when they simply are not there. Sade does not deny their presence. Justine, the virtuous sister, is a martyr for the moral law. Juliette draws the conclusion that the bourgeoisie wanted to ignore: she demonizes Catholicism as the most up-to-date mythology, and with it civilization as a whole. The energies which were devoted to the Blessed Sacrament are applied to sacrilege instead. But this reversal is merely attributed to society. In all this, Juliette is by no means fanatical, as Catholicism was in the case of the Incas; her procedure is enlightened and efficient as she goes about her work of sacrilege—which the Catholics also retained as an archaic inheritance. The primeval behaviors which civilization had made taboo had led a subterranean existence, having been transformed into destructive tendencies under the stigma of bestiality. Juliette practices them not as natural but as tabooed activities. She compensates the value judgment against them (which was unfounded because all value judgments are unfounded) by its opposite. Even though she repeats the primitive reactions in so doing, they are not really primitive but bestial. Not unlike Merteuil in the *Liaisons Dangeureuses,*[18] Juliette embodies (in psychological terms) neither unsublimated nor regressive libido, but intellectual pleasure in regression—*amor intellectualis diaboli*, the pleasure of attacking civilization with its own weapons. She favors system and consequence. She is a proficient manipulator of the organ of rational thought. In regard to self-control, her directions are at times related to Kant's as the special application is to its basic proposition: "Therefore virtue, to the extent that it is founded upon inner freedom, also contains an affirmative commandment for men, which is to bring all their abilities and inclinations under its control [i.e., of reason], and therefore under self-control, which prevails over the negative commandment not to be ruled by one's emotions and inclinations [the duty of apathy]; because, unless reason takes the reins of government into its hand, emotions and inclinations will be in control."[19] Juliette preaches on the self-discipline of the criminal: "Work out your plan a few days beforehand; consider all its consequences; be attentive to what might assist you . . . what might betray you, and weigh up all these things with the same callousness you would apply if you were certain to be discovered."[20] The murderer's face must display the greatest calm: "Let your features express calm and equanimity; and try to summon up an extreme degree of callousness . . . if you were not certain that no pangs of conscience would attack you (and you will be so assured only through constant habituation to crime) . . . all your efforts to control your features and gestures would be of no account."[21] For formalistic reason, freedom from the bite of conscience is as essential as the absence of love or hate. Repentance posits the past (which popular ideology, in contradistinction to the bourgeoisie, always considered null and void) as existent; it is reversion, to prevent which was, for bourgeois practice, its only justification. Spinoza echoes the Stoics: "*Poenitentia virtus non est, sive ex ratione non oritur, sed is, quem facti poenitet, bis miser seu impotens est.*"[22] Wholly in the spirit of Francavilla, he then goes on to remark: "*terret vulgus, nisi metuat*"[23] and therefore asserts (as a good Machiavellian) that humility and repentance, like fear and hope, can be very useful despite their irrationality. "Apathy (in the form of rigor)," says Kant, "is a necessary presupposition of virtue,"[24] and (not unlike Sade) he distinguishes this "moral apathy" from insensibility in the shape of indifference to sensory stimuli. Enthusiasm is bad. Calmness and decisiveness constitute the strength of virtue: "That is the state of health in the moral life; an emotion, on the other hand, even when awakened by the notion of good, is but a transient brilliance succeeded by languor."[25] Juliette's friend Clairwil affirms the same thing in regard to vice: "My soul is unyielding, and I am far from preferring sensibility to happy indifference, in which I rejoice. Oh Juliette . . . you are probably deluded as to that dangerous sensibility on which so many fools pride themselves."[26] Apathy appears at those turning points of bourgeois history (even in ancient times) when the sovereign historical tendency makes the *pauci beati* aware of their own impotence. Apathy indicates the reversion of individual human spontaneity into the private world which was thereby established as the bourgeois life-form proper. Stoicism (which is the bourgeois philosophy) makes it easier for the privileged, confronted with the suffering of others, to steel themselves to their own threats. It confirms the general by elevating private existence, as a protection from the generality, to the condition of a principle. The bourgeois' private sphere is upper-class cultural material that has lost its status.

Juliette believes in science. She wholly despises any form of worship whose rationality cannot be demonstrated: belief in God and his dead Son, obedience to the Ten Commandments, good rather than evil, not sin but salvation. She is attracted by the reactions proscribed by the legends of civilization. She operates with semantics and logical syntax like the most up-to-date positivism, but does not anticipate this servant of our own administration in directing her linguistic criticism primarily against thought and philosophy; instead, as a child of the aggressive Enlightenment, she fixes upon religion. "A dead god!" she says of Christ: "Nothing is more ridiculous than the Catholic dictionary's nonsequacious God = infinite, and death = finite. Idiotic Christians, what are you to do with your dead God?"[27] Her particular passion is to transform what has been damned as devoid of scientific proof into something worth aspiring after, to transform what is acknowledged without evidence into the object of abomination—the transvaluation of all values, the "courage to do what is forbidden"[28] (but without Nietzsche's telltale "Come!", without his biological idealism). "Are pretexts necessary in order to commit a crime?" asks Princess Borghese, Juliette's friend, wholly in Nietzsche's sense.[29] And he proclaims the quintessence of her theory:[30] "The weak and unsuccessful must perish; this is the first proposition of *our* philanthropy. And they should even be helped on their way. What is more injurious than any vice—the compassion of action for all failures and weaklings—Christianity. . . ."[31] Christianity: ". . . singularly desirous of subjugating tyrants and forcing them to acknowledge the doctrine of brotherhood . . . takes up the role of the weak; it represents them and has to speak and sound like them. . . . We should be persuaded that this bond [of fraternity] was, in truth, proposed by the weak and sanctioned by them when sacerdotal authority happened to fall into their hands."[32] This is the contribution of Noirceuil, Juliette's mentor, to the genealogy of morals. Nietzsche maliciously celebrates the powerful and their cruelty: "exerted without, where the alien world begins," against, that is, everything which does not belong to them:

> There they enjoy freedom from any social constraint, and dally in the wilderness to compensate themselves for the tension brought about by long enclosure in the peaceful atmosphere of their society; they return to the guiltlessness of a predatory conscience, as exultant beasts who amble off after, say, a frightful sequence of murder, arson, rape, and torture, as if it were all no more than some student's prank, yet convinced that they have provided their bards with something to celebrate for ages to come. . . . This "courage" displayed by superior races, which is outrageous, absurd, and sudden, the very incalculability and improbability of their enterprises . . . their indifference to and contempt for safety, body, life, comfort, their ghastly serenity and profound pleasure in all destruction and in all the debauchery of conquest and cruelty. . . .[33]

This courage that Nietzsche so emphatically describes also captivates Juliette. To "live dangerously" is her mission too: *"oser tout dorénavant sans peur."*[34] There are the weak and the strong; there are classes, races and nations which rule, and there are those who are defeated. "Where, I ask you," cries Verneuil:

> is the mortal stupid enough to swear against all the evidence to the contrary that men are born equal in justice and in fact? Only such an enemy of mankind as Rousseau could assert this paradox, because being so very weak himself he wished to draw down to his level those to whose height he could not ascend. But what impudence, I ask you, could allow the pygmy of four feet two inches to compare himself with the stature that nature has endowed with the strength and form of a Hercules? The fly might as well rank itself with the elephant. Strength, beauty, stature, eloquence: these were the virtues that in the dawn of society proved decisive when authority passed into the rulers' hands.[35]

"To require of strength," Nietzsche continues: "that it should not assert itself as strength, that it should not be a will to conquer, a will to overthrow, a will to be master, a thirst for enmity and resistance and triumph, is as senseless as to demand of weakness that it masquerade as strength."[36] "How in truth can you require," says Verneuil:

> that he who has been endowed by nature with an eminent capacity for crime, whether by virtue of the superiority of his powers, and the refinement of his physical organs, or through an education conformable to his station or through his riches; how, I repeat, can you require that this individual should have to obey the same law that calls all to virtue or to moderation? Is the law more just when it punishes the two men alike? Is it natural that he whom everything invites to commit evil should be treated exactly as he whom everything drives to behave prudently?[37]

*

Not to have glossed over or suppressed but to have trumpeted far and wide the impossibility of deriving from reason any fundamental argument against murder fired the hatred which the progressives (and they precisely) still direct against Sade and Nietzsche. They were significantly unlike the logical positivists in taking science at its word. The fact that Sade and Nietzsche insist on the *ratio* more decisively even than logical positivism implicitly liberates from its hiding-place the utopia contained in the Kantian notion of reason as in every great philosophy: the utopia of a humanity which, itself no longer distorted, has no further need to distort. Inasmuch as the merciless doctrines proclaim the identity of domination and reason, they are more merciful than those of the moralistic lackeys of the bourgeoisie. "Where do your greatest dangers lie?" was the question Nietzsche once posed himself[38] and answered thus: "In compassion." With his denial he redeemed the unshakeable confidence in man that is constantly betrayed by every form of assurance that seeks only to console.

Notes

1. Kant, *"Beantwortung der Frage: Was ist Aufklärung?"* ("An Answer to the Question: What is Enlightenment?") *Kants Werke* (Akademie-Ausgabe), vol. VIII, 35.
2. *Kritik der reinen Vernunft* (*Critique of Pure Reason*), vol. III, 427.
3. Ibid., 427.
4. Ibid., 435f.
5. Ibid., 428.
6. Ibid., 429.
7. *Kritik der reinen Vernunft*, vol. IV, 93.
8. *Kritik der Urteilskraft* (*Critique of Judgment*), vol. V, 185.
9. Ibid., 185.
10. *Metaphysische Anfänge der Tugendlehre* (*Metaphysical First Principles of the Doctrine of Virtue*), vol. VI, 449.
11. Spinoza, *Ethica* (*Ethics*), part III, *Praefatio*.
12. *Kritik der reinen Vernunft*, vol. III, 109.
13. *Histoire de Juliette* (Holland, 1797), vol. V, 319f.
14. Ibid., 322f.
15. Ibid., 324.
16. *Kritik der praktischen Vernunft* (*Critique of Practical Reason*), vol. V, 31, 47, 55, etc.
17. *Nouveaux essais sur l'entendement humain* (*New Essays Concerning Human Understanding*), ed. Erdmann (Berlin, 1840), book 1, chap. 2, 215.
18. Cf. Heinrich Man's introduction to the Insel Verlag edition.
19. *Metaphysische Anfänge de Tugendlehre*, vol. VI, 408
20. *Juliette*, vol. IV, 58.
21. Ibid., 60f.
22. Spinoza, *Ethica*, part IV, prop. LIV, 368.
23. Ibid., Schol.
24. *Metaphysische Anfänge der Tugendlehre*, vol. VI, 408.
25. Ibid., 409.
26. *Juliette*, vol. 11, 114.
27. *Juliette*, vol. 111, 282.
28. Nietzsche, *Umwertung aller Werte* (*Transvaluation of All Values*), *Werke* (Kröner), vol. VIII, 213.
29. *Juliette*, vol. IV, 204.
30. E. Dühren (in *Neue Forschungen*, Berlin, 1904, 453ff) has referred to the association.
31. Nietzsche, *Umwertung aller Werte*, vol. VIII, 218.
32. *Juliette*, vol. I, 315f.
33. *Zur Genealogie der Moral* (*On the Genealogy of Morals*), Vol. VII, 321ff.
34. *Juliette*, Vol. I, 300.

35. *Histoire de Justine* (Holland, 1797), vol. IV, 4.
36. *Zur Genealogie der Moral*, vol. VII, 326f.
37. *Justine*, vol. IV, 7.
38. *Die fröhliche Wissenschaft* (*The Gay Science*), vol. 5, 205.

13

HERBERT MARCUSE
(1898–1979)

Herbert Marcuse was born in Berlin 1898. He received his Ph.D. in literature in 1922 before moving to Freiburg in 1928 to study philosophy with Heidegger. Although he was impressed with Heidegger as a thinker, Marcuse—a German Jew and a radical—was dismayed by Heidegger's political involvement with the Nazis and in 1933 decided to leave Freiburg and join the Institute for Social Research (headed by Max Horkheimer). He followed the institute first to Geneva, then to Paris, and finally to New York. He became a U.S. citizen in 1940 and between 1942 and 1951 served in the Office of Strategic Services (forerunner of the CIA) and the U.S. State Department. Marcuse returned to academic life in 1952 and went on to teach at Brandeis University and the University of California at San Diego. He died in 1979.

As a member of the Institute for Social Research and heavily influenced by Georg Lukács, Marcuse spent his early career developing a Marxist critique of society, which bore fruit in 1941 with the publication of *Reason and Revolution*. In 1955 he published his most original book *Eros and Civilization*, a bold admixture of Marx and Freud in which Marcuse attempted to show how unconscious libidinal instincts (*eros*) tend toward a nonrepressive order where exploitative work is transformed into play. His radical critique of advanced capitalism was further developed in *One-Dimensional Man* (1964) and in his later works *An Essay on Liberation* (1969) and *Counterrevolution and Revolt* (1972). Marcuse's unique and influential blend of psychoanalysis, existentialism, and Marxism led the popular media to dub him the "father of the New Left." He was an inspiration for a generation of students during the countercultural revolution of the 1960s in the United States and Europe.

The featured selection is from Marcuse's widely read *One-Dimensional Man: Studies in the Ideology of Advanced Industrial Society*. Marcuse begins with the observation that Western democratic society is unfree and repressive, and that advanced technology and new forms of social control, such as advertising and the mass market, have diffused the revolutionary potential in society by generating "false needs." Marcuse argues that such needs lead individuals to relinquish their interiority, independence, and liberty and identify themselves with the prevailing ideology of society. This ideology is a "one-dimensional thought and behavior in which ideas, aspirations, and objectives that, by their content, transcend the established universe of discourse and action are either repelled or reduced to terms of this universe." To counteract this monocultural hegemony of "positivism," "consumerism," "self-validating hypotheses," "hypnotic definitions or dictations" (e.g., "the Free World"), Marcuse calls for a "pacification of existence," where the struggles between man and man, and man and nature, are no longer characterized by vested interests in domination and capital accumulation but are coordinated for the betterment of the human condition.

HERBERT MARCUSE (1898–1979)

Select Bibliography of Marcuse's Works in English

The Aesthetic Dimension: Toward a Critique of Marxist Aesthetics. Boston: Beacon Press, 1978.

Eros and Civilization: A Philosophical Inquiry into Freud. Boston: Beacon Press, 1974.

An Essay on Liberation. Boston: Beacon Press, 1969.

Five Lectures: Psychoanalysis, Politics, and Utopia. Trans. Jeremy J. Shapiro and Shierry M. Weber. Boston: Boston Beacon Press, 1970.

Hegel's Ontology and the Theory of Historicity. Trans. Seyla Benhabib. Cambridge, MA: MIT Press, 1987.

Negations: Essays in Critical Theory. London: Free Association Books, 1988.

One-Dimensional Man: Studies in the Ideology of Advanced Industrial Society. Boston: Beacon Press, 1966.

Reason and Revolution: Hegel and the Rise of Social Theory. Atlantic Highlands, NJ: Humanities Press, 1989.

Soviet Marxism: A Critical Analysis. Harmondsworth, UK: Penguin Books, 1971.

Studies in Critical Philosophy. Trans Joris De Bres. Boston: Beacon Press, 1973.

ONE-DIMENSIONAL MAN

A comfortable, smooth, reasonable, democratic unfreedom prevails in advanced industrial civilization, a token of technical progress. Indeed, what could be more rational than the suppression of individuality in the mechanization of socially necessary but painful performances; the concentration of individual enterprises in more effective, more productive corporations; the regulation of free competition among unequally equipped economic subjects; the curtailment of prerogatives and national sovereignties which impede the international organization of resources. That this technological order also involves a political and intellectual coordination may be a regrettable and yet promising development.

The rights and liberties which were such vital factors in the origins and earlier stages of industrial society yield to a higher stage of this society: they are losing their traditional rationale and content. Freedom of thought, speech, and conscience were—just as free enterprise, which they served to promote and protect—essentially *critical* ideas, designed to replace an obsolescent material and intellectual culture by a more productive and rational one. Once institutionalized, these rights and liberties shared the fate of the society of which they had become an integral part. The achievement cancels the premises.

To the degree to which freedom from want, the concrete substance of all freedom, is becoming a real possibility, the liberties which pertain to a state of lower productivity are losing their former content. Independence of thought, autonomy, and the right to political opposition are being deprived of their basic critical function in a society which seems increasingly capable of satisfying the needs of the individuals through the way in which it is organized. Such a society may justly demand acceptance of its principles and institutions, and reduce the opposition to the discussion and promotion of alternative policies *within* the status quo. In this respect, it seems to make little difference whether the increasing satisfaction of needs is accomplished by an authoritarian or a nonauthoritarian system. Under the conditions of a rising standard of living, nonconformity with the system itself appears to be socially useless, and the more so when it entails tangible economic and political disadvantages and threatens the smooth operation of the whole. Indeed, at least insofar as the necessities of life are involved, there seems to be no reason why the production and distribution of goods and services should proceed through the competitive concurrence of individual liberties.

Freedom of enterprise was from the beginning not altogether a blessing. As the liberty to work or to starve, it spelled toil, insecurity, and fear for the vast majority of the population. If the individual were no longer compelled to prove himself on the market, as a free economic subject, the disappearance of this kind of freedom would be one of the greatest achievements of civilization. The technological processes of mechanization and standardization might release individual energy into a yet uncharted realm of freedom beyond necessity. The very structure of human existence would be altered; the individual would be liberated from the work-world's imposing upon him alien needs and alien possibilities. The individual would be free to exert autonomy over a life that would be his own. If the productive apparatus could be organized and directed toward the satisfaction of the vital needs, its control might well be centralized; such control would not prevent individual autonomy, but render it possible.

This is a goal within the capabilities of advanced industrial civilization, the "end" of technological rationality. In actual fact, however, the contrary trend operates: the apparatus imposes its economic and political requirements for defense and expansion on labor time and free time, on the material and intellectual culture. By virtue of the way it has organized its technological base, contemporary industrial society tends to be totalitarian. For "totalitarian" is not only a terroristic political coordination of society, but also a nonterroristic economic-technical coordination which operates through the manipulation of needs by vested interests. It thus precludes the emergence of an effective opposition against the whole. Not only a specific form of government or party rule makes for totalitarianism, but also a specific system of production and distribution which may well be compatible with a "pluralism" of parties, newspapers, "countervailing powers," etc.

Today political power asserts itself through its power over the machine process and over the technical organization of the apparatus. The government of advanced and advancing industrial societies can maintain and secure itself only when it succeeds in mobilizing, organizing, and exploiting the technical, scientific, and mechanical productivity available to industrial civilization. And this productivity mobilizes society as a whole, above and beyond any particular individual or group interests. The brute fact that the machine's physical (only physical?) power surpasses that of the individual, and of any particular group of individuals, makes the machine the most effective political instrument in any society whose basic organization is that of the machine process. But the political trend may be reversed; essentially the power of the machine is only the stored-up and projected power of man. To the extent to which the work-world is conceived of as a machine and mechanized accordingly, it becomes the *potential* basis of a new freedom for man.

Contemporary industrial civilization demonstrates that it has reached the stage at which "the free society" can no longer be adequately defined in the traditional terms of economic, political, and intellectual liberties, not because these liberties have become insignificant, but because they are too significant to be confined within the traditional forms. New modes of realization are needed, corresponding to the new capabilities of society.

Such new modes can be indicated only in negative terms because they would amount to the negation of the prevailing modes. Thus economic freedom would mean freedom *from* the economy—from being controlled by economic forces and relationships; freedom from the daily struggle for existence, from earning a living. Political freedom would mean liberation of the individuals *from* politics over which they have no effective control.

Similarly, intellectual freedom would mean the restoration of individual thought now absorbed by mass communication and indoctrination, abolition of "public opinion" together with its makers. The unrealistic sound of these propositions is indicative, not of their utopian character, but of the strength of the forces which prevent their realization. The most effective and enduring form of warfare against liberation is the implanting of material and intellectual needs that perpetuate obsolete forms of the struggle for existence.

The intensity, the satisfaction and even the character of human needs, beyond the biological level, have always been preconditioned. Whether or not the possibility of doing or leaving, enjoying or destroying, possessing or rejecting something is seized as a *need* depends on whether or not it can be seen as desirable and necessary for the prevailing societal institutions and interests. In this sense, human needs are historical needs and, to the extent to which the society demands the repressive development of the individual, his needs themselves and their claim for satisfaction are subject to overriding critical standards.

We may distinguish both true and false needs. "False" are those which are superimposed upon the individual by particular social interests in his repression: the needs which perpetuate toil, aggressiveness, misery, and injustice. Their satisfaction might be most gratifying to the individual, but this happiness is not a condition which has to be maintained and protected if it serves to arrest the development of the ability (his own and others) to recognize the disease of the whole and grasp the chances of curing the disease. The result then is euphoria in unhappiness. Most of the prevailing needs to relax, to have fun, to behave and consume in accordance with the advertisements, to love and hate what others love and hate, belong to this category of false needs.

Such needs have a societal content and function which are determined by external powers over which the individual has no control; the development and satisfaction of these needs is heteronomous. No matter how much such needs may have become the individual's own, reproduced and fortified by the conditions of his existence; no matter how much he identifies himself with them and finds himself in their satisfaction, they continue to be what they were from the beginning—products of a society whose dominant interest demands repression.

The prevalence of repressive needs is an accomplished fact, accepted in ignorance and defeat, but a fact that must be undone in the interest of the happy individual as well as all those whose misery is the price of his satisfaction. The only needs that have an unqualified claim for satisfaction are the vital ones—nourishment, clothing, lodging at the attainable level of culture. The satisfaction of these needs is the prerequisite for the realization of *all* needs, of the unsublimated as well as the sublimated ones.

For any consciousness and conscience, for any experience which does not accept the prevailing societal interest as the supreme law of thought and behavior, the established universe of needs and satisfactions is a fact to be questioned—questioned in terms of truth and falsehood. These terms are historical throughout, and their objectivity is historical. The judgment of needs and their satisfaction, under the given conditions, involves standards of *priority*—standards which refer to the optimal development of the individual, of all individuals, under the optimal utilization of the material and intellectual resources available to man. The resources are calculable. "Truth" and "falsehood" of needs designate objective conditions to the extent to which the universal satisfaction of vital needs and, beyond it, the progressive alleviation of toil and poverty, are universally valid standards. But as historical standards, they do not only vary according to area and stage of development, they also can be defined only in (greater or lesser) *contradiction* to the prevailing ones. What tribunal can possibly claim the authority of decision?

In the last analysis, the question of what are true and false needs must be answered by the individuals themselves, but only in the last analysis; that is, if and when they are free to give their own answer. As long as they are kept incapable of being autonomous, as long as they are indoctrinated and manipulated (down to their very instincts), their answer to this question cannot be taken as their own. By the same token, however, no tribunal can justly arrogate to itself the right to decide which needs should be developed and satisfied. Any such tribunal is reprehensible, although our revulsion does not do away with the question: How can the people who have been the object of effective and productive domination by themselves create the conditions of freedom?

The more rational, productive, technical, and total the repressive administration of society becomes, the more unimaginable the means and ways by which the administered individuals might break their servitude and seize their own liberation. To be sure, to impose Reason upon an entire society is a paradoxical and scandalous idea—although one might dispute the righteousness of a society which ridicules this idea while making its own population into objects of total administration. All liberation depends on the consciousness of servitude, and the emergence of this consciousness is always hampered by the predominance of needs and satisfactions which, to a great extent, have become the individual's own. The process always replaces one system of preconditioning by another; the optimal goal is the replacement of false needs by true ones, the abandonment of repressive satisfaction.

The distinguishing feature of advanced industrial society is its effective suffocation of those needs which demand liberation—liberation also from that which is tolerable and rewarding and comfortable—while it sustains and absolves the destructive power and repressive function of the affluent society. Here, the social controls exact the overwhelming need for the production and consumption of waste; the need for stupefying work where it is no longer a real necessity; the need for modes of relaxation which soothe and prolong this stupefaction; the need for maintaining such deceptive liberties as free competition at administered prices, a free press which censors itself, free choice between brands and gadgets.

Under the rule of a repressive whole, liberty can be made into a powerful instrument of domination. The range of choice open to the individual is not the decisive factor in determining the degree of human freedom, but *what* can be chosen and what *is* chosen by the individual. The criterion for free choice can never be an absolute one, but neither is it entirely relative. Free election of masters does not abolish the masters or the slaves. Free choice among a wide variety of goods and services does not signify freedom if these goods and services sustain social controls over a life of toil and fear—that is, if they sustain alienation. And the spontaneous reproduction of superimposed needs by the individual does not establish autonomy; it only testifies to the efficacy of the controls.

Our insistence on the depth and efficacy of these controls is open to the objection that we overrate greatly the indoctrinating power of the "media," and that by themselves the people would feel and satisfy the needs which are now imposed upon them. The objection misses the point. The preconditioning does not start with the mass production of radio and television and with the centralization of their control. The people enter this stage as preconditioned receptacles of long standing; the decisive difference is in the flattening out of the contrast (or conflict) between the given and the possible, between the satisfied and the unsatisfied needs. Here, the so-called equalization of class distinctions reveals its ideological function. If the worker and his boss enjoy the same television program and visit the same resort places, if the typist is as attractively made up as the daughter of her employer, if the Negro owns a Cadillac, if they all read the same newspaper, then this assimilation indicates not the disappearance of classes, but the extent to which the needs and satisfactions that serve the preservation of the Establishment are shared by the underlying population.

Indeed, in the most highly developed areas of contemporary society, the transplantation of social into individual needs is so effective that the difference between them seems to be purely theoretical. Can one really distinguish between the mass media as instruments of information and entertainment, and as agents of manipulation and indoctrination? Between the automobile as nuisance and as convenience? Between the horrors and the comforts of functional architecture? Between the work for national defense and the work for corporate gain? Between the private pleasure and the commercial and political utility involved in increasing the birthrate?

We are again confronted with one of the most vexing aspects of advanced industrial civilization: the rational character of its irrationality. Its productivity and efficiency, its capacity to increase and spread comforts, to turn waste into need, and destruction into construction, the extent to which this civilization transforms the object world into an extension of man's mind and body make the very notion of alienation questionable. The people recognize themselves in their commodities; they find their soul in their automobile, hi-fi set, split-level home, kitchen equipment. The very mechanism which ties the individual to his society has changed, and social control is anchored in the new needs which it has produced.

The prevailing forms of social control are technological in a new sense. To be sure, the technical structure and efficacy of the productive and destructive apparatus have been a major instrumentality for subjecting the population to the established social division of labor throughout the modern period. Moreover, such integration has always been accompanied by more obvious forms of compulsion, loss of livelihood, the administration of justice, the police, the armed forces. It still is. But in the contemporary period, the technological controls appear to be the very embodiment of Reason for the benefit of all social groups and interests—to such an extent that all contradiction seems irrational and all counteraction impossible.

No wonder then that, in the most advanced areas of this civilization, the social controls have been introjected to the point where even individual protest is affected at its roots. The intellectual and emotional refusal "to go along" appears neurotic and impotent. This is the sociopsychological aspect of the political event that marks the contemporary period: the passing of the historical forces which, at the preceding stage of industrial society, seemed to represent the possibility of new forms of existence.

But the term "introjection" perhaps no longer describes the way in which the individual by himself reproduces and perpetuates the external controls exercised by his society. Introjection suggests a variety of relatively spontaneous processes by which a Self (Ego) transposes the "outer" into the "inner." Thus introjection implies the existence of an inner dimension distinguished from and even antagonistic to the external exigencies—an individual consciousness and an individual unconscious *apart from* public opinion and behavior.[1] The idea of "inner freedom" here has its reality: it designates the private space in which man may become and remain "himself."

Today this private space has been invaded and whittled down by technological reality. Mass production and mass distribution claim the *entire* individual, and industrial psychology has long since ceased to be confined to the factory. The manifold processes of introjection seem to be ossified in almost mechanical reactions. The result is not adjustment but *mimesis*: an immediate identification of the individual with *his* society and, through it, with the society as a whole.

This immediate, automatic identification (which may have been characteristic of primitive forms of association) reappears in high industrial civilization; its new "immediacy," however, is the product of a sophisticated, scientific management and organization. In this process, the "inner" dimension of the mind in which opposition to the status quo can take root is whittled down. The loss of this dimension, in which the power of negative thinking—the critical power of Reason—is at home, is the ideological counterpart to the very material process in which advanced industrial society silences and reconciles the opposition. The impact of progress turns Reason into submission to the facts of life, and to the dynamic capability of producing more and bigger facts of the same sort of life. The efficiency of the system blunts the individuals' recognition that it contains no facts which do not communicate the repressive power of the whole. If the individuals find themselves in the things which shape their life, they do so, not by giving, but by accepting the law of things—not the law of physics but the law of their society.

I have just suggested that the concept of alienation seems to become questionable when the individuals identify themselves with the existence which is imposed upon them and have in it their own development and satisfaction. This identification is not illusion but reality. However, the reality constitutes a more progressive stage of alienation. The latter has become entirely objective; the subject which is alienated is swallowed up by its alienated existence. There is only one dimension, and it is everywhere and in all forms. The achievements of progress defy ideological indictment as well as justification; before their tribunal, the "false consciousness" of their rationality becomes the true consciousness.

This absorption of ideology into reality does not, however, signify the "end of ideology." On the contrary, in a specific sense advanced industrial culture is *more* ideological than its predecessor, inasmuch as today the ideology is in the process of production itself.[2] In a provocative form, this proposition reveals the political aspects of the prevailing technological rationality. The productive apparatus and the goods and services which it produces "sell" or impose the social system as a whole. The means of mass transportation and communication, the commodities of lodging, food, and clothing, the irresistible output of the entertainment and information industry carry with them prescribed attitudes and habits, certain intellectual and emotional reactions which bind the consumers more or less pleasantly to the producers and, through the latter, to the whole. The products indoctrinate and manipulate; they promote a false consciousness which is immune against its falsehood. And as these beneficial products become available to more individuals in more social classes, the indoctrination they carry ceases to be publicity; it becomes a way of life. It is a good way of life—much better than before—and as a good way of life, it militates against qualitative change. Thus emerges a pattern of *one-dimensional thought and behavior* in which ideas, aspirations, and objectives that, by their content, transcend the established universe of discourse and action are either repelled or reduced to terms of this universe. They are redefined by the rationality of the given system and of its quantitative extension.

The trend may be related to a development in scientific method: operationalism in the physical, behaviorism in the social sciences. The common feature is a total empiricism in the treatment of concepts; their meaning is restricted to the representation of particular operations and behavior. The operational point of view is well illustrated by P.W. Bridgman's analysis of the concept of length:[3]

> We evidently know what we mean by length if we can tell what the length of any and every object is, and for the physicist nothing more is required. To find the length of an object, we have to perform certain physical operations. The concept of length is therefore fixed when the operations by which length is measured are fixed: that is, the concept of length involves as much and nothing more than the set of operations by which length is determined. In general, we mean by any concept nothing more than a set of operations; *the concept is synonymous with the corresponding set of operations.*

Bridgman has seen the wide implications of this mode of thought for the society at large:[4]

> To adopt the operational point of view involves much more than a mere restriction of the sense in which we understand "concept," but means a far-reaching change in all our habits of thought, in that we shall no longer permit ourselves to use as tools in our thinking concepts of which we cannot give an adequate account in terms of operations.

Bridgman's prediction has come true. The new mode of thought is today the predominant tendency in philosophy, psychology, sociology, and other fields. Many of the most seriously troublesome concepts are being "eliminated" by showing that no adequate account of them in terms of operations or behavior can be given. The radical empiricist onslaught . . . thus provides the methodological justification for the debunking of the mind by the intellectuals—a positivism which, in its denial of the transcending elements of Reason, forms the academic counterpart of the socially required behavior.

Outside the academic establishment, the "far-reaching change in all our habits of thought" is more serious. It serves to coordinate ideas and goals with those exacted by the prevailing system, to enclose them in the system, and to repel those which are irreconcilable with the system. The reign of such a one-dimensional reality does not mean that materialism rules, and that the spiritual, metaphysical, and bohemian occupations are petering out. On the contrary, there is a great deal of "Worship together this week," "Why not try God," Zen, existentialism, and beat ways of life, etc. But such modes of protest and transcendence are no longer contradictory to the status quo and no longer negative. They are rather the ceremonial part of practical behaviorism, its harmless negation, and are quickly digested by the status quo as part of its healthy diet.

One-dimensional thought is systematically promoted by the makers of politics and their purveyors of mass information. Their universe of discourse is populated by self-validating hypotheses which, incessantly and monopolistically repeated, become hypnotic definitions or dictations. For example, "free" are the institutions which operate (and are operated on) in the countries of the Free World; other transcending modes of freedom are by definition either anarchism, communism, or propaganda. "Socialistic" are all encroachments on private enterprises not undertaken by private enterprise itself (or by government contracts), such as universal and comprehensive health insurance, or the protection of nature from all-too-sweeping commercialization, or the establishment of public services which may hurt private profit. This totalitarian logic of accomplished facts has its Eastern counterpart. There, freedom is the way of life instituted by a communist regime, and all other transcending modes of freedom are either capitalistic, or revisionist, or leftist sectarianism. In both camps, nonoperational ideas are nonbehavioral and subversive. The movement of thought is stopped at barriers which appear as the limits of Reason itself.

Such limitation of thought is certainly not new. Ascending modern rationalism, in its speculative as well as empirical form, shows a striking contrast between extreme critical radicalism in scientific and philosophic method on the one hand, and an uncritical quietism in the attitude toward established and functioning social institutions. Thus Descartes' *ego cogitans* was to leave the "great public bodies" untouched, and Hobbes held that "the present ought always to be preferred, maintained, and accounted best." Kant agreed with Locke in justifying revolution *if and when* it has succeeded in organizing the whole and in preventing subversion.

However, these accommodating concepts of Reason were always contradicted by the evident misery and injustice of the "great public bodies" and the effective, more or less conscious rebellion against them. Societal conditions existed which provoked and permitted real dissociation from the established state of affairs; a private as well as political dimension was present in which dissociation could develop into effective opposition, testing its strength and the validity of its objectives.

With the gradual closing of this dimension by the society, the self-limitation of thought assumes a larger significance. The interrelation between scientific-philosophical and societal processes, between theoretical and practical Reason, asserts itself "behind the back" of the scientists and philosophers. The society bars a whole type of oppositional operations and behavior; consequently, the concepts pertaining to them are rendered illusory or meaningless. Historical transcendence appears as metaphysical transcendence, not acceptable to science and scientific thought. The operational and behavioral point of view, practiced as a "habit of thought" at large, becomes the view of the established universe of discourse and action, needs and aspirations. The "cunning of Reason" works, as it so often did, in the interest of the powers that be. The insistence on operational and behavioral concepts turns against the efforts to free thought and behavior *from* the given reality and *for* the suppressed alternatives. Theoretical and practical Reason, academic and social behaviorism meet on common ground: that of an advanced society which makes scientific and technical progress into an instrument of domination.

"Progress" is not a neutral term; it moves toward specific ends, and these ends are defined by the possibilities of ameliorating the human condition. Advanced industrial society is approaching the stage where continued progress would demand the radical subversion of the prevailing direction and organization of progress. This stage would be reached when material production (including the necessary services) becomes automated to the extent that all vital needs can be satisfied while necessary labor time is reduced to marginal time. From this point on, technical progress would transcend the realm of necessity, where it served as the instrument of domination and exploitation which thereby limited its rationality; technology would become subject to the free play of faculties in the struggle for the pacification of nature and of society.

Such a state is envisioned in Marx's notion of the "abolition of labor." The term "pacification of existence" seems better suited to designate the historical alternative of a world which—through an international conflict which transforms and suspends the contradictions within the established societies—advances on the brink of a global war. "Pacification of existence" means the development of man's struggle with man and with nature, under conditions where the competing needs, desires, and aspirations are no longer organized by vested interests in domination and scarcity—an organization which perpetuates the destructive forms of this struggle.

Today's fight against this historical alternative finds a firm mass basis in the underlying population, and finds its ideology in the rigid orientation of thought and behavior to the given universe of facts. Validated by the accomplishments of science and technology, justified by its growing productivity, the status quo defies all transcendence. Faced with the possibility of pacification on the grounds of its technical and intellectual achievements, the mature industrial society closes itself against this alternative. Operationalism, in theory and practice, becomes the theory and practice of *containment*. Underneath its obvious dynamics, this society is a thoroughly static system of life: self-propelling in its oppressive productivity and in its beneficial coordination. Containment of technical progress goes hand in hand with its growth in the established direction. In spite of the political fetters imposed by the status quo, the more technology appears capable of creating the conditions for pacification, the more are the minds and bodies of man organized against this alternative.

The most advanced areas of industrial society exhibit throughout these two features: a trend toward consummation of technological rationality, and intensive efforts to contain this trend within the established institutions. Here is the internal contradiction of this civilization: the irrational element in its rationality. It is the token of its achievements. The industrial society which makes technology and science its own is organized for the ever-more-effective domination of man and nature, for the ever-more-effective utilization of its resources. It becomes irrational when the success of these efforts opens new dimensions of human realization. Organization for peace is different from organization for war; the institutions which served the struggle for existence cannot serve the pacification of existence. Life as an end is qualitatively different from life as a means.

Such a qualitatively new mode of existence can never be envisaged as the mere by-product of economic and political changes, as the more or less spontaneous effect of the new institutions which constitute the necessary prerequisite. Qualitative change also involves a change in the *technical* basis on which this society rests—one which sustains the economic and political institutions through which the "second nature" of man as an aggressive object of administration is stabilized. The techniques of industrialization are political techniques; as such, they prejudge the possibilities of Reason and Freedom.

To be sure, labor must precede the reduction of labor, and industrialization must precede the development of human needs and satisfactions. But as all freedom depends on the conquest of alien necessity, the realization of freedom depends on the *techniques* of conquest. The highest productivity of labor can be used for the perpetuation of labor, and the most efficient industrialization can serve the restriction and manipulation of needs.

When this point is reached, domination—in the guise of affluence and liberty—extends to all spheres of private and public existence, integrates all authentic opposition, absorbs all alternatives. Technological rationality reveals its political character as it becomes the great vehicle of better domination, creating a truly totalitarian universe in which society and nature, mind and body are kept in a state of permanent mobilization for the defense of this universe.

Notes

1. The change in the function of the family here plays a decisive role: its "socializing" functions are increasingly taken over by outside groups and media. See my *Eros and Civilization* (Boston: Beacon Press, 1955), 96 ff.
2. Theodor W. Adorno, *Prismen: Kulturkritik und Gesellschaft* (Frankfurt: Suhrkamp, 1955), 24 f.
3. P.W. Bridgman, *The Logic of Modern Physics* (New York: Macmillan, 1928), 5. The operational doctrine has since been refined and qualified. Bridgman himself has extended the concept of "operation" to include the "paper-and-pencil" operations of the theorist (in Philipp J. Frank, *The Validation of Scientific Theories* [Boston: Beacon Press, 1954], Chap. II). The main impetus remains the same: it is "desirable" that the paper-and-pencil operations "be capable of eventual contact, although perhaps indirectly, with instrumental operations."
4. P.W. Bridgman, *The Logic of Modern Physics*, loc. cit., 31.

14

JÜRGEN HABERMAS
(1929–)

German philosopher and social theorist Jürgen Habermas was born in 1929 in Düsseldorf. He began his university studies at Göttingen, undertaking research in philosophy, history, and psychology, before transferring to Bonn to complete a dissertation on the Absolute and history in Friedrich Schelling's thought. In 1953, he made his definitive entry into the arena of political criticism with a newspaper article that took Heidegger to task for his remarks about the "inner truth and greatness" of National Socialism in *An Introduction to Metaphysics*. Habermas's continuing interest in political and cultural critique led him to become a researcher at the Institute for Social Research, where he served as Theodor Adorno's assistant from 1956 to 1959. From 1971 to 1981, he was codirector of the Max Planck Institute in Starnberg and has since held a number of prestigious research and teaching posts at such universities as Berkeley, Northwestern, and Frankfurt.

Habermas is widely regarded as the most eminent of the second generation of Frankfurt School theorists, a reputation that was secured by the publication of several influential early writings, including *The Structural Transformation of the Public Sphere* (1962), *Theory and Practice* (1963), and *Knowledge and Human Interests* (1968). Although he shares many concerns with first-generation Frankfurt School theorists such as Horkheimer and Adorno, Habermas has never espoused the wholly negative and critical attitude toward modernity characteristic of his predecessors. He has instead dedicated himself to reclaiming the project of Enlightenment critique over and against its dissolution among many contemporary theorists. Thus in his magnum opus, *The Theory of Communicative Action* (1981), Habermas argues that, despite the pervasive nature of instrumental rationality and success-oriented action in contemporary society, so strongly criticized by Horkheimer, Adorno, and others, there exists another type of rationality based on intersubjective communication. It is precisely this communicative form of rationality, which according to Habermas contains immense critical and emancipatory potential, that he accuses Bataille, Foucault, Derrida, and other postmodernists of seriously overlooking in his most widely read and polemical book, *The Philosophical Discourse of Modernity* (1985). Habermas maintains that the wholesale rejection of reason and the Enlightenment project prevents drawing a distinction between alienation and genuine emancipation, a distinction that is crucial to the establishment of any viable ethical or political position.

From this perspective, the most promising means of moving beyond the quandaries associated with postmodern relativism is to construct a moral theory grounded in communicative action and discourse. The central claim of Habermas's version of "discourse ethics" is that moral norms gain legitimacy if they are justified and agreed upon in the shared rational discourse of moral agents—a discourse that, due to its commitment to impartiality and universalizability, transcends contingent, cultural circumstances and avoids the dilemmas of moral skepticism. In our reading, "On the Pragmatic, the Ethical, and the Moral Employments of Practical Reason," Habermas offers a comprehensive examination of practical reason in an attempt to delimit its pragmatic, ethical, and moral aspects. With these determinations in place, he goes on to examine the relation of discourse ethics to practical reason with an eye toward the intersubjective tensions inherent in the specifically moral dimensions of practical life. In order to deal effectively with these tensions and to bring the disparate dimensions of practical reason under a single perspective, Habermas suggests that it is necessary to move beyond the realm of practical-moral discourse and enter the sphere of law and politics, where communicative action and discourse take on a more concrete institutional form.

Select Bibliography of Habermas's Works in English

Between Facts and Norms: Contributions to a Discourse Theory of Law and Democracy. Trans. William Rehg. Cambridge, MA: MIT Press, 1996.

The Inclusion of the Other: Studies in Political Theory. Ed. Ciaran Cronin and Pablo de Greiff. Cambridge, MA: MIT Press, 1988.

Justification and Application: Remarks on Discourse Ethics. Trans. Ciaran Cronin. Cambridge, MA: MIT Press, 1993.

Knowledge and Human Interests. Trans. Jeremy J. Shapiro. Boston: Beacon Press, 1971.

Legitimation Crisis. Trans. Thomas McCarthy. Boston: Beacon Press, 1975.

Moral Consciousness and Communicative Action. Trans. Christian Lenhardt and Shierry Weber Nicholsen. Cambridge, MA: MIT Press, 1990.

The New Conservatism: Cultural Criticism and the Historians' Debate. Trans. Shierry Weber Nicholsen. Cambridge, MA: MIT Press, 1989.

The Philosophical Discourse of Modernity. Trans. Frederick G. Lawrence. Cambridge, MA: MIT Press, 1987.

Postmetaphysical Thinking. Trans. William Mark Hohengarten. Cambridge, MA: MIT Press, 1992.

The Structural Transformation of the Public Sphere: An Inquiry into a Category of Bourgeois Society. Trans. Thomas Burger. Cambridge, MA: MIT Press, 1991.

The Theory of Communicative Action. Volume I. Reason and Rationalization on Society. Trans. Thomas McCarthy. Boston: Beacon Press, 1984.

The Theory of Communicative Action. Volume 2. Lifeworld and System: A Critique of Functionalist Reason. Trans. Thomas McCarthy. Boston: Beacon Press, 1987.

ON THE PRAGMATIC, THE ETHICAL, AND THE MORAL EMPLOYMENTS OF PRACTICAL REASONS

Contemporary discussions in practical philosophy draw, now as before, on three main sources: Aristotelian ethics, utilitarianism, and Kantian moral theory. Two of the parties to these interesting debates also appeal to Hegel, who tried to achieve a synthesis of the classical communal and modern individualistic conceptions of freedom with his theory of objective spirit and his "sublation" (*Aufhebung*) of morality into ethical life. Whereas the communitarians appropriate the Hegelian legacy in the form of an Aristotelian ethics of the good and abandon the universalism of rational natural law, discourse ethics takes its orientation for an intersubjective interpretation of the categorical imperative from Hegel's theory of recognition but without incurring the cost of a historical *dissolution* of morality in ethical life. Like Hegel it insists, though in a Kantian spirit, on the internal relation between justice and solidarity. It attempts to show that the meaning of the basic principle of morality can be explicated in terms of the content of the unavoidable presuppositions of an argumentative practice that can be pursued only in common with others. The moral point of view from which we can judge practical questions impartially is indeed open to different interpretations. But because it is grounded in the communicative structure of rational discourse as such, we cannot simply dispose of it at will. It forces itself intuitively on anyone who is at all open to this reflective form of communicative action. With this fundamental assumption, discourse ethics situates itself squarely in the Kantian tradition yet without leaving itself vulnerable to the objections with which the abstract ethics of conviction has met from its inception. Admittedly, it adopts a narrowly circumscribed conception of morality that focuses on questions of justice. But it neither has to neglect the calculation of the consequences of actions rightly emphasized by utilitarianism nor exclude from the sphere of discursive problematization the questions of the good life accorded prominence by classical ethics, abandoning them to irrational emotional dispositions or decisions. The term *discourse ethics* may have occasioned a misunderstanding in this connection. The theory of discourse relates in different ways to moral, ethical, and pragmatic questions. It is this differentiation that I propose to clarify here.

Classical ethics, like modern theories, proceeds from the question that inevitably forces itself upon an individual in need of orientation faced with a perplexing practical task in a particular situation: How should I proceed, what should I do?[1] The meaning of this "should" remains indeterminate as long as the relevant problem and the aspect under which it is to be addressed have not been more clearly specified. I will begin by taking the distinction between pragmatic, ethical, and moral questions as a guide to differentiating the various uses of practical reason. Different tasks are required of practical reason under the aspects of the purposive, the good, and the just. Correspondingly, the constellation of reason and volition changes as we move between pragmatic, ethical, and moral discourses. Finally, once moral theory breaks out of the investigative horizon of the first person singular, it encounters the reality of an alien will, which generates problems of a different order.

I

Practical problems beset us in a variety of situations. They "have to be" mastered; otherwise we suffer consequences that are at very least annoying. We *must* decide what to do when the bicycle we use every day is broken, when we are afflicted with illness, or when we lack the money necessary to realize certain desires. In such cases we look for reasons for a rational choice between different available courses of action in the light of a task that we *must* accomplish if we *want* to achieve a certain goal. The goals themselves can also become problematic, as, for example, when holiday plans fall through or when we must make a career decision. Whether one travels to Scandinavia or to Elba or stays at home or whether one goes directly to college or first does an apprenticeship, becomes a physician or a salesperson—such things depend in the first instance on our preferences and on the options open to us in such situations. Once again we seek reasons for a rational choice but in this case for a choice between the goals themselves.

In both cases the rational thing to do is determined in part by what one wants: it is a matter of making a rational choice of means in the light of fixed purposes or of the rational assessment of goals in the light of existing preferences. Our will is already fixed as a matter of fact by our wishes and values; it is open to further determination only in respect of alternative possible choices of means or specifications of ends. Here we are exclusively concerned with appropriate techniques—whether for repairing bicycles or treating disease—with strategies for acquiring money or with programs for planning vacations and choosing occupations. In complex cases decision-making strategies themselves must be developed; then reason seeks reassurance concerning its own procedure by becoming reflective— for example, in the form of a theory of rational choice. As long as the question "What should I do?" has such pragmatic tasks in view, observations, investigations, comparisons, and assessments undertaken on the basis of empirical data with a view to efficiency or with the aid of other decision rules are appropriate. Practical reflection here proceeds within the horizon of purposive rationality, its goal being to discover appropriate techniques, strategies, or programs.[2] It leads to recommendations that, in the most straightforward cases, are expressed in the semantic form of conditional imperatives. Kant speaks in this connection of rules of skill and of counsels of prudence and, correspondingly, of technical and pragmatic imperatives. These relate causes to effects in accordance with value preferences and prior goal determinations. The imperative meaning they express can be glossed as that of a *relative ought*, the corresponding directions for action specifying what one "ought" or "must" do when faced with a particular problem if one wants to realize certain values or goals. Of course, once the values themselves become problematic, the question "What should I do?" points beyond the horizon of purposive rationality.

In the case of complex decisions—for example, choosing a career—it may transpire that the question is not a pragmatic one at all. Someone who wants to become a manager of a publishing house might deliberate as to whether it is more expedient to do an apprenticeship first or go straight to college; but someone who is not clear about what he wants to do is in a completely different situation. In the latter case, the choice of a career or a direction of study is bound up with one's "inclinations" or interests, what occupation one would find fulfilling, and so forth. The more radically this question is posed, the more it becomes a matter of what life one would like to lead, and that means what kind of person one is and would like to be. When faced with crucial existential choices, someone who does not know what he wants to be will ultimately be led to pose the question, "Who am I, and who would I like to be?" Decisions based on weak or trivial preferences do not require justification; no one need give an account of his preferences in automobiles or sweaters, whether to himself or anyone else. In the contrasting case, I shall follow Charles Taylor in using the term *strong preferences* to designate preferences that concern not merely contingent dispositions and inclinations but the self-understanding of a person, his character and way of life; they are inextricably interwoven with each individual's identity.[3] This circumstance not only lends existential decisions their peculiar weight but also furnishes them with a context in which they both admit and stand in need of justification. Since Aristotle, important *value decisions* have been regarded as clinical questions of the good life. A decision based on illusions—attaching oneself to the wrong partner or choosing the wrong career—can lead to a failed life. The exercise of practical reason directed in this sense to the good and not merely to the possible and expedient belongs, following classical usage, to the sphere of ethics.

Strong evaluations are embedded in the context of a particular self-understanding. How one understands oneself depends not only on how one describes oneself but also on the ideals toward which one strives. One's identity is determined simultaneously by how one sees oneself and how one would like to see oneself, by what one finds oneself to be and the ideals with reference to which one fashions oneself and one's life. This existential self-understanding is evaluative in its core and, like all evaluations, is Janus-faced. Two components are interwoven in it: the descriptive component of the ontogenesis of the ego and the normative component of the ego-ideal. Hence, the clarification of one's self-understanding or the clinical reassurance of one's identity calls for an *appropriative* form of understanding—the appropriation of one's own life history and the traditions and circumstances of life that have shaped one's process of development.[4] If illusions are playing a role, this hermeneutic self-understanding can be raised to the level of a form of reflection that dissolves self-deceptions. Bringing one's life history and its normative context to awareness in a critical manner does not lead to a value-neutral self-understanding; rather, the hermeneutically generated self-description is logically contingent upon a critical relation to self. A more profound self-understanding alters the attitudes that sustain, or at least imply, a life project with normative substance. In this way, strong evaluations can be justified through hermeneutic self-clarification.

One will be able to choose between pursuing a career in management and training to become a theologian on better grounds after one has become clear about who one is and who one would like to be. Ethical questions are generally answered by unconditional imperatives such as the following: "You must embark on a career that affords you the assurance that you are helping other people." The meaning of this imperative can be understood as an "ought" that is not dependent on subjective purposes and preferences and yet is not absolute. What you "should" or "must" do has here the sense that it is "good" for you to act in this way in the long run, all things considered. Aristotle speaks in this connection of paths to the good and happy life. Strong evaluations take their orientation from a goal posited absolutely for me, that is, from the highest good of a self-sufficient form of life that has its value in itself.

The meaning of the question "What should I do?" undergoes a further transformation as soon as my actions affect the interests of others and lead to conflicts that should be regulated in an impartial manner, that is, from the moral point of view. A contrasting comparison will be instructive concerning the new discursive modality that thereby comes into play. Pragmatic tasks are informed by the perspective of an agent who takes his preferences and goals as his point of departure. Moral problems cannot even be conceived from this point of view because other persons are accorded merely the status of means or limiting conditions for the realization of one's own individual plan of action. In strategic action, the participants assume that each decides egocentrically in accordance with his own interests. Given these premises, there exists from the beginning at least a latent conflict between adversaries. This can be played out or curbed and brought under control; it can also be resolved in the mutual interest of all concerned. But without a radical shift in perspective and attitude, an interpersonal conflict cannot be perceived by those involved *as* a moral problem. If I can secure a loan only by concealing pertinent information, then from a pragmatic point of view all that counts is the probability of my deception's succeeding. Someone who raises the issue of its permissibility is posing a *different* kind of question—

the moral question of whether we all could will that anyone in my situation should act in accordance with the same maxim.

Ethical questions by no means call for a complete break with the egocentric perspective; in each instance they take their orientation from the telos of one's own life. From this point of view, other persons, other life histories, and structures of interests acquire importance only to the extent that they are interrelated or interwoven with my identity, my life history, and my interests within the framework of an intersubjectively shared form of life. My development unfolds against a background of traditions that I share with other persons; moreover, my identity is shaped by collective identities, and my life history is embedded in encompassing historical forms of life. To that extent the life that is good for me also concerns the forms of life that are common to us.[5] Thus, Aristotle viewed the *ethos* of the individual as embedded in the *polis* comprising the citizen body. But ethical questions point in a different direction from moral questions: the regulation of interpersonal conflicts of action resulting from opposed interests is not yet an issue. Whether I would like to be someone who in a case of acute need would be willing to defraud an anonymous insurance company just this one time is not a moral question, for it concerns my self-respect and possibly the respect that others show me, but not equal respect for all, and hence not the symmetrical respect that everyone should accord the integrity of all other persons.

We approach the moral outlook once we begin to examine our maxims as to their compatibility with the maxims of others. By maxims Kant meant the more or less trivial, situational rules of action by which an individual customarily regulates his actions. They relieve the agent of the burden of everyday decision-making and fit together to constitute a more or less consistent life practice in which the agent's character and way of life are mirrored. What Kant had in mind were primarily the maxims of an occupationally stratified, early capitalist society. Maxims constitute in general the smallest units in a network of operative customs in which the identity and life projects of an individual (or group) are concretized; they regulate the course of daily life, modes of interaction, the ways in which problems are addressed and conflicts resolved, and so forth. Maxims are the plane in which ethics and morality intersect because they can be judged alternately from ethical and moral points of view. The maxim to allow myself just one trivial deception may not be *good* for me—for example, if it does not cohere with the picture of the person who I would like to be and would like others to acknowledge me to be. The same maxim may also be *unjust* if its general observance is not equally good for all. A mode of examining maxims or a heuristic for generating maxims guided by the question of how I want to live involves a *different* exercise of practical reason from reflection on whether from my perspective a generally observed maxim is suitable to regulate our communal existence. In the first case, what is being asked is whether a maxim is good for me and is appropriate in the given situation, and in the second, whether I can will that a maxim should be followed by everyone as a general law.

The former is a matter for ethical deliberation, the latter for moral deliberation, though still in a restricted sense, for the outcome of this deliberation remains bound to the personal perspective of a particular individual. My perspective is structured by my self-understanding, and a casual attitude toward deception may be compatible with my preferred way of life if others behave similarly in comparable situations and occasionally make me the victim of their manipulations. Even Hobbes recognizes a golden rule with reference to which such a maxim could be justified under appropriate circumstances. For him it is a "natural law" that each should accord everyone else the rights he demands for himself.[6] But an egocentrically conceived universalizability test does not yet imply that a maxim would be accepted by all as the moral yardstick of their actions. This would follow only if my perspective necessarily cohered with that of everyone else. Only if my identity and my life project reflected a universally valid form of life would what from my perspective is equally good for all in fact be equally in the interest of all.[7]

A categorical imperative that specifies that a maxim is just only if *all* could will that it should be adhered to by everyone in comparable situations first signals a break with the egocentric character of the golden rule ("Do not do unto others what you would not have them do unto you"). *Everyone* must be able to will that the maxims of our action should become a universal law.[8] Only a maxim that can be generalized from the perspective of all affected counts as a norm that can command general assent and to that extent is worthy of recognition or, in other words, is morally binding. The question "What should I do?" is answered morally with reference to what *one* ought to do. Moral commands are categorical or unconditional imperatives that express valid norms or make implicit reference to them. The imperative meaning of these commands alone can be understood as an "ought" that is dependent on neither subjective goals and preferences nor on what is for me the absolute goal of a good, successful, or not-failed life. Rather, what one "should" or "must" do has here the sense that to act thus is just and therefore a duty.

II

Thus, the question "What should I do?" takes on pragmatic, an ethical, or a moral meaning depending on how the problem is conceived. In each case it is a matter of justifying choices among alternative available courses of action, but pragmatic tasks call for a different *kind of action*, and the corresponding question, a different *kind of answer*, from ethical or moral ones. Value-oriented assessments of ends and purposive assessments of available means facilitate rational decisions concerning how we must intervene in the objective world in order to bring about a desired state of affairs. This is essentially a matter of settling empirical questions and questions of rational choice, and the *terminus ad quem* of a corresponding pragmatic discourse is a recommendation concerning a suitable technology or a realizable program of action. The rational consideration of an important value decision that affects the whole course of one's life is quite a different matter. This latter involves hermeneutical clarification of an individual's self-understanding and clinical questions of a happy or not-failed life. The *terminus ad quem* of a corresponding ethical-existential discourse is advice concerning the correct conduct of life and the realization of a personal life project. Moral judgment of actions and maxims is again something different. It serves to clarify legitimate behavioral expectations in response to interpersonal conflicts resulting from the disruption of our orderly coexistence by conflicts of interests. Here we are concerned with the justification and application of norms that stipulate reciprocal rights and duties, and the *terminus ad quem* of a corresponding moral-practical discourse is an agreement concerning the just resolution of a conflict in the realm of norm-regulated action.

Thus, the pragmatic, ethical, and moral employments of practical reason have as their respective goals technical and strategic directions for action, clinical advice, and moral judgments. Practical reason is the ability to justify corresponding imperatives, where not just the illocutionary meaning of "must" or "ought" changes with the practical relation and the kind of decision impending but also the *concept of the will* that is supposed to be open to determination by rationally grounded imperatives in each instance. The "ought" of pragmatic recommendations relativized to subjective ends and values is tailored to the *arbitrary choice (Willkür)* of a subject who makes intelligent decisions on the basis of contingent attitudes and preferences that form his point of departure; the faculty of rational choice does not extend to the interests and value orientations themselves but presupposes them as given. The "ought" of clinical advice relativized to the *telos* of the good life is addressed to the striving for self-realization and thus to the *resoluteness* of an individual who has committed himself to an authentic life; the capacity for existential decisions or radical choice of self always operates within the horizon of a life history, in whose traces the individual can discern who he is and who he would like to become. The categorical "ought" of moral injunctions, finally, is directed to the *free will (freien Willen)*, emphatically construed, of a person who acts in accordance with self-given laws; this will alone is autonomous in the sense that it is completely open to determination by moral insights. In the sphere of validity of the moral law, neither contingent dispositions nor life histories and personal identities set limits to the determination of the will by practical reason. Only a will that is guided by moral insight, and hence is completely rational, can be called autonomous. All heteronomous elements of mere choice or of commitment to an idiosyncratic way of life, however authentic it may be, have been expunged from such a will. Kant confused the autonomous will with an omnipotent will and had to transpose it into the intelligible realm in order to conceive of it as absolutely determinative. But in the world as we experience it, the autonomous will is efficacious only to the extent that it can ensure that the motivational force of good reasons outweighs the power of other motives. Thus, in the plain language of everyday life, we call a correctly informed but weak will a "good will."

To summarize, practical reason, according to whether it takes its orientation from the purposive, the good, or the just, directs itself in turn to the choice of the purposively acting subject, to the resoluteness of the authentic, self-realizing subject, or to the free will of the subject capable of moral judgment. In each instance, the constellation of reason and volition and the concept of practical reason itself undergo alteration. Not only the addressee, the will of the agent who seeks an answer, changes its status with the meaning of the question "What should I do?" but also the addresser, the capacity of practical deliberation itself. According to the aspect chosen, there result three different though complementary interpretations of practical reason. But in each of the three major philosophical traditions, just one of these interpretations has been thematized. For Kant practical reason is coextensive with morality; only in autonomy do reason and the will attain unity. Empiricism assimilates practical reason to its pragmatic use; in Kantian terminology, it is reduced to the purposive exercise of the understanding. And in the Aristotelian tradition, practical reason assumes the role of a faculty of judgment that illuminates the life historical horizon of a customary *ethos*. In each case a *different* exercise is attributed to practical reason, as will become apparent when we consider the respective discourses in which they operate.

III

Pragmatic discourses in which we justify technical and strategic recommendations have a certain affinity with empirical discourses. They serve to relate empirical knowledge to hypothetical goal determinations and preferences and to assess the consequences of (imperfectly informed) choices in the light of underlying maxims. Technical or strategic recommendations ultimately derive their validity from the empirical knowledge on which they rest. Their validity does not depend on whether an addressee decides to adopt their directives. Pragmatic discourses take their orientation from *possible contexts* of application. They are related to the actual volitions of agents only though subjective goal determinations and preferences. There is no *internal* relation between reason and the will. In ethical-existential discourses, this constellation is altered in such a way that justifications become rational motives for changes of attitude.

The roles of agent and participant in discourse overlap in such processes of self-clarification. Someone who wishes to attain clarity about his life as a whole—to justify important value decisions and to gain assurance concerning his identity—cannot allow himself to be represented by someone else in ethical-existential discourse, whether in his capacity as the one involved or as the one who must weigh competing claims. Nevertheless, there is room here for discourse because here too the steps in argumentation should not be idiosyncratic but must be comprehensible in intersubjective terms. The individual attains reflective distance from his own life history only within the horizon of forms of life that he shares with others and that themselves constitute the context for different individual life projects. Those who belong to a shared life-world are potential participants who can assume the catalyzing role of impartial critics in processes of self-clarification. This role can be refined into the therapeutic role of an analyst once generalizable clinical knowledge comes into play. Clinical knowledge of this sort is first generated in such discourses.[9]

Self-clarification draws on the context of a specific life history and leads to evaluative statements about what is good for a particular person. Such evaluations, which rest on the reconstruction of a consciously appropriated life history, have a peculiar semantic status, for "reconstruction" here signifies not just the descriptive delineation of a developmental process through which one has become the individual one finds oneself to be; it signifies at the same time a critical sifting and rearrangement of the elements integrated in such a way that one's own past can be accepted in the light of existing possibilities of action as the developmental history of the person one would like to be and continue to be in the future. The existential figure of the "thrown projection" illuminates the Janus-faced character of the strong evaluations justified by way of a critical appropriation of one's own life history. Here genesis and validity can no longer be separated as they can in the case of technical and strategic recommendations. Insofar as I recognize what is good for me, I also already in a certain sense make the advice my own; that is what it means to make a conscious decision. To the extent that I have become convinced of the soundness of clinical advice, I also already made up my mind to transform my life in the manner suggested. On the other hand, my identity is only responsive to—even at the mercy of—the reflexive pressure of an altered self-understanding when it observes the same standards of authenticity as ethical existential discourse itself. Such a discourse already presupposes, on the part of the addressee, a striving to live an authentic life or the suffering of a patient who has become conscious of the "sickness unto death." In this respect, ethical-existential discourse remains contingent on the *prior telos* of a *consciously* pursued way of life.

IV

In ethical-existential discourses, reason and the will condition one another reciprocally, though the latter remains embedded in the life-historical context thematized. Participants in processes of self-clarification cannot distance themselves from the life histories and forms of life in which they actually find themselves. Moral-practical discourses, by contrast, require a break with all of the unquestioned truths of an established, concrete ethical life, in addition to distancing oneself from the contexts of life with which one's identity is inextricably interwoven. The higher-level intersubjectivity characterized by an intermeshing of the perspective of each with the perspectives of all is constituted only under the communicative presuppositions of a universal discourse in which all those possibly affected could take part and could adopt a hypothetical, argumentative stance toward the validity claims of norms and modes of action that have become problematic. This impartial standpoint overcomes the subjectivity of the individual participant's perspective without becoming disconnected from the performative attitude of the participants. The objectivity of the so-called ideal observer would impede access to the intuitive knowledge of the life-world. Moral-practical discourse represents the ideal extension of each individual communication community from within.[10] In this forum, only those norms proposed that express a common interest of all affected can win justified assent. To this extent, discursively justified norms bring to expression simultaneously both insight into what is equally in the interest of all and a general will that has absorbed into itself, *without repression*, the will of all. Understood in this way, the will determined by moral grounds does not remain external to argumentative reason; the autonomous will is completely internal to reason.

Hence, Kant believed that practical reason first completely comes into its own and becomes coextensive with morality in its role as a norm-testing court of appeal. Yet the discourse-ethical interpretation of the categorical imperative we have offered reveals the one-sidedness of a theory that concentrates exclusively on questions of justification. Once moral justifications rest on a principle of universalization constraining participants in discourse to examine whether disputed norms could command the well-considered assent of all concerned, detached from practical situations and without regard to current motives or existing institutions, the problem of how norms, thus grounded, could ever be *applied* becomes more acute.[11] Valid norms owe their abstract universality to the fact that they withstand the universalization test only in a decontextualized form. But in this abstract formulation, they can be applied without qualification only to standard situations whose salient features have been integrated from the outset into the conditional components of the rule as conditions of application. Moreover, every justification of a norm is necessarily subject to the normal limitations of a finite, historically situated outlook that is provincial in regard to the future. Hence *a fortiori* it cannot already explicitly allow for all of the salient features that at some time in the future will characterize the constellations of unforeseen individual cases. For this reason, the *application* of norms calls for argumentative clarification in its own right. In this case, the impartiality of judgment cannot again be secured through a principle of universalization; rather, in addressing questions of context-sensitive application, practical reason must be informed by a principle of appropriateness. What must be determined here is which of the norms already accepted as valid is appropriate in a given case in the light of all the relevant features of the situation conceived as exhaustively as possible.

Of course, discourses of application, like justificatory discourses, are a purely cognitive undertaking and as such cannot compensate for the uncoupling of moral judgment from the concrete motives that inform actions. Moral commands are valid regardless of whether the addressee can also summon the resolve to do what is judged to be right. The autonomy of his will is a function of whether he is capable of acting from moral insight, but moral insights do not of themselves lead to autonomous actions. The validity claim we associate with normative propositions certainly has obligatory force, and duty, to borrow Kant's terminology, is the affection of the will by the validity claim of moral commands. That the reasons underlying such validity claims are not completely ineffectual is shown by the pangs of conscience that plague us when we act against our better judgment. Guilt feelings are a palpable indicator of transgressions of duty, but then they express only the recognition that we lack good reasons to act *otherwise*. Thus, feelings of guilt reflect a split within the will itself.

V

The empirical will that has split off from the autonomous will plays an important role in the dynamics of our moral learning processes.[12] The division of the will is a symptom of weakness of will only when the moral demands against which it transgresses are in fact legitimate and it is *reasonable* to expect adherence to them under the given circumstances. In the revolt of a dissident will, there all too often also come to expression, as we know, the voice of the other who is excluded by rigid moral principles, the violated integrity of human dignity, recognition refused, interests neglected, and differences denied.

Because the principles of a will that has attained autonomy embody a claim analogous to that associated with knowledge, validity and genesis once again diverge here as they do in pragmatic discourse. Thus, behind the facade of categorical validity may lurk a hidden, entrenched interest that is susceptible only of being pushed through. This facade can be erected all the more easily because the rightness of moral commands, unlike the truth of technical or strategic recommendations, does not stand in a contingent relation to the will of the addressee but is intended to bind the will rationally from within. Liberating ourselves from the merely presumptive generality of selectively employed universalistic principles applied in a context-insensitive manner has always required, and today still requires, social movements and political struggles; we have to learn from the painful experiences and the irreparable suffering of those who have been humiliated, insulted, injured, and brutalized that nobody may be excluded in the name of moral universalism—neither underprivileged classes nor exploited nations, neither domesticated women nor marginalized minorities. Someone who in the name of universalism excludes another who has the right to *remain* alien or other betrays his own guiding idea. The universalism of equal respect for all and of solidarity with everything that bears the mark of humanity is first put to the test by radical freedom in the choice of individual life histories and particular forms of life.

This reflection already oversteps the boundaries of individual will formation. Thus far we have examined the pragmatic, ethical, and moral employments of practical reason, taking as a guide the traditional question, "What should *I* do?" But with the shift in horizon of our questions from the first person singular to the first person plural, more changes than just the forum of reflection. Individual will formation by its very nature is already guided by public argumentation, which it simply reproduces *in foro interno*. Thus, where moral life runs up against the boundaries of morality, it is not a matter of a shift in perspective from internal monological thought to public discourse but of a transformation in the problem at issue; what changes is the role in which other subjects are encountered.

Moral-practical discourse detaches itself from the orientation to personal success and one's own life to which both pragmatic and ethical reflection remain tied. But norm-testing reason still encounters the other as an opponent in an *imaginary*—because counterfactually extended and virtually enacted—process of argumentation. Once the other appears as a *real* individual with his own unsubstitutable will, new problems arise. *This* reality of the alien will belongs to the primary conditions of collective will formation.

The fact of the plurality of agents and the twofold contingency under which the reality of one will confronts that of another generate the additional problem of the communal pursuit of collective goals, and the problem of the regulation of communal existence under the pressure of social complexity also takes on a new form. Pragmatic discourses point to the necessity of compromise as soon as one's own interests have to be brought into harmony with those of others. Ethical-political discourses have as their goal the clarification of a collective identity that must leave room for the pursuit of diverse individual life projects. The problem of the conditions under which moral commands are reasonable motivates the transition from morality to law. And, finally, the implementation of goals and programs gives rise to questions of the transfer and neutral exercise of power.

Modern rational natural law responded to this constellation of problems, but it failed to do justice to the intersubjective nature of collective will formation, which cannot be correctly construed as individual will formation writ large. Hence, we must renounce the premises of the philosophy of the subject on which rational natural law is based. From the perspective of a theory of discourse, the problem of agreement among parties whose wills and interests clash is shifted to the plane of institutionalized procedures and communicative presuppositions of processes of argumentation and negotiation that must be actually carried out.[13]

It is only at the level of a discourse theory of law and politics that we can also expect an answer to the question invited by our analyses: Can we still speak of practical reason in the singular after it has dissolved into three different forms of argumentation under the aspects of the purposive, the good, and the right? All of these forms of argument are indeed related to the wills of possible agents, but as we have seen, concepts of the will change with the type of question and answer entertained. The unity of practical reason can no longer be grounded in the unity of moral argumentation in accordance with the Kantian model of the unity of transcendental consciousness, for there is no metadiscourse on which we could fall back to justify the choice between different forms of argumentation.[14] Is the issue of whether we wish to address a given problem under the standpoint of the purposive, the good, or the just not then left to the arbitrary choice, or at best the prediscursive judgment, of the individual? Recourse to a faculty of judgment that "grasps" whether a problem is aesthetic rather than economic, theoretical rather than practical, ethical rather than moral, political rather than legal, must remain suspect for anyone who agrees that Kant had good grounds for abandoning the Aristotelian concept of judgment. In any case, it is not the faculty of reflective judgment, which subsumes particular cases under general rules, that is relevant here but an aptitude for discriminating problems into different kinds.

As Peirce and the pragmatists correctly emphasize, real problems are always rooted in something objective. The problems we confront thrust themselves upon us; they have a situation-defining power and engage our minds with their own logics. Nevertheless, if each problem followed a unique logic of its own that had nothing to do with the logic of the next problem, our minds would be led in a new direction by every new kind of problem. A practical reason that saw its unity only in the blind spot of such a reactive faculty of judgment would remain an opaque construction comprehensible only in phenomenological terms.

Moral theory must bequeath this question unanswered to the philosophy of law; the unity of practical reason can be realized in an unequivocal manner only within a network of public forms of communication and practices in which the conditions of rational collective will formation have taken on concrete institutional form.

Notes

1. Ursula Wolf, *Das Problem des moralischen Sollens* (Berlin, 1984).
2. Hans Albert, *Treatise on Critical Reason,* trans. M. V. Rorty (Princeton, NJ, 1985).
3. Charles Taylor, "The Concept of a Person," in *Philosophical Papers* (New York, 1985)1:97ff.
4. Hans-Georg Gadamer, "Hermeneutics as Practical Philosophy," in *Reason in the Age of Science*, trans. F. Lawrence (Cambridge, MA: 1982), 88ff.
5. Michael Sandel, *Liberalism and the Limits of Justice* (New York, 1982).
6. Hobbes, *De Cive,* III, 14.
7. Ernst Tugendhat, "Antike und moderne Ethik," in *Probleme der Ethik* (Stuttgart, 1984), 33ff.
8. Kant, *Foundations of the Metaphysics of Morals*, trans. L. W. Beck (New York, 1959), p. 42 [425].
9. Cf. Tullio Maranhao, *Therapeutic Discourse and Socratic Dialogue* (Madison, WI: 1986).
10. Karl-Otto Apel, "The *a priori* of the Communication Community and the Foundations of Ethics," in *Towards a Transformation of Philosophy,* trans. G. Adey and D. Frisby (London, 1980), 225ff.
11. Klaus Günther, *Der Sinn für Angemessenheit* (Frankfurt, 1988).
12. Ernst Tugendhat, *Probleme der Ethik* (Stuttgart, 1984), 87ff.
13. Here I part company with Karl-Otto Apel and his "principle of complementarity"; see also Jürgen Habermas, "Volkssouveränität als Verfahren," in Forum für Philosophie (ed.), *Die Ideen von 1798 in der deutschen Rezeption* (Frankfurt, 1989), 7–36.
14. This objection is raised by Martin Seel in *Die Kunst der Entzweiung* (Frankfurt, 1976).

Part 4

POSTMODERNISM

15

GEORGES BATAILLE
(1897–1962)

The essayist, art critic, and novelist Georges Bataille was born in Billon, central France, in 1897. He served in the army in 1916 and 1917, but was discharged because of tuberculosis, an illness that was to plague him, along with recurrent bouts of depression, for the rest of his life. In 1917, he made plans to become a priest and joined the Catholic seminary at Saint-Fleur. He lost his faith three years later, whereupon he turned his attention to the study of thirteenth-century chivalric poetry. In 1922, he became a medievalist librarian at the Bibliothèque Nationale in Paris, a position he would hold for the next twenty years. From 1923, Bataille was involved with Surrealism, until its leader, the poet André Breton, officially excommunicated him from the movement. Bataille and Breton, however, reunited in 1935 to form the group Contre-Attaque in response to the rising tide of European fascism. In 1946, Bataille founded the influential journal *Critique*, which was the first journal to publish the work of Maurice Blanchot, Roland Barthes, Michel Foucault, and Jacques Derrida. He died in Paris in 1962.

Embracing a multiplicity of literary genres, including poetry, philosophy, fiction, and autobiography, Bataille's work displays an obsessive concern with the themes of excess, excrement, torture, religion, sacrifice, transgression, and eroticism. An antihumanist *par excellence*, he rejected traditional philosophical notions of subjectivity while attempting to think the means—sexual, violent, intellectual, artistic, religious—by which the rational individual risks "annihilation" in a transcendental act of communion with the "other." In *The Story of the Eye* (1928), *Blue of Noon* (1945), *The Abbot C* (1950), *Eroticism* (1957), and *The Accursed Share* (vol. 2, published posthumously in 1976), this transgression is located in the sexual union, which causes a momentary dissolution of identity between otherwise distinct individuals and opens the prospect of a continuity or "communication" between life and death. Bataille was heavily influenced by Nietzsche (see *On Nietzsche* [1945]), and, with Pierre Klossowski, helped introduce the "new" Nietzsche, untainted by the crude falsifications of the Nazis, to France. Bataille became a major influence on postmodernist thinkers such as Foucault, Deleuze, Derrida, and Kristeva, though he was criticized by Jean-Paul Sartre, who branded him the "new mystic."

The featured essay called "The Notion of Expenditure" (1933) is one of Bataille's earliest and clearest attempts to insert such heterogeneous elements as political economy, Marxism, sacrifice, and religion into a *general economy* (as he will later call it), governed by *surplus* rather than lack (see *The Accursed Share*,vol. 1 [1949]). Drawing on the anthropology of Marcel Mauss and his influential essay "The Gift" (1925), Bataille seeks to show how the "principle of loss" or "unconditioned expenditure" provides the impetus behind much of human behavior in its search for "the sacred." Human society has what Bataille calls "an *interest* in considerable losses, in catastrophes that, *while conforming to well-defined needs*, provoke tumultuous depressions, crises of dread, and, in the final analysis, a certain orgiastic state." This interest is represented in the complex *potlatch* ceremonies of American Indians as well as in the cultic sacrifice of human beings and animals, the lavish contributions made to the Church and monasteries in the Middle Ages, the desire for expensive jewelry, the financing of grand pastimes and sports, and the production of nonutilitarian art. However, it is the modern workers' revolutionary class struggle, waged against a parsimonious and largely rational capitalist bourgeoisie, that signifies for Bataille "the grandest form of social expenditure."

Select Bibliography of Bataille's Works in English

The Accursed Share: An Essay on General Economy (3 volumes in 2 books). Trans. Robert Hurley. New York: Zone Books, 1988–1991.

The Bataille Reader. Ed. Fred Botting and Scott Wilson. Oxford: Blackwell Publishers, 1997.

Eroticism: Death and Sensuality. Trans. Mary Dalwood. San Francisco: City Lights Books, 1986.

The Impossible. Trans. Robert Hurley. San Francisco: City Lights Books, 1991.

Inner Experience. Trans. Leslie Anne Boldt. Albany, NY: State University of New York, 1988.

Literature and Evil. Trans. Alastair Hamilton. New York: M. Boyars, 1985.

On Nietzsche. Trans. Bruce Boone. New York: Paragon House, 1992.

Story of the Eye. Trans. Joachim Neugroschel. San Francisco: City Lights Books, 1987.

Theory of Religion. Trans. Robert Hurley. New York: Zone Books, 1989.

Visions of Excess: Selected Writings, 1927–1939. Trans. Allan Stoekl, with Carl R. Lovitt, and Donald M. Leslie, Jr. Minneapolis, MN: University of Minnesota Press, 1986.

THE NOTION OF EXPENDITURE

I. The Insufficiency of the Principle of Classical Utility

Every time the meaning of a discussion depends on the fundamental value of the word *useful*—in other words, every time the essential question touching on the life of human societies is raised, no matter who intervenes and what opinions are expressed—it is possible to affirm that the debate is necessarily warped and that the fundamental question is eluded. In fact, given the more or less divergent collection of present ideas, there is nothing that permits one to define what is useful to man. This lacuna is made fairly prominent by the fact that it is constantly necessary to return, in the most unjustifiable way, to principles that one would like to situate beyond utility and pleasure: *honor* and *duty* are hypocritically employed in schemes of pecuniary interest and, without speaking of God, *Spirit* serves to mask the intellectual disarray of the few people who refuse to accept a closed system.

Current practice, however, is not deterred by these elementary difficulties, and common awareness at first seems able to raise only verbal objections to the principles of classical utility—in other words, to supposedly material utility. The goal of the latter is, theoretically, pleasure—but only in a moderate form, since violent pleasure is seen as *pathological*. On the one hand, this material utility is limited to acquisition (in practice, to production) and to the conservation of goods; on the other, it is limited to reproduction and to the conservation of human life (to which is added, it is true, the struggle against pain, whose importance itself suffices to indicate the negative character of the pleasure principle instituted, in theory, as the basis of utility). In the series of quantitative representations linked to this flat and untenable conception of existence only the question of reproduction seriously lends itself to controversy, because an exaggerated increase in the number of the living threatens to diminish the individual share. But on the whole, any general judgment of social activity implies the principle that all individual effort, in order to be valid, must be reducible to the fundamental necessities of production and conservation. Pleasure, whether art, permissible debauchery, or play, is definitively reduced, in the intellectual representations *in circulation*, to a concession; in other words it is reduced to a diversion whose role is subsidiary. The most appreciable share of life is given as the condition—sometimes even as the regrettable condition—of productive social activity.

It is true that personal experience—if it is a question of a youthful man, capable of wasting and destroying without reason—each time gives the lie to this miserable conception. But even when he does not spare himself and destroys himself while making allowance for nothing, the most lucid man will understand nothing, or imagine himself sick; he is incapable of a *utilitarian* justification for his actions, and it does not occur to him that a human society can have, just as he does, an *interest* in considerable losses, in catastrophes that, *while conforming to well-defined needs*, provoke tumultuous depressions, crises of dread, and, in the final analysis, a certain orgiastic state.

In the most crushing way, the contradiction between current social conceptions and the real needs of society recalls the narrowness of judgment that puts the father in opposition to the satisfaction of his son's needs. This narrowness is such that it is impossible for the son to express his will. The father's partially malevolent solicitude is manifested in the things he provides for his son: lodgings, clothes, food, and, when absolutely necessary, a little harmless recreation. But the son does not even have the right to speak about what really gives him a fever; he is obliged to give people the impression that for him no *horror* can enter into consideration. In this respect, it is sad to say that *conscious humanity has remained a minor*; humanity recognizes the right to acquire, to conserve, and to consume rationally, but it excludes in principle *nonproductive expenditure*.

It is true that this exclusion is superficial and that it no more modifies practical activities than prohibitions limit the son, who indulges in his unavowed pleasures as soon as he is no longer in his father's presence. Humanity can allow itself the pleasure of expressing, in the father's interest, conceptions marked with flat paternal sufficiency and blindness. In the practice of life, however, humanity acts in a way that allows for the satisfaction of disarmingly savage needs, and it seems able to subsist only at the limits of horror. Moreover, to the small extent that a man is incapable of yielding to considerations that either are official or are susceptible of becoming so, to the small extent that he is inclined to feel the attraction of a life devoted to the destruction of established authority, it is difficult to believe that a peaceful world, conforming to his interests, could be for him anything other than a convenient illusion.

The difficulties met with in the development of a conception that is not guided by the servile mode of father-son relations are thus not insurmountable. It is possible to admit the historical necessity of vague and disappointing images, used by a majority of people, who do not act without a minimum of error (which they use as if it were a drug)—and who, moreover, in all circumstances refuse to find their way in a labyrinth resulting from human inconsistencies. An extreme simplification represents, for the uncultivated or barely cultivated segments of the population, the only chance to avoid a diminution of aggressive force. But it would be cowardly to accept, as a limit to understanding, the conditions of poverty and necessity in which such simplified images are formed. And if a less arbitrary conception is condemned to remain esoteric, and if as such, in the present circumstances, it comes into conflict with an unhealthy repulsion, then one must stress that this repulsion is precisely the shame of a generation whose rebels are afraid of the noise of their own words. Thus one cannot take it into account.

II. The Principle of Loss

Human activity is not entirely reducible to processes of production and conservation, and consumption must be divided into two distinct parts. The first, reducible part is represented by the use of the minimum necessary for the conservation of life and the continuation of individuals' productive activity in a given society; it is therefore a question simply of the fundamental condition of productive activity. The second part is represented by so-called unproductive expenditures: luxury, mourning, war, cults, the construction of sumptuary monuments, games, spectacles, arts, perverse sexual activity (i.e., deflected from genital finality)—all these represent activities which, at least in primitive circumstances, have no end beyond themselves. Now it is necessary to reserve the use of the word *expenditure* for the designation of these unproductive forms, and not for the designation of all the modes of consumption that serve as a means to the end of production. Even though it is always possible to set the various forms of expenditure in opposition to each other, they constitute a group characterized by the fact that in each case the accent is placed on a *loss* that must be as great as possible in order for that activity to take on its true meaning.

This principle of loss, in other words, of unconditional expenditure, no matter how contrary it might be to the economic principle of balanced accounts (expenditure regularly compensated for by acquisition), only *rational* in the narrow sense of the word, can be illustrated through a small number of examples taken from common experience:

1. Jewels must not only be beautiful and dazzling (which would make the substitution of imitations possible): one sacrifices a fortune, preferring a diamond necklace; such a sacrifice is necessary for the constitution of this necklace's fascinating character. This fact must be seen in relation to the symbolic value of jewels, universal in psychoanalysis. When in a dream a diamond signifies excrement, it is not only a question of association by contrast; in the unconscious, jewels, like excrement, are cursed matter that flows from a wound: they are a part of oneself destined for open sacrifice (they serve, in fact, as sumptuous gifts charged with sexual love). The functional character of jewels requires their immense material value and alone explains the inconsequence of the most beautiful imitations, which are very nearly useless.

2. Cults require a bloody wasting of men and animals in *sacrifice*. In the etymological sense of the word, sacrifice is nothing other than the production of *sacred* things.

From the very first, it appears that sacred things are constituted by an operation of loss: in particular, the success of Christianity must be explained by the value of the theme of the Son of God's ignominious crucifixion, which carries human dread to a representation of loss and limitless degradation.

3. In various competitive games, loss in general is produced under complex conditions. Considerable sums of money are spent for the maintenance of quarters, animals, equipment, or men. As much energy as possible is squandered in order to produce a feeling of stupefaction—in any case with an intensity infinitely greater than in productive enterprises. The danger of death is not avoided; on the contrary, it is the object of a strong unconscious attraction. Besides, competitions are sometimes the occasion for the public distribution of prizes. Immense crowds are present; their passions most often burst forth beyond any restraint, and the loss of insane sums of money is set in motion in the form of wagers. It is true that this circulation of money profits a small number of professional bettors, but it is no less true that this circulation can be considered to be a real *charge* of the passions unleashed by competition and that, among a large number of bettors, it leads to losses disproportionate to their means; these even attain such a level of madness that often the only way out for gamblers is prison or death. Beyond this, various modes of unproductive expenditure can be linked, depending on the circumstances, to great competitive spectacles, just as elements moving separately are caught up in a mightier whirlwind. Thus horse races are associated with a sumptuary process of social classification (the existence of Jockey Clubs need only be mentioned) and the ostentatious display of the latest luxurious fashions. It is necessary in any case to observe that the complex of expenditure represented by present-day racing is insignificant when compared to the extravagance of the Byzantines, who tied the totality of their public activity to equestrian competition.

4. From the point of view of expenditure, artistic productions must be divided into two main categories, the first constituted by architectural construction, music, and dance. This category is comprised of *real* expenditures. Nevertheless, sculpture and painting, not to mention the use of sites for ceremonies and spectacles, introduce even into architecture the principle of the second category, that of *symbolic* expenditure. For their part, music and dance can easily be charged with external significations.

In their major form, literature and theater, which constitute the second category, provoke dread and horror through symbolic representations of tragic loss (degradation or death); in their minor form, they provoke laughter through representations which, though analogously structured, exclude certain seductive elements. The term poetry, applied to the least degraded and least intellectualized forms of the expression of a state of loss, can be considered synonymous with expenditure; it in fact signifies, in the most precise way, creation by means of loss. Its meaning is therefore close to that of *sacrifice*. It is true that the word "poetry" can only be appropriately applied to an extremely rare residue of what it commonly signifies and that, without a preliminary reduction, the worst confusions could result; it is, however, impossible in a first, rapid exposition to speak of the infinitely variable limits separating subsidiary formations from the residual element of poetry. It is easier to indicate that, for the rare human beings who have this element at their disposal, poetic expenditure ceases to be symbolic in its consequences; thus, to a certain extent, the function of representation engages the very life of the one who assumes it. It condemns him to the most disappointing forms of activity, to misery, to despair, to the pursuit of inconsistent shadows that provide nothing but vertigo or rage. The poet frequently can use words only for his own loss; he is often forced to choose between the destiny of a reprobate, who is as profoundly separated from society as dejecta are from apparent life, and a renunciation whose price is a mediocre activity, subordinated to vulgar and superficial needs.

III. Production, Exchange, and Unproductive Activity

Once the existence of expenditure as a social function has been established, it is then necessary to consider the relations between this function and those of production and acquisition that are opposed to it. These relations immediately present themselves as those of an *end* with *utility*. And if it is true that production and acquisition in their development and changes of form introduce a variable that must be understood in order to comprehend historical processes, they are, however, still only means subordinated to expenditure. As dreadful as it is, human poverty has never had a strong enough hold on societies to cause the concern for conservation—which gives production the appearance of an end—to dominate the concern for unproductive expenditure. In order to maintain this preeminence, since power is exercised by the classes that expend, poverty was excluded from all social activity. And the poor have no other way of reentering the circle of power than through the revolutionary destruction of the classes occupying that circle—in other words, through a bloody and in no way limited social expenditure.

The secondary character of production and acquisition in relation to expenditure appears most clearly in primitive economic institutions, since exchange is still treated as a sumptuary loss of ceded objects: thus at its *base* exchange presents itself as a process of expenditure, over which a process of acquisition has developed. Classical economics imagined that primitive exchange occurred in the form of barter; it had no reason to assume, in fact, that a means of acquisition such as exchange might have as its origin not the need to acquire that it satisfies today, but the contrary need, the need to destroy and to lose. The traditional conceptions of the origins of economy have only recently been disproved—even so recently that a great number of economists continue arbitrarily to represent barter as the ancestor of commerce.

In opposition to the artificial notion of barter, the archaic form of exchange has been identified by Mauss under the name *potlatch*,[1] borrowed from the Northwestern American Indians who provided such a remarkable example of it. Institutions analogous to the Indian *potlatch*, or their traces, have been very widely found.

The *potlatch* of the Tlingit, the Haida, the Tsimshian, and the Kwakiutl of the northwestern coast has been studied in detail since the end of the nineteenth century (but at that time it was not compared with the archaic forms of exchange of other countries). The least advanced of these American tribes practice *potlatch* on the occasion of a person's change in situation—initiations, marriages, funerals—and, even in a more evolved form, it can never be separated from a festival; whether it provides the occasion for this festival, or whether it takes place on the festival's occasion. *Potlatch* excludes all bargaining and, in general, it is constituted by a considerable gift of riches, offered openly and with the goal of humiliating, defying, and *obligating* a rival. The exchange value of the gift results from the fact that the donee, in order to efface the humiliation and respond to the challenge, must satisfy the obligation (incurred by him at the time of acceptance) to respond later with a more valuable gift, in other words, to return with interest.

But the gift is not the only form of *potlatch*; it is equally possible to defy rivals through the spectacular destruction of wealth. It is through the intermediary of this last form that *potlatch* is reunited with religious sacrifice, since what is destroyed is theoretically offered to the mythical ancestors of the donees. Relatively recently a Tlingit chief appeared before his rival to slash the throats of some of his own slaves. This destruction was repaid at a given date by the slaughter of a greater number of slaves. The Tchoukchi of far northwestern Siberia, who have institutions analogous to *potlatch*, slaughter dog teams in order to stifle and humiliate another group. In northwestern America, destruction goes as far as the burning of villages and the smashing of flotillas of canoes. Emblazoned copper ingots, a kind of money on which the fictive value of an immense fortune is sometimes placed, are broken or thrown into the sea. The delirium of the festival can be associated equally with hecatombs of property and with gifts accumulated with the intention of stunning and humiliating.

Usury, which regularly appears in these operations as obligatory surplus at the time of the returned *potlatch*, gives rise to the observation that the loan with interest must be substituted for barter in the history of the origins of exchange. It must be recognized, in fact, that wealth is multiplied in *potlatch* civilizations in a way that recalls the inflation of credit in banking civilizations; in other words, it would be impossible to realize at once all the wealth possessed by the total number of donors resulting from the obligations contracted by the total number of donees. But this comparison applies only to a secondary characteristic of *potlatch*.

It is the constitution of a positive property of loss—from which spring nobility, honor, and rank in a hierarchy—that gives the institution its significant value. The gift must be considered as a loss and thus as a partial destruction, since the desire to destroy is in part transferred onto the recipient. In unconscious forms, such as those described by psychoanalysis, it symbolizes excretion, which itself is linked to death, in conformity with the fundamental connection between anal eroticism and sadism. The excremental symbolism of emblazoned coppers, which on the Northwest Coast are the gift objects *par excellence*, is based on a very rich mythology. In Melanesia, the donor designates as his excrement magnificent gifts, which he deposits at the feet of the rival chief.

The consequences in the realm of acquisition are only the unwanted result—at least to the extent that the drives that govern the operation have remained primitive—of a process oriented in the opposite direction. "The ideal," indicates Mauss, "would be to give a *potlatch* and not have it returned." This ideal is realized in certain forms of destruction to which custom allows no possible response. Moreover, since the yields of *potlatch* are in some ways pledged in advance in a new *potlatch*, the archaic principle of wealth is displayed with none of the attenuations that result from the avarice developed at later stages; wealth appears as an acquisition to the extent that power is acquired by a rich man, but it is entirely directed toward loss in the sense that this power is characterized as power to lose. It is only through loss that glory and honor are linked to wealth.

As a game, *potlatch* is the opposite of a principle of conservation: it puts an end to the stability of fortunes as it existed within the totemic economy, where possession was hereditary. An activity of excessive exchange replaced heredity (as source of possession) with a kind of deliriously formed ritual poker. But the players can never retire from the game, their fortunes made; they remain at the mercy of provocation. At no time does a fortune serve to *shelter its owner from need*. On the contrary, it functionally remains—as does its possessor—*at the mercy of a need for limitless loss*, which exists endemically in a social group.

The nonsumptuary production and consumption upon which wealth depends thus appear as relative utility.

IV. The Functional Expenditure of the Wealthy Classes

The notion of *potlatch*, strictly speaking, should be reserved for expenditures of an agonistic type, which are instigated by challenges and which lead to responses. More precisely, it should be reserved for forms which, for archaic societies, are not distinguishable from *exchange*.

It is important to know that exchange, at its origin, was *immediately* subordinated to a human *end*; nevertheless it is evident that its development, linked to progress in the modes of production, only started at the stage at which this subordination ceased to be immediate. The very principle of the function of production requires that products be exempt from loss, at least provisionally.

In the market economy, the processes of exchange have an acquisitive sense. Fortunes are no longer placed on a gambling table; they have become relatively stable. It is only to the extent that stability is assured and can no longer be compromised by even considerable losses that these losses are submitted to the regime of unproductive expenditure. Under these new conditions, the elementary components of *potlatch* are found in forms that are no longer as directly agonistic.[2] Expenditure is still destined to acquire or maintain rank, but in principle it no longer has the goal of causing another to lose his rank.

In spite of these attenuations, ostentatious loss remains universally linked to wealth, as its ultimate function.

More or less narrowly, social rank is linked to the possession of a fortune, but only on the condition that the fortune be partially sacrificed in unproductive social expenditures such as festivals, spectacles, and games. One notes that in primitive societies, where the exploitation of man by man is still fairly weak, the products of human activity not only flow in great quantities to rich men because of the protection or social leadership services these men supposedly provide, but also because of the spectacular collective expenditures for which they must pay. In so-called civilized societies, the fundamental *obligation* of wealth disappeared only in a fairly recent period. The decline of paganism led to a decline of the games and cults for which wealthy Romans were obliged to pay; thus it has been said that Christianity individualized property, giving its possessor total control over his products and abrogating his social function. It abrogated at least the obligation of this expenditure, for Christianity replaced pagan expenditure prescribed by custom with voluntary alms, either in the form of distributions from the rich to the poor, or (and above all) in the form of extremely significant contributions to churches and later to monasteries. And these churches and monasteries precisely assumed, in the Middle Ages, the major part of the spectacular function.

Today the great and free forms of unproductive social expenditure have disappeared. One must not conclude from this, however, that the very principle of expenditure is no longer the end of economic activity.

A certain evolution of wealth, whose symptoms indicate sickness and exhaustion, leads to shame in oneself accompanied by petty hypocrisy. Everything that was generous, orgiastic, and excessive has disappeared; the themes of rivalry upon which individual activity still depends develop in obscurity, and are as shameful as belching. The representatives of the bourgeoisie have adopted an effaced manner; wealth is now displayed behind closed doors, in accordance with depressing and boring conventions. In addition, people in the middle class—employees and small shopkeepers—having attained mediocre or minute fortunes, have managed to debase and subdivide ostentatious expenditure, of which nothing remains but vain efforts tied to tiresome rancor.

Such trickery has become the principal reason for living, working, and suffering for those who lack the courage to condemn this moldy society to revolutionary destruction. Around modern banks, as around the totem poles of the Kwakiutl, the same desire to dazzle animates individuals and leads them into a system of petty displays that blinds them to each other, as if they were staring into a blinding light. A few steps from the bank, jewels, dresses, and cars wait behind shop windows for the day when they will serve to establish the augmented splendor of a sinister industrialist and his even more sinister old wife. At a lower level, gilded clocks, dining room buffets, and artificial flowers render equally shameful service to a grocer and his wife. Jealousy arises between human beings, as it does among the savages, and with an equivalent brutality; only generosity and nobility have disappeared, and with them the dazzling contrast that the rich provided to the poor.

As the class that possesses the wealth—having received with wealth the obligation of functional expenditure—the modern bourgeoisie is characterized by the refusal in principle of this obligation. It has distinguished itself from the aristocracy through the fact that it has consented only to *spend for itself*, and within itself—in other words, by hiding its expenditures as much as possible from the eyes of the other classes. This particular form was originally due to the development of its wealth in the shadow of a more powerful noble class. The rationalist conceptions developed by the bourgeoisie, starting in the seventeenth century, were a response to these humiliating conceptions of restrained expenditure; this rationalism meant nothing other than the strictly economic representation of the world—economic in the vulgar sense, the bourgeois sense, of the word. The hatred of expenditure is the *raison d'être* of and the justification for the bourgeoisie; it is at the same time the principle of its horrifying hypocrisy. A fundamental grievance of the bourgeois was the prodigality of feudal society and, after coming to power, they believed that, because of their habits of accumulation, they were capable of acceptably dominating the poorer classes. And it is right to recognize that the people are incapable of hating them as much as their former masters, to the extent that they are incapable of loving them, for the bourgeois are incapable of concealing a sordid face, a face so rapacious and lacking in nobility, so frighteningly small, that all human life, upon seeing it, seems degraded.

In opposition, the people's consciousness is reduced to maintaining profoundly the principle of expenditure by representing bourgeois existence as the shame of man and as a sinister cancellation.

V. Class Struggle

In trying to maintain sterility in regard to expenditure, in conformity with a reasoning that balances *accounts*, bourgeois society has only managed to develop a universal meanness. Human life only rediscovers agitation on the scale of irreducible needs through the efforts of those who push the consequences of current rationalist conceptions as far as they will go. What remains of the traditional modes of expenditure has become atrophied, and living sumptuary tumult has been lost in the unprecedented explosion of *class struggle*.

The components of *class struggle* are seen in the process of expenditure, dating back to the archaic period. In *potlatch,* the rich man distributes products furnished him by other, impoverished, men. He tries to rise above a rival who is rich like himself, but the ultimate stage of his foreseen elevation has no more necessary a goal than his further separation from the nature of destitute men. Thus expenditure, even though it might be a social function, immediately leads to an agonistic and apparently antisocial act of separation. The rich man consumes the poor man's losses, creating for him a category of degradation and abjection that leads to slavery. Now it is evident that, from the endlessly transmitted heritage of the sumptuary world, the modern world has received slavery, and has reserved it for the proletariat. Without a doubt bourgeois society, which pretends to govern according to rational principles, and which, through its own actions, moreover, tends to realize a certain human homogeneity, does not accept without protest a division that seems destructive to man himself; it is incapable, however, of pushing this resistance further than theoretical negation. It gives the workers rights equal to those of the masters, and it announces this *equality* by inscribing that word on walls. But the masters, who act as if they were the expression of society itself, are preoccupied—more seriously than with any other concern—with showing that they do not in any way share the abjection of the men they employ. *The end of the workers' activity is to produce in order to live, but the bosses' activity is to produce in order to condemn the working producers to a hideous degradation*—for there is no disjunction possible between, on the one hand, the characterization the bosses seek through their modes of expenditure, which tend to elevate them high above human baseness, and on the other hand this baseness itself, of which this characterization is a function.

In opposition to this conception of agonistic social expenditure, there is the representation of numerous bourgeois efforts to ameliorate the lot of the workers—but this representation is only the expression of the cowardice of the modern upper classes, who no longer have the force to recognize the results of their own destructive acts. The expenditures taken on by the capitalists in order to aid the proletarians and give them a chance to pull themselves up on the social ladder only bear witness to their inability (due to exhaustion) to carry out thoroughly a sumptuary process. Once the loss of the poor man is accomplished, little by little the pleasure of the rich man is emptied and neutralized; it gives way to a kind of apathetic indifference. Under these conditions, in order to maintain a neutral state rendered relatively agreeable by apathy (and which exists in spite of troublesome elements such as sadism and pity), it can be useful to compensate for the expenditure that engenders abjection with a new expenditure, which tends to attenuate it. The bosses' political sense, together with certain partial developments of prosperity, has allowed this process of compensation to be, at times, quite extensive. Thus in the Anglo-Saxon countries, and in particular in the United States of America, the primary process takes place at the expense of only a relatively small portion of the population: to a certain extent, the working class itself has been led to participate in it (above all when this was facilitated by the preliminary existence of a class held to be abject by common accord, as in the case of the blacks). But these subterfuges, whose importance is in any case strictly limited, do not modify in any way the fundamental division between noble and ignoble men. The cruel game of social life does not vary among the different civilized countries, where the insulting splendor of the rich loses and degrades the human nature of the lower class.

It must be added that the attenuation of the masters' brutality—which in any case has less to do with destruction itself than with the psychological tendencies to destroy—corresponds to the general atrophy of the ancient sumptuary processes that characterizes the modern era.

Class struggle, on the contrary, becomes the grandest form of social expenditure when it is taken up again and developed, this time on the part of the workers, and on such a scale that it threatens the very existence of the masters.

VI. Christianity and Revolution

Short of revolt, it has been possible for the provoked poor to refuse all moral participation in a system in which men oppress men; in certain historical circumstances, they succeeded, through the use of symbols even more striking than reality, in lowering all of "human nature" to such a horrifying ignominy that the pleasure found by the rich in measuring the poverty of others suddenly became too acute to be endured without vertigo. Thus, independently of all ritual forms, an exchange of exasperated challenges was established, exacerbated above all by the poor, a *potlatch* in which real refuse and revealed moral filth entered into a rivalry of horrible grandeur with everything in the world that was rich, pure, and brilliant; and an exceptional outlet was found for this form of spasmodic convulsion in religious despair, which was its unreserved exploitation.

In Christianity, the alternations between the exaltation and dread, tortures and orgies constituting religious life were conjoined in a more tragic way and were merged with a sick social structure, which was tearing itself apart with the dirtiest cruelty. The triumphal song of the Christians glorifies God because he has entered into the bloody game of social war, and because he has "hurled the powerful from the heights of their grandeur and has exalted the miserably poor." Their myths associate social ignominy and the cadaverous degradation of the torture victim with divine splendor. In this way religion assumes the total oppositional function manifested by contrary forces, which up to this point had been divided between the rich and the poor, with the one group condemning the other to ruin. It is closely tied to terrestrial despair, since it itself is only an epiphenomenon of the measureless hate that divides men—but an epiphenomenon that tends to substitute itself for the totality of divergent processes it summarizes. In conformity with the words attributed to Christ, who said he came to divide and not to reign, religion thus does not at all try to do away with what others consider the scourge of man. On the contrary, in its immediate form, it wallows in a revolting impurity that is indispensable to its ecstatic torment.

The meaning of Christianity is given in the development of the delirious consequences of the expenditure of classes, in a mental agonistic orgy practiced at the expense of the real struggle.

However, in spite of the importance that it has had in human activity, Christian *humiliation* is only an episode in the historic struggle of the ignoble against the noble, of the impure against the pure. It is as if society, conscious of its own intolerable splitting, had become for a time dead drunk in order to enjoy it sadistically. But the heaviest drunkenness has not done away with the consequences of human poverty, and, with the exploited classes opposing the superior classes with greater lucidity, no conceivable limit can be assigned to hatred. In historical agitation, only the word Revolution dominates the customary confusion and carries with it the promise that answers the unlimited demands of the masses. As for the masters and the exploiters, whose function is to create the contemptuous forms that exclude human nature—causing this nature to exist at the limits of the earth, in other words in mud—a simple law of reciprocity requires that they be condemned to fear, to the great night when their beautiful phrases will be drowned out by death screams in riots. That is the bloody hope which, each day, is one with the existence of the people, and which sums up the insubordinate content of the class struggle.

Class struggle has only one possible end: the loss of those who have worked to lose "human nature."

But whatever form of development is foreseen, be it revolutionary or servile, the general convulsions constituted eighteen hundred years ago by the religious ecstasy of the Christians, and today by the workers' movement, must equally be represented as a decisive impulse *constraining* society to use the exclusion of one class by another to realize a mode of expenditure as tragic and as free as possible, and at the same time *constraining* it to introduce sacred forms so human that the traditional forms become relatively contemptible. It is the tropic character of such movements that accounts for the total human value of the workers' Revolution, a Revolution capable of exerting a force of attraction as strong as the force that directs simple organisms toward the sun.

VII. The Insubordination of Material Facts

Human life, distinct from juridical existence, existing as it does on a globe isolated in celestial space, from night to day and from one country to another—human life cannot in any way be limited to the closed systems assigned to it by reasonable conceptions. The immense travail of recklessness, discharge, and upheaval that constitutes life could be expressed by stating that life starts only with the deficit of these systems; at least what it allows in the way of order and reserve has meaning only from the moment when the ordered and reserved forces liberate and lose themselves for ends that cannot be subordinated to anything one can account for. It is only by such insubordination—even if it is impoverished—that the human race ceases to be isolated in the unconditional splendor of material things.

In fact, in the most universal way, isolated or in groups, men find themselves constantly engaged in processes of expenditure. Variations in form do not in any way alter the fundamental characteristics of these processes, whose principle is loss. A certain excitation, whose sum total is maintained at a noticeably constant level, animates collectivities and individuals. In their intensified form, the *states of excitation*, which are comparable to toxic states, can be defined as the illogical and irresistible impulse to reject material or moral goods that it would have been possible to utilize rationally (in conformity with the balancing of accounts). Connected to the losses that are realized in this way—in the case of the "lost woman" as well as in the case of military expenditure—is the creation of unproductive values; the most absurd of these values, and the one that makes people the most rapacious, is glory. Made complete through degradation, *glory*, appearing in a sometimes sinister and sometimes brilliant form, has never ceased to dominate social existence; it is impossible to attempt to do anything without it when it is dependent on the blind practice of personal or social loss.

In this way the boundless refuse of activity pushes human plans—including those associated with economic operations—into the game of characterizing universal matter; matter, in fact, can only be defined as the *nonlogical difference* that represents in relation to the *economy* of the universe what *crime* represents in relation to the law. The glory that sums up or symbolizes (without exhausting) the object of free expenditure, while it can never exclude crime, cannot be distinguished—at least if one takes into account the only characterization that has a value comparable to matter—from the *insubordinate characterization*, which is not the condition for anything else.

If in addition one demonstrates the interest, concurrent with glory (as well as with degradation), which the human community necessarily sees in the qualitative change constantly realized by the movement of history, and if, finally, one demonstrates that this movement is impossible to contain or direct toward a limited end, it becomes possible, having abandoned all reserves, to assign a *relative* value to utility. Men assure their own subsistence or avoid suffering, not because these functions themselves lead to a sufficient result, but in order to accede to the insubordinate function of free expenditure.

Notes

1. On *potlatch*, see above all Marcel Mauss, "Essai sur le don, form archaïque de l'échange" in *Année sociologique*, 1925. [Translated as *The Gift: Forms and Functions of Exchange in Archaic Societies*, trans. I. Cunnison (New York: Norton, 1967). Tr.]
2. In other words, involving rivalry and struggle.

16

EMMANUEL LEVINAS
(1906–1995)

(See Chapter 5 for a biographical sketch and bibliography of Levinas.) Our second essay by Emmanuel Levinas is "Substitution." The essay was presented as a lecture in 1967 before being revised for publication the following year. It was further modified in 1974 to become the "centerpiece" of Levinas's second great work, *Otherwise Than Being or Beyond Essence*.

At the end of his short autobiography "Signature" (1976), Levinas wrote:

> The ontological language which *Totality and Infinity* [1961] still uses in order to exclude the purely psychological significance of the proposed analyses is hereafter avoided. And the analyses themselves refer not to the *experience* in which the subject always thematizes what he equals, but to the *transcendence* in which he answers for that which his intentions have not encompassed. (*Difficult Freedom*, 295)

"Substitution" is a clear example of Levinas's attempt to avoid the earlier "ontological language" of *Totality and Infinity*. Here we encounter terms such as "obsession," "hostage," "persecution," and "proximity" that compose the "ethical language" of his later thought. According to Levinas, ethical language derives from "nonphilosophical experiences" that cannot be reduced to consciousness and thematization and are "beyond" phenomenological description. Levinas is acutely aware of the contradiction involved in making what allegedly cannot be thematized the theme of his discussion! The problem of speaking about the identity of the Ego (or self) in relationship with the Other while calling into question the philosophical concept of identity itself is acknowledged in a note to the essay. There he tells us that the "enigma" of ethics can never present itself within discourse as an *arche* (from Greek, meaning "beginning" or "rule") that unites the terms of the discussion under the sovereign order of Being, but signifies "an-archically" as the "trace" of the Other's transcendence. The trace, which plays a role in Levinas's later thought similar to that of "the face" in his earlier work, features within philosophical discourse as a contradiction, as evidenced by the expression, "passivity more passive than all passivity." The idea of radical passivity is repeatedly invoked by Levinas in the following essay to refer to the situation of the self who is under obligation to the Other prior to freedom and consciousness, but who is not mechanically or psychically determined all the same.

The underlying claim of the essay is that the self does not enter into relationship with the Other already constituted as such (as was perhaps claimed in *Totality and Infinity*), but attains its identity only *through* the relationship with the Other. Thus I am unique and irreplaceable only insofar as I am "one-for-the-other," which amounts to putting myself in the place of the Other and shouldering his or her responsibility. This painful situation of taking the place of the Other is what Levinas calls "substitution."

SUBSTITUTION

1. Principle and Anarchy

In the relationship with beings which is called consciousness, we identify these beings through the dispersion of "adumbrations" in which they appear.[1] Similarly, in self-consciousness, we identify ourselves through a multiplicity of temporal phases. It is as though subjective life, in the form of consciousness, involved being's losing and rediscovering itself, so as *to possess itself* by showing itself, proposing itself as a *theme*, exposing itself in the truth. This identification is not the counterpart of any image. It is a *claim* of the mind, proclamation, saying, kerygma. It is by no means arbitrary, however, resting as it does on a mysterious operation of schematism,[2] through which an ideality corresponds with the dispersion of aspects and images, adumbrations or phases. Consciousness is therefore always the grasping of a being through an ideality. Even an empirical, individual being appears through the ideality of the logos. Subjectivity as consciousness is thus interpreted as an ontological event, namely, the rediscovery of being on the basis of an ideal principle or *arche* in its thematic exposition. The detour of ideality leads to a coinciding with oneself, that is, to the certainty which remains the guide and guarantee of the whole spiritual adventure of Being. That is why the "adventure" is not exactly an adventure. It is never dangerous. It is always a self-possession, sovereignty, *arche*. What arrives of the *unknown* is already disclosed, open, manifest, cast in the mold of the *known*, and can never come as a complete surprise. For the Western philosophical tradition, all spirituality is consciousness, the thematic exposition of Being, that is to say, knowledge.

In starting with *touching*, interpreted not as palpation but as caress, and *language*, interpreted not as the traffic of information but as contact, we have tried to describe *proximity* as irreducible to consciousness and thematization.[3] Proximity is a relationship with what cannot be resolved into "images" and exposed. It is a relationship not with what is inordinate with respect to a theme but with what is incommensurable with it; with what cannot be identified in the kerygmatic logos, frustrating any schematism.

Incapable of remaining in a theme and of appearing, this invisibility that becomes contact does not result from the nonsignifyingness of what is approached but rather from a way of signifying wholly other than that of exhibition from a *beyond* of the visible. Not that the "beyond" would be "further" than everything that appears, or "present in absence," or revealed by a symbol, which would again be to submit to a principle and to give oneself to consciousness. Here what is essential lies in the refusal to let oneself be domesticated or subdued by a theme. The "beyond" loses its proper signifyingness and becomes immanence as soon as the logos interrogates, invests, presents, and exposes it, although its attachment in proximity is absolute exteriority. Without any common measure with the present, proximity is always "already past," above the "now" which it troubles and obsesses. This way of passing, troubling the present, without allowing itself to be invested by the *arche* of consciousness, this

178

striation of rays across the clarity or the exposable, we have called "trace."[4] *Anarchically*, proximity is a relationship with a singularity, without the mediation of any principle or ideality. In the concrete, it describes my relationship with the neighbor, a relationship whose signifyingness is prior to the celebrated "sense bestowing." This incommensurability with regard to consciousness, emerging as a trace from *I know not where*, is neither the inoffensive relation of knowledge where everything is equivalent nor the indifference of spatial contiguity. It is the summoning of myself by the other (*autrui*), it is a responsibility toward those whom we do not even know. The relation of proximity does not amount to any modality of distance or geometrical contiguity, nor to the simple "representation" of the neighbor. It is *already* a summons of extreme exigency, an obligation which is *anachronistically* prior to every engagement. An anteriority that is older than the *a priori*. This formulation expresses a way of being affected that can in no way be invested by spontaneity: the subject is affected without the source of the affection becoming a theme of re-presentation. The term *obsession* designates this relation which is irreducible to consciousness.

Irreducible to consciousness, even if this relation overturns consciousness and manifests itself there—obsession traverses consciousness contrariwise, inscribing itself there as something foreign, as disequilibrium, as delirium, undoing thematization, eluding *principle*, origin, and will, all of which are affirmed in every gleam of consciousness. This movement is, in the original sense of the term, anarchic. In no way, then, is obsession to be confused with a hypertrophy of consciousness.

An-archy is not a matter of disorder as opposed to order, just as the withdrawal from a theme is not a putative return to a diffuse "field of consciousness" awaiting attention. Disorder is but another order, and the diffuse can possibly be thematized.[5] Anarchy troubles being beyond these alternatives. It halts the ontological play, which, precisely as play, is consciousness in which being loses and rediscovers itself and is thereby lit up. Anachronistically *lagging* behind its present, incapable of recovering this lag and of thinking what touches it,[6] the Ego is evinced in the ascendancy of the Other over the Same to the point of interruption, leaving it speechless: an-archic, obsession is persecution. Here persecution does not amount to consciousness gone mad; it designates the manner in which the Ego is affected and a defection from consciousness. This inversion of consciousness is without doubt a passivity, but a passivity this side of all passivity, defined in terms totally different from those of intentionality, where *submission* is always also an *assuming*, that is, an experience always forestalled and sanctioned, attached once more to an origin. The intentionality of consciousness certainly does not refer solely to a voluntary intention. And yet it does retain the initiating and inchoate motif of a voluntary intention. Thought recognizes and invests its very project in the given which enters it. The given manifests itself *a priori*—from the first, it re-presents itself—but it does not knock at the door unannounced, allowing, across the interval of space and time, the leisure necessary for welcome. The *for itself* is thus the power that a being exercises over itself, its will and sovereignty, where it is equal to itself and in possession of itself. Domination is within consciousness as such and Hegel thought that the *I* is simply consciousness mastering itself in equality with itself, what he called "the freedom of this infinite equality."

The obsession we have recognized in proximity contrasts strongly with this view of a being possessing itself in equality with itself. How can the passivity of obsession find a place in consciousness, where everything is intentionally assumed? Consciousness is total freedom, or is ultimately that; and it is total equality, equality of self with self, but also equality to the extent that, for consciousness, responsibility is always strictly measured in terms of freedom, and thus always limited. How can there be in consciousness an undergoing, or a Passion, whose "active" source would not in any way fall into consciousness? It is important to stress this exteriority, which is neither objective nor spatial. Irrecuperable in immanence, and thus outside the order (or command) of consciousness, exteriority is obsessional, nonthematizable, and, in the sense defined above, an-archic. We might go so far as to say "extra-ordinary."

It is in a *responsibility that is justified by no prior commitment*—in the responsibility for the other (*autrui*)—an ethical situation, that the me-ontological and meta-logical structure of this Anarchy is outlined, undoing the logos framing the apology through which consciousness still recovers itself and commands. This Passion is absolute in that it takes hold without any *a priori*. Consciousness is thus afflicted before entertaining an image of what reaches it, afflicted in spite of itself. Under these characteristics, we recognize persecution, a placing in question anterior to questioning, a responsibility beyond the logos of the response, as though persecution by the other (*autrui*) were the basis of solidarity with the other (*autrui*). How can such a Passion[7] have a place and time in consciousness?

2. Recurrence and the Hither Side

Does consciousness exhaust the notion of subjectivity? Is there not a condition in the Ego that is still tacitly reduced to consciousness? Does the Ego coincide with the *for itself* of consciousness? We have long since treated subjectivity and consciousness as equivalent concepts, without interrogating the dimension masked by the controversial notion of soul. We must ask ourselves whether the notion of the Ego can be reduced to the *for itself* of consciousness.

But to speak of the hither side of consciousness is not to turn toward the unconscious. The unconscious, in its clandestinity, rehearses the game played out in consciousness,[8] namely, the search for meaning and truth as the search for the self. While this opening onto the self is certainly occluded and repressed, psychoanalysis still manages to break through and restore self-consciousness. It follows that our study will not be following the way of the unconscious.

The reduction of subjectivity to consciousness dominates philosophical thought, which, since Hegel, has striven to overcome the dualism of being and thought by identifying, under different forms, substance, and subject. Philosophy itself would be the ongoing and progressive disclosure of Being to itself. Consequently, disclosure is not annexed to the being of beings, to *essence* (if the term *essence* may be used in italics as an abstract noun of action[9] for the "being of beings"), but is constitutive of this *essence* as a perpetual vigilance and self-possession. The philosophy that proposes an ontology consummates this *essence* through this proposition, through the logos, whence the idea of consciousness fulfilling the very being of beings.

The disclosure of being to itself involves a *recurrence*, which poses a problem. *Essence* is drawn out like a colorless thread woven from the distaff of the Parcae. For there to be a return, must not the knot of ipseity be tied at some point? Were this not so, *essence* would continually elude itself, stretching out like a destiny. How can a jolt, an expulsion outside of the Same, an awakening and tracking down of the Same, the very play of *consciousness*, occur in the stretching out of *essence*? How can this distance with regard *to the self* and nostalgia of the self or retention of the self, according to which every present is a re-presentation, be produced? Must not all the articulations of this movement require the "rhythm" or the "pulse" of ipseity? Is not this rhythm in its turn but the disclosure of being to itself, the representation of being by itself, the identity of this "itself" being without mystery? Does not everything take place as if the disclosure of self to self came to be added to the identity of the object, an identity originating in the idealizing identification that thematizing thought bestows kerygmatically on adumbrations?[10] What is the relation between the "oneself" and the *for self* of representation? Is the "oneself" a recurrence of the same type as consciousness, knowledge, and representation, all of which would be sublimated in consciousness conceived as Mind? Is the "oneself" consciousness in its turn, or is it not a quite distinct event, one which would justify the use of separate terms: Self, I, Ego, soul?

Philosophers have for the most part described the identity of the *oneself* in terms of the return to self of consciousness. For Sartre, like Hegel, the oneself is posited as a *for itself*. The identity of the I would thus be reducible to a turning back of *essence* upon itself, a return to itself of essence as both subject and condition of the identification of the Same. The sovereignty of the "oneself," positing itself as one being among others, or as a central being, would only be an abstraction referring back to the concrete process of Truth where this return is accomplished; referring back, consequently, to the exposition of being—lost and rediscovered—to the expatiation and stretching out of time, referring back to the logos. This approach must be placed in question.

The identity of ipseity is not due to any kind of distinguishing characteristic, a *unicum* or a *hapax*, like fingerprints, and which as a principle of individuation would win for this identity a proper noun and thus a place in speech. The identity of the "oneself" is not the inertia of an individuated quiddity resulting from any incomparable quality inherent in the body or character, or the unicity of a natural or historical conjuncture.

The identity of the *oneself* is not equivalent to the identity of identification. This is so even if one seeks a source for the individual in the logos, wherein an ideal identity is proclaimed across an indefinite multiplicity of adumbrations via the schematism of discourse; and it is so even if the identity of the subject is bound to a process of identification through the structure of intentionality, be it that of immanent time in the Husserlian sense, in which is displayed not inertia but the scission of "eternal rest," nostalgia and rediscovery. The oneself which lives (we are almost tempted to say, without metaphor, which palpitates) alongside the movements of consciousness or intentionality, which are said to constitute it, does not bear its identity as do identical beings, themes, or parts of discourse, where they show themselves and where it is necessary that they remain identical; that is to say, they say themselves without being unsaid. The identity of ipseity is to be distinguished from the identity which allows a being to enter into discourse, to be thematized, and to appear to consciousness.

To be sure, reflection *upon* the self is possible, but this reflection does not *constitute* the living recurrence of subjectivity, a *recurrence* without duality, but a unity without rest, whose un-rest is due neither to dispersion of exterior givens nor to the flux of time biting into the future while conserving a past. The living identity of oneself is not distinguished from the self and does not lend itself to either a synthetic activity or recollection or anticipation. To present the knot of ipseity which is tied into the straight thread of *essence* according to the model of intentionality of the *for itself*, or as an opening on the self, is to presuppose a new ipseity behind ipseity. Ipseity is an indefeasible unity that has never been separated from the self. Perhaps it is this that explains Leibniz's mysterious formula: "the ego is innate to itself." The oneself guards the secret of its identification as a contraction, as an "entrance within." Unlike consciousness, which loses itself so as to find itself again in the retentions and protentions of its time, the oneself does not slacken the knot attaching it to the self only to tie it once more. It does not enter into the indiscreet play of concealments and unconcealments known as the phenomenon (or phenomenology, since the appearing of the phenomenon is already discourse). It is not a question of keeping or telling a secret, a concern for nondivulgence. The oneself is the irremissible identity that has no need to prove or thematize this identity. The oneself is "in itself" as one is in one's skin.

The fulcrum where the return of being to itself as knowledge or Mind is produced thus indicates the singularity par excellence. To be sure, this singularity may appear in an indirect language as a proper noun, as a being, situated at the threshold of generality, characteristic of every signification, whereby it is capable of referring to *essence*. But, as an original nonquiddity—no one—clothed as a being by a pure borrowing that masks its nameless singularity by bestowing it with a role, the fulcrum of the mind is a personal pronoun. If the return to self of knowledge, which is consciousness, the original truth of being, can be accomplished, this is because the recurrence of ipseity has already been produced. An inversion in the process of *essence* is a move *outside the game* that being plays in consciousness. It is precisely a withdrawal *in itself*, an exile *in itself*, without foundation in anything else, a noncondition. It is a withdrawal without spontaneity, and thus always already over, always already past. Ipseity is not an abstract point, a center of rotation, identifiable by way of the trajectory traced by a movement of consciousness. It is here and now identified without having to identify itself in the present, nor having to "decline" its identity, already older than the time of consciousness.

The identity of singularity does not issue from the identification of a being within *essence*.[11] It does not result from a synthesis of phases, nor, as identity, is it modified by the erosion of aging. An identity unutterable, shameful, and hence unjustifiable—these negative qualifications of subjectivity pertaining to the *oneself* do not hallow some ineffable mystery. They confirm a unity of the self which is presynthetic, prelogical, and (in some way) atomic, precluding the splitting up or separation of the self from itself, preventing it from showing itself (since no longer under a mask) and from being named otherwise than by a pro-noun. This prevention is the positivity of the One. But how this unity can be a tension, irreducible to the function carried out by the oneself in the ontology accomplished by consciousness, where, through the one-self, it operates its return upon itself—this is the question.

The oneself does not rest in peace under its identity. And yet its unrest is neither a splitting nor a process which levels difference. Its unity is not simply attached to some content of ipseity, like an indefinite article which substantifies even verbs in "nominalizing" and thematizing them. Here, unity precedes every article and every process. It is, in a sense, the content itself. The oneself, a unity in both form and content, is a singularity this side of the distinction between the particular and the universal.

This relation is not a pure and simple repetition of consciousness where being gathers itself, as the sea gathers the waves that lap the shore. It is a relation without a disjunction of the terms that are in relation, a relation which does not lead back to the intentional opening upon the self. The ego is *in itself* not like matter is in itself, which, perfectly wedded to its form, is what it is. The ego is in itself like one is in one's skin, that is to say, cramped, ill at ease in one's skin, as though the identity of matter weighing on itself concealed a dimension allowing a withdrawal this side of immediate coincidence, as though it concealed a materiality more material than all matter. The ego is an irritability, a susceptibility, or an exposure to wounding and outrage, delineating a passivity more passive still than any passivity relating to an effect. This *hither side* of identity is not reducible to the *for itself*, where a being recognizes itself in its difference beyond its immediate identity. Here we are obliged to speak of the irremissibility and the anguish (in the etymological sense of the term) of this *in itself* of the Oneself. This anguish is not the existential "being-toward-death" but the constriction of an "entry within," which is not a flight into the void but a passage into the fullness of the anxiety of contraction.[12] Such is the relation in which a being is immolated without taking leave of itself—without becoming ecstatic. Unable to take a distance from itself, it is hunted down in itself, on the hither side of resting in itself and of self-coincidence. This recurrence, which could certainly be called negativity (albeit a negativity prior to discourse as the indisputable homeland of dialectical negativity)—this recurrence of contraction—is the Self.

The negativity of the *in itself* (in the dual sense of *an sich* and *in sich*) has none of the openness of nothingness, but is a passage into fullness. Behind the distinction between rest and motion, between being *at home with oneself* and adventure, between equality and difference, this negativity brings to mind the formulae of the *Parmenides* describing the moment where the One "being in motion . . . comes to rest, and when being at rest . . . changes to motion," and where "it must itself be in no time at all" (156c). This "strange kind of nature," which "is interposed between motion and rest" (156d),[13] is not a break in time dynamically preserving a potential contradiction between present and future, or between present and past. Nor is it an extratemporal ideality governing temporal dispersion. Both of these in their own way imply the ontological adventure. This "strange kind of nature" is a *hither side* outside of all dialectical germination and all reference (even references to references, growing like an "itch"). Absolutely sterile and pure, completely cut off from adventure and reminiscence. No-place. A wrong time or between time (or bad-time)—nonbeing, but on this side of being and nothingness thematizable as being.

The expression "in one's skin" is not simply a metaphor for the *in itself*. It relates to a recurrence in the dead time or the *between-time* separating inspiration and expiration, the diastole and systole of the heart beating softly against the lining of one's own skin. The body is not merely an image or a figure; above all, it is the in-oneself and contraction of ipseity.[14]

The fundamental concept of ipseity, while tied to incarnation, is not a biological concept. (Indeed, must not the original meaning of the "lived body" be sought in the "in-itself" conceived as "in one's skin"?) The ontological (or me-ontological) movement of contraction takes us further. It outlines a schema in corporeality which permits us to attach the biological to a higher structure. Let us indicate this briefly for the moment: negativity without the void of nonbeing, negativity entangled in its own impossibility, outside of all initiative, an incredible withdrawal into fullness, without any detachment from self, is an impossibility of slipping away, a responsibility anterior to any free commitment. The oneself is a responsibility for the freedom of others.

3. The Self and Persecution

To return to our initial development, we wish to know if the passive folding back upon the self of ipseity (which, though it does not have the virtue of being an *act* of folding back, still makes possible the act of consciousness returning to itself) coincides with the an-archic passivity of obsession. Is not obsession a relationship with the outside, prior to the act that would open up the outside? Obsession is a total passivity, more passive still than the passivity of things. Things as "prime matter" bear the weight of the kerygmatic logos, which gives this matter its characteristics. Through falling under the directives of this saying, matter takes on a meaning and shows itself as this or that, i.e., a thing. This fall (or case), this pure submission to the logos, without considering the proposition whereby the thing becomes a narrative to which the logos belongs, is the essence of the accusative. The logos that informs prime matter in calling it to order is an accusation or a category. Obsession, however, is anarchic. It accuses me on the hither side of prime matter seized by the category, still modeled on what remains of obduracy, or potency, in the matter. As a potential being, prime matter remains a power which form takes into account. It is not by chance that Plato speaks of the indestructibility of matter or that Aristotle views matter as a *cause*. Such is the truth appropriate to the order of *things*. Western philosophy, arguably reification itself, has remained faithful to this order. It does not know the absolute passivity, this side of activity and passivity, conveyed by the idea of creation.[15] Philosophers have always been inclined to think of creation in terms of ontology, that is, in terms of a preexisting and indestructible matter.

In obsession, the accusation corresponding to the category is transformed into an absolute accusative in which the ego proper to free consciousness is caught up. Without foundation, prior to every will, the obsessional accusation is a persecution. It strips the Ego of its self-conceit and its dominating imperialism. The subject is in the accusative, without recourse in being, expelled from being, that is to say, *in itself*. In itself one. The recourse that being would offer the Ego brought back to itself would be the splitting of absolute unity, as in the first hypothesis of the *Parmenides*, where the existence of the One would be the negation of the One. The return of the Ego to the Self through obsession is not a self-reflection, a contemplative turning back on the self, but the reduction of the ego to the self. It is a return of the Ego to the passivity of the self, an anarchic passivity whose active source is not thematizable. Subjectivity in this sense is not a for-itself but an in-itself. In the approach, the subject does not detach itself from itself so as to recover itself. It is not like the instant which, through retention and protention in the temporality of consciousness, rediscovers itself already separated from itself. In the obsessive approach, the subject is not detached from itself so as then to become its own object and to have care for the self. It is an intrigue other than of egoism. In itself, the ego is divested of the ego that recovers and masks it. For, in the ego, the One is already contaminated by being, an exasperated and intrusive being. In its persecution, the ego returns to the self, not to reflect on the self but to denude itself in the absolute simplicity of identity. The absolutely individuated identity of the interior, in-itself, without recourse to any system of references. To be sure, this identity cannot be individuated as the "pole" of a self-identifying consciousness, nor even as an existence which, in its existence, would care for itself. The reflexive pronoun "itself," or the self, remains the great secret to be divulged. The return upon the self proper to reflection already implies the initial recurrence of the "itself."

Obsessed with responsibilities which do not result from decisions taken by a "freely contemplating" subject, consequently accused of what it never willed or decreed, accused of what it did not do, subjectivity is thrown back on itself—in itself—by a persecuting accusation. Concretely, this means to be accused of what others do and to be responsible for what others do. It is to be pushed to the limit, responsible for the very persecution undergone. Subjectivity is subject to the limitless passivity of an accusative that is not a mere declension derived from a nominative. Everything begins here in the accusative. Such is the exceptional condition—or noncondition—of the Self (even in our Latin grammars). Backed up against itself, because the self is in itself without recourse to anything, in itself as one is in one's skin (and this incarnation is not metaphorical, since to be in one's skin is an extreme way of being exposed, different from things). Does not the self take hold of itself through the very impossibility of slipping away from its identity, an identity toward which it is driven back by persecution? Does not a beginning dawn in this passivity?

Certainly. But how can the passivity of the self become a "hold on oneself"? Leaving aside a play on words, does this not presuppose an activity, a hidden and clandestine freedom, behind the absolutely an-archic passivity of obsession? Indeed, has any progress been made in the study so far?

4. Substitution

In speaking of the in-itself of persecuted subjectivity have we been faithful enough to the an-archy of passivity? In speaking of the recurrence of the ego to the self have we freed ourselves sufficiently from the postulates of ontological thinking, where eternal being always assumes what it undergoes and, whatever the nature of this undergoing, always reappears as the *principle* of what happens to it? It is perhaps here that ontological thinking ultimately differs from the thought which speaks of the creature rather than of being. Does not this thought, in its absolute diachrony, in the noninstant of creation, where the self called to being is not there to hear the call which it obeys, conceive an unlimited and an-archic passivity of the creature? In the absolute passivity of the creature, the Self is thought to the very end: the total passivity of the Self, suggested by the idea of creation, is a recurrence to the self, on this side of the self. A does not come back to A, as in an identity, but withdraws behind its point of departure. Must we not speak of a responsibility that is not assumed? Far from recognizing itself in the freedom of consciousness losing and rediscovering itself, slackening the order of being so as to reintegrate it in a free responsibility, the responsibility of obsession implies an absolute passivity of a self that has never been able to depart from itself so as to return within its limits and identify itself by recognizing itself in its past; an absolute passivity whose contraction is a movement this side of identity. Responsibility for the other does not wait for the freedom of commitment to the other. Without ever having done anything, I have always been under accusation: I am persecuted. Responsibility is not a return to self but an irremovable and implacable crispation, which the limits of identity cannot contain. In obsession, the self's responsibility is, as it were, a deficit. Its recurrence breaks open the limits of identity, the *principle* of being that lies in me, the intolerable resting in oneself proper to definition. Such is the ego's responsibility for what it did not will, that is to say, responsibility for others. This anarchy of self-recurrence, beyond the predictable play of action and passion in which the identity of being is maintained, is a passivity that is undergone in proximity. On this side of the limits of identity, the passivity of self-recurrence is not, however, an alienation. What can it be if not a substitution for others? In its passivity without the *arche* of identity, ipseity is a hostage. The word "I" means to be answerable for everything and for everyone.

In this substitution whereby identity is inverted, a passivity more passive still than all passivity, beyond the passivity of the identical, the self is freed from itself. This freedom is not that of a free initiative, an absolution which, in substituting for others, escapes relationship with them. At the extreme of passivity, it escapes passivity or the inevitable limitation to which every term in a relation is subject. In the incomparable relation of *responsibility*, the other is not merely a contestation but is supported by what it contests. Here we observe the overdetermination of ontological categories, transforming them into ethical notions. In this most passive passivity, the *Self* is freed from every Other and from itself.

In contrast to Hegel and the tradition, in which the ego is equal to itself (and thus a return of being to itself through the concept), the affirmation called forth by obsession, from the an-archic passivity of the self, can be stated only in terms of inequality. Yet inequality cannot be taken to mean an inadequation of the apparent being with respect to a profound or sublime being, nor is it a return toward an original innocence (such as the inequality of the ego to itself spoken of by Nabert). Rather, it signifies the passage of the identical to the other in substitution, which makes possible sacrifice.

The upsurge of the oneself in persecution, the anarchic passivity of substitution, is not some event whose history we might recount but a conjunction which describes the ego. It is the very gravity of being, a gravity which is perhaps the first meaning imported to being, over and above the simple "that's how it is." Being is recast as the unity of the universe insofar as it rests on the self: subject to being and subject to every being. The self bears the weight of the world; it is responsible for everyone. The subject is the one who, as in Lamentations 3:30, "presents his cheek to he who strikes him and is filled with shame." Here it is not a question of humiliating oneself, as if suffering were in itself, in its empirical essence, a magical power of atonement. But because, in suffering, in the original traumatism and return to self, where I am responsible for what I did not will, absolutely responsible for the persecution I undergo, outrage is done to me. The self is what in being inverts the work, upright, imperturbable, and without exemption, inverts the unfolding of the essence of being. Being in-itself, backed up against the self, to the point of being substituted for all that drives you into this non-Place, is the way in which the ego is in-itself, or "beyond essence."

Contrary to Eugen Fink and Jeanne Delhomme, both of whom demand an unconditional freedom without responsibility, a freedom of play, we discern in obsession a responsibility not resting on any free commitment, that is, a responsibility without freedom, a responsibility of the creature; a responsibility of one who comes too late into being to avoid supporting it in its entirety. This way of being, without prior commitment, responsible for the other (*autrui*), amounts to the fact of human fellowship, prior to freedom.

Being takes on a meaning and becomes a universe not because there exists among thinking beings a being pursuing ends, a being thereby structured as an Ego. There is abandonment, obsession, responsibility, and a Self because the trace of the Infinite (exceeding the present, turning its *arche* into anarchy) is inscribed in proximity.[16] The noninterchangeable *par excellence*, the I, substitutes itself for others. Nothing is a game. Thus being is transcended.

The ego is not merely a being endowed with certain so-called moral qualities, qualities it would bear as attributes. Its exceptional unicity in the passivity of the Passion of the self is the incessant event of substitution, the fact of being emptied of its being, of being turned inside out, the fact of *nonbeing*. In speaking of an *event*, we do not mean to reduce the being which is the Ego to the *act of substituting itself*, which would be the *being* of this *being*. Substitution is not an act but contrary to the act; it is a passivity inconvertible into an act, on this side of the act-passivity alternative. It is the ex-ceptional, which cannot serve as the grammatical *category* of Noun or Verb, the recurrence that can only be stated as an *in itself*, or as an *inside-out of being*, or as *nonbeing*. Nonbeing is a matter of bearing the burden of the misery and failure of the other, and even the responsibility that the other can have for me. To be a "self" is always to have one degree of responsibility more.[17] The responsibility for the other (*autrui*) is perhaps the concrete event designated by the verb "not to be," in an attempt to distinguish it both from nothingness and from the product of the transcendental imagination.

It is through the condition of being a hostage that there can be pity, compassion, pardon, and proximity in the world—even the little there is, even the simple "after you Sir." All the transfers of sentiment which theorists of original war and egoism use to explain the birth of generosity (it isn't clear, however, that there was war at the beginning; before wars there were altars) could not take root in the ego were it not, in its entire being, or rather its entire nonbeing, subjected not to a category, as in the case of matter, but to an unlimited accusative, that is to say, persecution, self, hostage, already substituted for others.

The ego is not a being which is capable of expiating for others; it is this original expiation which is involuntary because prior to the initiative of the will. It is as though the Ego's unity and unicity were already the hold over the self exerted by the gravity of being, abandoned by the unrepresentable withdrawal of the Infinite. This hold over the self is the Self, outside of any place where its load may be set down, a nonlocation where the "I" is an other (but without the alienation Rimbaud speaks of). *In itself*, this side of identity and the autonomy of autoaffection, subjectivity is not a substance; it is in itself through the absolute passivity that comes to it anarchically from the Other and where we are perhaps justified in rejecting the activity-passivity alternative in order to speak of expiation.

It is from subjectivity understood as a self, from the *excidence* and dispossession of contraction, whereby the Ego does not appear but immolates itself, that the relationship with the other is possible as communication and transcendence. This relation is not simply another quest for certainty, a self-coincidence paradoxically claimed to be the basis of communication. Consequently, all one can say of communication and transcendence is their incertitude. As an adventure of subjectivity which is not governed by the concern to rediscover oneself, an adventure other than the coinciding of consciousness, communication rests on incertitude (here a positive condition) and is possible only as deliberately sacrificed. Communication with the other (*autrui*) can be transcendence only as a dangerous life, as a fine risk to be run. These words receive their full weight when, instead of merely designating a lack of certainty, they express the gratuity of sacrifice. In speaking of a fine risk to be run, the word *fine* has not been given sufficient thought. In their antithesis to certainty, indeed to consciousness, these terms take on a positive meaning and are no longer makeshift expressions.

The ethical language we have resorted to does not derive from a special moral experience which would be independent of the description hitherto developed. It proceeds from what Alphonse de Waelhens called nonphilosophical experiences, arising from the very meaning of the approach that cuts across knowledge, from the face that cuts across the phenomenon. Phenomenology is able to follow the reversion of thematization into an-archy in the description of the approach. Ethical language succeeds in expressing the paradox in which phenomenology suddenly finds itself, since ethics, beyond politics, features at the level of this reversion. Beginning with the approach, the description refers to the neighbor who bears the trace of a withdrawal, ordering it as a face. The signifyingness of the trace in respect of behavior is a signifyingness whose anarchic insinuation should not be forgotten and confused with indication, that is, with the monstration of the signified in the signifier, with the itinerary taken by theological and edifying thinking in deducing too readily the truths of faith, whereby obsession is contained as a principle in a theme and the very an-archy of its movement is annulled.[18] The trace in which the face is ordered is not reducible to a sign, for the sign and its relation to the signified are synchronous in a theme. The approach is not the thematization of any relation but that very relation which resists thematization inasmuch as it is an-archic. To thematize it is already to lose it and to depart from the absolute passivity of self. The passivity which is this side of the passivity-activity alternative, a passivity more passive than any inertia, is expressed in ethical terms: accusation, persecution, responsibility for others. The persecuted one is expelled from its place and has nothing left but itself, has nothing in the world upon which to rest its head. Accused beyond any fault, persecuted, one is unable to offer a self-defense in language, because the disqualification of the apology is the very characteristic of persecution, so that persecution is the precise moment where the subject is reached or touched without the mediation of the logos.[19]

5. Before Freedom

In coming to the end of our discussion we may ask ourselves whether we have not been so imprudent as to affirm that the first word of the mind, that which makes all the others possible, including the words *negativity* and *consciousness*, is an unconditional *Yes* of submission. A *Yes* of submission which negates truth and all the highest values!

An unconditional *Yes* certainly, but not a naïve one: a *Yes* older than naïve spontaneity. We still reason as though the ego had been present at the creation of the world and as though the world, henceforth in its charge, had issued from an act of free will. Such are the presumptions of philosophers, the presumptions of idealists. Indeed, it is for this that Scripture reproaches Job. No doubt he could have understood his misfortunes had they been the result of his faults. But he never wanted to do evil! His so-called friends thought as he did: in an orderly world one is responsible only for one's *own* actions. Ergo, Job must have been guilty of an oversight. But the meaning of the world is not inscribed in being as a theme that exhibits itself in this world. Job does not have at his disposal all that is required for deliberating in matters of justice. Entering too late into a world created without him, he is responsible over and above what he experiences. And yet, in the same way, he is *better* for not being a mere effect of this world. The distinction between the free and the nonfree is not therefore ultimate. Prior to the Ego taking a decision, the *outside of being*, where the Ego arises or is accused, is necessary. This occurs not through freedom but through an unlimited susceptibility, anarchical and *without assumption*, which, unlike the susceptibility of matter determined by the energy of a cause, is overdetermined by a valuing.[20] The birth of the Ego in a gnawing remorse, which is precisely a withdrawing into oneself; this is the absolute recurrence of substitution. The condition, or noncondition, of the Self is not originally an autoaffection presupposing the Ego but is precisely an affection by the Other, an anarchic traumatism this side of autoaffection and self-identification,[21] a traumatism of responsibility and not causality.

A disengagement outside (or this side) of being is not the result of an inconsequential game played out in some corner of being where the ontological plot is relaxed. An exit made possible by the weight exerted at a single point by the remainder of its substance: responsibility. It is this responsibility for the creature that constitutes the "self." Responsibility for the creature, for that which the ego had not been the author. To be a "self" is to be responsible before having done anything. It is in this sense to substitute oneself for others. In no way does this represent servitude, for the distinction between master and slave already assumes a preestablished ego.

To say that subjectivity begins in the person, that the person begins in freedom, that freedom is the primary causality, is to blind oneself to the secret of the self and its relation to the past. This relation does not amount to placing oneself at the beginning of this past so as to be responsible within the strict limits of intention, nor to being the simple result of the past. All the suffering and failure of the world weighs on that point where a singling out occurs, an inversion of being's *essence*. A point is subject to everything. The impossibility of slipping away is the very singling out of the subject. The notion of hostage overturns the position that starts from presence (of the ego to the self) as a beginning of philosophy. I am not merely the origin of myself, but I am disturbed by the Other. Not judged by the Other, but condemned without being able to speak, persecuted. But we have shown that it is necessary to go further: to be substitutable for the persecutor, whence the idea of responsibility preceding freedom.

Of course, the notion of the subject to which the analysis of proximity leads us does not coincide with the notion of Mind, but the notion of soul does not correspond either. It is Me who is a substitution and sacrifice and not another, not the Other (*Autrui*), in whom I would like to discover a soul identical to my own. To say that the soul should sacrifice itself for others would be to preach human sacrifice. To say that the ego is a substitution is not to proclaim the universality of a principle, the "essence" of an Ego, but, quite the contrary, it is to restore to the soul its egoity, which supports no generalization. From this situation, the way by which the logos attains to the essence of the ego passes through the third party.[22]

Modern antihumanism, which denies the primacy that the human person, a free end in itself, has for the signification of being, is true over and above the reasons it gives itself. It makes a place for subjectivity positing itself in abnegation, in sacrifice, and in substitution. Its great intuition is to have abandoned the idea of person as an end in itself. The Other (*Autrui*) is the end, and me, I am a hostage.

Shall we say that the world, with all its sufferings and all its failings, weighs on the ego because the ego is a free consciousness, capable of sympathy and compassion? Shall we say that only a being which is free is susceptible to the weight of the world that it takes upon itself? Let us suppose for a moment that the ego is free and capable of deciding in favor of solidarity with others. At least it will be recognized that this freedom has no time to assume this urgent weight and that, consequently, it appears collapsed and defeated under its suffering. In the impossibility of evading the neighbor's call, in the impossibility of distancing ourselves—perhaps we approach the other (*autrui*) in contingency, but henceforth we are not free to distance ourselves from him or her—the assumption of the suffering and failings of the other (*autrui*) in no way goes beyond passivity: it is passion. This condition, or noncondition, of the hostage will therefore be nothing less than the primary and essential modality of freedom and not an empirical accident of the Ego's freedom (in itself proud).

Certainly—but this would be another paper—my responsibility for everyone can manifest itself while also limiting itself. The ego may be called, in the name of this unlimited responsibility, to be concerned also with itself. The fact that the other, my neighbor, is also a third in relation to another, likewise a neighbor, is the birth of thought, of consciousness, of justice, and of philosophy. The unlimited and initial responsibility that justifies this concern for justice, for the self, and for philosophy can be forgotten. In this forgetfulness, consciousness is pure egoism. But the egoism is neither first nor last. The impossibility of escaping God—the adventure of Jonas—dwells in the depths of myself as a self, as an absolute passivity. (I pronounce the word *God* without suppressing the intermediaries that lead to this word and, as it were, the anarchy of its entrance into discourse, just as phenomenology announces concepts without ever destroying the scaffoldings by which they are reached. Here, at least, God is not merely a value among values.) This passivity is not simply the possibility of death within being, the possibility of impossibility, but is an impossibility anterior to this possibility, an impossibility of slipping away, an absolute susceptibility, a gravity without any frivolity, the birth of a meaning in the obtuseness of being, a "being able to die," submitted to sacrifice.

SUBSTITUTION

Notes

1. "La substitution" was part of a public lecture given at the Faculté Universitaire Saint-Louis, Brussels, November 30, 1967. It was a continuation of the discussion held the day before entitled "Proximité," which was based on the study "Langage et proximité" and subsequently appeared in the second edition of *En découvrant l'existence avec Husserl et Heidegger* (Paris: Vrin, 1967), 217–36 ["Language and Proximity," in *Collected Philosophical Papers*, trans. A. Lingis (The Hague: Martinus Nijhoff, 1987), 109–26]. The two lectures "Proximity" and "Substitution" were given under the general title "Beyond Essence." The present text [as published in the *Revue philosophique de Louvain* 66 (1968), 487–508] represents the final version of the discussion. Certain themes have been formulated in a more strenuous manner for the reader, who can "withstand" more than the listener. Some notes have been added in an attempt to clarify perspectives opened by the particular subject matter.
2. Here there can be no question of analyzing this "mystery," which is realized in "narration."
3. See "Language and Proximity" in *Collected Philosophical* Papers, trans. Alphonso Lingis (The Hague: Martinus Nijhoff, 1987), 109–10.
4. If the anarchical were not signaled *within* consciousness, it would reign in its own way. The anarchical is possible only when contested by the discourse which betrays, and yet translates, without annulling, its an-archy. The notion of an *abuse of language* demands stringent thought.
5. See Bergson's *Creative Evolution* regarding the notion of disorder, which warrants close attention. Subversion and revolution are still within order. To recall Hegel, that which appears to consciousness in the experience of a "new object" as the "nothingness of the first" shows itself to the philosopher, who is in a position to see "behind the back of consciousness," as the result of a genesis, born in the midst of the same dialectical order (*Phenomenology of Spirit*, trans. A. V. Miller [Oxford: Oxford University Press, 1977], 55–6). This movement of genesis, traversing the State, ends in absolute knowledge as the accomplishment of consciousness. The notion of anarchy introduced here precedes the political (or antipolitical) meaning popularly ascribed to it. It cannot, under pain of contradiction, be set up as a principle (in the sense the anarchists intend when, for example, they maintain that anarchy is the mother of order). Anarchy, unlike *arche*, cannot be sovereign. It can only disturb, albeit in a radical way, the State, prompting isolated moments of negation *without any* affirmation. The State, then, cannot set itself up as a Whole. But, in return, anarchy is allowed a say.
6. An inability which is *said* all the same. An-archy does not reign, and so remains ambiguous and enigmatic. It leaves a trace which discourse, in the pain of expression, tries to say. Yet it leaves only a trace.
7. Such is a relation without any *a priori* deriving from spontaneity, be it that spontaneity which ontology asks of finite thought, and which, as pure receptivity and in order to welcome a being, must operate as a transcendental imagination, formative of the imaginary, cavity of nothingness.
8. Consciousness is the game *par excellence,* a "transcendental imagination."
9. We do not go so far as to write *essance,* like Jacques Derrida (whose remarkable work must be given the highest praise) writes *différance*.
10. Cf. "Language and Proximity," 109–15.
11. Within the amphibology, that is, of being and beings—verb and noun—"temporalized" in time.
12. Heidegger's analysis describes the anguish arising from the limitation of being. To the extent that the analysis is not to be read merely as psychological or anthropological, it teaches us that form (which according to our philosophical tradition *defines* being) is always too small for being. Definition in terms of form, "formness," beauty, luster, and appearing, is also a strangulation, that is, anguish itself. The disproportion between being and its phenomenality, the fact that being is cramped in its manifestation, would be produced under the anthropological modes of finite being, as a being-existing-toward-death. The measure of determination would thus be the ill-fitting measure of a Nessus tunic. Yet anguish as being-toward-death is also the hope of reaching the space of nonbeing. This possibility of deliverance (and the temptation of suicide) arises in the anxiety of death. As nothingness, death is an opening in which along with being the anguish arising from being's definition is engulfed. By contrast, anxiety, as the narrowness of a "passage into fullness," is the recurrence of the Oneself, a recurrence without evasion or defection. Such is a responsibility stronger than death, affirmed by Plato in his own fashion in the *Phaedo* when condemning suicide (62b).
13. The very notion of the *hither side* is without doubt justified by this extract from the *Parmenides.* It is a question of a retreat, a reclusion which remains a presence in the world and in history, and which does not go outside the World so as to become, in chimerical fashion, a force liberated from the world, endowed with spiritual powers capable of triumphs or failures. Triumphs and failures presuppose personal freedom and, consequently, an Ego endowed with a political and religious sovereignty and principality. On *this side,* the Ego is a self, no longer part of being or history; neither an effect at rest nor a cause in movement.

189

14. The body is neither an obstacle opposed to the soul nor a tomb that imprisons it. It is the very susceptibility of the Self, a susceptibility to wounding and sacrifice.

15. This freedom enveloped in a responsibility that it cannot shoulder is the *way* of a creature, the unlimited passivity of the self, the noncondition of the self.

16. In the final three studies of the second edition of our book *En découvrant l'existence avec Husserl et Heidegger*, all the descriptions of the *face* which refer to the ambiguity or the very enigma of anarchy: the Illeity of the infinite in the face, as the trace of the withdrawal of the Infinite as Infinite, accomplished before arrival, whereby the Other (*Autrui*) commands my responsibility—remain descriptions of the nonthematizable, of the anarchic, and consequently do not lead to any theological thesis. Language is nevertheless able to speak of it, thereby confirming the impossibility of the an-archic constituting itself as a sovereignty; whence the very noncondition of anarchy. Yet the hold of language over the anarchic is not a mastery, for otherwise anarchy would be subordinated to the *arche* of consciousness. This hold is the struggle and pain of expression, giving rise to discourse along with the necessity of the State and the *arche* of sovereignty. (We allude to this in the final paragraph of the present study, and hope to speak of it further at a later date.) It is also clear that in our interpretation of signifyingness, the practical order (and the religious which is inseparable from the practical) is defined in terms of the an-archic. Theology is possible only as a contestation of the religious, which is nevertheless confirmed through the struggles or failures of theology. [The last three essays in *En découvrant l'existence avec Husserl et Heidegger* are "The Trace of the Other," "Enigma and Phenomenon," and "Language and Proximity."]

17. The suffering of the other, my pity for this suffering, the other's sorrow over my pity, my sorrow over this sorrow, and so on—this vortex stops with me. Throughout this sequence it is I who admit of one movement more. My suffering is the focus of all sufferings—and all faults. Even the faults of my persecutors, which amounts to suffering the ultimate persecution, that is, suffering absolutely.

18. In this way theological language destroys the religious situation of transcendence. The infinite presents itself an-archically, and thematization is deprived of "the experience" which alone could lend it credence. Language *about* God rings false or turns into myth.

19. We have said that proximity, obsession, and subjectivity do not lead back to consciousness. But, rather than attesting to a preconscious stage or to a repression which would suppress them, their nonconsciousness confirms their exception from the totality, that is to say, their refusal of manifestation. To the extent that essence is inseparable from exhibition and thus from the ideality of the logos and the kerygmatic principality, this exception is nonbeing or anarchy, this side of the, still ontological, alternative of being and nothingness, this side of essence. To be sure, nonconsciousness is the distinguishing feature of mechanical phenomena or the repression of psychic structures, whence the pretension of mechanism or psychologism to universality. But the nonconscious may be read otherwise, in terms of its traces, undoing the categories of mechanism. The nonconscious is understood as the nonvoluntariness of persecution, which, as persecution, interrupts every justification, every apology, and every logos. This reduction to silence is a passivity this side of all material passivity. This side of the neutrality of things, absolute passivity becomes incarnation, corporeality, that is to say, susceptibility to pain, outrage, and unhappiness. In its susceptibility, it bears the trace of this *hither side* of things as a responsibility for what the persecuted, in her or his ipseity, did not will, that is, a responsibility for the very persecution she or he undergoes.

20. Perhaps the notion of anarchy accounts for the notion of valuing, whose dimension is so difficult to distinguish from the being of beings. To value is indeed "to weigh" on the subject, although otherwise than in terms of a cause weighing on an effect, a being weighing on the thought to which it presents itself, an end weighing on the tendency or will it solicits. What does this *otherwise* mean? We think that in valuing there arises a susceptibility which is incapable of thematizing or assuming what it receives, a susceptibility that makes itself responsible in *spite of itself.* In its original influence, prior to any intentional movement, without the possibility of a free attitude towards it, value renders things "pure" or "impure." The death of the Other makes me impure owing to its proximity and explains the "*Noli me tangere.*" There is not here a phenomenon of mystical mentality, but an indelible moment, which the notion of value recalls.

21. If obsession is suffering and "contrariness," it is because the altruism of the hostage-subjectivity is not an inclination, is not the *natural* benevolence associated with the moral philosophers of sentiment. It is contrary to nature, a nonvoluntary election, inseparable from the persecution to which no consent is thinkable—anarchic. Persecution reduces the ego to the self, to the absolute accusative whereby the Ego is accused of a fault which it neither willed nor committed, and which disturbs its freedom. Persecution is a traumatism, violence *par excellence*, without warning, without *a priori*, without the possibility of apology, without logos. Persecution leads back to a resignation without consent and as a result traverses a night of the unconscious. This is the meaning of

the unconscious, the night where the ego comes back to itself in the traumatism of persecution, a passivity more passive still than all passivity, on this side of identity, becoming the responsibility of substitution.

22. The Ego is not universalizable: I remain *here*, despite every ecstasis (except the ecstasis of death) and despite every "concept of the Ego." I cannot absolve myself, that is to say, detach myself from myself (a matter of suspending the original responsibility of the hither side, outside of the free dialogical exchange of questions and answers that persecution paralyses by placing in question), although I am in a position to pardon others in their alterity or in their subsumption under the concept of the Ego. Such is the priority of the Self prior to all freedom, or nonfreedom.

17

JEAN-FRANÇOIS LYOTARD
(1924–1998)

Jean-François Lyotard is the most prominent French theorist of postmodernism. Born in Versailles in 1924, Lyotard studied philosophy and literature at the Sorbonne in Paris. He passed the *agrégation* in 1950, whereupon he taught for one year in a lycée in Constantine, Algeria. In Constantine, Lyotard read Marx and became a severe critic of the French occupation of Algeria. In 1954, he joined the radical left-wing group Socialism or Barbarism, led by Cornelius Castoriadis, though he broke with the group ten years later and formed his own socialist revolutionary organization, Workers Power. He resigned from this group in 1966 after losing faith in the totalizing implications of Marxist theory, and returned to the study and writing of philosophy. He taught at the University of Nanterre, where he took a leading role in the events of May 1968, and at the University of Paris, Vincennes. During the eighties and nineties, he held positions as visiting professor at numerous universities in the United States, including the University of California, San Diego, John Hopkins University, University of Minnesota, and the University of California, Irvine. Lyotard died in Paris at the age of 73.

Lyotard's first book, *Phenomenology* (1954), confronted the limitations of Husserlian phenomenology from the perspective of Marxism. However, as he came to distance himself from Marxist theory, he turned in his second book, *Discours, figure* (1971), to the revolutionary potential of nondiscursive or figurative art and its capacity to disrupt dialectical philosophy. The transgressive elements of sensuous experience are related to Freud's theory of libido in Lyotard's most provocative and demanding work, *Libidinal Economy* (1974), a powerful critique of Marxism and other "hegemonic" political systems that serve to inhibit and limit "libidinal intensities." While Lyotard soon abandoned libidinal materialism, his trenchant criticism of philosophical pretensions to ground claims made by the sciences and arts was carried over into his most famous book, *The Postmodern Condition: A Report on Knowledge* (1979). It is in this work that we find Lyotard's celebrated formulation of postmodernism as "incredulity toward metanarratives." Such a crisis of legitimation corresponds to an age of fragmentation and pluralism in which the totalizing discourse of modernity from the Enlightenment to Marx gives way to "little narratives" that are incommensurable and self-legitimating, rather like Wittgensteinian "language games."

Our reading is taken from *The Differend: Phrases in Dispute* (1983), which Lyotard considered his most important book. A "differend" is a dispute between at least two parties that cannot be equitably resolved for lack of a common rule of judgment applicable to all of the arguments. It differs from ordinary litigation in that the aggrieved party (the "victim") is deprived of the language or means necessary to present the wrong done to him or her. Lyotard uses the example of Holocaust survivors confronted with revisionist historian Robert Faurrison's demands for proof that the gas chambers existed. The only proof that Faurisson will accept is from eyewitnesses who were themselves victims of the gas chambers. Obviously, such witnesses are not able to testify because they are dead. Thus the Holocaust survivors are deprived of the possibility of presenting their case due to the very terms in which Faurisson has set up the debate. The task, according to Lyotard, is first, to acknowledge differends whenever they occur, and second, to bear witness to the injustice that occurs whenever the incommensurability of different language games produces a victim who is deprived of the means of arguing and thus unable to rectify the wrong done to him or her. Lyotard invokes Levinas at the end of his essay to show how the discourse of moral prescriptives is heterogeneous and irreducible to descriptive language—an observation also made by Hume, of course.

Select Bibliography of Lyotard's Works in English

The Differend: Phrases in Dispute. Trans. Georges Van Den Abbeele. Minneapolis, MN: University of Minnesota Press, 1987.

Heidegger and "the jews." Trans. Andreas Michel and Mark S. Roberts. Minneapolis, MN: University of Minnesota Press, 1987.

The Inhuman: Reflections on Time. Trans. Geoffrey Bennington and Rachel Bowlby. Stanford, CA: Stanford University Press, 1991.

Just Gaming (with Jean-Loup Thebaud). Trans. Wlad Godzich. Minneapolis, MN: University of Minnesota Press, 1985.

Lessons on the Analytic of the Sublime: Kant's Critique of Judgment, 23–29. Trans. Elizabeth Rottenberg. Stanford, CA: Stanford University Press, 1994.

Libidinal Economy. Trans. Iain Hamilton Grant. Bloomington, IN: Indiana University Press, 1993.

The Lyotard Reader. Ed. Andrew Benjamin. Oxford: Blackwell Publishers, 1989.

Phenomenology. Trans. Brian Beakley. Albany, NY: State University of New York Press, 1991.

Political Writings. Trans. Bill Readings and Kevin Paul Geiman. Minneapolis, MN: University of Minnesota Press, 1993.

The Postmodern Condition: A Report on Knowledge. Trans. Geoffrey Bennington and Brian Massumi. Minneapolis, MN: University of Minnesota Press, 1984.

Toward the Postmodern. Trans. Robert Harvey and Mark S. Roberts. Atlantic Highlands, NJ: Humanities Press, 1993.

THE DIFFEREND

Differend

1. You are informed that human beings endowed with language were placed in a situation such that none of them is now able to tell about it. Most of them disappeared then, and the survivors rarely speak about it. When they do speak about it, their testimony bears only upon a minute part of this situation. How can you know that the situation itself existed? That it is not the fruit of your informant's imagination? Either the situation did not exist as such. Or else it did exist, in which case your informant's testimony is false, either because he or she should have disappeared, or else because he or she should remain silent, or else because, if he or she does speak, he or she can bear witness only to the particular experience he or she had, it remaining to be established whether this experience was a component of the situation in question.

2. "I have analyzed thousands of documents. I have tirelessly pursued specialists and historians with my questions. I have tried in vain to find a single former deportee capable of proving to me that he had really seen, with his own eyes, a gas chamber" (Faurisson).[1] To have "really seen with his own eyes" a gas chamber would be the condition which gives one the authority to say that it exists and to persuade the unbeliever. Yet it is still necessary to prove that the gas chamber was used to kill at the time it was seen. The only acceptable proof that it was used to kill is that one died from it. But if one is dead, one cannot testify that it is on account of the gas chamber. The plaintiff complains that he has been fooled about the existence of gas chambers, fooled that is about the so-called Final Solution. His argument is: in order for a place to be identified as a gas chamber, the only eyewitness I will accept would be a victim of this gas chamber; now, according to my opponent, there is no victim that is not dead; otherwise, this gas chamber would not be what he or she claims it to be. There is, therefore, no gas chamber.

3. Can you give me, says an editor defending his or her profession, the title of a work of major importance which would have been rejected by every editor and which would therefore remain unknown? Most likely, you do not know any masterpiece of this kind because, if it does exist, it remains unknown. And if you think you know one, since it has not been made public, you cannot say that it is of major importance, except in your eyes. You do not know of any, therefore, and the editor is right.— This argument takes the same form as those in the preceding numbers. Reality is not what is "given" to this or that "subject," it is a state of the referent (that about which one speaks) which results from the effectuation of establishment procedures defined by a unanimously agreed-upon protocol, and from the possibility offered to anyone to recommence this effectuation as often as he or she wants. The publishing industry would be one of these protocols, historical inquiry another. . . .

6. The plaintiff's conclusion (No. 2) should have been that since the only witnesses are the victims, and since there are no victims but dead ones, no place can be identified as a gas chamber. He should not

have said that there are none, but rather that his opponent cannot prove that there are any, and that should have been sufficient to confound the tribunal. It is up to the opponent (the victim) to adduce the proof of the wrong done to him or her!

7. This is what a wrong would be: a damage accompanied by the loss of the means to prove the damage. This is the case if the victim is deprived of life, or of all his or her liberties, or of the freedom to make his or her ideas or opinions public, or simply of the right to testify to the damage, or even more simply if the testifying phrase is itself deprived of authority. In all of these cases, to the privation constituted by the damage there is added the impossibility of bringing it to the knowledge of others, and in particular to the knowledge of a tribunal. Should the victim seek to bypass this impossibility and testify anyway to the wrong done to him or to her, he or she comes up against the following argumentation: either the damages you complain about never took place, and your testimony is false; or else they took place, and since you are able to testify to them, it is not a wrong that has been done to you, but merely a damage, and your testimony is still false. . . .

Obligation

161. The splitting of the self would, at least, have the finality of destroying its presumptuousness. Of recalling that the law is transcendent to all intellection. And this under the guise of an abhorrent buffoonery, as David Rousset calls it.[2] Certainly, someone who decides the law instead of being its addressee cannot be a judge but is necessarily a criminal. And someone who submits to a law decided in this way can only be a victim. Judge, he or she is not judged. Condemned or acquitted, he or she is not expiated. Still, the speculative non-sense of "Auschwitz" could conceal a paradox of faith (Kierkegaard).[3]

162. Is the order Abraham receives to sacrifice his son any more intelligible than a memorandum directing roundups, convoys, concentratings, and either slow or quick death? Isn't it a matter of idiolect? Abraham hears: *That Isaac die, that is my law*, and he obeys. The Lord speaks at this moment only to Abraham, and Abraham is answerable only to the Lord. Since the reality, if not of the Lord, then at least of the phrase imputed to Him, cannot be established, how can it be known that Abraham isn't a paranoiac subject to homicidal (infanticidal) urges? Or a fake?

163. The question is not even that of obedience, but of obligation. The question is to know whether, when one hears something that might resemble a call, one is held to be held by it. One can resist it or answer it, but it will first have to be received as a call, rather than, for instance, as a fantasy. One must find oneself placed in the position of addressee for a prescription (the request being a modality of prescription).

164. But the request that harries President Schreber [see Freud's case history], the one that overwhelms Abraham, and the one that galvanizes the SS are all different!—What do you mean to say? That one emanates from a fantasmatic figure, another from God, and a third from a political leader? You know that the addressor's identity is subject to differends: the phantom that, according to Flechsig, calls upon Schreber is called God in the Schreberian idiom, etc.—But these various authorities at least are not prescribing the same acts! They can be recognized by what they order done!—I am not saying that the content of the law is indifferent, but it does not allow one to distinguish the rightful authority from its imposture. Above all, the question, which is so to speak preliminary, is that the request emanating from this entity be received as though it were law. The only sign capable of guiding a third party in this is that the addressee is obligated. By the very assumption (of an idiolect), the third party has access neither to the addressor nor to the phrase. He is like Charcot [Freud's teacher] faced with a hysteric, or like the friend you tell your dream to.

165. A phrase is obligatory if its addressee is obligated. Why he or she is obligated is something he or she can perhaps think to explain. In any case, the explanation requires further phrases, in which he or she is no longer situated as the addressee but as the addressor, and whose stakes are no longer those of obeying, but those of convincing a third party of the reasons one has for obeying. Phrases of commentary. The I's blindness may regain the upper hand on the occasion of such phrases.

166.—Why *blindness* (no. 165)?—Because it is impossible to deduce a prescription from a description. The fact that two million people are unemployed in a country does not explain that the unemployment must be remedied. For this to take place, a minor premise must be understood or presupposed, namely, the prescription that all those who can work ought to work. The blindness or transcendental illusion resides in the pretension to found the good or the just upon the true, or what ought to be upon what is. By found, I simply mean the seeking and articulating of implications which allow a prescriptive phrase to be concluded from cognitive phrases. The same goes for Abraham. God orders that Isaac be sacrificed to Him. Abraham obeys "because" God is the one giving the order. It is understood or presupposed that orders given by God are just. This commandment (from God) is just because God's commandments are all just and cannot be unjust. Now, nothing can be ascertained about a totality (which is never given), be it the totality of divine orders. Nor, therefore, can anything be affirmed about it cognitively. As for the ethos of God "Himself," it is accessible only through the totality of his commandments. But, as we have just said, this totality etc. (And finally, supposing that God and His orders are just, how can it be known that God is the one giving the orders?) (No. 162.)

167. The angels themselves are prey to this blindness. "Driven out of Abraham's house," Levinas writes, "Hagar and Ishmael wandered in the desert. When their water supply was spent, God opened Hagar's eyes and she saw a well and gave drink to her dying son."[4] So far, nothing abnormal, and we wouldn't expect anything less from a God who is The Good. Still, this generosity aroused some reproach from the divine counselors (or bad aeons) that are the angels: they see farther than the ends of their noses and are acquainted with the ruses of history: "The angels protested: Wilt Thou bring up a well for one who will one day make Israel suffer?" God undoes the Hegelian trap: "What does the end of history matter, says the Eternal. I judge each for what he is now and not for what he will become." Even God does not and should not know the totality of events. It would be unjust were He to take into consideration what will be done tomorrow in order to judge what is now. It is possible then that He would have given something to drink to Hitler when Hitler was thirsty.

168. To talk in terms of a holocaust is to signify that God commanded the hand of the Nazi butcher, with the Jewish people in the place of Isaac. It is admitted, though, that if the Lord of Abraham asked the father for the sacrifice of his son, it was in order to test Abraham's faithfulness to the Lord. Did God want to test the SS's faithfulness to Him? Was there an alliance between them? And did the SS love the Jew as a father does his son? If not, how could the crime have the value of a sacrifice in the eyes of its victim? And in those of its executioner? And in those of its beneficiary? Or else, was it God who offered up part of His people in sacrifice? But to what god could He offer them up? It is also said that Israel had to be punished for its faults, or fault: pride. Not one of these phrases, which describe the divinity's intention (testing, punishing) with a view to explaining the sacrifice, is falsifiable. Not one of them can stand as an explanation of the order to kill, that is, as its legitimation. The only way you can make a "beautiful death" out of "Auschwitz" death is by means of a rhetoric.

169. The blindness is in putting yourself in the place of the other, in saying *I* in his or her place, in neutralizing his or her transcendence. If you were to lay bare the Lord's intentions, you would then know His idiolect, how it is spoken, the phrases whose addressor and addressee He is and which presumably engender the commandment, and the senses of those phrases. "Auschwitz" is deduced, for instance, from the Lord's anger against His people. But alone by itself, this implication is a crime against ethics: the people would be obligated by an order because they could understand its sense!

170. Instead, obligation should be described as a scandal for the one who is obligated: deprived of the "free" use of oneself, abandoned by one's narcissistic image, opposed in this, inhibited in that, worried over not being able to be oneself without further ado.—But these are phenomenological or psychoanalytic descriptions of a dispossessed or cloven consciousness. Which are far too human, and humanist. They maintain the self even in the very acknowledgment of its dispersion. Could we begin with the dispersion, without any nostalgia for the self? And think therefore the splitting of the self apart from any finality, if it is true that finality is still the action of a self which is exerted upon an object beforehand and from a distance, even if this action momentarily cleaves that self? Of course, the idea of a splitting would also have to be abandoned then, since it presupposes a beautiful totality: the result.

Notes

1. In Pierre Vidal-Naquet, "A Paper Eichmann," trans. M. Jolas, *Democracy* 1, 2 (1981): 81.
2. David Rousset, *Le pitre ne rit pas* (Paris, 1979).
3. Søren Kierkegaard, *Fear and Trembling* [see Chapter 6 above].
4. Emmanuel Levinas, *Difficult Freedom*, trans. Séan Hand (Baltimore, MD: Johns Hopkins University Press, 1990).

18

MICHEL FOUCAULT
(1926–1984)

French philosopher and historian Michel Foucault was born in Poitiers in 1926. He received his *agré-gation* in philosophy in 1952 from the École Normale Supérieure and taught in Sweden, Poland, and Germany before accepting an academic appointment to teach at the University of Clermont-Ferrand in France in 1960. In 1968 he became head of the philosophy department at the University of Vincennes and in 1970 he was elected to the Collège de France, the nation's most prestigious institution of higher research and learning. Politically active throughout the 1970s, he petitioned against American involvement in Vietnam and helped form the Groupe d'Information sur les Prisons, an organization that sought to publicize the poor conditions in prisons. He was an enthusiastic and outspoken defender of the Iranian revolution (1979), a political stance that was to damage his reputation in the short term. In the 1980s, he abandoned the bloody rhetoric of "revolt," and embraced a more "liberal" version of politics, actively supporting, among other things, gay rights. He was frequently invited to lecture outside of France, particularly in the United States, where he taught annually at the University of California at Berkeley. His name became indelibly linked to the oft-quoted and ill-understood phrase the "death of man." He died—probably of AIDS—in 1984.

Foucault's writings may be grouped under three headings: archaeology, genealogy, and ethics. "Archaeology," which Foucault defined as the "science of the archive," refers to a type of historical analysis that eschews teleology and traditional assumptions associated with the humanist subject since Kant (see *Madness and Civilization* [1961], *The Birth of the Clinic* [1963], *The Order of Things* [1966], and *The Archaeology of Knowledge* [1969]). Archaeology's quasi-structuralist focus on discourse, however, meant that it was inadequate to the task of explaining the practical conditions that govern the formation of a particular type of discursivity. Thus Foucault found it necessary to replace archaeology with "genealogy," where greater emphasis is placed on the unconscious operations of "power" dispersed throughout the social body, especially in factories, schools, hospitals, and prisons (see *Discipline and Punish* [1975]).

Foucault claimed that such power functions best when it masks its operations by presenting itself as "knowledge" and adopting the appearance of objective science. Through various "disciplines" (in both senses of the term) and techniques used to subjugate bodies and control populations, power becomes embodied in the modern state apparatus as "biopower." This was the theme of *History of Sexuality: An Introduction*, vol. 1 (1976), in which Foucault sought to show how the proliferation of sexual discourse during the last hundred and fifty years has turned Western man into a "confessing animal." The projected six-volume *History of Sexuality*, however, was never completed. As always with Foucault, who was famous for his protean views, he found himself dissatisfied with his earlier findings, which left unexplained the relationship between the modern subject and previous modes of subjectivity. Thus he was forced to go back to the Greeks (vol. 2, *The Use of Pleasure* [1984]) and then forward to medieval Christianity (*The Confessions of the Flesh* [unpublished]), and back again to the Greeks (vol. 3, *The Care of the Self* [1984]). It was during this odyssey that Foucault forged the predominant interest in ethics that characterizes the last period of his work.

Our reading is taken from one of Foucault's final interviews (1983) and presents what is perhaps his clearest statement concerning the positive role of ethics in our lives. The interview is remarkable both for the candor with which Foucault speaks, using phrases like "personal choice," which would have seemed unthinkable ten years earlier, but also for the way in which Foucault adopts Nietzsche's injunction in *The Gay Science* to "'give style' to one's 'character'" (section 290). Foucault interprets this as the ethical requirement to create oneself and one's life as a work of art, in contradistinction to Christianity, which requires "renouncing the self and deciphering its truth."

Select Bibliography of Foucault's Works in English

The Archeology of Knowledge. Trans. Alan Sheridan. New York: Pantheon, 1972.

The Birth of the Clinic: An Archeology of Medical Perception. Trans. Alan Sheridan. New York: Vintage Books, 1973.

The Care of the Self. The History of Sexuality, Vol. 3. Trans. Robert Hurley. New York Vintage, 1988.

Discipline and Punish: The Birth of the Prison. Trans. Alan Sheridan. New York: Pantheon, 1977.

Essential Works of Foucault, 1954–1984, Vol. 1: Ethics. Ed. Paul Rabinow. Trans. Robert Hurley. New York: The New Press, 1998.

Essential Works of Foucault, 1954–1984, Vol. 2: Aesthetics, Method, and Epistemology. Ed. James D. Faubion. Trans. Robert Hurley. New York: The New Press, 1999.

Essential Works of Foucault, 1954–1984, Vol. 3: Power. Ed. James D. Faubion. Trans. Robert Hurley. New York: The New Press, 2000.

The Foucault Reader. Ed. Paul Rabinow. New York: Pantheon, 1984.

History of Sexuality, Vol. 1: An Introduction. Trans. Robert Hurley. New York Vintage, 1978.

Language, Counter-Memory, Practice: Selected Essays and Interviews. Trans. Donald F. Bouchard and Sherry Simon. Ithaca, NY: Cornell University Press, 1977.

Madness and Civilization: A History of Insanity in the Age of Reason. Trans. Richard Howard. London: Tavistock, 1971.

Politics, Philosophy, Culture: Interviews and Other Writings 1977–1984. Ed. Lawrence D. Kritzman. New York: Routledge, 1988.

Power/Knowledge: Selected Interviews and Other Writings, 1972–1977. Ed. Colin Gordon. New York: Pantheon, 1980.

The Order of Things: An Archeology of the Human Sciences. Trans. Alan Sheridan. London: Tavistock, 1970.

The Use of Pleasure. The History of Sexuality, Vol. 2. Trans. Robert Hurley. New York: Vintage, 1985.

ON THE GENEALOGY OF ETHICS

·

MF. What strikes me is that in Greek ethics people were concerned with their moral conduct, their ethics, their relations to themselves and to others much more than with religious problems.[1] For instance, what happens to us after death? What are the gods? Do they intervene or not?—these are very, very unimportant problems for them, and they are not directly related to ethics, to conduct. The second thing is that ethics was not related to any social—or at least to any legal—institutional system. For instance, the laws against sexual misbehavior were very few and not very compelling. The third thing is that what they were worried about, their theme, was to constitute a kind of ethics which was an aesthetics of existence.

Well, I wonder if our problem nowadays is not, in a way, similar to this one, since most of us no longer believe that ethics is founded in religion, nor do we want a legal system to intervene in our moral, personal, private life. Recent liberation movements suffer from the fact that they cannot find any principle on which to base the elaboration of a new ethics. They need an ethics, but they cannot find any other ethics than an ethics founded on so-called scientific knowledge of what the self is, what desire is, what the unconscious is and so on. I am struck by this similarity of problems.

Q. Do you think that the Greeks offer an attractive and plausible alternative?

MF. No! I am not looking for an alternative; you can't find the solution of a problem in the solution of another problem raised at another moment by other people. You see, what I want to do is not the history of solutions, and that's the reason why I don't accept the word "alternative." I would like to do genealogy of problems, of *problématiques*. Mypoint is not that everything is bad, but that everything is dangerous, which is not exactly the same as bad. If everything is dangerous, then we always have something to do. So my position leads not to apathy but to a hyper- and pessimistic activism.

I think that the ethicopolitical choice we have to make every day is to determine which is the main danger. Take as an example Robert Castel's analysis of the history of the antipsychiatry movement (*La Gestion des risques*). I agree completely with what Castel says, but that does not mean, as some people suppose, that the mental hospitals were better than antipsychiatry; that does not mean that we were not right to criticize those mental hospitals. I think it was good to do that, because *they* were the danger. And now it's quite clear that the danger has changed. For instance, in Italy they have closed all the mental hospitals, and there are more free clinics, and so on—and they have new problems. . . .

Q. So, Greek life may not have been altogether perfect; still it seems an attractive alternative to endless Christian self-analysis.

MF. The Greek ethics was linked to a purely virile society with slaves, in which women were underdogs whose pleasure had no importance, whose sexual life had to be only oriented towards, determined by their status as wives, and so on. . . .

Q. So, despite the German Hellenists, classical Greece was not a Golden Age. Yet, surely we can learn something from it?

MF. I think there is no exemplary value in a period which is not our period . . . it is not anything to get back to. But we do have an example of an ethical experience which implied a very strong connection between pleasure and desire. If we compare that to our experience now, where everybody—the philosopher or the psychoanalyst—explains that what is important is desire, and pleasure is nothing at all, we can wonder whether this disconnection wasn't an historical event, one which was not at all necessary, not linked to human nature, or to any anthropological necessity.

Q. But you already illustrated that in *The History of Sexuality* by contrasting our science of sexuality with the oriental *ars erotica.*

MF. One of the numerous points where I was wrong in that book was what I said about this *ars erotica*. I should have opposed our science of sex to a contrasting practice in our own culture. The Greeks and Romans did not have any *ars erotica* to be compared with the Chinese *ars erotica* (or at least it was not something very important in their culture). They had a *techne tou biou* in which the economy of pleasure played a very large role. In this "art of life" the notion of exercising a perfect mastery over oneself soon became the main issue. And the Christian hermeneutics of the self constituted a new elaboration of this *techne*.

Q. But, after all you have told us about nonreciprocity and obsession with health, what can we learn from this third possibility?

MF. What I want to show is that the general Greek problem was not the *techne* of the self, it was the *techne* of life, the *techne tou biou,* how to live. It's quite clear from Socrates to Seneca or Pliny, for instance, that they didn't worry about the afterlife, what happened after death, or whether God exists or not. That was not really a great problem for them; the problem was which *techne* do I have to use in order to live as well as I ought to live. And I think that one of the main evolutions in ancient culture has been that this *techne tou biou* became more and more a *techne* of the self. A Greek citizen of the fifth or fourth century would have felt that his *techne* for life was to take care of the city, of his companions. But for Seneca, for instance, the problem is to take care of himself.

With Plato's *Alcibiades*, it's very clear: you have to take care of yourself because you have to rule the city. But taking care of yourself for its own sake starts with the Epicureans—it becomes something very general with Seneca, Pliny, and so on: everybody has to take care of himself. Greek ethics is centered on a problem of personal choice, of aesthetics of existence.

The idea of the *bios* as a material for an aesthetic piece of art is, something which fascinates me. The idea also that ethics can be a very strong structure of existence, without any relation with the juridical *per se,* with an authoritarian system, with a disciplinary structure. All that is very interesting. . . .

Q. So, what kind of ethics can we build now, when we know that between ethics and other structures there are only historical coagulations and not a necessary relation?

MF. What strikes me is the fact that in our society, art has become something which is related only to objects and not to individuals, or to life. That art is something which is specialized or which is done by experts who are artists. But couldn't everyone's life become a work of art? Why should the lamp or the house be an art object, but not our life?

Q. Of course, that kind of project is very common in places like Berkeley [California] where people think that everything from the way they eat breakfast, to the way they have sex, to the way they spend their day, should itself be perfected.

MF. But I am afraid in most of those cases, most of the people think if they do what they do, if they live as they live, the reason is that they know the truth about desire, life, nature, body, and so on.

Q. But if one is to create oneself without recourse to knowledge or universal rules, how does your view differ from Sartrean existentialism?

MF. I think that from the theoretical point of view, Sartre avoids the idea of the self as something which is given to us, but through the moral notion of authenticity, he turns back to the idea that we have to be ourselves—to be truly our true self. I think that the only acceptable practical consequence of what Sartre has said is to link his theoretical insight to the practice of creativity—and not of authenticity. From the idea that the self is not given to us, I think that there is only one practical consequence: we have to create ourselves as a work of art. In his analyses of Baudelaire, Flaubert, etc., it is interesting to see that Sartre refers the work of creation to a certain relation to oneself—the author to himself— which has the form of authenticity or of inauthenticity. I would like to say exactly the contrary: we should not have to refer the creative activity of somebody to the kind of relation he has to himself, but should relate the kind of relation one has to oneself to a creative activity.

Q. That sounds like Nietzsche's observation in *The Gay Science* that one should create one's life by giving style to it through long practice and daily work.

MF. Yes. My view is much closer to Nietzsche's than to Sartre's. . . .

Q. Would it be fair to say that you're not doing the genealogy of morals, because you think the moral codes are relatively stable, but what you're doing is a genealogy of ethics?

MF. Yes, I'm writing a genealogy of ethics. The genealogy of the subject as a subject of ethical actions, or the genealogy of desire as an ethical problem. So, if we take ethics in classical Greek philosophy or medicine, what is the ethical substance? It is the *aphrodisia,* which are at the same time acts, desire, and pleasure. What is the *mode d'assujettissement?* It is that we have to build our existence as a beautiful existence; it is an aesthetic mode. You see, what I tried to show is that nobody is obliged in classical ethics to behave in such a way as to be truthful to their wives, to not touch boys, and so on. But, if they want to have a beautiful existence, if they want to have a good reputation, if they want to be able to rule others, they have to do that. So, they accept those obligations in a conscious way for the beauty or glory of existence. The choice, the aesthetic choice or the political choice, for which they decide to accept this kind of existence—that's the *mode d'assujettissement.*It's a choice, it's a personal choice.

In late Stoicism, when they start saying "Well, you are obliged to do that because you are a human being" something changes. It's not a problem of choice; you have to do it because you are a rational being. The *mode d'assujettissement* is changing.

In Christianity what is very interesting is that the sexual rules for behavior were, of course, justified through religion. The institutions by which they were imposed were religious institutions. But the form of the obligation was a legal form. There was a kind of the internal juridification of religious law inside Christianity. For instance, all the casuistic practice was typically a juridical practice.

Q. After the Enlightenment, though, when the religious drops out, is the juridical what's left?

MF. Yes, after the eighteenth century, the religious framework of those rules disappears in part, and then between a medical or scientific approach and a juridical framework there was competition, with no resolution.

Q. Could you sum this all up?

MF. Well, the *substance éthique* for the Greeks was the *aphrodisia*; *mode d'assujettissement* was a politicoaesthetic choice; the *form d'ascèse* was the *techne* which were used—and there we find, for example, the *techne* about the body, or economics as the rules by which you define your role as husband, or the erotic as a kind of asceticism toward oneself in loving boys, and so on—and the *téléologie* was the mastery of oneself. So, that's the situation I describe in the two first parts of *L' Usage des plaisirs.* . . .

Q. What is the care of the self which you have decided to treat separately in *Le Souci de soi*?

MF. What interests me in the Hellenistic culture, in the Greco-Roman culture, starting from about the third century B.C. and continuing until the second or third century after Christ, is a precept for which the Greeks had a specific word, *epimeleia heautou,*which means taking care of one's self. It does not mean simply being interested in oneself, nor does it mean having a certain tendency to self-attachment or self-fascination. *Epimeleia heautou* is a very powerful word in Greek which means working on or being concerned with something. For example, Xenophon used the word *epimeleia heautou* to describe agricultural management. The responsibility of a monarch for his fellow citizens was also *epimeleia heautou*. That which a doctor does in the course of caring for a patient is *epimeleia heautou*. It is, therefore, a very powerful word; it describes a sort of work, an activity; it implies attention, knowledge, technique.

Q. But isn't the application of knowledge and technology to the self a modern invention?

MF. Knowledge played a different role in the classical care of the self. There are very interesting things to analyze about relations between scientific knowledge and the *epimeleia heautou*. The one who cared for himself had to choose among all the things that you can know through scientific knowledge only those kinds of things which were relative to him and important to life.

Q. So theoretical understanding, scientific understanding, was secondary to and guided by ethical and aesthetic concerns?

MF. Their problem and their discussion concerned what limited sorts of the knowledge were useful for *epimeleia*. For instance, for the Epicureans, the general knowledge of what is the world, of what is the necessity of the world, the relation between world, necessity and the gods—all that was very important for the care of the self. Because it was first a matter of meditation: if you were able exactly to understand the necessity of the world, then you could master passions in a much better way, and so on. So, for the Epicureans there was a kind of adequation between all possible knowledge and the care of the self. The reason that one had to become familiar with physics or cosmology was that one had to take care of the self. For the Stoics, the true self is defined only by what I can be master of.

Q. So knowledge is subordinated to the practical end of mastery?

MF. Epictetus is very clear on that. He gives as an exercise to walk every morning in the streets looking, watching. And if you meet a consular figure you say, "Is the consul something I can master?" No, so I have nothing to do. If I meet a beautiful girl or beautiful boy, is their beauty, their desirability, something which depends on me, and so on? For the Christians things are quite different; for Christians the possibility that Satan can get inside your soul and give you thoughts you cannot recognize as Satanic but that you might interpret as coming from God leads to uncertainty about what is going on inside your soul. You are unable to know what the real root of your desire is, at least without hermeneutic work.

Q. So, to what extent did the Christians develop new techniques of self-mastery?

MF. What interests me about the classical concept of care of the self is that we see here the birth and development of a certain number of ascetic themes ordinarily attributed to Christianity. Christianity is usually given credit for replacing the generally tolerant Greco-Roman lifestyle with an austere lifestyle marked by a series of renunciations, interdictions, or prohibitions. Now, we can see that in this activity of the self on itself, the ancients developed a whole series of austerity practices that the Christians later directly borrowed from them. So, we see that this activity became linked to a certain sexual austerity which was subsumed directly into the Christian ethic. We are not talking about a moral rupture between tolerant antiquity and austere Christianity.

Q. In the name of what does one choose to impose this lifestyle upon oneself?

MF. In antiquity, this work on the self with its attendant austerity is not imposed on the individual by means of civil law or religious obligation, but is a choice about existence made by the individual. People decide for themselves whether or not to care for themselves.

I don't think it is to attain eternal life after death, because they were not particularly concerned with that. Rather they acted so as to give to their life certain values (reproduce certain examples, leave behind them an exalted reputation, give the maximum possible brilliance to their lives). It was a question of making one's life into an object for a sort of knowledge, for a *techne*—for an art.

We have hardly any remnant of the idea in our society, that the principal work of art which one has to take care of, the main area to which one must apply aesthetic values is oneself, one's life, one's existence. We find this in the Renaissance, but in a slightly academic form, and yet again in nineteenth-century dandyism, but those were only episodes.

Q. But isn't the Greek concern with the self just an early version of our self-absorption which many consider a central problem in our society?

MF. You have a certain number of themes—and I don't say that you have to reutilize them in this way—which indicate to you that in a culture to which we owe a certain number of our most important constant moral elements, there was a practice of the self, a conception of the self, very different from our present culture of the self. In the California cult of the self, one is supposed to discover one's true self, to separate it from that which might obscure or alienate it, to decipher its truth thanks to psychological or psychoanalytic science, which is supposed to be able to tell you what your true self is. Therefore, not only do I not identify this ancient culture of the self with what you might call the Californian cult of the self, I think they are diametrically opposed.

What happened in between is precisely an overturning of the classical culture of the self. This took place when Christianity substituted the idea of a self which one had to renounce because clinging to the self was opposed to God's will for the idea of a self which had to be created as a work of art.

Q. We know that one of the studies for *Le Souci de soi* concerns the role of writing in the formation of the self. How is the question of the relation of writing and the self posed by Plato?

MF. First, to bring out a certain number of historical facts which are often glossed over when posing this problem of writing, we must look into the famous question of the *hypomnemata*. Current interpreters see in the critique of the *hypomnemata* in the *Phaedrus* a critique of writing as a material support for memory. Now, in fact, *hypomnemata* has a very precise meaning. It is a copybook, a notebook. Precisely this type of notebook was coming into vogue at Plato's time for personal and administrative use. This new technology was as disrupting as the introduction of the computer into private life today. It seems to me the question of writing and the self must be posed in terms of the technical and material framework in which it arose.

Secondly, there are problems of interpretation concerning the famous critique of writing as opposed to the culture of memory in the *Phaedrus*. If you read the *Phaedrus,* you will see that this passage is secondary with respect to another one which is fundamental and which is in line with the theme which runs throughout the end of the text. It does not matter whether a text is written or oral—the problem is whether or not the discourse in question gives access to truth. Thus the written/oral question is altogether secondary with respect to the question of truth.

Thirdly, what seems remarkable to me is that these new instruments were immediately used for the constitution of a permanent relationship to oneself—one must manage oneself as a governor manages the governed, as a head of an enterprise manages his enterprise, a head of household manages his household. This new idea that virtue consists essentially in perfectly governing oneself, that is, in exercising upon oneself as exact a mastery as that of a sovereign against whom there would no longer be revolts, is something very important which we will find for centuries—practically until Christianity. So, if you will, the point at which the question of the *hypomnemata* and the culture of the self come together in a remarkable fashion is the point at which the culture of the self takes as its goal the perfect government of the self—a sort of permanent political relationship between self and self. The ancients carried on this politics of themselves with these notebooks just as governments and those who manage enterprises administered by keeping registers. This is how writing seems to me to be linked to the problem of the culture of the self. . . .

Q. But how does writing connect up with ethics and the self?

MF. No technique, no professional skill can be acquired without exercise; neither can one learn the art of living, the *techne tou biou*, without an *askesis* which must be taken as a training of oneself by oneself: this was one of the traditional principles to which the Pythagoreans, the Socratics, the Cynics had for a long time attributed great importance. Among all the forms this training took (and which included abstinences, memorizations, examinations of conscience, meditations, silence and listening to others), it seems that writing—the fact of writing for oneself and for others—came quite late to play a sizeable role.

Q. What specific role did the notebooks play when they finally became influential in late antiquity?

MF. As personal as they were, the *hypomnemata* must nevertheless not be taken for intimate diaries or for those accounts of spiritual experience (temptations, struggles, falls, and victories) which can be found in later Christian literature. They do not constitute an "account of oneself"; their objective is not to bring the *arcana conscientiae* to light, the confession of which—be it oral or written—has a purifying value. The movement that they seek to effect is the inverse of this last one. The point is not to pursue the indescribable, not to reveal the hidden, not to say the nonsaid, but on the contrary, to collect the already-said, to reassemble that which one could hear or read, and this to an end which is nothing less than the constitution of oneself.

The *hypomnemata* are to be resituated in the context of a very sensitive tension of that period. Within a culture very affected by traditionality, by the recognized value of the already-said, by the recurrence of discourse, by the "citational" practice under the seal of age and authority, an ethic was developing which was very explicitly oriented to the care of oneself, toward definite objectives such as retiring into oneself, reaching oneself, living with oneself, being sufficient to oneself, profiting by and enjoying oneself. Such is the objective of the *hypomnemata*: to make of the recollection of the fragmentary *logos* transmitted by teaching, listening, or reading a means to establish as adequate and as perfect a relationship of oneself to oneself as possible.

Q. Could you tell us something about how Greco-Roman austerity differs from Christian austerity?

MF. One thing that has been very important is that in Stoic ethics the question of purity was nearly inexistent or rather marginal. It was important in Pythagorean circles and also in the neo-Platonic schools and became more and more important through their influence and also through religious influences. At a certain moment, the problem of an aesthetics of existence is covered over by the problem of purity, which is something else and which requires another kind of technique. In Christian ascetism the question of purity becomes more and more important; the reason why you have to take control of yourself is to keep yourself pure. The problem of virginity, this model of feminine integrity, becomes much more important in Christianity. The theme of virginity has nearly nothing to do with sexual ethics in Greco-Roman ascetism. There the problem is a problem of self-domination. It was a virile model of self-domination and a woman who was temperate was as virile to herself as a man. The paradigm of sexual self-restraint becomes a feminine paradigm through the theme of purity and virginity, based on the model of physical integrity. Physical integrity rather than self-regulation became important. So the problem of ethics as an aesthetics of existence is covered over by the problem of purification.

This new Christian self had to be constantly examined because in this self were lodged concupiscence and desires of the flesh. From that moment on, the self was no longer something to be made but something to be renounced and deciphered. Consequently, between paganism and Christianity, the opposition is not between tolerance and austerity, but between a form of austerity which is linked to an aesthetic of existence and other forms of austerity which are linked to the necessity of renouncing the self and deciphering its truth.

Q. So Nietzsche, then, must be wrong, in *The Genealogy of Morals,* when he credits Christian asceticism for making us the kind of creatures that can make promises?

MF. Yes, I think he has given mistaken credit to Christianity, given what we know about the evolution of pagan ethics from the fourth century B.C. to the fourth century after.

Notes

1. The following is the result of a series of working sessions with Michel Foucault conducted by Paul Rabinow and Hubert Dreyfus at Berkeley, California, in April 1983.

19

JACQUES DERRIDA
(1930–)

French philosopher and deconstructionist Jacques Derrida was born in 1930 into a Jewish family in El-Biar, Algiers. At the age of eighteen he earned his baccalaureate degree and decided to take up the study of philosophy after hearing a radio broadcast on teaching philosophy as a vocation. During his early years as a philosophy student at the École Normale Supérieure, Derrida studied widely in structuralism, phenomenology, literary criticism, and especially the history of philosophy. In 1956, he received a grant to study at Harvard University, where he worked on a translation and introduction to Edmund Husserl's *Origin of Geometry* and read the works of James Joyce, to whom Derrida would later devote two important essays. From 1960 to 1964, Derrida taught philosophy and logic at the Sorbonne before eventually returning to the École Normale Supérieure in 1965 to teach the history of philosophy. Since the mid-1970s, Derrida has spent a significant portion of his time teaching and lecturing abroad, particularly in the United States, where he has held visiting professorship at such universities as Yale, Cornell, and, more recently, the University of California, Irvine, where he is currently professor of Humanities.

Although he published a number of important essays and translations during the early 1960s, it was not until 1967 that Derrida gained any sort of philosophical renown. In that year, he published three seminal works: *Speech and Phenomena*, *Writing and Difference*, and *Of Grammatology*. In these works, Derrida offered a "deconstructive" analysis of the "logocentrism" characteristic of the Western metaphysical tradition, which has tended to privilege self-present speech (*logos*) over "writing" (or *arché-writing*), a technical term for Derrida that refers to the "trace" of the author's absence in the text of philosophy entailing an irreducible and irretrievable loss of meaning. These works were followed in 1972 with the publication of *Positions*, *Dissemination*, and *Margins of Philosophy*, which extended Derrida's deconstructive approach to philosophy and literature through painstaking analyses of texts written by authors as diverse as Plato, Mallarmé, Austin, and Heidegger. While these early writings often gestured toward quasi-ethical and political themes, it was not until the mid-1980s that Derrida's work took on an overtly ethical and political character. In his writings on the Heidegger and Paul de Man "affairs" (*Of Spirit* [1987] and *Mémoires: for Paul de Man* [1989]), Derrida sought to elucidate the complex relation between deconstruction and concrete ethical and political positions. His writings from 1990 onward (e.g., *Gift of Death* [1992], *Specters of Marx* [1993], and *Politics of Friendship* [1994]) have become increasingly concerned with the elaboration of a thought of what proceeds or serves as the conditions of possibility for ethics and politics—what he sometimes calls "the ethical" or "the political."

Our selection, entitled "Passions" (1991), belongs to this recent period of Derrida's writings in which classical ethical themes are submitted to careful analysis in order to probe their foundations and radicalize their meaning. The occasion for the essay was an invitation from David Wood to Derrida to contribute an opening essay to an anthology of critical essays on Derrida's work entitled *Derrida: A*

Critical Reader. Derrida interprets Wood's request as an invitation to "respond," which naturally raises the question of what "responsivity" and responsibility actually entail in this instance. This leads Derrida into a complex analysis of "the secret," at the end of which he confides his taste for "literature," here equated with the democratic "right to say everything." This democratic space of freedom is what deconstruction incessantly seeks out inasmuch as it opens the possibility of critically questioning all dogmas and discourses, "even those of the ethics or the politics of responsibility."

Select Bibliography of Derrida's Works in English

Adieu to Emmanuel Levinas. Trans. Pascale-Anne Brault and Michael Naas. Stanford, CA: Stanford University Press, 1999.

Dissemination. Trans. Barbara Johnson. Chicago: Chicago University Press, 1981.

Edmund Husserl's "Origin of Geometry": An Introduction. Trans. John P. Leavey. New Jersey: Humanities Press, 1978.

The Gift of Death. Trans. David Wills. Chicago: Chicago University Press, 1995.

Margins of Philosophy. Trans. Alan Bass. Chicago: University of Chicago Press, 1982.

Of Grammatology. Trans. Gayatri C. Spivak. Baltimore, MD: Johns Hopkins University Press, 1974.

Of Spirit: Heidegger and the Question. Trans. Geoffrey Bennington and Rachel Bowlby. Chicago: Chicago University Press, 1989.

On the Name. Ed. Thomas Dutoit. Stanford, CA: Stanford University Press, 1995.

Positions. Trans. Alan Bass. Chicago: University of Chicago Press, 1981.

Politics of Friendship. Trans. George Collins. London: Verso, 1996.

Specters of Marx. Trans. Peggy Kamuf. New York: Routledge, 1994.

Speech and Phenomena. Trans. David Allison. Evanston, IL: Northwestern University Press, 1973.

Spurs: Nietzsche's Styles. Trans. Barbara Harlow. Chicago: University of Chicago Press, 1979.

Writing and Difference. Trans. Alan Bass. Chicago: University of Chicago Press, 1978.

PASSIONS

Whoever ponders the necessity, the genealogy and therefore also the limits of the concept of responsibility cannot fail to wonder at some point what is meant by "respond," and *responsiveness* [English in original—Tr.], a precious word for which I can find no strict equivalent in my language. And to wonder whether "to respond" has an opposite, which would consist, if common sense is to be believed, in not responding. Is it possible to make a decision on the subject of "responding" and of "responsiveness"?

One can today, in many different places, attend to or participate in a congenial and disturbing task: restoring morality and, especially, reassuring those who had serious reasons for being troubled by this topic. Some souls believe themselves to have found in Deconstruction—as if there were one, and only one—a modern form of immorality, of amorality, or of irresponsibility (etc.: a discourse too well known; I do not need to continue), while others, more serious, in less of a hurry, better disposed toward so-called Deconstruction, today claim the opposite; they discern encouraging signs and in increasing numbers (at times, I must admit, in some of my texts) which would testify to a permanent, extreme, direct, or oblique, in any event, increasingly intense attention, to those things which one could identify under the fine names of "ethics," "morality," "responsibility," "subject," etc. Before reverting to not-responding, it would be necessary to declare in the most direct way that if one had the *sense* of duty and of responsibility, it would compel breaking with both these moralisms, with these two restorations of morality, including, therefore, the remoralization of deconstruction, which naturally seems more attractive than that to which it is rightly opposed, but which at each moment risks reassuring itself in order to reassure the other and to promote the consensus of a new dogmatic slumber. And it is so that one not be in too much of a hurry to say that it is in the name of a *higher* responsibility and a more intractable moral exigency that one declares one's distaste, uneven as it may be, for both moralisms. Undoubtedly, it is always following the affirmation of a certain excess that one can suspect the well-known immorality, indeed the denigrating hypocrisy of moralisms. But nothing allows one to assert that the best names or the most suitable figures for this affirmation are ethics, morality, politics, responsibility, or the subject. Furthermore, would it be moral and responsible to act morally because one has a *sense* (the word emphasized above) of duty and responsibility? Clearly not; it would be too easy and, precisely, natural, programmed by nature: it is hardly moral to be moral (responsible, etc.) because one has the *sense* of the moral, of the highness of the law, etc. This is the well-known problem of "respect" for the moral law, itself the "cause" of respect in the Kantian sense; this problem draws all of its interest from the disturbing paradox that it inscribes in the heart of a morality incapable of giving an account of being inscribed in an affect or in a sensibility of what should not be inscribed there or should only enjoin the sacrifice of everything that would only obey this sensible inclination. It is well known that sacrifice and the sacrificial offering are at the heart of Kantian morality, under their own name (cf., for example, Kant's *Critique of Practical Reason*, bk. 1, pt. 1, ch. 3). The object of sacrifice there is always of the order of the sensuous motives, of the secretly "pathological" interest which must, says Kant, be "humbled" before the moral law; this concept of sacrificial offering, thus of sacrifice in general, requires the whole apparatus of the "critical" distinctions of Kantianism: sensible/intelligible, passivity/spontaneity, *intuitus derivativus/intuitus originarius,* etc.; the same goes for the concept of *passion*; what I am looking for here, passion according to me, would be a concept of passion that would be non-"pathological" in Kant's sense.)

All this, therefore, still remains open, suspended, undecided, questionable even beyond the question, indeed, to make use of another figure, absolutely aporetic. What is the ethicity of ethics? The morality of morality? What is responsibility? What is the "What is?" in this case? etc. These questions are always urgent. In a certain way they must remain urgent and unanswered, at any rate without a general and rule-governed response, without a response other than that which is linked specifically each time, to the occurrence of a decision without rules and without will in the course of a new test of the undecidable. And let it not be said too precipitately that these questions or these propositions are *already* inspired by a concern that could by right be called ethical, moral, responsible, etc. For sure, in saying that ("And let it not be said too precipitately . . ." etc.), one gives ammunition to the officials of antideconstruction, but all in all isn't that preferable to the constitution of a consensual euphoria or, worse, a community of complacent deconstructionists, reassured and reconciled with the world in ethical certainty, good conscience, satisfaction of service rendered, and the consciousness of duty accomplished (or, more heroically still, yet to be accomplished)?

So the nonresponse. Clearly, it will always be possible to say, and it will be true, that nonresponse is a response. One always has, one always must have, the right not to respond, and this liberty belongs to responsibility itself, that is, to the liberty that one believes must be associated with it. One must always be free not to respond to an appeal or to an invitation—and it is worth remembering this, reminding oneself of the essence of this liberty. Those who think that responsibility or the sense of responsibility is a good thing, a prime virtue, indeed the Good itself, are convinced, however, that one must always answer (for oneself, to the other, before the other, or before the law) and that, moreover, a nonresponse is always a modality determined in the space opened by an unavoidable responsibility. Is there then nothing more to say about nonresponse? On it or on the subject of it, if not in its favor?

Let us press on and, in the attempt to convince more quickly, let us take an example, whether or not it is valid for the law. What example? This one. And certainly, when I say this very example, I already say something more and something else; I say something which goes beyond the *tode ti,* the this of the example. The example itself, as such, overflows its singularity as much as its identity. This is why there are no examples, while at the same time there are only examples; I have said this, too, often about many examples, no doubt. The exemplarity of the example is clearly never the exemplarity of the example. We can never be sure of having put an end to this very old children's game in which all the discourses, philosophical or not, which have ever inspired deconstructions are entangled by the performative fiction which consists in saying, starting up the game again, "take precisely this example."

If, for example, I respond to the invitation which is made to me to respond to the texts collected here, which do me the honor or the kindness of taking an interest in certain of my earlier publications, am I not going to be heaping up errorsand therefore conduct myself in an irresponsible way—by taking on false responsibilities? What faults?

1. First of all, that of endorsing a situation, of subscribing to it and acting as if I found myself at ease in such a strange place, as if I found it normal or natural to speak here, as if we were sitting down at the table in the midst of twelve people who were speaking on the whole about "me" or addressing themselves to "me." "I" [*Moi*], who am both a twelfth insofar as I am part of a group, one among others, and already, being thus split or redoubled, the thirteenth insofar as I am not one example among others in the series of twelve. What would it look like if I supposed I could reply to all these men and this woman at the same time, or if I supposed I could *begin by responding,* thus disregarding the very

scholarly and very singular strategy of each of these eleven or twelve discourses, at once so generous and so unself-satisfied and so overdetermined? By speaking last, both in conclusion and in introduction, in twelfth or thirteenth place, am I not taking the insane risk and adopting the odious attitude of treating all these thinkers as disciples, indeed the apostles, among whom some would be preferred by me, others potential evil traitors? Who would be Judas here? What is someone to do who does not want to be and who knows himself not to be (but how can one be sure about these things, and how can one extricate oneself from these matrices?) either an apostle (*apostolas,* a messenger of God), or Jesus, or Judas? Because it dawned on me a little late, counting the number of participants gathered here, exactly twelve (who is still to come?), then noticing the words "oblique offering" and "passion" in his letter, that David Wood was perhaps the perverse producer of a mystery—and that in fact the "oblique offering," which was no less his than mine, had a flavor that was ironically, sarcastically, eucharistic (no vegetarian—there are at least two among the guests—will ever be able to break with the sublimity of mystical cannibalism): the "this is my body which is given for you, keep this in remembrance of me," is this not the most oblique offering?Is this not what I commented on all year long in *Glas* or in my last seminars on "eating—the other" and the "rhetoric of cannibalism"? All the more reason not to respond. This is no Last Supper, and the ironic friendship which brings us together consists in knowing this, while peering with a "squinty eye" toward this cannibalism in mourning.

2. If I did respond I would put myself in the situation of someone who felt *capable of responding*: he has an answer for everything, he takes himself to be up to answering each of us, each question, each objection or criticism; he does not see that each of the texts gathered here has its force, its logic, its singular strategy, that it would be necessary to reread everything, to reconstitute the work and its trajectory, the themes and arguments of each, the discursive tradition and the many texts set to work, etc. To claim to do all this, and to do it in a few pages, would smack of a *hybris* and a naïveté without limit—and from the outset a flagrant lack of respect for the discourse, the work, and the offering of the other. More reasons for not responding.

3. From these two arguments we can glimpse that a certain *nonresponse* can attest to this politeness (without rules) of which we spoke above, and finally to respect for others, that is to say, also to an exigency of responsibility. It will perhaps be said that this nonresponse is the best response, that it is still a response and a sign of responsibility. Perhaps. Let us wait and see. In any case, one thinks of that pride, that self-satisfaction, that elementary confidence which it would take to answer when a good education teaches children that they must not "answer back" (at any rate in the sense and tradition of French manners) when grown-ups speak to them, they must not reproach them or criticize them, and certainly not ask them questions.

4. The overweening presumption from which *no response will ever be free* not only has to do with the fact that the response claims to measure up to the discourse of the other, to situate it, understand it, indeed circumscribe it by responding thus *to* the other and *before* the other. The respondent presumes, with as much frivolity as arrogance, that he can respond to the other and before the other because first of all he is able to answer for himself and for all he has been able to do, say, or write. To answer for oneself would here be to presume to know all that one could do, say, or write, to gather it together in an intelligible and coherent synthesis, to stamp it with one and the same seal (whatever the genre, the place, or the date, the discursive form, the contextual strategy, etc.), to posit that the same "I think" accompanies all "my" representations, which themselves form a systematic, homogeneous tissue of "theses," "themes," "objects," of "narratives," of "critiques," or of "evaluations," a tissue which can be subjectivized and of which I would have a total and intact memory, would know all the premises and all the consequences, etc.; this would also be to suppose that deconstruction is of the same order as the critique whose concept and history it precisely deconstructs. So many dogmatic naïvetes that one will never discourage, but all the more reason not to respond, not to act as if one could respond to the other,

before the other, and for oneself. Someone will retort: indeed, but then this nonresponse is still a response, the most polite, the most modest, the most vigilant, the most respectful—both of the other and of truth. This nonresponse would again be a respectable form of politeness and respect, a responsible form of the vigilant exercise of responsibility. In any case, this would confirm that one cannot or that one ought not fail to respond. One cannot, one ought not to respond with nothing. The ought and the can are here strangely coimplicated. Perhaps. Let us wait and see.

Continuing these four preceding arguments, I would avoid errors (errors of politeness, moral errors, etc.) by not responding, by responding elliptically, by responding obliquely. I would have said to myself: it would be better, it is fairer, it is more decent, and more moral, not to respond. It is more respectful to the other, more responsible in the face of the imperative of critical, hypercritical, and above all "deconstructive" thought which insists on yielding as little as possible to dogmas and presuppositions. So you see—if I took heed of all these reasons, and if, still believing that this nonresponse was the best response, I decided not to respond, then I would run even worse risks.

Which ones?

1. To start with, the first injury or injustice: seeming not to take sufficiently seriously the persons and the texts offered here, to evince toward them an inadmissible ingratitude and a culpable indifference.

2. And then to exploit the "good reasons" for not responding to make use of silence in a way that is still strategic: because there is an art of the nonresponse, or of the deferred response, which is a rhetoric of war, a polemical ruse. Polite silence can become the most insolent weapon and the most deadly irony. On the pretext of waiting to have read through, pondered, labored to be able to begin to reply seriously (which will in fact be necessary and which could take forever), nonresponse as postponed or elusive, indeed absolutely elliptical response can always shelter one comfortably, safe from all objection. And on the pretext of feeling incapable of responding *to* the other, and answering *for* oneself, does one not undermine, both theoretically and practically, the concept of responsibility, which is actually the very essence of the *socius*?

3. To justify one's nonresponse by all these arguments, one can still refer to rules, to general norms, but then one falls short of the principle of politeness and of responsibility that we recalled above: never to believe oneself free of any debt and hence never to act simply according to a rule, in conformity to duty, not even *out of duty*, still less "out of politeness." Nothing would be more immoral and more impolite.

4. Certainly, nothing would be worse than substituting for an inadequate response, but one still giving evidence of a sincere, modest, finite, resigned effort, an interminable discourse. Such a discourse would pretend to provide, instead of a response or a nonresponse, a performative (more or less *performante* [literally: performing, also dynamic, effective] and more or less metalinguistic) for all these questions, nonquestions, or nonresponses. Such an operation would be open to the most justified critiques, it would offer its body, it would surrender, as if in sacrifice, the most vulnerable body to the most just blows. Because it would suffer from a *double* failure, it would combine two apparently contradictory faults: first, the claim to mastery or to an overview(be it meta-linguistic, meta-logical, meta-metaphysical, etc.) and second, the becoming–work of art (literary performance or performative, fiction, work), the aestheticizing play of a discourse from which one expects a serious, thoughtful, or philosophical response.

So, what are we to do? It is impossible to respond here. It is impossible to respond to this question about the response. It is impossible to respond to the question by which we precisely ask ourselves whether it is necessary to respond or not to respond, whether it is necessary, possible, or impossible. This aporia without end paralyzes us because it binds us doubly. (I must and I need not, I must not, it is necessary and impossible, etc.) In one and the same place, on the same apparatus, I have my two hands tied or nailed down. What are we to do? But also how is it that it does not prevent us from speaking, from continuing to describe the situation, from trying to make oneself understood? What is the nature of this language, since already it no longer belongs, no longer belongs simply, either to the question or to the response whose limits we have just verified and are continuing to verify? Of what does this verification consist, when nothing happens without some sacrifice? Will one call this a testimony in a sense that neither the martyr, the attestation nor the testament would exhaust? And, as with every testimony, providing that it never be reducible, precisely, to verification, to proof or to demonstration, in a word, to knowledge?

Among other things, to return to the start of the scene, we find that the analyst, the one to whom we have given the name, can no longer describe or objectify the programmed development of a ritual, still less of a sacrificial offering. No one wanted to play the role of the sacrificeable or of the sacrificer, all the *agents* (priests, victims, participants, spectators, readers) not only *refuse to act,* but even if they wanted to make the prescribed gestures they would find themselves brought to a halt when faced with these contradictory orders. And it is not only a religious sociality whose identity is thus menaced, it is a philosophical sociality, insofar as it presupposes the order (preferably circular) of the appeal, of the question and the response. Some will say that this is the very principle of the community which sees itself thus exposed to disruption. Others will say that the threat of disruption threatens nothing, that it has always been the instituting or constitutive origin of religious or philosophical ties, of the social bond in general: the community lives and feeds on this vulnerability, and so it should. If the analyst in fact discovers limits to his work of scientific objectification, that is quite normal: he is a participant in a process which he would like to analyze, he can virtually play all the roles in it (that is to say, also mime them). This limit furnishes positively the condition of his intelligence, of his reading, of his interpretations. But what would be the condition of this condition? The fact that the *Critical Reader* is *a priori* and endlessly exposed to a *critical reading*.

What could escape this sacrificial verification and so secure the very space of *this very discourse, for example*? No question, no response, no responsibility. Let us say that there is a secret here. Let us testify: *There* is something secret. [*Il y a là du secret*.] We will leave the matter here for today, but not without an exercise on the essence and existence of such a secret, an exercise that will have an apophatic aspect. The apophatic is not here necessarily dependent on negative theology, even if it makes it possible, too. And what we are attempting to put to the test is the possibility, in truth the impossibility, for any testimony to guarantee itself by expressing itself in the following form and grammar: "Let us testify that. . . ."

We testify to a secret that is without content, without a content separable from its performative experience, from its performative tracing. (We shall not say from its performative *enunciation* or from its *propositional argumentation;* and we keep in reserve a number of questions about performativity in general.)

Let us say, therefore: *There is something secret*. It would not be a matter of an artistic or technical secret reserved for someone—or for several, such as style, ruse, the signature of talent or the mark of a genius, the know-how that is thought to be incommunicable, untransmittable, unteachable, inimitable. It would not even be a matter of that psychophysical secret, the art hidden in the depths of the human soul, of which Kant speaks in connection with the transcendental schematism, and of the imagination (*eine verborgene Kunst in den Tiefen der menschlichen Seele*).

There is something secret. It would not be a question of a secret as a representation dissimulated by a conscious subject, nor, moreover, of the content of an unconscious representation, some secret or mysterious motive that the moralist or the psychoanalyst might have the skill to detect, or, as they say, to demystify. This secret would not even be of the order of absolute subjectivity, in the rather unorthodox sense, with respect to a history of metaphysics, that Kierkegaard gave to *existence* and to all that resists the concept or frustrates the system, especially the Hegelian dialectic. This secret would not belong to any of the stages (aesthetic, ethical, religious A or B) that Kierkegaard distinguishes. It would be neither sacred nor profane.

There is something secret. But to take account of what we have just suggested, the being-there of the secret belongs no more to the private than to the public. It is not a deprived interiority that one would have to reveal, confess, announce, that is, to which one would have to respond by accounting for it and thematizing it in broad daylight. Who would ever determine the proper extent of a thematization so as to judge it finally adequate? And is there any worse violence than that which consists in calling for the response, demanding that one *give an account of* everything, and preferably *thematically?* Because this secret is not phenomenalizable. Neither phenomenal nor noumenal. No more than religion can philosophy, morality, politics, or the law accept the unconditional respect of this secret. These authorities are constituted as authorities who may properly ask for accounts, that is, responses, from those with accepted responsibilities. No doubt they allow sometimes that there are conditional secrets (the secret of confession, the professional secret, the military secret, the manufacturing secret, the state secret). But the *right to secrets* is in all these cases a conditional right. Because the secret can be shared there, and limited by given conditions. The secret becomes simply a *problem.* It can and must be made known under other circumstances. Everywhere that a response and a responsibility are required, the right to a secret becomes conditional. There are no secrets, only problems for the knowledges which in this respect include not only philosophy, science, and technology, but also religion, morality, politics, and the law.

There is something secret. [*Il y a du secret.*] It concerns neither that into which a revealed religion *initiates* us nor that which it *reveals* (namely a mystery of passion), nor a learned ignorance (in a Christian brotherhood practicing a kind of negative theology), nor the content of an esoteric doctrine (for example, in a Pythagorean, Platonic, or neo-Platonic community). In any case it cannot be reduced to these because it makes them possible. The secret is not mystical.

There is something secret. But it does not conceal itself. Heterogeneous to the hidden, to the obscure, to the nocturnal, to the invisible, to what can be dissimulated and indeed to what is nonmanifest in general, it cannot be unveiled. It remains inviolable even when one thinks one has revealed it. Not that it hides itself forever in an indecipherable crypt or behind an absolute veil. It simply exceeds the play of veiling/unveiling, dissimulation/revelation, night/day, forgetting/anamnesis, earth/heaven, etc. It does not belong therefore to the truth, neither to the truth as *homoiosis* oradequation, nor to the truth as memory (Mnemosyne, *aletheia),* nor to the given truth, nor to the promised truth, nor to the inaccessible truth. Its nonphenomenality is without relation, even negative relation, to phenomenality. Its reserve is no longer of the intimacy that one likes to call secret, of the very close or very proper which sucks in or inspires so much profound discourse (the *Geheimnis* or, even richer, the inexhaustible *Unheimliche*).

Certainly, one could speak this secret in other names, whether one finds them or gives them to it. Moreover, this happens at every instant. It remains secret under all names and it is its irreducibility to the very name which makes it secret, even when one *makes the truth* in its name as Augustine put it so originally. The secret is that one here calls it secret, putting it for once in relation to all the secrets which bear the same name but cannot be reduced to it. The secret would also be homonymy, not so much a hidden resource of homonymy, but the functional possibility of homonymy or of *mimesis.*

There is something secret. One can always speak about it, that is not enough to disrupt it. One can speak of it *ad infinitum,* tell stories about it, utter all the discourses which it puts to work and the stories which it unleashes or enchains, because the secret often makes one think of these secret histories and it even gives one a taste for them. And the secret will remain secret, mute, impassive as the *khōra,* as *Khōra* foreign to every history, as much in the sense of *Geschichte* or *res gestae* as of knowledge and of historical narrative (*epistémè, historia rerum gestarom*), and outside all periodization, all epochalization. It remains silent, not to keep a word in reserve or withdrawn, but because it remains foreign to speech, without our even being able to say in that distinguished syntagm: "the secret is that in speech which is foreign to speech." It is no more in speech than foreign to speech. It does not answer to speech, it does not say "I, the secret," it does not correspond, it does not answer: either for itself or to anyone else, before anyone or anything whatsoever. Absolute nonresponse which one could not even call to account or for something on account, grant indemnities, excuses, or "discounts"—so many ruses, always, to draw it into a *process* that is philosophical, ethical, political, juridical, etc. The secret gives rise to no *process*. It may appear to give rise to one (indeed it always does so), it may lend itself to it, but it never surrenders to it. The ethics of the discussion may always not respect it (according to me it owes it respect, even if this seems difficult or contradictory, because the secret is intractable), but it will never reduce it. Moreover, no discussion would either begin or continue without it. And whether one respects it or not, the secret remains there impassively, at a distance, out of reach. In this one cannot not respect it, whether one likes it or not, whether one knows it or not.

There, there is no longer time nor place.

A confidence to end with today. Perhaps all I wanted to do was to confide or confirm my taste (probably unconditional) for literature, more precisely for literary writing. Not that I like literature in general, nor that I prefer it to something else, to philosophy, for example, as they suppose who ultimately discern neither one nor the other. Not that I want to reduce everything to it, especially not philosophy. Literature I could fundamentally do without, in fact, rather easily. If I had to retire to an island, it would be particularly history books, memoirs, that I would doubtless take with me, and that I would read in my own way, perhaps to make literature out of them, unless it would be the other way round, and this would be true for other books (art, philosophy, religion, human or natural sciences, law, etc.). But if, without liking literature in general and for its own sake, I like something *about it*, which above all cannot be reduced to some aesthetic quality, to some source of formal pleasure, this would be *in place of the secret*. In place of an absolute secret. There would be the passion. There is no passion without secret, this very secret, indeed no secret without this passion. *In place of the secret*: there where nevertheless everything is said and where what remains is nothing—but the remainder, not even of literature.

I have often found myself insisting on the necessity of distinguishing between literature and belles lettres or poetry. Literature is a modern invention, inscribed in conventions and institutions which, to hold on to just this trait, secure in principle its *right to say everything*. Literature thus ties its destiny to a certain noncensure, to the space of democratic freedom (freedom of the press, freedom of speech, etc.). No democracy without literature; no literature without democracy. One can always want neither one nor the other, and there is no shortage of doing without them under all regimes; it is quite possible to consider neither of them to be unconditional goods and indispensable rights. But in no case can one dissociate one from the other. No analysis would be equal to it. And each time that a literary work is censured, democracy is in danger, as everyone agrees. The possibility of literature, the legitimation that a society gives it, the allaying of suspicion or terror with regard to it, all that goes together—politically—with the unlimited right to ask any question, to suspect all dogmatism, to analyze every presupposition, even those of the ethics or the politics of responsibility.

But this authorization to say everything paradoxically makes the author an author who is not responsible to anyone, not even to himself, for whatever the persons or the characters of his works, thus of what he is supposed to have written himself, say and do, for example. And these "voices" speak, allow or make to come—even in literatures without persons and without characters. This authorization to say everything (which goes together with democracy, as the apparent hyperresponsibility of a "subject") acknowledges a right to absolute nonresponse, just where there can be no question of responding, of being able to or having to respond. This nonresponse is more original and more secret than the modalities of power and duty because it is fundamentally heterogeneous to them. We find there a hyperbolic condition of democracy which seems to contradict a certain determined and historically limited concept of such a democracy, a concept which links it to the concept of a subject that is calculable, accountable, imputable, and responsible, a subject having-to-respond, having to tell the truth, having to testify according to the sworn word ("the whole truth, nothing but the truth"), before the law, having to reveal the secret, with the exception of certain situations that are determinable and regulated by law (confession, the professional secrets of the doctor, the psychoanalyst, or the lawyer, secrets of national defense or state secrets in general, manufacturing secrets, etc.). This contradiction also indicates the task (task of thought, also theoreticopractical task) for any democracy to come.

There is in literature, in the *exemplary* secret of literature, a chance of saying everything without touching upon the secret. When all hypotheses are permitted, groundless and *ad infinitum,* about the meaning of a text, or the final intentions of an author, whose person is no more represented than non-represented by a character or by a narrator, by a poetic or fictional sentence, which detaches itself from its presumed source and thus remains *locked away,*when there is no longer even any sense in making decisions about some secret behind the surface of a textual manifestation (and it is this situation which I would call text or trace), when it is the call of this secret, however, which points back to the other or to something else, when it is this itself which keeps our passion aroused, and holds us to the other, then the secret impassions us. Even if there is none, even if it does not exist, hidden behind anything whatever. Even if the secret is no secret, even if there has never been a secret, a single secret. Not one.

Can one ever finish with obliqueness? The secret, if there is one, is not hidden at the corner of an angle, it does not lay itself open to a double view or to a squinting gaze. It cannot be seen, quite simply. No more than a word. As soon as there are words—and this can be said of the trace in general, and of the chance that it is—direct intuition no longer has any chance. One can reject, as we have done, the word "oblique"; one cannot deny the destinerrant indirection as soon as there is a trace. Or, if you prefer, one can only deny it.

One can stop and examine a secret, make it say things, make out that there is something there when there is not. One can lie, cheat, seduce by making use of it. One can play with the secret as with a simulacrum, with a lure or yet another strategy. One can cite it as an impregnable resource. One can try in this way to secure for oneself a phantasmatic power over others. That happens every day. But this very simulacrum still bears witness to a possibility which exceeds it. It does not exceed it in the direction of some ideal community, rather toward a solitude without any measure common to that of an isolated subject, a solipsism of the *ego* whose sphere of belonging (*Eigentlichkeit*) would give rise to some analogical appresentation of the alter ego and to some genesis constitutive of intersubjectivity (Husserl), or with that of a *Jemeinigkeit* of *Dasein* whose solitude, Heidegger tells us, is still a modality of *Mitsein.* Solitude, the other name of the secret to which the simulacrum still bears witness, is neither of consciousness, nor of the subject, nor of *Dasein,* not even of *Dasein* in its authentic being-able, whose testimony or attestation (*Bezeugung*) Heidegger analyzes (cf. *Being and Time,* par. 54ff). It makes them possible, but what it makes possible does not put an end to the secret. The secret never allows itself to be captured or covered over by the relation to the other, by being-with or by any form of "social bond." Even if it makes them possible, it does not answer to them, it is what does not answer. No *responsiveness* [English in original—Tr.]. Shall we call this death? Death dealt? Death dealing? I see no reason not to call that life, existence, trace. And it is not the contrary.

Consequently, if the simulacrum still bears witness to a possibility which exceeds it, this exceeding remains, it (is) *the* remainder, and it remains such even if one precisely cannot here trust any definite witness, nor even any guaranteed value to bearing witness, or, to put it another way, as the name suggests, to the history of any *martyrdom (martyria).* For one will never reconcile the value of a testimony with that of knowledge or of certainty—it is impossible and it ought not be done. One will never reduce the one to the other—it is impossible and it ought not be done.

That remains, according to me, the absolute solitude of a passion without martyrdom.

20

RICHARD RORTY
(1931–)

Richard Rorty is one of the most important philosophers working in the United States today. Born in New York in 1931, he studied at the universities of Chicago and Yale, obtaining his doctorate in philosophy in 1956. After spending two years in the army, he taught for three years at Wellesley College before accepting an appointment to teach Greek philosophy at Princeton University in 1961. He remained at Princeton for twenty-two years, after which he joined the University of Virginia as Kenan Professor of the Humanities. In 1998, he joined the Department of Comparative Literature at Stanford University, where he currently teaches.

Rorty is best known for his attempt to bridge the gap between philosophical traditions as diverse as pragmatism, analytic philosophy, and contemporary Continental philosophy. He emerged on the philosophical scene in 1967 with the publication of an edited collection of writings by prominent analytic philosophers called *The Linguistic Turn: Essays in Philosophical Method*. The anthology included a lengthy introduction in which Rorty spoke of the failure of Western philosophy to construct immutable and unshakable foundations for knowledge and thus fulfill the goal of being transformed into a science. The critique of the Cartesian aspirations of philosophy was continued in *Philosophy and the Mirror of Nature* (1979) when Rorty undertook to dismantle the traditional conception of the mind as a mirror that faithfully represents reality. Rorty showed that such an epistemological ideal is thwarted by historical, cultural, and linguistic practices that are always contingent and self-justifying ("epistemological behaviorism"). Here Rorty claimed to be merely following in the footsteps of Dewey, Heidegger, and Wittgenstein, thinkers "whose aim is to edify—to help their readers, or society as a whole, break free from outworn vocabularies and attitudes, rather than to provide 'grounding' for the intuitions and customs of the present." What Rorty brings to the dance is his own brand of "neopragmatism," expressed in a number of essays written between 1972 and 1980 and collected under the title *Consequences of Pragmatism* (1982). Defining pragmatism in terms of three basic features of "antiessentialism," "practical wisdom," and "contingency," Rorty argued that philosophy should direct its efforts away from theory toward more practical concerns so that, after careful deliberation, we are in a position to decide the relative merits of alternative courses of action having an important bearing on our lives. This requires more imaginative ways of thinking and the invention of new vocabularies—something that Rorty acknowledged in *Contingency, Irony, and Solidarity* (1989) is more suited to literature and literary criticism than to traditional philosophy.

In our selection from "Private Irony and Liberal Hope" (see *Contingency, Irony, and Solidarity*, chap. 4), Rorty offers a description of what he calls the "liberal ironist." Ironists are persons who "are never quite able to take themselves seriously because always aware that the terms in which they describe themselves are subject to change, always aware of the contingency and fragility of their final vocabularies, and thus of their selves." They are furthermore classified as "liberal" if they are against suffering and consider "cruelty the worst thing we do." This cruelty can take many forms, including ignoring the capacity of individuals to create themselves by constraining them to adopt universally shared human goals. To question the metaphysical pretensions to truth through the invention of more pluralistic vocabularies and behaviors is thus, according to Rorty, tantamount to achieving something like "human solidarity"—albeit one devoid of common goals and truth, with only "hope" remaining.

Select Bibliography of Rorty's Works in English

Achieving Our Country: Leftist Thought in Twentieth-Century America. Cambridge, MA: Harvard University Press, 1998.

Consequences of Pragmatism. Minneapolis: University of Minnesota Press, 1982.

Contingency, Irony, and Solidarity. Cambridge: Cambridge University Press, 1989.

Essays on Heidegger and Others: Philosophical Papers, Volume 2. Cambridge: Cambridge University Press, 1991.

The Linguistic Turn (Edited). Chicago: University of Chicago Press, 1992.

Objectivity, Relativism, and Truth: Philosophical Papers, Volume 1. Cambridge: Cambridge University Press, 1991.

Philosophy and the Mirror of Nature. Princeton, NJ: Princeton University Press, 1979.

Truth and Progress: Philosophical Papers, Volume 3. Cambridge: Cambridge University Press, 1998.

PRIVATE IRONY AND LIBERAL HOPE

All human beings carry about a set of words which they employ to justify their actions, their beliefs, and their lives. These are the words in which we formulate praise of our friends and contempt for our enemies, our long-term projects, our deepest self-doubts, and our highest hopes. They are the words in which we tell, sometimes prospectively and sometimes retrospectively, the story of our lives. I shall call these words a person's "final vocabulary."

It is "final" in the sense that if doubt is cast on the worth of these words, their user has no noncircular argumentative recourse. Those words are as far as he can go with language; beyond them there is only helpless passivity or a resort to force. A small part of a final vocabulary is made up of thin, flexible, and ubiquitous terms such as "true," "good," "right," and "beautiful." The larger part contains thicker, more rigid, and more parochial terms, for example, "Christ," "England," "professional standards," "decency," "kindness," "the Revolution," "the Church," "progressive," "rigorous," "creative." The more parochial terms do most of the work.

I shall define an "ironist" as someone who fulfills three conditions: (1) She has radical and continuing doubts about the final vocabulary she currently uses, because she has been impressed by other vocabularies, vocabularies taken as final by people or books she has encountered; (2) she realizes that arguments phrased in her present vocabulary can neither underwrite nor dissolve these doubts; (3) insofar as she philosophizes about her situation, she does not think that her vocabulary is closer to reality than others, that it is in touch with a power not herself. Ironists who are inclined to philosophize see the choice between vocabularies as made neither within a neutral and universal metavocabulary nor by an attempt to fight one's way past appearances to the real, but simply by playing the new off against the old.

I call people of this sort "ironists" because their realization that anything can be made to look good or bad by being redescribed, and their renunciation of the attempt to formulate criteria of choice between final vocabularies, puts them in the position which Sartre called "metastable": never quite able to take themselves seriously because always aware that the terms in which they describe themselves are subject to change, always aware of the contingency and fragility of their final vocabularies, and thus of their selves.

The opposite of irony is common sense. For that is the watchword of those who unself-consciously describe everything important in terms of the final vocabulary to which they and those around them are habituated. To be commonsensical is to take for granted that statements formulated in that final vocabulary suffice to describe and judge the beliefs, actions, and lives of those who employ alternative final vocabularies.

When common sense is challenged, its adherents respond at first by generalizing and making explicit the rules of the language game they are accustomed to play (as some of the Greek Sophists did, and as Aristotle did in his ethical writings). But if no platitude formulated in the old vocabulary suffices to meet an argumentative challenge, the need to reply produces a willingness to go beyond platitudes. At that point, conversation may go Socratic. The question "What is x?" is now asked in such a way that it cannot be answered simply by producing paradigm cases of x-hood. So one may demand a definition, an essence.

To make such Socratic demands is not yet, of course, to become an ironist in the sense in which I am using this term. It is only to become a "metaphysician," in a sense of that term which I am adapting from Heidegger. In this sense, the metaphysician is someone who takes the question "What is the intrinsic nature of (e.g., justice, science, knowledge, Being, faith, morality, philosophy)?" at face value. He assumes that the presence of a term in his own final vocabulary ensures that it refers to something which has a real essence. The metaphysician is still attached to common sense, in that he does not question the platitudes which encapsulate the use of a given final vocabulary, and in particular the platitude which says there is a single permanent reality to be found behind the many temporary appearances. He does not redescribe but, rather, analyzes old descriptions with the help of other old descriptions.

The ironist, by contrast, is a nominalist and a historicist. She thinks nothing has an intrinsic nature, a real essence. So she thinks that the occurrence of a term like "just" or "scientific" or "rational" in the final vocabulary of the day is no reason to think that Socratic inquiry into the essence of justice or science or rationality will take one much beyond the language games of one's time. The ironist spends her time worrying about the possibility that she has been initiated into the wrong tribe, taught to play the wrong language game. She worries that the process of socialization which turned her into a human being by giving her a language may have given her the wrong language, and so turned her into the wrong kind of human being. But she cannot give a criterion of wrongness. So, the more she is driven to articulate her situation in philosophical terms, the more she reminds herself of her rootlessness by constantly using terms like "*Weltanschauung,*" "perspective," "dialectic," "conceptual framework," "historical epoch," "language game," "redescription," "vocabulary," and "irony."

The metaphysician responds to that sort of talk by calling it "relativistic" and insisting that what matters is not what language is being used but what is true. Metaphysicians think that human beings by nature desire to know. They think this because the vocabulary they have inherited, their common sense, provides them with a picture of knowledge as a relation between human beings and "reality," and the idea that we have a need and a duty to enter into this relation. It also tells us that "reality," if properly asked, will help us determine what our final vocabulary should be. So metaphysicians believe that there are, out there in the world, real essences which it is our duty to discover and which are disposed to assist in their own discovery. They do not believe that anything can be made to look good or bad by being redescribed—or, if they do, they deplore this fact and cling to the idea that reality will help us resist such seductions.

By contrast, ironists do not see the search for a final vocabulary as (even in part) a way of getting something distinct from this vocabulary right. They do not take the point of discursive thought to be knowing, in any sense that can be explicated by notions like "reality," "real essence," "objective point of view," and "the correspondence of language of reality." They do not think its point is to find a vocabulary which accurately represents something, a transparent medium. For the ironists, "final vocabulary" does not mean "the one which puts all doubts to rest" or "the one which satisfies our criteria of ultimacy, or adequacy, or optimality." They do not think of reflection as being governed by criteria. Criteria, on their view, are never more than the platitudes which contextually define the terms of a final vocabulary currently in use. Ironists agree with Davidson about our inability to step outside our language in order to compare it with something else, and with Heidegger about the contingency and historicity of that language.

The typical strategy of the metaphysician is to spot an apparent contradiction between two platitudes, two intuitively plausible propositions, and then propose a distinction which will resolve the contradiction. Metaphysicians then go on to embed this distinction within a network of associated distinctions—a philosophical theory—which will take some of the strain off the initial distinction. This sort of theory construction is the same method used by judges to decide hard cases, and by theologians to interpret hard texts. That activity is the metaphysician's paradigm of rationality. He sees philosophical theories as converging—a series of discoveries about the nature of such things as truth and personhood, which get closer and closer to the way they really are, and carry the culture as a whole closer to an accurate representation of reality.

The ironist, however, views the sequence of such theories—such interlocked patterns of novel distinctions—as gradual, tacit substitutions of a new vocabulary for an old one. She calls "platitudes" what the metaphysician calls "intuitions." She is inclined to say that when we surrender an old platitude (e.g., "The number of biological species is fixed" or "Human beings differ from animals because they have sparks of the divine with them" or "Blacks have no rights which whites are bound to respect"), we have made a change rather than discovered a fact. The ironist, observing the sequence of "great philosophers" and the interaction between their thought and its social setting, sees a series of changes in the linguistic and other practices of the Europeans. Whereas the metaphysician sees the modern Europeans as particularly good at discovering how things really are, the ironist sees them as particularly rapid in changing their self-image, in re-creating themselves.

The metaphysician thinks that there is an overriding intellectual duty to present arguments for one's controversial views—arguments which will start from relatively uncontroversial premises. The ironist thinks that such arguments—logical arguments—are all very well in their way, and useful as expository devices, but in the end not much more than ways of getting people to change their practices without admitting they have done so. The ironist's preferred form of argument is dialectical in the sense that she takes the unit of persuasion to be a vocabulary rather than a proposition. Her method is redescription rather than inference. Ironists specialize in redescribing ranges of objects or events in partially neologistic jargon, in the hope of inciting people to adopt and extend that jargon. An ironist hopes that by the time she has finished using old words in new senses, not to mention introducing brand-new words, people will no longer ask questions phrased in the old words. So the ironist thinks of logic as ancillary to dialectic, whereas the metaphysician thinks of dialectic as a species of rhetoric, which in turn is a shoddy substitute for logic.

The rise of literary criticism to preeminence within the high culture of the democracies—its gradual and only semiconscious assumption of the cultural role once claimed (successively) by religion, science, and philosophy—has paralleled the rise in the proportion of ironists to metaphysicians among the intellectuals. This has widened the gap between the intellectuals and the public. For metaphysics is woven into the public rhetoric of modern liberal societies. So is the distinction between the moral and the "merely" aesthetic—a distinction which is often used to relegate "literature" to a subordinate position within culture and to suggest that novels and poems are irrelevant to moral reflection. Roughly speaking, the rhetoric of these societies takes for granted most of the oppositions which I claimed have become impediments to the culture of liberalism.

This situation has led to accusations of "irresponsibility" against ironist intellectuals. Some of these accusations come from know-nothings—people who have not read the books against which they warn others, and are just instinctively defending their own traditional roles. The know-nothings include religious fundamentalists, scientists who are offended at the suggestion that being "scientific" is not the highest intellectual virtue, and philosophers for whom it is an article of faith that rationality requires the deployment of general moral principles of the sort put forward by Mill and Kant. But the same accusations are made by writers who know what they are talking about, and whose views are entitled to respect. As I have already suggested, the most important of these writers is Habermas, who has mounted a sustained, detailed, carefully argued polemic against critics of the Enlightenment (e.g., Adorno, Foucault) who seem to turn their back on the social hopes of liberal societies. In Habermas's view, Hegel (and Marx) took the wrong tack in sticking to a philosophy of "subjectivity"—of self-reflection—rather than attempting to develop a philosophy of intersubjective communication.

I want to defend ironism, and the habit of taking literary criticism as the presiding intellectual discipline, against polemics such as Habermas's. My defense turns on making a firm distinction between the private and the public. Whereas Habermas sees the line of ironist thinking which runs from Hegel through Foucault and Derrida as destructive of social hope, I see this line of thought as largely irrelevant to public life and to political questions. Ironist theorists like Hegel, Nietzsche, Derrida, and Foucault seem to me invaluable in our attempt to form a private self-image, but pretty much useless when it comes to politics. Habermas assumes that the task of philosophy is to supply some social glue which will replace religious belief, and to see Enlightenment talk of "universality" and "rationality" as the best candidate for this glue. So he sees this kind of criticism of the Enlightenment, and of the idea of rationality, as dissolving the bonds between members of liberal societies. He thinks of the contextualism and perspectivalism for which I praised Nietzsche as irresponsible subjectivism.

Habermas shares with the Marxists, and with many of those whom he criticizes, the assumption that the real meaning of a philosophical view consists in its political implications, and that the ultimate frame of reference within which to judge a philosophical, as opposed to a merely "literary," writer, is a political one. For the tradition within which Habermas is working, it is as obvious that political philosophy is central to philosophy as, for the analytic tradition, that philosophy of language is central. But, it would be better to avoid thinking of philosophy as a "discipline" with "core problems" or with a social function. It would also be better to avoid the idea that philosophical reflection has a natural starting point—that one of its subareas is, in some natural order of justification, prior to the others. For, in the ironist view I have been offering, there is no such thing as a "natural" order of justification for beliefs or desires. Nor is there much occasion to use the distinctions between logic and rhetoric, or between philosophy and literature, or between rational and nonrational methods of changing other people's mind. If there is no center to the self, then there are only different ways of weaving new candidates for belief and desire into antecendently existing webs of belief and desire. The only important political distinction in the area is that between the use of force and the use of persuasion.

Habermas, and other metaphysicians who are suspicious of a merely "literary" conception of philosophy, think that liberal political freedoms require some consensus about what is universally human. We ironists who are also liberals think that such freedoms require no consensus on any topic more basic than their own desirability. From our angle, all that matters for liberal politics is the widely shared conviction that we shall call "true" or "good" whatever is the outcome of free discussion—that if we take care of political freedom, truth and goodness will take care of themselves.

"Free discussion" here does not mean "free from ideology," but simply the sort which goes on when the press, the judiciary, the elections, and the universities are free, social mobility is frequent and rapid, literacy is universal, higher education is common, and peace and wealth have made possible the leisure necessary to listen to lots of different people and think about what they say. I share with Habermas the Peircelike claim that the only general account to be given of our criteria for truth is one which refers to "undistorted communication" but I do not think there is much to be said about what counts as "undistorted" except "the sort you get when you have democratic political institutions and the conditions for making these institutions function."

The social glue holding together the ideal liberal society consists in little more than a consensus that the point of social organization is to let everybody have a chance at self-creation to the best of his or her abilities, and that that goal requires, besides peace and wealth, the standard "bourgeois freedoms." This conviction would not be based on a view about universally shared human ends, human rights, the nature of rationality, the Good for Man, nor anything else. It would be a conviction based on nothing more profound than the historical facts which suggest that without the protection of something like the institutions of bourgeois liberal society, people will be less able to work out their private salvations, create their private self-images, reweave their webs of belief and desire in the light of whatever new people and books they happen to encounter. In such an ideal society, discussion of public affairs will revolve around (1) how to balance the needs for peace, wealth, and freedom when conditions require that one of these goals be sacrificed to one of the others, and (2) how to equalize opportunities for self-creation and then leave people alone to use, or neglect, their opportunities.

The suggestion that this is all the social glue liberal societies need is subject to two main objections. The first is that as a practical matter, this glue is just not thick enough—that the (predominantly) metaphysical rhetoric of public life in the democracies is essential to the continuation of free institutions. The second is that it is psychologically impossible to be a liberal ironist—to be someone for whom "cruelty is the worst thing we do" [to use Judith Shklar's definition of "liberal"] and to have no metaphysical beliefs about what all human beings have in common.

The first objection is a prediction about what would happen if ironism replaced metaphysics in our public rhetoric. The second is a suggestion that the public-private split I am advocating will not work: that no one can divide herself up into a private self-creator and a public liberal, that the same person cannot be, in alternate moments, Nietzsche and J.S. Mill.

I want to dismiss the first of these objections fairly quickly, in order to concentrate on the second. The former amounts to the prediction that the prevalence of ironist notions among the public at large, the general adoption of antimetaphysical, antiessentialist views about the nature of morality and rationality and human beings, would weaken and dissolve liberal societies. It is possible that this prediction is correct, but there is at least one excellent reason for thinking it false. This is the analogy with the decline of religious faith. That decline, and specifically the decline of people's ability to take the idea of postmortem rewards seriously, has not weakened liberal societies, and indeed has strengthened them. Lots of people in the eighteenth and nineteenth centuries predicted the opposite. They thought that hope of heaven was required to supply moral fiber and social glue—that there was little point, for example, in having an atheist swear to tell the truth in a court of law. As it turned out, however, willingness to endure suffering for the sake of future reward was transferable from individual rewards to social ones, from one's hopes for paradise to one's hopes for one's grandchildren.

The reason liberalism has been strengthened by this switch is that whereas belief in an immortal soul kept being buffeted by scientific discoveries and by philosophers' attempts to keep pace with natural science, it is not clear that any shift in scientific or philosophical opinion could hurt the sort of social hope which characterizes modern liberal societies—the hope that life will eventually be freer, less cruel, more leisured, richer in goods and experiences, not just for our descendants but for everybody's descendants. If you tell someone whose life is given meaning by this hope that philosophers are waxing ironic over real essence, the objectivity of truth, and the existence of an ahistorical human nature, you are unlikely to arouse much interest, much less do any damage. The idea that liberal societies are bound together by philosophical beliefs seems to me ludicrous. What bind societies together are common vocabularies and common hopes. The vocabularies are, typically, parasitic on the hopes—in the sense that the principal function of the vocabularies is to tell stories about future outcomes which compensate for present sacrifices.

Modern, literate, secular societies depend on the existence of reasonably concrete, optimistic, and plausible political scenarios, as opposed to scenarios about redemption beyond the grave. To retain social hope, members of such a society need to be able to tell themselves a story about how things might get better, and to see no insuperable obstacles to this story's coming true. If social hope has become harder lately, this is not because the clerks have been committing treason but because, since the end of

World War II, the course of events has made it harder to tell a convincing story of this sort. The cynical and impregnable Soviet Empire, the continuing shortsightedness and greed of the surviving democracies, and the exploding, starving populations of the Southern Hemisphere make the problems our parents faced in the 1930s—Fascism and unemployment—look almost manageable. People who try to update and rewrite the standard social democratic scenario about human equality, the scenario which their grandparents wrote around the turn of the century, are not having much success. The problems which metaphysically inclined social thinkers believe to be caused by our failure to find the right sort of theoretical glue—a philosophy which can command wide assent in an individualistic and pluralistic society—are, I think, caused by a set of historical contingencies. These contingencies are making it easy to see the last few hundred years of European and American history—centuries of increasing public hope and private ironism—as an island in time, surrounded by misery, tyranny, and chaos. As Orwell put it, "The democratic vistas seem to end in barbed wire."

For the moment, I am simply trying to disentangle the public question "Is absence of metaphysics politically dangerous?" from the private question "Is ironism compatible with a sense of human solidarity?" To do so, it may help to distinguish the way nominalism and historicism look at present, in a liberal culture whose public rhetoric—the rhetoric in which the young are socialized—is still metaphysical, from the way they might look in a future whose public rhetoric is borrowed from nominalists and historicists. We tend to assume that nominalism and historicism are the exclusive property of intellectuals, of high culture, and that the masses cannot be so blasé about their own final vocabularies. But remember that once upon a time atheism, too, was the exclusive property of intellectuals.

In the ideal liberal society, the intellectuals would still be ironists, although the nonintellectuals would not. The latter would, however, be commonsensically nominalist and historicist. So they would see themselves as contingent through and through, without feeling any particular doubts about the contingencies they happened to be. They would not be bookish, nor would they look to literary critics as moral advisers. But they would be commonsensical nonmetaphysicians, in the way in which more and more people in the rich democracies have been commonsensical nontheists. They would feel no more need to answer the questions "Why are you a liberal? Why do you care about the humiliation of strangers?" than the average sixteenth-century Christian felt to answer the question "Why are you a Christian?" or than most people nowadays feel to answer the question "Are you saved?" Such a person would not need a justification for her sense of human solidarity, for she was not raised to play the language game in which one asks and gets justifications for that sort of belief. Her culture is one in which doubts about the public rhetoric of the culture are met not by Socratic requests for definitions and principles, but by Deweyan requests for concrete alternatives and programs. Such a culture could, as far as I can see, be every bit as self-critical and every bit as devoted to human equality as our own familiar, and still metaphysical, liberal culture—if not more so.

But even if I am right in thinking that a liberal culture whose public rhetoric is nominalist and historicist is both possible and desirable, I cannot go on to claim that there could or ought to be a culture whose public rhetoric is ironist. I cannot imagine a culture which socialized its youth in such a way as to make them continually dubious about their own process of socialization. Irony seems inherently a private matter. On my definition, an ironist cannot get along without the contrast between the final vocabulary she inherited and the one she is trying to create for herself. Irony is, if not intrinsically resentful, at least reactive. Ironists have to have something to have doubts about, something from which to be alienated.

This brings me to the second of the two objections I listed above, and thus to the idea that there is something about being an ironist which unsuits one for being a liberal, and that a simple split between private and public concerns is not enough to overcome the tension.

One can make this claim plausible by saying that there is at least a *prima facie* tension between the idea that social organization aims at human equality and the idea that human beings are simply incarnated vocabularies. The idea that we all have an overriding obligation to diminish cruelty, to make human beings equal in respect to their liability to suffering, seems to take for granted that there is something within human beings which deserves respect and protection quite independently of the language they speak. It suggests that a nonlinguistic ability, the ability to feel pain, is what is important, and that differences in vocabulary are much less important.

Metaphysics—in the sense of a search for theories which will get at real essence—tries to make sense of the claim that human beings are something more than centerless webs of beliefs and desires. The reason many people think such a claim essential to liberalism is that if men and women were, indeed, nothing more than sentential attitudes—nothing more than the presence or absence of dispositions toward the use of sentences phrased in some historically conditioned vocabulary—then not only human nature, but human solidarity, would begin to seem an eccentric and dubious idea. For solidarity with all possible vocabularies seems impossible. Metaphysicians tell us that unless there is some sort of common ur-vocabulary, we have no "reason" not to be cruel to those whose final vocabularies are very unlike ours. A universalistic ethics seems incompatible with ironism, simply because it is hard to imagine stating such an ethic without some doctrine about the nature of man. Such an appeal to real essence is the antithesis of ironism.

So the fact that greater openness, more room for self-creation, is the standard demand made by ironists on their societies is balanced by the fact that this demand seems to be merely for the freedom to speak a kind of ironic theoretical metalanguage which makes no sense to the man in the street. One can easily imagine an ironist badly wanting more freedom, more open space, for the Baudelaires and the Nabokovs, while not giving a thought to the sort of thing Orwell wanted: for example, getting more fresh air down into the coal mines, or getting the Party off the backs of the proles. This sense that the connection between ironism and liberalism is very loose, and that between metaphysics and liberalism pretty tight, is what makes people distrust ironism in philosophy and aestheticism in literature as "elitist."

The liberal metaphysician, by contrast, wants a final vocabulary with an internal and organic structure, one which is not split down the middle by a public-private distinction, not just a patchwork. He thinks that acknowledging that everybody wants to be taken on their own terms commits us to finding a least common denominator of those terms, a single description which will suffice for both public and private purposes, for self-definition and for one's relations with others. He prays, with Socrates, that the inner and the outer man will be as one—that irony will no longer be necessary. He is prone to believe, with Plato, that the parts of the soul and of the state correspond, and that distinguishing the essential from the accidental in the soul will help us distinguish justice from injustice in the state. Such metaphors express the liberal metaphysician's belief that the metaphysical public rhetoric of liberalism must remain central to the final vocabulary of the individual liberal, because it is the portion which expressed what she shares with the rest of humanity—the portion that makes solidarity possible.

But that distinction between a central, shared, obligatory portion and a peripheral, idiosyncratic, optional portion of one's final vocabulary is just the distinction which the ironist refuses to draw. She thinks that what unites her with the rest of the species is not a common language but just susceptibility to pain and in particular to that special sort of pain which the brutes do not share with the humans—humiliation. On her conception, human solidarity is not a matter of sharing a common truth or a common goal but of sharing a common selfish hope, the hope that one's world—the little things around which one has woven into one's final vocabulary—will not be destroyed. For public purposes, it does not matter if everybody's final vocabulary is different, as long as there is enough overlap so that everybody has some words with which to express the desirability of entering into other people's fantasies as well as into one's own. But those overlapping words—words like "kindness" or "decency" or "dignity"—do not form a vocabulary which all human beings can reach by reflection on their natures. Such reflection will not produce anything except a heightened awareness of the possibility of suffering. It will not produce a reason to care about suffering. What matters for the liberal ironist is not finding such a reason but making sure that she notices suffering when it occurs. Her hope is that she will not be limited by her own final vocabulary when faced with the possibility of humiliating someone with a quite different final vocabulary.

For the liberal ironist, skill at imaginative identification does the work which the liberal metaphysician would like to have done by a specifically moral motivation—rationality, or the love of God, or the love of truth. The ironist does not see her ability to envisage, and desire to prevent, the actual and possible humiliation of others—despite differences of sex, race, tribe, and final vocabulary—as more real or central or "essentially human" than any other part of herself. Indeed, she regards it as an ability and a desire which, like the ability to formulate differential equations, arose rather late in the history of humanity and is still a rather local phenomenon. It is associated primarily with Europe and America in the last three hundred years. It is not associated with any power larger than that embodied in a concrete historical situation, for example, the power of the rich European and American democracies to disseminate their customs to other parts of the world, a power which was enlarged by certain past contingencies and has been diminished by certain more recent contingencies.

Whereas the liberal metaphysician thinks that the good liberal knows certain crucial propositions to be true, the liberal ironist thinks the good liberal has a certain kind of know-how. Whereas he thinks of the high culture of liberalism as centering around theory, she thinks of it as centering around literature (in the older and narrower sense of that term—plays, poems, and, especially, novels). He thinks that the task of the intellectual is to preserve and defend liberalism by backing it up with some true propositions about large subjects, but she thinks that this task is to increase our skill at recognizing and describing the different sorts of little things around which individuals or communities center their fantasies and their lives. The ironist takes the words which are fundamental to metaphysics, and in particular to the public rhetoric of the liberal democracies, as just another text, just another set of little human things. Her ability to understand what it is like to make one's life center around these words is not distinct from her ability to grasp what it is like to make one's life center around the love of Christ or of Big Brother. Her liberalism does not consist in her devotion to those particular words but in her ability to grasp the function of many different sets of words.

These distinctions help explain why ironist philosophy has not done, and will not do, much for freedom and equality. But they also explain why "literature" (in the older and narrower sense), as well as ethnography and journalism, is doing a lot. As I said earlier, pain is nonlinguistic: it is what we human beings have that ties us to the non-language-using beasts. So victims of cruelty, people who are suffering, do not have much in the way of a language. That is why there is no such thing as the "voice of the oppressed" or the "language of the victims." The language the victims once used is not working anymore, and they are suffering too much to put new words together. So the job of putting their situation into language is going to have to be done for them by somebody else. The liberal novelist, poet, or journalist is good at that. The liberal theorist usually is not.

The suspicion that ironism in philosophy has not helped liberalism is quite right, but that is not because ironist philosophy is inherently cruel. It is because liberals have come to expect philosophy to do a certain job—namely, answering questions like "Why not be cruel?" and "Why be kind?"—and they feel that any philosophy which refuses this assignment must be heartless. But that expectation is a result of a metaphysical upbringing. If we could get rid of the expectation, liberals would not ask ironist philosophy to do a job which it cannot do, and which it defines itself as unable to do.

The metaphysician's association of theory with social hope and of literature with private perfection is, in an ironist liberal culture, reversed. Within a liberal metaphysical culture the disciplines which were charged with penetrating behind the many private appearances to the one general common reality—theology, science, philosophy—were the ones which were expected to bind human beings together, and thus to help eliminate cruelty. Within an ironist culture, by contrast, it is the disciplines which specialize in thick description of the private and idiosyncratic which are assigned this job. In particular, novels and ethnographies which sensitize one to the pain of those who do not speak our language must do the job which demonstrations of a common human nature were supposed to do. Solidarity has to be constructed out of little pieces, rather than found already waiting, in the form of an ur-language which all of us recognize when we hear it.

Conversely, within our increasingly ironist culture, philosophy has become more important for the pursuit of private perfection rather than for any social task.

Part 5

PSYCHOANALYSIS AND FEMINISM

21

SIGMUND FREUD
(1856–1939)

The founder of psychoanalysis, Sigmund Freud, was born in the Moravian town of Freiberg (now in the Czech Republic) in 1856. Three years later, his family moved to Vienna, Austria, where Freud lived and worked for much of the rest of his life. Freud was an exceptional student, and after planning initially to study law at university, he ultimately chose a career in medicine. In 1885, Freud studied in Paris with the French neurologist Jean-Martin Charcot. Charcot's work with patients classified as "hysterics" had an immense impact on the young Freud, as it introduced the possibility that certain mental disorders might have psychological rather than purely physiological causes. Upon his return to Vienna in 1886, Freud established a medical practice in neuropsychiatry, and went on to publish a number of remarkably influential case studies and theoretical works that helped to develop and refine the practice and theory of psychoanalysis. Late in his life, in June 1938, Freud fled to London to escape Nazi persecution, and, as he put it, "to die in freedom." He passed away soon thereafter, succumbing to the cancer of the mouth that had plagued him for the last two decades of his life.

Freud's first major work, *The Interpretation of Dreams*, was published in 1900. In this book, he argued for his celebrated thesis that dreams should be understood as the fulfillment of repressed wishes or desires; he also began developing a comprehensive theory of the structure of the mind that would inform his later investigations. Freud extended the scope of psychoanalysis with his subsequent works *The Psychopathology of Everyday Life* (1901), *Three Essays on the Theory of Sexuality* (1905), and "Fragment of an Analysis of a Case of Hysteria" (1905), which almost overnight won him the reputation—rightly or wrongly—as a pansexualist. Although Freud did not always take well to having his ideas criticized by others, he was not averse to self-criticism. One of the major shifts in Freud's work occurred in 1923 with the publication of *The Ego and the Id*, where he replaced his original theory of mind (with its division between the conscious and unconscious) with a more complicated, tripartite structure (ego, id, and super-ego). Another notable shift in Freud's later writings was his concern to extend psychoanalytic insights gained from the analysis of individuals to the wider stage of cultural and social analysis. From the 1920s onward, Freud presented these sociocultural investigations in such works as *Group Psychology and the Analysis of the Ego* (1921), *The Future of an Illusion* (1927), *Civilization and Its Discontents* (1930), and his last major work, *Moses and Monotheism* (1939).

The reading for this chapter, "The Super-ego," is drawn from *Civilization and Its Discontents*. In this book, Freud moves between analyses of wide-ranging phenomena, including religion, human nature, sexuality, aggression, and the origins of civilized life. In the book's final chapter, he seeks to explain the greatest cause of human unhappiness within civilized life, namely, the acquisition of a super-ego. According to Freud, the super-ego represents the internalization of a previously external agency. Prior to the acquisition of a super-ego, the ego is punished only for those inadmissible acts witnessed by an external authority. But with the emergence of the super-ego, which has the function of "keeping a watch over" not only the ego's *actions* but also its hidden *intentions*, the ego becomes permanently racked with guilt. Freud suggests that a similar phenomenon takes place at the level of society where a cultural super-ego provides us with a set of strict ethical norms governing social behavior. The question for Freud, and for society as a whole, as he sees it, is whether a form of ethical life is possible that will not create the same neuroses at the social level as those which are created by the super-ego at the level of the individual.

Select Bibliography of Freud's Works in English

The Standard Edition of the Complete Psychological Works of Sigmund Freud (24 volumes). Trans. and ed. James Strachey in collaboration with Anna Freud. London: Hogarth Press, 1953–1974.

Beyond the Pleasure Principle (1920). *Standard Edition*, vol. XVIII.

Civilization and Its Discontents (1930). *Standard Edition*, vol. XXI.

The Ego and the Id (1923). *Standard Edition*, vol. XIX.

The Future of an Illusion (1927). *Standard Edition*, vol. XXI.

Group Psychology and the Analysis of the Ego (1921). *Standard Edition*, vol. XVIII.

Three Essays on the Theory of Sexuality (1905). *Standard Edition*, vol. VII.

The Interpretation of Dreams (1900). *Standard Edition*, vols. IV–V.

Moses and Monotheism (1939). *Standard Edition*, vol. XXIII.

New Introductory Lectures on Psycho-Analysis (1933). *Standard Edition*, vol. XXII.

An Outline of Psychoanalysis (1940). *Standard Edition*, vol. XXIII.

The Psychopathology of Everyday Life (1901). *Standard Edition*, vol. VI.

Totem and Taboo (1912). *Standard Edition*, vol. XIII.

THE SUPER-EGO

My intention [is] to represent the sense of guilt as the most important problem in the development of civilization and to show that the price we pay for our advance in civilization is a loss of happiness through the heightening of the sense of guilt.[1] Anything that still sounds strange about this statement, which is the final conclusion of our investigation, can probably be traced to the quite peculiar relationship—as yet completely unexplained—which the sense of guilt has to our consciousness. In the common case of remorse, which we regard as normal, this feeling makes itself clearly enough perceptible to consciousness. Indeed, we are accustomed to speak of a "consciousness of guilt" instead of a "sense of guilt." Our study of the neuroses, to which, after all, we owe the most valuable pointers to an understanding of normal conditions, brings us up against some contradictions. In one of those affections, obsessional neurosis, the sense of guilt makes itself noisily heard in consciousness; it dominates the clinical picture and the patient's life as well, and it hardly allows anything else to appear alongside of it. But in most other cases and forms of neurosis it remains completely unconscious, without on that account producing any less important effects. Our patients do not believe us when we attribute an "unconscious sense of guilt" to them. In order to make ourselves at all intelligible to them, we tell them of an unconscious need for punishment, in which the sense of guilt finds expression. But its connection with a particular form of neurosis must not be overestimated. Even in obsessional neurosis there are types of patients who are not aware of their sense of guilt, or who only feel it as a tormenting uneasiness, a kind of anxiety, if they are prevented from carrying out certain actions. It ought to be possible eventually to understand these things; but as yet we cannot. Here perhaps we may be glad to have it pointed out that the sense of guilt is at bottom nothing else but a topographical variety of anxiety; in its later phases it coincides completely with *fear of the super-ego.* And the relations of anxiety to consciousness exhibit the same extraordinary variations. Anxiety is always present somewhere or other behind every symptom; but at one time it takes noisy possession of the whole of consciousness, while at another it conceals itself so completely that we are obliged to speak of unconscious anxiety or, if we want to have a clearer psychological conscience, since anxiety is in the first instance simply a feeling, of possibilities of anxiety. Consequently it is very conceivable that the sense of guilt produced by civilization is not perceived as such either, and remains to a large extent unconscious, or appears as a sort of *malaise*, a dissatisfaction, for which people seek other motivations. Religions, at any rate, have never overlooked the part played in civilization by a sense of guilt. Furthermore—a point which I failed to appreciate elsewhere—they claim to redeem mankind from this sense of guilt, which they call sin. From the manner in which, in Christianity, this redemption is achieved—by the sacrificial death of a single person, who in this manner takes upon himself a guilt that is common to everyone—we have been able to infer what the first occasion may have been on which this primal guilt, which was also the beginning of civilization, was acquired.

Though it cannot be of great importance, it may not be superfluous to elucidate the meaning of a few words such as "super-ego," "conscience," "sense of guilt," "need for punishment" and "remorse," which we have often, perhaps, used too loosely and interchangeably. They all relate to the same state of affairs, but denote different aspects of it. The super-ego is an agency which has been inferred by us, and conscience is a function which we ascribe, among other functions, to that agency. This function consists in keeping a watch over the actions and intentions of the ego and judging them, in exercising a censorship. The sense of guilt, the harshness of the super-ego, is thus the same thing as the severity of the conscience. It is the perception which the ego has of being watched over in this way, the assessment of the tension between its own strivings and the demands of the super-ego. The fear of this critical agency (a fear which is at the bottom of the whole relationship), the need for punishment, is an instinctual manifestation on the part of the ego, which has become masochistic under the influence of a sadistic super-ego; it is a portion, that is to say, of the instinct towards internal destruction present in the ego, employed for forming an erotic attachment to the super-ego. We ought not to speak of a conscience until a super-ego is demonstrably present. As to a sense of guilt, we must admit that it is in existence before the super-ego, and therefore before conscience, too. At that time it is the immediate expression of fear of the external authority, a recognition of the tension between the ego and that authority. It is the direct derivative of the conflict between the need for the authority's love and the urge towards instinctual satisfaction, whose inhibition produces the inclination to aggression. The superimposition of these two strata of the sense of guilt—one coming from fear of the *external* authority, the other from fear of the *internal* authority—has hampered our insight into the position of conscience in a number of ways. Remorse is a general term for the ego's reaction in a case of sense of guilt. It contains, in little altered form, the sensory material of the anxiety which is operating behind the sense of guilt; it is itself a punishment and can include the need for punishment. Thus remorse, too, can be older than conscience.

Nor will it do any harm if we once more review the contradictions which have for a while perplexed us during our enquiry. Thus, at one point the sense of guilt was the consequence of acts of aggression that had been abstained from; but at another point—and precisely at its historical beginning, the killing of the father—it was the consequence of an act of aggression that had been carried out. But a way out of this difficulty was found. For the institution of the internal authority, the super-ego, altered the situation radically. Before this, the sense of guilt coincided with remorse. (We may remark, incidentally, that the term "remorse" should be reserved for the reaction after an act of aggression has actually been carried out.) After this, owing to the omniscience of the super-ego, the difference between an aggression intended and an aggression carried out lost its force. Henceforward a sense of guilt could be produced not only by an act of violence that is actually carried out (as all the world knows), but also by one that is merely intended (as psychoanalysis has discovered). Irrespectively of this alteration in the psychological situation, the conflict arising from ambivalence—the conflict between the two primal instincts—leaves the same result behind. We are tempted to look here for the solution of the problem of the varying relation in which the sense of guilt stands to consciousness. It might be thought that a sense of guilt arising from remorse for an evil *deed* must always be conscious, whereas a sense of guilt arising from the perception of an evil *impulse* may remain unconscious. But the answer is not so simple as that. Obsessional neurosis speaks energetically against it.

The second contradiction concerned the aggressive energy with which we suppose the super-ego to be endowed. According to one view, that energy merely carries on the punitive energy of the external authority and keeps it alive in the mind; while, according to another view, it consists, on the contrary, of one's own aggressive energy which has not been used and which one now directs against that inhibiting authority. The first view seemed to fit in better with the *history*, and the second with the *theory*, of the sense of guilt. Closer reflection has resolved this apparently irreconcilable contradiction almost too completely; what remained as the essential and common factor was that in each case we were dealing with an aggressiveness which had been displaced inwards. Clinical observation, moreover, allows us in fact to distinguish two sources for the aggressiveness which we attribute to the super-ego; one or the other of them exercises the stronger effect in any given case, but as a general rule they operate in unison.

This is, I think, the place at which to put forward for serious consideration a view which I have earlier recommended for provisional acceptance. In the most recent analytic literature a predilection is shown for the idea that any kind of frustration, any thwarted instinctual satisfaction, results, or may result, in a heightening of the sense of guilt. A great theoretical simplification will, I think, be achieved if we regard this as applying only to the *aggressive* instincts, and little will be found to contradict this assumption. For how are we to account, on dynamic and economic grounds, for an increase in the sense of guilt appearing in place of an unfulfilled *erotic* demand? This only seems possible in a roundabout way—if we suppose, that is, that the prevention of an erotic satisfaction calls up a piece of aggressiveness against the person who has interfered with the satisfaction, and that this aggressiveness has itself to be suppressed in turn. But if this is so, it is after all only the aggressiveness which is transformed into a sense of guilt, by being suppressed and made over to the super-ego. I am convinced that many processes will admit of a simpler and clearer exposition if the findings of psychoanalysis with regard to the derivation of the sense of guilt are restricted to the aggressive instincts. Examination of the clinical material gives us no unequivocal answer here, because, as our hypothesis tells us, the two classes of instinct hardly ever appear in a pure form, isolated from each other; but an investigation of extreme cases would probably point in the direction I anticipate.

I am tempted to extract a first advantage from this more restricted view of the case by applying it to the process of repression. As we have learned, neurotic symptoms are, in their essence, substitutive satisfactions for unfulfilled sexual wishes. In the course of our analytic work we have discovered to our surprise that perhaps every neurosis conceals a quota of unconscious sense of guilt, which in its turn fortifies the symptoms by making use of them as a punishment. It now seems plausible to formulate the following proposition. When an instinctual trend undergoes repression, its libidinal elements are turned into symptoms, and its aggressive components into a sense of guilt. Even if this proposition is only an average approximation to the truth, it is worthy of our interest.

Some readers of this work may further have an impression that they have heard the formula of the struggle between Eros and the death instinct too often. It was alleged to characterize the process of civilization which mankind undergoes but it was also brought into connection with the development of the individual, and, in addition, it was said to have revealed the secret of organic life in general. We cannot, I think, avoid going into the relations of these three processes to one another. The repetition of the same formula is justified by the consideration that both the process of human civilization and of the development of the individual are also vital processes—which is to say that they must share in the most general characteristic of life. On the other hand, evidence of the presence of this general characteristic fails, for the very reason of its general nature, to help us to arrive at any differentiation [between the processes], so long as it is not narrowed down by special qualifications. We can only be satisfied, therefore, if we assert that the process of civilization is a modification which the vital process experiences under the influence of a task that is set it by Eros and instigated by Ananke—by the exigencies of reality; and that this task is one of uniting separate individuals into a community bound together by libidinal ties. When, however, we look at the relation between the process of human civilization and the developmental or educative process of individual human beings, we shall conclude without much hesitation that the two are very similar in nature, if not the very same process applied to different kinds of object. The process of the civilization of the human species is, of course, an abstraction of a higher order than is the development of the individual and it is therefore harder to apprehend in concrete terms, nor should we pursue analogies to an obsessional extreme; but in view of the similarity between the aims of the two processes—in the one case the integration of a separate individual into a human group, and in the other case the creation of a unified group out of many individuals—we cannot be surprised at the similarity between the means employed and the resultant phenomena.

In view of its exceptional importance, we must not long postpone the mention of one feature which distinguishes between the two processes. In the developmental process of the individual, the program of the pleasure principle, which consists in finding the satisfaction of happiness, is retained as the main aim. Integration in, or adaptation to, a human community appears as a scarcely avoidable condition which must be fulfilled before this aim of happiness can be achieved. If it could be done without that condition it would perhaps be preferable. To put it in other words, the development of the individual seems to us to be a product of the interaction between two urges, the urge towards happiness, which we usually call "egoistic," and the urge towards union with others in the community, which we call "altruistic." Neither of these descriptions goes much below the surface. In the process of individual development, as we have said, the main accent falls mostly on the egoistic urge (or the urge towards happiness); while the other urge, which may be described as a "cultural" one, is usually content with the role of imposing restrictions. But in the process of civilization things are different. Here by far the most important thing is the aim of creating a unity out of the individual human beings. It is true that the aim of happiness is still there, but it is pushed into the background. It almost seems as if the creation of a great human community would be most successful if no attention had to be paid to the happiness of the individual. The developmental process of the individual can thus be expected to have special features of its own which are not reproduced in the process of human civilization. It is only insofar as the first of these processes has union with the community as its aim that it need coincide with the second process.

Just as a planet revolves around a central body as well as rotating on its own axis, so the human individual takes part in the course of development of mankind at the same time as he pursues his own path in life. But to our dull eyes the play of forces in the heavens seems fixed in a never-changing order; in the field of organic life we can still see how the forces contend with one another, and how the effects of the conflict are continually changing. So, also, the two urges, the one towards personal happiness and the other towards union with other human beings, must struggle with each other in every individual; and so, also, the two processes of individual and of cultural development must stand in hostile opposition to each other and mutually dispute the ground. But this struggle between the individual and society is not a derivative of the contradiction—probably an irreconcilable one—between the primal instincts of Eros and death. It is a dispute within the economics of the libido, comparable to the contest concerning the distribution of libido between ego and objects; and it does admit of an eventual accommodation in the individual, as, it may be hoped, it will also do in the future of civilization, however much that civilization may oppress the life of the individual today.

The analogy between the process of civilization and the path of individual development may be extended in an important respect. It can be asserted that the community, too, evolves a super-ego under whose influence cultural development proceeds. It would be a tempting task for anyone who has a knowledge of human civilizations to follow out this analogy in detail. I will confine myself to bringing forward a few striking points. The super-ego of an epoch of civilization has an origin similar to that of an individual. It is based on the impression left behind by the personalities of great leaders—men of overwhelming force of mind or men in whom one of the human impulsions has found its strongest and purest, and therefore often its most one-sided, expression. In many instances the analogy goes still further, in that during their lifetime these figures were—often enough, even if not always—mocked and maltreated by others and even dispatched in a cruel fashion. In the same way, indeed, the primal father did not attain divinity until long after he had met his death by violence. The most arresting example of this fateful conjunction is to be seen in the figure of Jesus Christ—if, indeed, that figure is not a part of mythology, which called it into being from an obscure memory of that primal event. Another point of agreement between the cultural and the individual super-ego is that the former, just like the latter, sets up strict ideal demands, disobedience to which is visited with "fear of conscience." Here, indeed, we come across the remarkable circumstance that the mental processes concerned are actually more familiar to us and more accessible to consciousness as they are seen in the group than they can be in the individual man. In him, when tension arises, it is only the aggressiveness of the super-ego which, in the form of reproaches, makes itself noisily heard; its actual demands often remain unconscious in the background. If we bring them to conscious knowledge, we find that they coincide with the precepts of the prevailing cultural super-ego. At this point the two processes, that of the cultural development of the group and that of the cultural development of the individual, are, as it were, always interlocked. For that reason some of the manifestations and properties of the super-ego can be more easily detected in its behavior in the cultural community than in the separate individual.

The cultural super-ego has developed its ideals and set up its demands. Among the latter, those which deal with the relations of human beings to one another are comprised under the heading of ethics. People have at all times set the greatest value on ethics, as though they expected that it in particular would produce especially important results. And it does in fact deal with a subject which can easily be recognized as the sorest spot in every civilization. Ethics is thus to be regarded as a therapeutic attempt—as an endeavor to achieve, by means of a command of the super-ego, something which has so far not been achieved by means of any other cultural activities. As we already know, the problem before us is how to get rid of the greatest hindrance to civilization—namely, the constitutional inclination of human beings to be aggressive towards one another; and for that very reason we are especially interested in what is probably the most recent of the cultural commands of the super-ego, the commandment to love one's neighbor as oneself. In our research into, and therapy of, a neurosis, we are led to make two reproaches against the super-ego of the individual. In the severity of its commands and prohibitions it troubles itself too little about the happiness of the ego, in that it takes insufficient account of the resistances against obeying them—of the instinctual strength of the id [in the first place], and of the difficulties presented by the real external environment [in the second]. Consequently we are very often obliged, for therapeutic purposes, to oppose the super-ego, and we endeavor to lower its demands. Exactly the same objections can be made against the ethical demands of the cultural super-ego. It, too, does not trouble itself enough about the facts of the mental constitution of human beings. It issues a command and does not ask whether it is possible for people to obey it. On the contrary, it assumes that a man's ego is psychologically capable of anything that is required of it, that his ego has unlimited mastery over his id. This is a mistake; and even in what are known as normal people the id cannot be controlled beyond certain limits. If more is demanded of a man, a revolt will be produced in him or a neurosis, or he will be made unhappy. The commandment, "Love thy neighbor as thyself," is the strongest defense against human aggressiveness and an excellent example of the unpsychological proceedings of the cultural super-ego. The commandment is impossible to fulfill; such an enormous inflation of love can only lower its value, not get rid of the difficulty. Civilization pays no attention to all this; it merely admonishes us that the harder it is to obey the precept the more meritorious it is to do so. But anyone who follows such a precept in present-day civilization only puts himself at a disadvantage *vis-à-vis* the person who disregards it. What a potent obstacle to civilization aggressiveness must be, if the defense against it can cause as much unhappiness as aggressiveness itself! "Natural" ethics, as it is called, has nothing to offer here except the narcissistic satisfaction of being able to think oneself better than others. At this point the ethics based on religion introduces its promises of a better afterlife. But so long as virtue is not rewarded here on earth, ethics will, I fancy, preach in vain. I too think it quite certain that a real change in the relations of human beings to possessions would be of more help in this direction than any ethical commands; but the recognition of this fact among socialists has been obscured and made useless for practical purposes by a fresh idealistic misconception of human nature.

I believe the line of thought which seeks to trace in the phenomena of cultural development the part played by a super-ego promises still further discoveries. I hasten to come to a close. But there is one question which I can hardly evade. If the development of civilization has such a far-reaching similarity to the development of the individual and if it employs the same methods, may we not be justified in reaching the diagnosis that, under the influence of cultural urges, some civilizations, or some epochs of civilization—possibly the whole of mankind—have become "neurotic"? An analytic dissection of such neuroses might lead to therapeutic recommendations which could lay claim to great practical interest. I would not say that an attempt of this kind to carry psychoanalysis over to the cultural community was absurd or doomed to be fruitless. But we should have to be very cautious and not forget that, after all, we are only dealing with analogies and that it is dangerous, not only with men but also with concepts, to tear them from the sphere in which they have originated and been evolved. Moreover, the diagnosis of communal neuroses is faced with a special difficulty. In an individual neurosis we take as our starting point the contrast that distinguishes the patient from his environment, which is assumed to be "normal." For a group all of whose members are affected by one and the same disorder no such background could exist; it would have to be found elsewhere. And as regards the therapeutic application of our knowledge, what would be the use of the most correct analysis of social neuroses, since no one possesses authority to impose such a therapy upon the group? But in spite of all these difficulties, we may expect that one day someone will venture to embark upon a pathology of cultural communities.

For a wide variety of reasons, it is very far from my intention to express an opinion upon the value of human civilization. I have endeavored to guard myself against the enthusiastic prejudice which holds that our civilization is the most precious thing that we possess or could acquire and that its path will necessarily lead to heights of unimagined perfection. I can at least listen without indignation to the critic who is of the opinion that when one surveys the aims of cultural endeavor and the means it employs, one is bound to come to the conclusion that the whole effort is not worth the trouble, and that the outcome of it can only be a state of affairs which the individual will be unable to tolerate. My impartiality is made all the easier to me by my knowing very little about all these things. One thing only do I know for certain and that is that man's judgments of value follow directly his wishes for happiness—that, accordingly, they are an attempt to support his illusions with arguments. I should find it very understandable if someone were to point out the obligatory nature of the course of human civilization and were to say, for instance, that the tendencies to a restriction of sexual life or to the institution of a humanitarian ideal at the expense of natural selection were developmental trends which cannot be averted or turned aside and to which it is best for us to yield as though they were necessities of nature. I know, too, the objection that can be made against this, to the effect that in the history of mankind, trends such as these, which were considered insurmountable, have often been thrown aside and replaced by other trends. Thus I have not the courage to rise up before my fellowmen as a prophet, and I bow to their reproach that I can offer them no consolation: for at bottom that is what they are all demanding—the wildest revolutionaries no less passionately than the most virtuous believers.

The fateful question for the human species seems to me to be whether and to what extent their cultural development will succeed in mastering the disturbance of their communal life by the human instinct of aggression and self-destruction. It may be that in this respect precisely the present time deserves a special interest. Men have gained control over the forces of nature to such an extent that with their help they would have no difficulty in exterminating one another to the last man. They know this, and hence comes a large part of their current unrest, their unhappiness and their mood of anxiety. And now it is to be expected that the other of the two "Heavenly Powers," eternal Eros, will make an effort to assert himself in the struggle with his equally immortal adversary. But who can foresee with what success and with what result?

Notes

1. "Thus conscience does make cowards of us all. . . ." That the education of young people at the present day conceals from them the part which sexuality will play in their lives is not the only reproach which we are obliged to make against it. Its other sin is that it does not prepare them for the aggressiveness of which they are destined to become the objects. In sending the young out into life with such a false psychological orientation, education is behaving as though one were to equip people starting on a Polar expedition with summer clothing and maps of the Italian Lakes. In this it becomes evident that a certain misuse is being made of ethical demands. The strictness of those demands would not do so much harm if education were to say: "This is how men ought to be, in order to be happy and to make others happy; but you have to reckon on their not being like that." Instead of this the young are made to believe that everyone else fulfills those ethical demands—that is, that everyone else is virtuous. It is on this that the demand is based that the young, too, shall become virtuous.

22

JACQUES LACAN
(1901–1981)

French psychoanalyst Jacques Lacan was born in 1901. Trained in psychiatry at the Faculté de Medi-cine de Paris, he received his doctorate in 1932 for a thesis on paranoia. In the early 1950s, Lacan began developing his unique version of psychonanalysis based on structural lingustics (Saussure) and anthropology (Lévi-Strauss) in what he dubbed a "return to Freud." His unorthodox approach to analysis, which included truncated therapy sessions and even the absence of the analyst, eventually led to his expulsion in 1953 from the International Psychoanalytic Association. Lacan went on to cre-ate the Société Française de Psychanalyse and for the next twenty years presented annual seminars in which he offered highly original, if controversial, reinterpretations of Freudian psychoanalysis. These seminars were attended by some of the most famous French intellectuals of the time and drew the attention of the mass media because of their polemical and often volatile manner. Shortly before his death, Lacan formed the Ecole de la Cause Freudienne, which continues to champion Lacanian psychoanalysis to this day.

Throughout his work, Lacan challenged several of the founding assumptions of standard psychoan-alytic practice, beginning with the commonplace notion that the task of therapy is to restore the true identity of the ego in order to render it capable of functioning properly in the world. For Lacan, the very notion of a stable and unified ego is a fiction that belongs to the realm of the "Imaginary." This illu-sory notion of a fully rational and autonomous ego stands in sharp contrast to Lacan's notion of the subject, or the "I," which never attains complete self-identity. On Lacan's account, the subject is con-stituted by unconscious desires that operate through social and linguistic structures belonging to the domain of the "Symbolic." Accordingly, the unconscious is said to be "the discourse of the Other" inasmuch as its functioning is radically different from the intentional speech acts of the conscious ego. The goal of psychoanalysis, according to Lacan, is to release the patient from the Imaginary order of self-possession ("identity," "harmony," "self-sufficiency," etc.) into the Symbolic order of lan-guage in which the self acknowledges its more fundamental relation to the Other. Hence Lacan's fa-mous statement (reminiscent of Rimbaud): "The I is other."

In his 1959 to 1960 seminar, *The Ethics of Psychoanalysis*, from which our present reading is ex-cerpted, Lacan seeks to explain the complex relation between "desire," "the Other," and "the moral law." Lacan argues that unconscious desire is structured in such a way that it serves to dissemble its object. He gives various names to this object of desire, which is situated "beyond the pleasure princi-ple," including "*das Ding*," "Other," and "the Real." Lacan likens the search for *das Ding* to the tradi-tional concept of ethics in its search for "the Good." However, he makes it clear that "ethics is not simply concerned with the fact that there are obligations, that there is a bond that binds, orders, and makes the social law." Rather than casting ethics in the repressive role of the superego, which is how Freud understood it, Lacan construes it as the law or motivating force behind the subject's uncon-scious drive toward the "prehistoric Other," who/which is prior to social norms and practices. We should not be surprised, then, to find what is perhaps the most rigorous theory of ethics in the tradition, namely, Kantianism, aligned with the kind of "antimorality" exemplified in the writings of the Marquis de Sade. Indeed, Lacan finds three important points of convergence between Kant's and Sade's thinking: (1) the importance attached to the law of nature; (2) the elimination of sentiment (and sentimentality) as a guide for action; and (3) the characterization of lawlike action as painful, which, according to Kant, is due to the humbling of self-love through respect for the law, and which, according to Sade, results from the pain ("the other's pain as well as the pain of the subject himself") that attends sexual *jouissance* itself.

Select Bibliography of Lacan's Works in English

Ecrits: A Selection. Trans. Alan Sheridan. New York: W.W. Norton, 1987.

Feminine Sexuality: Jacques Lacan and the École Freudienne. Ed. Juliet Mitchell and Jacqueline Rose. New York: W.W. Norton, 1985.

The Four Fundamental Concepts of Psychoanalysis. Trans. Alan Sheridan. New York: W.W. Norton, 1978.

The Seminar of Jacques Lacan: Book I. Freud's Technical Papers. Trans. John Forrester. New York: W.W. Norton, 1988.

The Seminar of Jacques Lacan: Book II. The Ego in Freud's Theory and in the Techniques of Psychoanlysis. Trans. Dennis Porter. New York: W.W. Norton, 1992.

The Seminar of Jacques Lacan: Book VII. The Ethics of Psychoanalysis. Trans. Dennis Porter. New York: W.W. Norton, 1992.

Television: A Challenge to the Psychoanalytic Establishment. Ed. Joan Copjec. New York: W.W. Norton, 1990.

THE ETHICS OF PSYCHOANALYSIS

What if we brought a simple soul into this lecture hall, set him down in the front row, and asked him what Lacan means.

The simple soul will get up, go to the board and will give the following explanation:

> Since the beginning of the academic year Lacan has been talking to us about *das Ding* in the following terms. He situates it at the heart of a subjective world which is the one whose economy he has been describing to us from a Freudian perspective for years. This subjective world is defined by the fact that the signifier in man is already installed at the level of the unconscious, and that it combines its points of reference with the means of orientation that his functioning as a natural organism of a living being also gives him.

Simply by writing it on the board and putting *das Ding* at the center, with the subjective world of the unconscious organized in a series of signifying relations around it, you can see the difficulty of topographical representation. The reason is that *das Ding* is at the center only in the sense that it is excluded. That is to say, in reality *das Ding* has to be posited as exterior, as the prehistoric Other that it is impossible to forget—the Other whose primacy of position Freud affirms in the form of something *entfremdet*, something strange to me, although it is at the heart of me, something that on the level of the unconscious only a representation can represent.

1

I said "something that only a representation can represent." Do not look upon that as a simple pleonasm, for "represent" and "representation" here are two different things, as *Vorstellungsrepräsentanz* indicates. It is a matter of that which in the unconscious represents, in the form of a sign, representation as a function of apprehending—of the way in which every representation is represented insofar as it evokes the good that *das Ding* brings with it.

But to speak of "the good" is already a metaphor, an attribute. Everything that qualifies representations in the order of the good is caught up in refraction, in the atomized system that the structure of the unconscious facilitations imposes, in the complex mechanism of a signifying system of elements. It is only in that way that the subject relates to that which presents itself on the horizon as his good. His good is already pointed out to him as the significant result of a signifying composition that is called up at the unconscious level or, in other words, at a level where he has no mastery over the system of directions and investments that regulate his behavior in depth.

I will use a term here that only those who have present in their minds the Kantian formulas of *The Critique of Practical Reason* will be able to appreciate. I invite those who do not have them present in their minds or who have not yet encountered what is, from more than one point of view, an extraordinary book to make good their memories or their general knowledge.

It is impossible for us to make any progress in this seminar relative to the questions posed by the ethics of psychoanalysis if you do not have this book as a reference point.

So as to motivate you to look at it, let me emphasize that it is certainly extraordinary from the point of view of its humor. To remain poised at the limit of the most extreme conceptual necessity produces an effect of plenitude and content as well as of vertigo, as a result of which you will not fail to sense at some point in the text the abyss of the comic suddenly open up before you. Thus I do not see why it is a door that you would refuse to open. We will in any case see in a minute how we can open it here.

It is then, to be explicit, the Kantian term *Wohl* that I propose in order to designate the good in question. It has to do with the comfort of the subject insofar as, whenever he refers to *das Ding* as his horizon, it is the pleasure principle that functions for him. And it does so in order to impose the law in which a resolution of the tension occurs that is linked to something that, using Freud's phrase, we will call the successful lures—or, better yet, the signs that reality may or may not honor. The sign here is very close to a representative currency, and it suggests an expression that I incorporated into one of my first lectures, that on physical causality, in a phrase that begins one of its paragraphs, i.e., "more inaccessible to our eyes that are made for the signs of the money changer."

Let me carry the image further. "The signs of the money changer" are already present at the base of the structure which is regulated according to the law of *Lust* and *Unlust*, according to the rule of the indestructible *Wunsch* that pursues repetition, the repetition of signs. It is in that way that the subject regulates his initial distance to *das Ding*, the source of all *Wohl* at the level of the pleasure principle, and which at its heart already gives rise to what we may call *das Gut des Objekts*, the good object—following the Kantian example, as the practitioners of psychoanalysis have not failed to do.

On the horizon, beyond the pleasure principle, there rises up the *Gut, das Ding*, thus introducing at the level of the unconscious something that ought to oblige us to ask once again the Kantian question of the *causa noumenon. Das Ding* presents itself at the level of unconscious experience as that which already makes the law. Although it is necessary to give this verbal phrase, "makes the law," the emphasis it receives in one of the most brutal games of elementary society and that is evoked in a recent book by Roger Vailland. It is a capricious and arbitrary law, the law of the oracle, the law of signs in which the subject receives no guarantee from anywhere, the law in relation to which he has no *Sicherung*, to use another Kantian term. That is also at bottom the bad object that Kleinian theory is concerned with.

Although it must be said that at this level *das Ding* is not distinguished as bad. The subject makes no approach at all to the bad object, since he is already maintaining his distance in relation to the good object. He cannot stand the extreme good that *das Ding* may bring him, which is all the more reason why he cannot locate himself in relation to the bad. However much he groans, explodes, curses, he still does not understand; nothing is articulated here even in the form of a metaphor. He produces symptoms, so to speak, and these symptoms are at the origin of the symptoms of defense.

And how should we conceive of defense at this level? There is organic defense. Here the ego defends itself by hurting itself as the crab gives up its claw, revealing thereby the connection I developed between the motor system and pain. Yet in what way does man defend himself that is different from an animal practicing self-mutilation? The difference is introduced here by means of the signifying structuralization in the human unconscious. But the defense or the mutilation that is proper to man does not occur only at the level of substitution, displacement, or metaphor—everything that structures its gravitation with relation to the good object. Human defense takes place by means of something that has a name, and which is, to be precise, lying about evil.

At the level of the unconscious, the subject lies. And this lying is his way of telling the truth of the matter. The *orthos logos* of the unconscious at this level—as Freud indicates clearly in the *Entwurf* in relation to hysteria—is expressed as *prōton pseudos*, the first lie.

Given the amount of time I have been discussing the *Entwurf* with you, do I need to remind you of the example that he gives of a female patient called Emma, whom he doesn't mention elsewhere and who is not the Emma of the *Studies on Hysteria*? It is the case of a woman who has a phobia about going into stores by herself because she is afraid people will make fun of her on account of her clothes.

Everything is related to an early memory. At the age of twelve she went into a store and the shop assistants apparently laughed at her clothes. One of them attracted her and even stirred her in some strange way in her emerging puberty. Behind that we find a causal memory, that of an act of aggression she suffered in a shop at the hands of a *Greis*. The French translation, modeled on the English, which was itself particularly careless, says "shopkeeper"—but an old fogey is involved, an elderly man, who pinched her somewhere under her dress in a very direct manner. This memory thus echoes the idea of a sexual attraction experienced in the other.

All that remains in the symptom is attached to clothes, to the mockery of her clothes. But the path of truth is suggested in a masked form, in the deceiving *Vorstellung* of her clothes. In an opaque way, there is an allusion to something that did not happen on the occasion of the first memory, but on the second. Something that wasn't apprehended in the beginning is apprehended retroactively, by means of the deceitful transformation—*prōton pseudos*. Thus in that way we have confirmation of the fact that the relationship of the subject to *das Ding* is marked as bad—but the subject can only formulate this fact through the symptom.

That is what the experience of the unconscious has forced us to add to our premises when we take up again the question of ethics as it has been posed over the centuries, and as it has been bequeathed us in Kantian ethics, insofar as the latter remains, in our thought if not in our experience, the point to which these questions have been brought.

The way in which ethical principles are formulated when they impose themselves on consciousness or when about to emerge from preconsciousness, as commandments, has the closest relationship to the second principle introduced by Freud, namely, the reality principle.

The reality principle is the dialectical correlative of the pleasure principle. One is not simply, as one at first imagines, the application of the consequence of the other; each one is really the correlative of the other. Without this neither one would make any sense. Once again we are led to deepen the reality principle in a way I suggested in connection with the experience of paranoia.

As I have already told you, the reality principle isn't simply the same as it appears in the *Entwurf*, the testing that sometimes takes place at the level of the ω system or the *Wahrnehmungsbewusstsein* system. It doesn't function only on the level of that system in which the subject, probing in reality that which communicates the sign of a present reality, is able to adjust correctly the deceptive emergence of the *Vorstellung* as it is provoked by repetition at the level of the pleasure principle. It is something more. Reality faces man—and that is what interests him in it—both as having already been structured and as being that which presents itself in his experience as something that always returns to the same place.

I pointed it out when I was discussing the case of President Schreber. The function of the stars in the delirious system of that exemplary subject shows us, just like a compass, the polar star of the relation of man to the real. The history of science makes something similar seem plausible. Isn't it strange, paradoxical even, that it was the observations of shepherds and Mediterranean sailors of the return to the same place of an object which might seem to interest human experience least, namely, a star, that revealed to the farmer when he should sow his seeds? Think of the important role that the Pleiades played for Mediterranean navigators. Isn't it remarkable that it was the observation of the return of the stars to the very same places that, repeated over the centuries, led to the structuralization of reality by physics, which is what we mean by science? The fruitful laws involved came down to earth from the sky, to Galileo from the physics of the peripatetic philosophers. However, from that earth, where the laws of the heavens had been rediscovered, Galilean physics returned to the sky by demonstrating that the stars are by no means what we had believed them to be, that they are not incorruptible, that they are subject to the same laws as the terrestrial globe.

Furthermore, if a decisive step in the history of science was already taken by Nicolas of Cuse, who was one of the first to formulate the idea that the stars were not incorruptible, we know something else, we know that they might not be in the same place.

Thus that first demand that made us explore the structuralization of the real down through history in order to produce a supremely efficient and supremely deceptive science, that first demand is the demand of *das Ding* it seeks whatever is repeated, whatever returns, and guarantees that it will always return, to the same place—and it has driven us to the extreme position in which we find ourselves, a position where we can cast doubt on all places, and where nothing in that reality which we have learned to disrupt so admirably responds to that call for the security of a return.

Yet it is to this search for something that always returns to the same place that what is known as ethics has attached itself over the centuries. Ethics is not simply concerned with the fact that there are obligations, that there is a bond that binds, orders, and makes the social law. There is also something that we have frequently referred to here by the term "the elementary structures of kinship"—the elementary structures of property and of the exchange of goods as well. And it is as a result of these structures that man transforms himself into a sign, unit, or object of a regulated exchange in a way that Claude Lévi-Strauss has shown to be fixed in its relative unconsciousness. That which over generations has presided over this new supernatural order of the structures is exactly that which has brought about the submission of man to the law of the unconscious. But ethics begins beyond that point.

It begins at the moment when the subject poses the question of that good he had unconsciously sought in the social structures. And it is at that moment, too, that he is led to discover the deep relationship as a result of which that which presents itself as a law is closely tied to the very structure of desire. If he doesn't discover right away the final desire that Freudian inquiry has discovered as the desire of incest, he discovers that which articulates his conduct so that the object of his desire is always maintained at a certain distance. But this distance is not complete; it is a distance that is called proximity, which is not identical to the subject, which is literally close to it, in the way that one can say that the *Nebenmensch* that Freud speaks of as the foundation of the thing is his neighbor.

If at the summit of the ethical imperative something ends up being articulated in a way that is as strange or even scandalous for some people as "Thou shalt love thy neighbor as thyself," this is because it is the law of the relation of the subject to himself that he make himself his own neighbor, as far as his relationship to his desire is concerned.

My thesis is that the moral law is articulated with relation to the real as such, to the real insofar as it can be the guarantee of the Thing. That is why I invite you to take an interest in what I have called the high point of the crisis in ethics, and that I have designated from the beginning as linked to the moment when *The Critique of Practical Reason* appeared.

2

Kantian ethics appears at the moment when the disorienting effect of Newtonian physics is felt, a physics that has reached a point of independence relative to *das Ding*, to the human *Ding*.

It was Newtonian physics that forced Kant to revise radically the function of reason in its pure form. And it is also in connection with the questions raised by science that a form of morality has come to engage us; it is a morality whose precise structure could not have been perceived until then—one that detaches itself purposefully from all reference to any object of affection, from all reference to what Kant called the *pathologisches Objekt*, a pathological object, which simply means the object of any passion whatsoever.

No *Wohl*, whether it be our own or that of our neighbor, must enter into the finality of moral action. The only definition of moral action possible is that which was expressed in Kant's well-known formula: "Act in such a way that the maxim of your action may be accepted as a universal maxim." Thus action is moral only when it is dictated by the motive that is articulated in the maxim alone. To translate *allgemeine* as "universal" is not quite right, since it is closer to "common." Kant contrasts "general" with "universal," which he takes up in its Latin form. All of which proves that something here is left in an undetermined state. *Handle so, dass die Maxime deines Willens jederzeit zugleich als Prinzip einer allgemeinen Gesetzgebung gelten könne.* "Act so that the maxim of your will may always be taken as the principle of laws that are valid for all."

That formula, which is, as you know, the central formula of Kant's ethics, is pursued by him to the limit of its consequences. His radicalism even leads to the paradox that in the last analysis the *gute Wille*, good will, is posited as distinct from any beneficial action. In truth, I believe that the achievement of a form of subjectivity that deserves the name of contemporary, that belongs to a man of our time, who is lucky enough to be born now, cannot ignore this text. I simply emphasize it as we continue on our merry way, for one can, in fact, get by with very little—the person to our right and the person to our left are nowadays, if not neighbors, then at the very least people who, from the point of view of volume, are close enough to prevent us from falling down. But one must have submitted oneself to the test of reading this text in order to measure the extreme, almost insane character of the corner that we have been backed into by something that is after all present in history, namely, the existence, indeed the insistence, of science.

If, of course, no one has ever been able to put such a moral axiom into practice—even Kant himself did not believe it possible—it is nevertheless useful to see how far things have gone. In truth, we have built another bridge in our relation to reality. For some time transcendental aesthetics itself—I am referring to that which is designated as such in *The Critique of Pure Reason*—is open to challenge, at the very least on the level of that play of writing where theoretical physics is currently registering a hit. Henceforth, given the point we have reached in the light of our science, a renewal or updating of the Kantian imperative might be expressed in the following way, with the help of the language of electronics and automation: "Never act except in such a way that your action may be programmed." All of which takes us a step further in the direction of an even greater, if not the greatest, detachment from what is known as a Sovereign Good.

Let us be clear about this: when we reflect on the maxim that guides our action, Kant is inviting us to consider it for an instant as the law of a nature in which we are called upon to live. That is where one finds the apparatus that would have us reject in horror some maxim or other that our instincts would gladly lead us to. In this connection he gives us examples that are worth taking note of in a concrete sense, for however obvious they may seem, they perhaps suggest, at least to the analyst, a line of reflection. But note that he affirms the laws of *nature*, not of *society*. It is only too clear that not only do societies live very well by reference to laws that are far from promoting their universal application, but even more remarkably . . . these societies prosper as a result of the transgression of these maxims.

It is a matter then of a mental reference to a nature that is organized according to the laws of an object constructed at the moment when we raise the question of our rule of conduct.

So as to produce the kind of shock or eye-opening effect that seems to me necessary if we are to make progress, I simply want to draw your attention to this: if *The Critique of Practical Reason* appeared in 1788, seven years after the first edition of *The Critique of Pure Reason*, there is another work which came out six years after *The Critique of Practical Reason*, a little after Thermidor in 1795, and which is called *Philosophy in the Boudoir*.

As I suppose you all know, *Philosophy in the Boudoir* is the work of a certain Marquis de Sade, who is famous for more than one reason. His notoriety was accompanied from the beginning by great misfortunes, and one might add by the abuse of power concerning him—he did after all remain a prisoner for twenty-five years, which is a long time for someone who, my goodness, as far as we know, never committed a serious crime, and who in certain of our modern ideologies has been promoted to a point where one can also say that there is at the very least some confusion, if not excess.

Although in the eyes of some the work of the Marquis de Sade seems to promise a variety of entertainments, it is not strictly speaking much fun. Moreover, the parts that seem to give the most pleasure can also be regarded as the most boring. But one cannot claim that his work lacks coherence. And, in a word, it is precisely the Kantian criteria he advances to justify his positions that constitute what can be called a kind of antimorality.

The paradox of this is argued with the greatest coherence in the work that is entitled *Philosophy in the Boudoir*. A short passage is included in it that, given the number of attentive ears here, is the only one that I expressly recommend you read—"Frenchmen, one more effort to become republicans."

As a result of this appeal, which supposedly came from a number of cells that were active at that time in revolutionary Paris, the Marquis de Sade proposes that, given the ruin of those authorities on which (according to the work's premises) the creation of a true republic depends, we should adopt the opposite of what was considered up to that point as the essential minimum of a viable and coherent morality.

And, in truth, he does quite a good job in defending that proposal. It is no accident if we first find in *Philosophy in the Boudoir* the praise of calumny. Calumny, he writes, can in no sense be injurious; if it imputes to our neighbor worse things than one can justifiably impute to him, it nevertheless has the merit that it puts us on guard against his activities. And the author proceeds in like manner to justify point by point the reversal of the fundamental imperatives of the moral law, extolling incest, adultery, theft, and everything else you can think of. If you adopt the opposite of all the laws of the Decalogue, you will end up with the coherent exposition of something which in the last instance may be articulated as follows: "Let us take as the universal maxim of our conduct the right to enjoy any other person whatsoever as the instrument of our pleasure."

Sade demonstrates with great consistency that, once universalized, this law, although it gives libertines complete power over all women indifferently, whether they like it or not, conversely also liberates those same women from all the duties that civilized society imposes on them in their conjugal, matrimonial, and other relations. This conception opens wide the floodgates that in imagination he proposes as the horizon of our desire; everyone is invited to pursue to the limit the demands of his lust, and to realize them.

If the same opening is given to all, one will be able to see what a natural society is like. Our repugnance may be legitimately related to that which Kant himself claims to eliminate from the criteria of the moral law, namely, to the realm of sentiment.

If one eliminates from morality every element of sentiment, if one removes or invalidates all guidance to be found in sentiments, then in the final analysis the Sadian world is conceivable—even if it is its inversion, its caricature—as one of the possible forms of the world governed by a radical ethics, by the Kantian ethics as elaborated in 1788.

Believe me, there is no lack of Kantian echoes in the attempts to articulate moral systems that one finds in a vast literature that might be called libertine, the literature of the man of pleasure, which is an equally caricatural form of the problem that for a long time preoccupied the *ancién regime*, and from Fénelon on, the education of girls. You can see that pushed to its comically paradoxical limit in *The Raised Curtain* by Mirabeau.

Well now, we are coming to that on account of which, in its search for justification, for a base and support, in the sense of reference to the reality principle, ethics encounters its own stumbling block, its failure—I mean there where an aporia opens up in that mental articulation we call ethics. In the same way that Kantian ethics has no other consequence than that gymnastic exercise whose formative function for anyone who thinks I have called to your attention, so Sadian ethics has had no social consequences at all.

Understand that I don't know if the French have really tried to become republicans, but it is certain that just like all the other nations of the world, including those who had their revolutions after them—bolder, more ambitious, and more radical revolutions, too—they have left what I will call the religious bases of the Ten Commandments completely intact, even pushing them to a point where their puritan character is increasingly marked. We've reached a situation where the leader of a great socialist state on a visit to other contemporary cultures is scandalized to see dancers on the Pacific coast of the noble country of America raising their legs a little too high.

We are thus faced here with a question, that is to say, the question of the relationship to *das Ding*.

This relationship seems to me to be sufficiently emphasized in the third chapter of *The Critique of Practical Reason* concerning the motives of practical pure reason. In effect, Kant acknowledges after all the existence of *one* sentient correlative of the moral law in its purity, and strangely enough, I ask you to note, it is nothing other than pain itself. I will read you the passage concerned, the second paragraph of the third part:

> Consequently, we can see *a priori* that the moral law as the determining principle of will, by reason of the fact that it sets itself against our inclinations, must produce a feeling that one could call pain. And this is the first and perhaps only case, where we are allowed to determine, by means of *a priori* concepts, the relationship between a knowledge, which comes from practical pure reason, and a feeling of pleasure or pain.

In brief, Kant is of the same opinion as Sade. For in order to reach *das Ding* absolutely, to open the floodgates of desire, what does Sade show us on the horizon? In essence, pain. The other's pain as well as the pain of the subject himself, for on occasions they are simply one and the same thing. To the degree that it involves forcing an access to the Thing, the outer extremity of pleasure is unbearable to us. It is this that explains the absurd or, to use a popular expression, maniacal side of Sade that strikes us in his fictional constructions. We are aware at every moment of the discomfort in living constructions, the kind of discomfort that makes it so difficult for our neurotic patients to confess certain of their phantasms.

In fact, to a certain degree, at a certain level, phantasms cannot bear the revelation of speech.

3

We are then brought back again to the moral law insofar as it is incarnated in a certain number of commandments. I mean the Ten Commandments, which in the beginning, at a period that is not so remote in the past, were collected by a people that sets itself apart as a chosen people.

As I said, it is appropriate to reconsider these commandments. I noted last time that there is a study to be done for which I would gladly call upon one of you as the representative of a tradition of moral theology. A great many questions deserve our attention. I spoke of the number of commandments. There is also the matter of their form and the way in which they are transmitted to us in the future tense. I would be glad to call upon the help of someone who knows enough Hebrew to answer my questions. In the Hebrew version is it a future tense or a form of the volitive that is used in Deuteronomy and Numbers, where we see the first formulations of the Decalogue?

The issue I want to raise today concerns their privileged structure in relation to the structure of the law. I want today to consider two of them.

I must leave to one side the huge questions posed by the promulgation of these commandments by something that announces itself in the following form: "I am what I am." It is, in effect, necessary not to draw the text in the direction of Greek metaphysics by translating as "he who is," or "he who am." The English translation, "I am that I am," is, according to Hebrew scholars, the closest to what is meant by the formulation of the verse. Perhaps I am mistaken, but since I do not know Hebrew and while I wait on further information on the subject, I rely on the best authorities, and they are of one mind on the question.

That "I am what I am" is announced first of all to a small people in the form of that which saved it from the misfortunes of Egypt, and it begins by affirming, "You will adore no God but me, before my countenance." I leave open the question of what "before my countenance" means. Does it mean that beyond the countenance of God, i.e., outside Canaan, the adoration of other gods is not inconceivable for a believing Jew? A passage from the Second Book of Samuel, spoken by David, seems to confirm this.

It is nevertheless the case that the Second Commandment, the one that formally excludes not only every cult, but also every image, every representation of what is in heaven, on earth, or in the void, seems to me to show that what is involved is in a very special relationship to human feeling as a whole. In a nutshell, the elimination of the function of the imaginary presents itself to my mind, and, I think, to yours, as the principle of the relation to the symbolic, in the meaning we give that term here; that is to say, to speech. Its principal condition is there.

I leave aside the question of rest on the Sabbath day. But I believe that that extraordinary commandment according to which, in a land of masters, we observe one day out of seven without work—such that, according to humorous proverbs, the common man is left no happy medium between the labor of love and the most stultifying boredom—that suspension, that emptiness, clearly introduces into human life the sign of a gap, a beyond relative to every law of utility. It seems to me, therefore, that it has the most intimate relationship to something that we are on the track of here.

I leave aside the prohibition on murder, for we will have to come back to that in connection with the respective significance of the act and its retribution. I want to take up the prohibition on lying insofar as it is related to what presented itself to us as that essential relationship of man to the Thing, insofar as it is commanded by the pleasure principle, namely, the lie that we have to deal with every day in our unconscious.

"Thou shalt not lie" is the commandment in which the intimate link between desire, in its structuring function, with the law is felt most tangibly. In truth, this commandment exists to make us feel the true function of the law. And I can do no better than to place it beside the sophism in which is manifested most strikingly the type of ingenuity that is furthest from the Jewish or Talmudic tradition, namely, the paradox of Epimenides, he who affirmed that all men are liars. What am I saying, in proposing the articulation of the unconscious that I gave you; what am I saying, responds the sophism?—except that I, too, lie, and, consequently, I can affirm nothing valid concerning not simply the function of truth, but even the significance of lying.

"Thou shalt not lie" as a negative precept has as its function to withdraw the subject of enunciation from that which is enunciated. Remember the graph. It is there that I can say "Thou shalt not lie"—there where I lie, where I repress, where I, the liar, speak. In "Thou shalt not lie" as law is included the possibility of the lie as the most fundamental desire.

I am going to give you a proof that is to my mind nevertheless valid. It concerns Proudhon's famous phrase: "Property is theft." Another proof is that of the cries of anguish lawyers emit whenever it is a question, in some more or less grotesque and mythical form, of using a lie detector. Must we conclude from this that the respect of the human person involves the right to lie? Surely, it is a question and not an answer to reply "yes, certainly." One might say, it's not so simple.

What is the source of that rebellion against the fact that something exists which may reduce the question of the subject's speech to a universally objectified application? The point is that speech doesn't itself know what it is saying when it lies, and that, on the other hand, in lying it also speaks some truth. Moreover, it is in this antinomic function between the law and desire, as conditioned by speech, that resides the primordial authority which makes this commandment among all ten one of the cornerstones of that which we call the human condition, to the extent that that condition merits our respect.

Since time is getting on, I will skip quickly forward to the issue that is the object of our discussion today relative to the relationship between desire and the law. It is the famous commandment that affirms the following—it makes one smile, but when one thinks about it, one doesn't smile for long: "Thou shalt not covet thy neighbor's house, thou shalt not covet thy neighbor's wife, neither his manservant, nor his maidservant, neither his ox, nor his ass, nor anything that belongs to thy neighbor."

Putting the wife between the house and the donkey has given rise to more than one idea that one can recognize there the exigencies of a primitive society—a society of Bedouins, "wogs," and "niggers." Well, I don't agree.

The law affirmed there, the part concerning one's neighbor's wife at least, is still alive in the hearts of men who violate it every day, and it doubtless has a relationship to that which is the object of our discussion today, namely, *das Ding*.

It is not after all a question of just any good here. It is not a question of that which creates the law of exchange and covers with a kind of amusing legality, a kind of social *Sicherung*, the movements, the *impetus*, of human instincts. It is a question of something whose value resides in the fact that none of these objects exists without having the closest possible relationship to that in which the human being can rest as if it were *die Trude*, *das Ding*—not insofar as it is his good, but insofar as it is the good in which he may find rest. Let me add *das Ding* insofar as it is the very correlative of the law of speech in its most primitive point of origin, and in the sense that this *Ding* was there from the beginning, that it was the first thing that separated itself from everything the subject began to name and articulate, that the covetousness that is in question is not addressed to anything that I might desire but to a thing that is my neighbor's Thing.

It is to the extent that the commandment in question preserves the distance from the Thing as founded by speech itself that it assumes its value.

But where does this take us?

Is the Law the Thing? Certainly not. Yet I can only know of the Thing by means of the Law. In effect, I would not have had the idea to covet it if the Law hadn't said: "Thou shalt not covet it." But the Thing finds a way by producing in me all kinds of covetousness thanks to the commandment, for without the Law the Thing is dead. But even without the Law, I was once alive. But when the commandment appeared, the Thing flared up, returned once again, I met my death. And for me, the commandment that was supposed to lead to life turned out to lead to death, for the Thing found a way and thanks to the commandment seduced me; through it I came to desire death.

I believe that for a little while now some of you at least have begun to suspect that it is no longer I who have been speaking. In fact, with one small change, namely, "Thing" for "sin," this is the speech of Saint Paul on the subject of the relations between the law and sin in the Epistle to the Romans, chapter 7, paragraph 7.

Whatever some may think in certain milieus, you would be wrong to think that the religious authors aren't a good read. I have always been rewarded whenever I have immersed myself in their works. And Saint Paul's Epistle is a work that I recommend to you for your vacation reading; you will find it very good company.

The relationship between the Thing and the Law could not be better defined than in these terms. And we will come back to it now. The dialectical relationship between desire and the Law causes our desire to flare up only in relation to the Law, through which it becomes the desire for death. It is only because of the Law that sin, *hamartia*—which in Greek means lack and nonparticipation in the Thing—takes on an excessive, hyperbolic character. Freud's discovery—the ethics of psychoanalysis—does it leave us clinging to that dialectic? We will have to explore that which, over the centuries, human beings have succeeded in elaborating that transgresses the Law, puts them in a relationship to desire that transgresses interdiction, and introduces an erotics that is above morality.

I don't think that you should be surprised by such a question. It is after all precisely something that all religions engage in, all mysticisms, all that Kant disdainfully calls the *Religionsschwärmereien*, religious enthusiasms—it's not an easy term to translate. What is all this except a way of rediscovering the relationship to *das Ding* somewhere beyond the law? There are no doubt other ways. No doubt, in talking about erotics, we will have to talk about the kind of rules of love that have been elaborated over the centuries. Freud said somewhere that he could have described his doctrine as an erotics, but, he went on, "I didn't do it, because that would have involved giving ground relative to words, and he who gives ground relative to words also gives ground relative to things. I thus spoke of the theory of sexuality."

It's true: Freud placed in the forefront of ethical inquiry the simple relationship between man and woman. Strangely enough, things haven't been able to move beyond that point. The question of *das Ding* is still attached to whatever is open, lacking, or gaping at the center of our desire. I would say— you will forgive the play on words—that we need to know what we can do to transform this damage into our "dame" in the archaic French sense, our lady.

Don't laugh at this sleight of hand; it was in the language before I used it. If you look up the etymology of the word "danger," you will see that exactly the same ambiguity exists from the beginning in French: "danger" was originally "domniarium," domination. The word "dame" gradually came to contaminate that word. And, in effect, when we are in another's power, we are in great danger.

23

GILLES DELEUZE
(1925–1995)

FÉLIX GUATTARI
(1930–1992)

French philosopher Gilles Deleuze was born in Paris in 1925. He entered the Sorbonne in 1945, where he was a student of Jean Hyppolite and Georges Canguilhem. He passed his *agrégation* in 1948 and taught in various high schools before becoming an assistant professor at the Sorbonne in 1957. In 1969, he accepted an academic position at the University of Paris–Vincennes, where he taught until his retirement in 1987. In the same year, he met Félix Guattari, with whom he collaborated on *Capitalism and Schizophrenia*, vol. 1, *Anti-Oedipus* (1972), and vol. 2, *A Thousand Plateaus* (1980). Smelted in the revolutionary and political fervor of May 1968, the former became one of the best-selling works of recent philosophy. Throughout the 1970s, Deleuze was politically active, helping to form (with Michel Foucault and others) the Groupe d'Information sur les Prisons and supporting various causes, from gay rights to Palestinian repatriation. In the 1980s, Deleuze wrote various books on painting (*Francis Bacon: The Logic of Sensation* [1981]) and cinema (*The Movement-Image* [1983]; *The Time-Image* [1985]). His final collaboration with Guattari was *What Is Philosophy?* (1991). In 1995, at the end of an academic career that spanned over forty years, during which time he published over twenty major works, including a number of studies on individual philosophers and writers (Hume, Kant, Nietzsche, Bergson, Spinoza, Leibniz, Foucault, Sacher-Masoch, Sade, Kafka, and Proust), and after a long and debilitating illness, Deleuze committed suicide.

French psychoanalyst Félix Guattari was born at Villeneuve-les-Sablons, Oise, in 1930. Trained in psychoanalysis under Lacan, he became codirector of La Borde, Cour-Cheverny, a private, experimental psychiatric clinic providing training for philosophers, psychologists, ethnologists, and social workers. An ultraleftist, and Trotskyite for a limited time, he was a harsh critic of French colonialism and took a leading role in the events of May 1968. In the 1980s, Guattari broke away from the École Freudienne to found a European Alternative Network for Psychiatry with fellow antipsychiatrist R.D. Laing. During the same decade, he become politically active in the ecology movement (*The Three Ecologies* [1989]), in which he sought to address Green issues outside the traditional political antagonism between the left and the right. Among his many independent works, particular mention should be made of *Molecular Revolution: Psychiatry and Politics* (1977), and his last work, *Chaosmosis: An Ethicoaesthetic Paradigm*, published the year of his death in 1992.

In his 1977 Preface to the English edition of *Anti-Oedipus*, the book from which our reading is taken, Michel Foucault writes:

> I would say that *Anti-Oedipus* (may its authors forgive me) is a book of ethics, the first book of ethics to be written in France in quite a long time. . . . How does one keep oneself from being a fascist, even (especially) when one believes oneself to be a militant? How do we rid our speech and our acts, our hearts and our pleasures, of fascism? How do we ferret out the fascism that is ingrained in our hearts? (*Anti-Oedipus*, xiii)

Anti-Oedipus does not call itself a book on ethics, but its ethical implications become clear once we step back from the scientific language of machines, connections, flows, and productions, and see it as primarily concerned with developing a new model of subjectivity. In opposition to traditional subjectivity that has all too easily succumbed to the ternary relations of Freud's Oedipus complex, which Deleuze and Guattari call the "paranoic machine," the revolutionary "schizo" is championed as someone who has *naturally* albeit *miraculously* escaped the forces of repression and Oedipalization unleashed by modern capitalism. The schizo operates in accordance with libidinal desire that is "productive" in that it *produces* its object through various "connective syntheses." (This may be contrasted with the traditional notion of Platonic-Lacanian desire, which is governed by the lack of what is desired). However, the same desire can also take the form of "antiproduction," according to Deleuze and Guattari, which they call "the body without organs" (a term borrowed from Antonin Artaud). Although we might expect the body without organs, lacking as it does the means to couple with the other "desiring machines," to terminate desire, it also functions as the condition for desire, which precisely requires the dis-organ-ization of the body in a free state so as to enable future couplings with alternative machines. It is clear from the tenor of Deleuze's and Guattari's materialist psychiatry that they consider the schizo—which is to be sharply distinguished from the "artificial schizophrenic found in mental institutions"—to be healthier than and hence *preferable* to the paranoid existence that wants to conserve its organ-ization at all costs, which manifests itself in terms of the traditional belief in God, for example.

Select Bibliography of Deleuze's Works in English

Anti-Oedipus: Capitalism and Schizophrenia (with Guattari). Trans. Robert Hurley, Mark Seem, and Helen R. Lane. Minneapolis, MN: University of Minnesota Press, 1989.

The Deleuze Reader. Ed. Constantin V. Boundas. New York: Columbia University Press, 1993.

Dialogues (with Claire Parnet). Trans. Hugh Tomlinson and Barbara Habberjam. New York: Columbia University Press, 1987.

Difference and Repetition. Trans. Paul Patton. New York: Columbia University Press, 1994.

Expressionism in Philosophy: Spinoza. Trans. Martin Joughin. New York: Zone Books, 1990.

Kant's Critical Philosophy. Trans. Hugh Tomlinson and Barbara Habberjam. Minneapolis, MN: University of Minnesota Press, 1983.

The Logic of Sense. Trans. Mark Lester and Charles Stivale. New York: Columbia University Press, 1990.

Nietzsche and Philosophy. Trans. Hugh Tomlinson. New York: Columbia University Press, 1983.

A Thousand Plateaus: Capitalism and Schizophrenia (with Guattari). Trans. Brian Massumi. Minneapolis, MN: University of Minnesota Press, 1987.

What Is Philosophy? (with Guattari). Trans. Hugh Tomlinson and Graham Burchell. New York: Columbia University Press, 1996.

Select Bibliography of Guattari's Works in English

Chaosmosis: An Ethicoaesthetic Paradigm. Trans. Paul Bains and Julian Pefanis. Bloomington, IN: Indiana University Press, 1995.

Chaosophy. Trans. Chet Wiener. New York: Semiotext(e), 1995.

Communists Like Us (with Antonio Negri). Trans. Michael Ryan. New York: Semiotext(e), 1990.

A Guattari Reader. Ed. Gary Genosko. Oxford: Blackwell, 1996.

Molecular Revolution: Psychiatry and Politics. Trans. Rosemary Sheed. New York: Penguin, 1984.

Soft Subversions. Trans. David L. Sweet and Chet Wiener. New York: Semiotext(e), 1996.

The Three Ecologies. Trans. Ian Pindar and Paul Sutton. London: Athlone, 2001.

DESIRING MACHINES

1. Desiring-Production

It is at work everywhere, functioning smoothly at times, at other times in fits and starts. It breathes, it heats, it eats. It shits and fucks. What a mistake to have ever said *the* id. Everywhere *it* is machines—real ones, not figurative ones: machines driving other machines, machines being driven by other machines, with all the necessary couplings and connections. An organ-machine is plugged into an energy-source-machine: the one produces a flow that the other interrupts. The breast is a machine that produces milk, and the mouth a machine coupled to it. The mouth of the anorexic wavers between several functions: its possessor is uncertain as to whether it is an eating-machine, an anal-machine, a talking-machine, or a breathing-machine (asthma attacks). Hence we are all handymen: each with his little machines. For every organ-machine, an energy-machine: all the time, flows and interruptions. Judge Schreber [see Freud's case history] has sunbeams in his ass. *A solar anus.* And rest assured that it works: Judge Schreber feels something, produces something, and is capable of explaining the process theoretically. Something is produced: the effects of a machine, not mere metaphors.

A schizophrenic out for a walk is a better model than a neurotic lying on the analyst's couch. A breath of fresh air, a relationship with the outside world. Lenz's stroll, for example, as reconstructed by Büchner. This walk outdoors is different from the moments when Lenz finds himself closeted with his pastor, who forces him to situate himself socially, in relationship to the God of established religion, in relationship to his father, to his mother. While taking a stroll outdoors, on the other hand, he is in the mountains, amid falling snowflakes, with other gods or without any gods at all, without a family, without a father or a mother, with nature. "What does my father want? Can he offer me more than that? Impossible. Leave me in peace."[1] Everything is a machine. Celestial machines, the stars or rainbows in the sky, alpine machines—all of them connected to those of his body. The continual whirr of machines. "He thought that it must be a feeling of endless bliss to be in contact with the profound life of every form, to have a soul for rocks, metals, water, and plants, to take into himself, as in a dream, every element of nature, like flowers that breathe with the waxing and waning of the moon."[2] To be a chlorophyll- or a photosynthesis-machine, or at least slip his body into such machines as one part among the others. Lenz has projected himself back to a time before the man-nature dichotomy, before all the coordinates based on this fundamental dichotomy have been laid down. He does not live nature as nature, but as a process of production. There is no such thing as either man or nature now, only a process that produces the one within the other and couples the machines together. Producing-machines, desiring-machines everywhere, schizophrenic machines, all of species life: the self and the non-self, outside and inside, no longer have any meaning whatsoever.

Now that we have had a look at this stroll of a schizo, let us compare what happens when Samuel Beckett's characters decide to venture outdoors. Their various gaits and methods of self-locomotion constitute, in and of themselves, a finely tuned machine. And then there is the function of the bicycle in Beckett's works: what relationship does the bicycle-horn machine have with the mother-anus machine? "What a rest to speak of bicycles and horns. Unfortunately it is not of them I have to speak, but of her who brought me into the world, through the hole in her ass if my memory is correct."[3] It is often thought that Oedipus is an easy subject to deal with, something perfectly obvious, a "given" that is there from the very beginning. But that is not so at all: Oedipus presupposes a fantastic repression of desiring-machines. And why are they repressed? To what end? Is it really necessary or desirable to submit to such repression? And what means are to be used to accomplish this? What ought to go inside the Oedipal triangle, what sort of thing is required to construct it? Are a bicycle horn and my mother's ass sufficient to do the job? Aren't there more important questions than these, however? Given a certain effect, what machine is capable of producing it? And given a certain machine, what can it be used for? Can we possibly guess, for instance, what a knife rest is used for if all we are given is a geometrical description of it? Or yet another example: on being confronted with a complete machine made up of six stones in the right-hand pocket of my coat (the pocket that serves as the source of the stones), five stones in the right-hand pocket of my trousers, and five in the left-hand pocket (transmission pockets), with the remaining pocket of my coat receiving the stones that have already been handled, as each of the stones moves forward one pocket, how can we determine the effect of this circuit of distribution in which the mouth, too, plays a role as a stone-sucking machine? Where in this entire circuit do we find the production of sexual pleasure? At the end of *Malone Dies*, Lady Pedal takes the schizophrenics out for a ride in a van and a rowboat, and on a picnic in the midst of nature: an infernal machine is being assembled. "Under the skin the body is an over-heated factory,/ and outside,/ the invalid shines,/ glows,/ from every burst pore."[4]

This does not mean that we are attempting to make nature one of the poles of schizophrenia. What the schizophrenic experiences, both as an individual and as a member of the human species, is not at all any one specific aspect of nature, but nature as a process of production. What do we mean here by process? It is probable that at a certain level nature and industry are two separate and distinct things: from one point of view, industry is the opposite of nature; from another, industry extracts its raw materials from nature; from yet another, it returns its refuse to nature; and so on. Even within society, this characteristic man-nature, industry-nature, society-nature relationship is responsible for the distinction of relatively autonomous spheres that are called production, distribution, consumption. But in general this entire level of distinctions, examined from the point of view of its formal developed structures, presupposes (as Marx has demonstrated) not only the existence of capital and the division of labor, but also the false consciousness that the capitalist being necessarily acquires, both of itself and of the supposedly fixed elements within an overall process. For the real truth of the matter—the glaring, sober truth that resides in delirium—is that there is no such thing as relatively independent spheres or circuits: production is immediately consumption and a recording process, without any sort of mediation, and the recording process and consumption directly determine production, though they do so within the production process itself. Hence everything is production: *production of productions*, of actions and of passions; *productions of recording processes*, of distributions and of coordinates that serve as points of reference; *productions of consumptions*, of sensual pleasures, of anxieties, and of pain. Everything is production, since the recording processes are immediately consumed, immediately consummated, and these consumptions directly reproduced. This is the first meaning of process as we use the term: incorporating recording and consumption within production itself, thus making them the productions of one and the same process.

Second, we make no distinction between man and nature: the human essence of nature and the natural essence of man become one within nature in the form of production or industry, just as they do within the life of man as a species. Industry is then no longer considered from the extrinsic point of view of utility, but rather from the point of view of its fundamental identity with nature as production of man and by man.[5] Not man as the king of creation, but rather as the being who is in intimate contact with the profound life of all forms or all types of beings, who is responsible for even the stars and animal life, and who ceaselessly plugs an organ-machine into an energy-machine, a tree into his body, a breast into his mouth, the sun into his asshole: the eternal custodian of the machines of the universe. This is the second meaning of process as we use the term: man and nature are not like two opposite terms confronting each other—not even in the sense of bipolar opposites within a relationship of causation, ideation, or expression (cause and effect, subject and object, etc.); rather, they are one and the same essential reality, the producer-product. Production as process overtakes all idealistic categories and constitutes a cycle whose relationship to desire is that of an immanent principle. That is why desiring-production is the principal concern of a materialist psychiatry, which conceives of and deals with the schizo as *Homo natura*. This will be the case, however, only on one condition, which in fact constitutes the third meaning of process as we use the term: it must not be viewed as a goal or an end in itself, nor must it be confused with an infinite perpetuation of itself. Putting an end to the process or prolonging it indefinitely—which, strictly speaking, is tantamount to ending it abruptly and prematurely—is what creates the artificial schizophrenic found in mental institutions: a limp rag forced into autistic behavior, produced as an entirely separate and independent entity. D.H. Lawrence says of love: "We have pushed a process into a goal. The aim of any process is not the perpetuation of that process, but the completion thereof. . . . The process should work to a completion, not to some horror of intensification and extremity wherein the soul and body ultimately perish."[6] Schizophrenia is like love: there is no specifically schizophrenic phenomenon or entity; schizophrenia is the universe of productive and reproductive desiring-machines, universal primary production as "the essential reality of man and nature."

Desiring-machines are binary machines, obeying a binary law or set of rules governing associations: one machine is always coupled with another. The productive synthesis, the production of production, is inherently connective in nature: "and . . ." "and then. . . ." This is because there is always a flow-producing machine, and another machine connected to it that interrupts or draws off part of this flow (the breast—the mouth). And because the first machine is in turn connected to another whose flow it interrupts or partially drains off, the binary series is linear in every direction. Desire constantly couples continuous flows and partial objects that are by nature fragmentary and fragmented. Desire causes the current to flow, itself flows in turn, and breaks the flows. "I love everything that flows, even the menstrual flow that carries away the seed unfecund."[7] Amniotic fluid spilling out of the sac and kidney stones; flowing hair; a flow of spittle, a flow of sperm, shit, or urine that are produced by partial objects and constantly cut off by other partial objects, which in turn produce other flows, interrupted by other partial objects. Every "object" presupposes the continuity of a flow; every flow, the fragmentation of the object. Doubtless each organ-machine interprets the entire world from the perspective of its own flux, from the point of view of the energy that flows from it: the eye interprets everything—speaking, understanding, shitting, fucking—in terms of seeing. But a connection with another machine is always established, along a transverse path, so that one machine interrupts the current of the other or "sees" its own current interrupted.

Hence the coupling that takes place within the partial object-flow connective synthesis also has another form: product/producing. Producing is always something "grafted onto" the product; and for that reason desiring-production is production of production, just as every machine is a machine connected to another machine. We cannot accept the idealist category of "expression" as a satisfactory or sufficient explanation of this phenomenon. We cannot, we must not attempt to describe the schizophrenic object without relating it to the process of production. The *Cahiers de l'art brut* are a striking confirmation of this principle, since by taking such an approach they deny that there is any such thing as a specific, identifiable schizophrenic entity. Or to take another example, Henri Michaux describes a schizophrenic table in terms of a process of production which is that of desire:

> Once noticed, it continued to occupy one's mind. It even persisted, as it were, in going about its own business. . . . The striking thing was that it was neither simple nor really complex, initially or intentionally complex, or constructed according to a complicated plan. Instead, it had been desimplified in the course of its carpentering. . . . As it stood, it was a table of additions, much like certain schizophrenics' drawings, described as "overstuffed," and if finished it was only insofar as there was no way of adding anything more to it, the table having become more and more an accumulation, less and less a table. . . . It was not intended for any specific purpose, for anything one expects of a table. Heavy, cumbersome, it was virtually immovable. One didn't know how to handle it (mentally or physically). Its top surface, the useful part of the table, having been gradually reduced, was disappearing, with so little relation to the clumsy framework that the thing did not strike one as a table, but as some freak piece of furniture, an unfamiliar instrument . . . for which there was no purpose. A dehumanized table, nothing cozy about it, nothing "middle-class," nothing rustic, nothing countrified, not a kitchen table or a work table. A table which lent itself to no function, self-protective, denying itself to service and communication alike. There was something stunned about it, something petrified. Perhaps it suggested a stalled engine.[8]

The schizophrenic is the universal producer. There is no need to distinguish here between producing and its product. We need merely note that the pure "thisness" of the object produced is carried over into a new act of producing. The table continues to "go about its business." The surface of the table, however, is eaten up by the supporting framework. The nontermination of the table is a necessary consequence of its mode of production. When Claude Lévi-Strauss defines *bricolage*, he does so in terms of a set of closely related characteristics: the possession of a stock of materials or of rules of thumb that are fairly extensive, though more or less a hodgepodge—multiple and at the same time limited; the ability to rearrange fragments continually in new and different patterns or configurations; and as a consequence, an indifference toward the act of producing and toward the product, toward the set of instruments to be used and toward the overall result to be achieved. The satisfaction the handyman experiences when he plugs something into an electric socket or diverts a stream of water can scarcely be explained in terms of "playing mommy and daddy," or by the pleasure of violating a taboo. The rule of continually producing production, of grafting producing onto the product, is a characteristic of desiring-machines or of primary production: the production of production. A painting by Richard Lindner, *"Boy with Machine,"* shows a huge, pudgy, bloated boy working one of his little desiring-machines, after having hooked it up to a vast technical social machine—which, as we shall see, is what even the very young child does.

Producing, a product: a producing/product identity. It is this identity that constitutes a third term in the linear series: an enormous undifferentiated object. Everything stops dead for a moment, everything freezes in place—and then the whole process will begin all over again. From a certain point of view it would be much better if nothing worked, if nothing functioned. Never being born, escaping the wheel of continual birth and rebirth, no mouth to suck with, no anus to shit through. Will the machines run so badly, their component pieces fall apart to such a point that they will return to nothingness and thus allow us to return to nothingness? It would seem, however, that the flows of energy are still too closely connected, the partial objects still too organic, for this to happen. What would be required is a pure fluid in a free state, flowing without interruption, streaming over the surface of a full body. Desiring-machines make us an organism; but at the very heart of this production, within the very production of this production, the body suffers from being organized in this way, from not having some other sort of organization, or no organization at all. "An incomprehensible, absolutely rigid stasis" in the very midst of process, as a third stage: *"No mouth. No tongue. No teeth. No larynx. No esophagus. No belly. No anus."* The automata stop dead and set free the unorganized mass they once served to articulate. The full body without organs is the unproductive, the sterile, the unengendered, the unconsumable. Antonin Artaud discovered this one day, finding himself with no shape or form whatsoever, right there where he was at that moment. The death instinct: that is its name, and death is not without a model. For desire desires death also, because the full body of death is its motor, just as it desires life, because the organs of life are the *working machine*. We shall not inquire how all this fits together so that the machine will run: the question itself is the result of a process of abstraction.

Desiring-machines work only when they break down, and by continually breaking down. Judge Schreber "lived for a long time without a stomach, without intestines, almost without lungs, with a torn oesophagus, without a bladder, and with shattered ribs; he used sometimes to swallow part of his own larynx with his food, etc."[9] The body without organs is nonproductive; nonetheless it is produced, at a certain place and a certain time in the connective synthesis, as the identity of producing and the product: the schizophrenic table is a body without organs. The body without organs is not the proof of an original nothingness, nor is it what remains of a lost totality. Above all, it is not a projection; it has nothing whatsoever to do with the body itself, or with an image of the body. It is the body without an image. This imageless, organless body, the nonproductive, exists right there where it is produced, in the third stage of the binary-linear series. It is perpetually reinserted into the process of production. The catatonic body is produced in the water of the hydrotherapy tub. The full body without organs belongs to the realm of antiproduction; but yet another characteristic of the connective or productive synthesis is the fact that it couples production with antiproduction, with an element of antiproduction.

2. The Body without Organs

An apparent conflict arises between desiring-machines and the body without organs. Every coupling of machines, every production of a machine, every sound of a machine running, becomes unbearable to the body without organs. Beneath its organs it senses there are larvae and loathsome worms, and a God at work messing it all up or strangling it by organizing it. "The body is the body/it is all by itself/and has no need of organs/the body is never an organism/organisms are the enemies of the body."[10] Merely so many nails piercing the flesh, so many forms of torture. In order to resist organ-machines, the body without organs presents its smooth, slippery, opaque, taut surface as a barrier. In order to resist linked, connected, and interrupted flows, it sets up a counterflow of amorphous, undifferentiated fluid. In order to resist using words composed of articulated phonetic units, it utters only gasps and cries that are sheer unarticulated blocks of sound. We are of the opinion that what is ordinarily referred to as "primary repression" means precisely that: it is not a "countercathexis," but rather this *repulsion* of desiring-machines by the body without organs. This is the real meaning of the paranoiac machine: the desiring-machines attempt to break into the body without organs, and the body without organs repels them, since it experiences them as an overall persecution apparatus. Thus we cannot agree with Victor Tausk when he regards the paranoiac machine as a mere projection, of "a person's own body" and the genital organs.[11] The genesis of the machine lies precisely here: in the opposition of the process of production of the desiring-machines and the nonproductive stasis of the body without organs. The anonymous nature of the machine and the nondifferentiated nature of its surface are proof of this. Projection enters the picture only secondarily, as does counterinvestment, as the body without organs invests a counterinside or a counteroutside, in the form of a persecuting organ or some exterior agent of persecution. But in and of itself the paranoiac machine is merely an avatar of the desiring-machines: it is a result of the relationship between the desiring-machines and the body without organs, and occurs when the latter can no longer tolerate these machines.

If we wish to have some idea of the forces that the body without organs exerts later on in the uninterrupted process, we must first establish a parallel between desiring-production and social production. We intend such a parallel to be regarded as merely phenomenological: we are here drawing no conclusions whatsoever as to the nature and the relationship of the two productions, nor does the parallel we are about to establish provide any sort of *a priori* answer to the question whether desiring-production and social production are really two separate and distinct productions. Its one purpose is to point out the fact that the forms of social production, like those of desiring-production, involve an unengendered nonproductive attitude, an element of antiproduction coupled with the process, a full body that functions as a socius. This socius may be the body of the earth, that of the tyrant, or capital. This is the body that Marx is referring to when he says that it is not the product of labor, but rather appears as its natural or divine presupposition. In fact, it does not restrict itself merely to opposing productive forces in and of themselves. It falls back on all production, constituting a surface over which the forces and agents of production are distributed, thereby appropriating for itself all surplus production and arrogating to itself both the whole and the parts of the process, which now seem to emanate from it as a quasi-cause. Forces and agents come to represent a miraculous form of its own power: they appear to be "miraculated" by it. In a word, the socius as a full body forms a surface where all production is recorded, whereupon the entire process appears to emanate from this recording surface. Society constructs its own delirium by recording the process of production; but it is not a conscious delirium, or rather is a true consciousness of a false movement, a true perception of an apparent objective movement, a true perception of the movement that is produced on the recording surface.

Capital is indeed the body without organs of the capitalist, or rather of the capitalist being. But as such, it is not only the fluid and petrified substance of money, for it will give to the sterility of money the form whereby money produces money. It produces surplus value, just as the body without organs reproduces itself, puts forth shoots, and branches out to the farthest corners of the universe. It makes the machine responsible for producing a relative surplus value, while embodying itself in the machine as fixed capital. Machines and agents cling so closely to capital that their very functioning appears to be miraculated by it. Everything seems objectively to be produced by capital as quasi-cause. As Marx observes, *in the beginning* capitalists are necessarily conscious of the opposition between capital and labor, and of the use of capital as a means of extorting surplus labor. But a perverted, bewitched world quickly comes into being, as capital increasingly plays the role of a recording surface that falls back on all of production. (Furnishing or realizing surplus value is what establishes recording rights.)

> With the development of relative surplus-value in the actual specifically capitalist mode of production, whereby the productive powers of social labor are developed, these productive powers and the social interrelations of labor in the direct labor-process seem transferred from labor to capital. Capital thus becomes a very mystic being since all of labor's social productive forces appear to be due to capital, rather than labor as such, and seem to issue from the womb of capital itself.[12]

What is specifically capitalist here is the role of money and the use of capital as a full body to constitute the recording or inscribing surface. But some kind of full body, that of the earth or the despot, a recording surface, an apparent objective movement, a fetishistic, perverted, bewitched world are characteristic of all types of society as a constant of social reproduction.

The body without organs now falls back on desiring-production, attracts it, and appropriates it for its own. The organ-machines now cling to the body without organs as though it were a fencer's padded jacket, or as though these organ-machines were medals pinned onto the jersey of a wrestler who makes them jingle as he starts toward his opponent. An attraction-machine now takes the place, or may take the place, of a repulsion-machine: a miraculating-machine succeeding the paranoiac machine. But what is meant here by "succeeding"? The two coexist, rather, and black humor does not attempt to resolve contradictions, but to make it so that there are none, and never were any. The body without organs, the unproductive, the unconsumable, serves as a surface for the recording of the entire process of production of desire, so that desiring-machines seem to emanate from it in the apparent objective movement that establishes a relationship between the machines and the body without organs. The organs are regenerated, "miraculated" on the body of Judge Schreber, who attracts God's rays to himself. Doubtless the former paranoiac machine continues to exist in the form of mocking voices that attempt to "demiraculate" the organs, the Judge's anus in particular. But the essential thing is the establishment of an enchanted recording or inscribing surface that arrogates to itself all the productive forces and all the organs of production, and that acts as a quasi-cause by communicating the apparent movement (the fetish) to them. So true is it that the schizo practices political economy, and that all sexuality is a matter of economy.

Production is not recorded in the same way it is produced, however. Or rather, it is not reproduced within the apparent objective movement in the same way in which it is produced within the process of constitution. In fact, we have passed imperceptibly into a domain of the production of recording, whose law is not the same as that of the production of production. The law governing the latter was connective synthesis or coupling. But when the productive *connections* pass from machines to the body without organs (as from labor to capital), it would seem that they then come under another law that expresses a *distribution* in relation to the nonproductive element as a "natural or divine presupposition" (the disjunctions of capital). Machines attach themselves to the body without organs as so many points of disjunction, between which an entire network of new syntheses is now woven, marking the surface off into coordinates, like a grid. The "either . . . or . . . or" of the schizophrenic takes over from the "and then": no matter what two organs are involved, the way in which they are attached to the body without organs must be such that all the disjunctive syntheses between the two amount to the same on the slippery surface. Whereas the "either/or" claims to mark decisive choices between immutable terms (the alternative: either this or that), the schizophrenic "either . . . or . . . or" refers to the system of possible permutations between differences that always amount to the same as they shift and slide about. As in the case of Beckett's mouth that speaks and feet that walk:

> He sometimes halted without saying anything. Either he had finally nothing to say, or while having something to say he finally decided not to say it. . . . Other main examples suggest themselves to the mind. Immediate continuous communication with immediate redeparture. Same thing with delayed redeparture. Delayed continuous communication with immediate redeparture. Same thing with delayed redeparture. Immediate discontinuous communication with immediate redeparture. Same thing with delayed redeparture. Delayed discontinuous communication with immediate redeparture. Same thing with delayed redeparture.[13]

Thus the schizophrenic, the possessor of the most touchingly meager capital—Malone's belongings, for instance—inscribes on his own body the litany of disjunctions, and creates for himself a world of parries where the most minute of permutations is supposed to be a response to the new situation or a reply to the indiscreet questioner. The disjunctive synthesis of recording therefore comes to overlap the connective syntheses of production. The process as process of production extends into the method as method of inscription. Or rather, if what we term libido is the connective "labor" of desiring-production, it should be said that a part of this energy is transformed into the energy of disjunctive inscription

(Numen). A transformation of energy. But why call this new form of energy divine, why label it Numen, in view of all the ambiguities caused by a problem of the unconscious that is only apparently religious? The body without organs is not God, quite the contrary. But the energy that sweeps through it is divine, when it attracts to itself the entire process of production and server as its miraculate, enchanted surface, inscribing it in each and every one of its disjunctions. Hence the strange relationship that Schreber has with God. To anyone who asks: "Do you believe in God?" we should reply in strictly Kantian or Schreberian terms: "Of course, but only as the master of the disjunctive syllogism, or as its *a priori* principle (God defined as the *Omnitudo realitatis*, from which all secondary realities are derived by a process of division)."

Hence the sole thing that is divine is the nature of an energy of disjunctions. Schreber's divine is inseparable from the disjunctions he employs to divide himself up into parts: earlier empires, later empires; later empires of a superior God, and those of an inferior God. Freud stresses the importance of these disjunctive syntheses in Schreber's delirium in particular, but also in delirium as a general phenomenon. "A process of decomposition of this kind is very characteristic of paranoia. Paranoia decomposes just as hysteria condenses. *Or rather*, paranoia resolves once more into their elements the products of the condensations and identifications which are effected in the unconscious."[14] But why does Freud thus add that, on second thought, hysterical neurosis comes first, and that disjunctions appear only as a result of the projection of a more basic, primordial condensed material? Doubtless this is a way of maintaining intact the rights of Oedipus in the God of delirium and the schizoparanoiac recording process. And for that very reason we must pose the most far-reaching question in this regard: does the recording of desire go by way of the various stages in the formation of the Oedipus complex? Disjunctions are the form that the genealogy of desire assumes; but is this genealogy Oedipal, is it recorded in the Oedipal triangulation? Is it not more likely that Oedipus is a requirement or a consequence of social reproduction, insofar as this latter aims at domesticating a genealogical form and content that are in every way intractable? For there is no doubting the fact that the schizo is constantly subjected to interrogation, constantly cross-examined. Precisely because his relationship with nature does not constitute a specific pole, the questions put to him are formulated in terms of the existing social code: your name, your father, your mother? In the course of his exercises in desiring-production, Beckett's Molloy is cross-examined by a policeman:

> Your name is Molloy, said the sergeant. Yes, I said, now I remember. And your mother? said the sergeant. I didn't follow. Is your mother's name Molloy too? said the sergeant. I thought it over. Your mother, said the sergeant, is your mother's—Let me think! I cried. At least I imagine that's how it was. Take your time, said the sergeant. Was mother's name Molloy? Very likely. Her name must be Molloy too, I said. They took me away, to the guardroom I suppose, and there I was told to sit down. I must have tried to explain.[15]

We cannot say that psychoanalysis is very innovative in this respect: it continues to ask its questions and develop its interpretations from the depths of the Oedipal triangle as its basic perspective, even though today it is acutely aware that this frame of reference is not at all adequate to explain so-called psychotic phenomena. The psychoanalyst says that we must *necessarily* discover Schreber's daddy beneath his superior God, and doubtless also his elder brother beneath his inferior God. At times the schizophrenic loses his patience and demands to be left alone. Other times he goes along with the whole game and even invents a few tricks of his own, introducing his own reference points in the model put before him and undermining it from within ("Yes, that's my mother, all right, but my mother's the Virgin Mary, you know"). One can easily imagine Schreber answering Freud: "Yes, I quite agree, naturally the talking birds are young girls, and the superior God is my daddy and the inferior God my brother." But little by little he will surreptitiously "reimpregnate" the series of young girls with all talking birds, his father with the superior God, and his brother with the inferior God, all of them divine forms that become complicated, or rather "desimplified," as they break through the simplistic terms and functions of the Oedipal triangle. As Artaud put it:

> I don't believe in father
>   in mother
>
> got no
> papamummy

Desiring-production forms a binary-linear system. The full body is introduced as a third term in the series, without destroying, however, the essential binary-linear nature of this series: 2, 1, 2, 1. . . . The series is completely refractory to a transcription that would transform and mold it into a specifically ternary and triangular schema such as Oedipus. The full body without organs is produced as antiproduction, that is to say it intervenes within the process as such for the sole purpose of rejecting any attempt to impose on it any sort of triangulation implying that it was produced by parents. How could this body have been produced by parents, when by its very nature it is such eloquent witness of its own self-production, of its own engendering of itself? And it is precisely here on this body, right where it is, that the Numen is distributed and disjunctions are established, independent of any sort of projection. *Yes, I have been my father and I have been my son.* "I, Antonin Artaud, am my son, my father, my mother, and myself."[16] The schizo has his own system of coordinates for situating himself at his disposal, because, first of all, he has at his disposal his very own recording code, which does not coincide with the social code, or coincides with it only in order to parody it. The code of delirium or of desire proves to have an extraordinary fluidity. It might be said that the schizophrenic passes from one code to the other, that he deliberately *scrambles all the codes*, by quickly shifting from one to another, according to the questions asked him, never giving the same explanation from one day to the next, never invoking the same genealogy, never recording the same event in the same way. When he is more or less forced into it and is not in a touchy mood, he may even accept the banal Oedipal code, so long as he can stuff it full of all the disjunctions that this code was designed to eliminate.

Adolf Wölfli's drawings reveal the workings of all sorts of clocks, turbines, dynamos, celestial machines, house-machines, and so on. And these machines work in a connective fashion, from the perimeter to the center, in successive layers or segments. But the "explanations" that he provides for them, which he changes as often as the mood strikes him, are based on genealogical series that constitute the recording of each of his drawings. What is even more important, the recording process affects the drawings themselves, showing up in the form of lines standing for "catastrophe" or "collapse" that are so many disjunctions surrounded by spirals.[17] The schizo maintains a shaky balance for the simple reason that the result is always the same, no matter what the disjunctions. Although the organ-machines attach themselves to the body without organs, the latter continues nonetheless to be without organs and does not become an organism in the ordinary sense of the word. It remains fluid and slippery. Agents of production likewise alight on Schreber's body and cling to it—the sunbeams, for instance, that he attracts, which contain thousands of tiny spermatozoids. Sunbeams, birds, voices, nerves enter into changeable and genealogically complex relationships with God and forms of God derived from the godhead by division. But all this happens and is all recorded on the surface of the body without organs: even the copulations of the agents, even the divisions of God, even the genealogies marking it off into squares like a grid, and their permutations. The surface of this uncreated body swarms with them, as a lion's mane swarms with fleas.

Notes

1. See Georg Büchner, *Lenz,* in *Complete Plays and Prose*, trans. Carl Richard Mueller (New York: Hill & Wang, 1963), 14.
2. Ibid.
3. Samuel Beckett, *Molloy,* in *Three Novels by Samuel Beckett* (New York: Grove Press, 1959), 16.
4. Antonin Artaud, *Van Gogh, the Man Suicided by Society*, trans. Mary Beach and Lawrence Ferlinghetti, in *Artaud Anthology* (San Francisco: City Lights Books, 1965), 158.
5. On the identity of nature and production, and species life in general, according to Marx, see the commentaries of Gerard Granel, "L'ontologie marxiste de 1844 et la question de la coupure," in *L'endurance de la pensée* (Paris: Plon, 1968), 301–10.
6. D.H. Lawrence, *Aaron's Rod* (New York: Penguin, 1976), 200–1.
7. Henry Miller, *Tropic of Cancer*, Ch. 13. See in this came chapter the celebration of desire-as-flux expressed in the phrase: ". . . and my guts spilled out in a grand schizophrenic rush, an evacuation that leaves me face to face with the Absolute."
8. Henri Michaux, *The Major Ordeals of the Mind*, trans. Richard Howard (New York: Harcourt Brace Jovanovich, 1974), 125–7.
9. Sigmund Freud, "Psycho-Analytic Notes upon an Autobiographical Case of Paranoia (Dementia Paranoides)," *Collected Papers: Authorized Translation under the Supervision of Joan Riviere* (New York: Basic Books, 1959), Vol. 3, 396.
10. Antonin Artaud, in *84*, nos. 5–6 (1948).
11. Victor Tausk, "On the Origin of the Influencing Machine in Schizophrenia," *Psychoanalytic Quarterly,* no. 2 (1933), 519–56.
12. Karl Marx, *Capital*, trans. Ernest Untermann (New York: International Publishers, 1967), Vol. 3, 827. See in Louis Althusser, *Lire le capital* (Paris: Maspero, 1965), the commentaries of Etienne Balibar, Vol. 2, 213ff., and of Pierre Macherey, Vol. 1, 201ff.
13. Samuel Beckett, "Enough," in *First Love and Other Shorts* (New York: Grove Press, 1974).
14. Freud, "Psycho-Analytic Notes," 432 (emphasis added).
15. Beckett, *Molloy*, 29.
16. Antonin Artaud, "Here Lies," trans. F. Teri Wehn and Jack Hirschman, in *Artaud Anthology* (San Francisco: City Lights Books, 1965), 247 and 238 respectively.
17. W. Morgenthaler, "Adolf Wölfli." French translation in *L'Art brut*, no. 2.

24

LUCE IRIGARAY
(1930–)

Feminist philosopher, psychoanalyst, and linguist Luce Irigaray was born in Belgium in 1930. She received a Master's degree in philosophy and literature at the University of Louvain in 1955, after which she taught high school in Brussels for three years. In 1959, Irigaray moved to Paris and attended the University of Paris, where she received a Master's degree in psychology and later a Diploma in psychopathology. In 1964, she began research for her two doctorates. Her first doctorate, in linguistics, was awarded by the University of Nanterre in 1968 and the second, in philosophy and psychoanalysis, was awarded in 1974 by the University of Vincennes. Her dissertation for this second degree, *Speculum of the Other Woman* (1974), won Irigaray international fame despite provoking the indignation of Lacanian psychoanalysts, who perceived her work as an indirect attack on Lacan. Throughout the 1970s, Irigaray was heavily active in the feminist movement in France and abroad, especially in Italy, where her work continues to have a large following. She is currently director of research in philosophy at the Centre National Recherche Scientifique in Paris.

By her own account, Irigaray's work comprises three phases, with each phase corresponding to a different elaboration of the question of sexual difference. The first phase—which includes her most widely read works, *Speculum of the Other Woman* and *This Sex Which Is Not One* (1977)—critically analyzes the manner in which the world has been constructed and interpreted in accordance with the classical masculine subject of Western metaphysics. The second phase builds on the first by supplementing the negative critique of phallocentrism with the positive construction of a specifically feminine subjectivity (see *Sexes and Genealogies* [1987] and *An Ethics of Sexual Difference* [1984]). Irigaray's most recent work, including such writings as *I Love to You* (1992), marks the third phase of her career. Here she seeks to disclose various ethico-political relations between the sexes that avoid hierarchy and domination altogether. Beyond this tripartite division, special mention should also be made of Irigaray's writings on the role of "the elemental" (the natural elements, such as water and air) in the works of such philosophers as Friedrich Nietzsche (*Marine Lover of Friedrich Nietzsche* [1980]) and Martin Heidegger (*The Forgetting of Air in Martin Heidegger* [1983]).

Our reading for this chapter is taken from Irigaray's ambitious work, *An Ethics of Sexual Difference*. As Irigaray notes at the beginning of her essay, sexual difference is not one issue among others, but rather one that "could be our 'salvation' if we thought it through." In order for this to occur, she maintains that a revolution in thought and ethics must take place, a revolution that would require us to challenge many of the founding concepts (e.g., space, time, relation, etc.) of Western thought. In a gesture inspired in part by Descartes and Levinas, Irigaray argues that an ethics that seeks to do justice to sexual difference must proceed from the passion of "wonder." In this mode, a man and a woman would approach each other as radically different, in "surprise" and "astonishment," leaving each other subjective and free. For Irigaray, then, a genuinely ethical relation to "one who differs from me sexually" is a relation to someone I cannot fully comprehend or possess, an other who remains to a certain extent "forever unknowable."

Select Bibliography of Irigaray's Works in English

Elemental Passions. Trans. Joanne Collie and Judith Still. New York: Routledge, 1992.

An Ethics of Sexual Difference. Trans. Carolyn Burke and Gillian C. Gill. Ithaca, NY: Cornell University Press, 1993.

The Forgetting of Air in Martin Heidegger. Trans. Mary Beth Mader. Austin, TX: University of Texas Press, 1999.

I Love to You: Sketch for a Felicity within History. Trans. Alison Martin. New York: Routledge, 1993.

Je, Tu, Nous: Toward a Culture of Difference. Trans. Alison Martin. New York: Routledge, 1993.

Marine Lover of Friedrich Nietzsche. Trans. Gillian C. Gill. New York: Columbia University Press, 1991.

Sexes and Genealogies. Trans. Gillian C. Gill. New York: Columbia University Press, 1993.

Speculum of the Other Woman. Trans. Gillian C. Gill. Ithaca, NY: Cornell University Press, 1985.

Thinking the Difference: For a Peaceful Revolution. Trans. Karin Montin. New York: Routledge, 1994.

This Sex Which Is Not One. Trans. Catherine Porter. Ithaca, NY: Cornell University Press, 1985.

THE ETHICS OF SEXUAL DIFFERENCE

Sexual difference is one of the major philosophical issues, if not the issue, of our age. According to Heidegger, each age has one issue to think through, and one only. Sexual difference is probably the issue in our time which could be our "salvation" if we thought it through.

But, whether I turn to philosophy, to science, or to religion, I find this underlying issue still cries out in vain for our attention. Think of it as an approach that would allow us to check the many forms that destruction takes in our world, to counteract a nihilism that merely affirms the reversal or the repetitive proliferation of status quo values—whether you call them the consumer society, the circularity of discourse, the more or less cancerous diseases of our age, the unreliability of words, the end of philosophy, religious despair or regression to religiosity, scientistic or technical imperialism that fails to consider the living subject.

Sexual difference would constitute the horizon of worlds more fecund than any known to date—at least in the West—and without reducing fecundity to the reproduction of bodies and flesh. For loving partners this would be a fecundity of birth and regeneration, but also the production of a new age of thought, art, poetry, and language: the creation of a new *poetics*.

Both in theory and in practice, everything resists the discovery and affirmation of such an advent or event. In theory, philosophy wants to be literature or rhetoric, wishing either to break with ontology or to regress to the ontological. Using the same ground and the same framework as "first philosophy," working toward its disintegration but without proposing any other goals that might assure new foundations and new works.

In politics, some overtures have been made to the world of women. But these overtures remain partial and local: some concessions have been made by those in power, but no new values have been established. Rarely have these measures been thought through and affirmed by women themselves, who consequently remain at the level of critical demands. Has a worldwide erosion of the gains won in women's struggles occurred because of the failure to lay foundations different from those on which the world of men is constructed? Psychoanalytic theory and therapy, the scenes of sexuality as such, are a long way from having effected their revolution. And with a few exceptions, sexual practice today is often divided between two parallel worlds: the world of men and the world of women. A nontraditional, fecund encounter between the sexes barely exists. It does not voice its demands publicly, except through certain kinds of silence and polemics.

A revolution in thought and ethics is needed if the work of sexual difference is to take place. We need to reinterpret everything concerning the relations between the subject and discourse, the subject and the world, the subject and the cosmic, the microcosmic and the macrocosmic. Everything, beginning with the way in which the subject has always been written in the masculine form, as *man*, even when it claimed to be universal or neutral. Despite the fact that *man*—at least in French—rather than being neutral, is sexed.

266

Man has been the subject of discourse, whether in theory, morality, or politics. And the gender of God, the guardian of every subject and every discourse, is always *masculine and paternal*, in the West. To women are left the so-called minor arts: cooking, knitting, embroidery, and sewing; and, in exceptional cases, poetry, painting, and music. Whatever their importance, these arts do not currently make the rules, at least not overtly.

Of course, we are witnessing a certain reversal of values: manual labor and art are being revalued. But the relation of these arts to sexual difference is never really thought through and properly apportioned. At best, it is related to the class struggle.

In order to make it possible to think through, and live, this difference, we must reconsider the whole problematic of *space* and *time*.

In the beginning there was space and the creation of space, as is said in all theogonies. The gods, God, first create *space*. And time is there, more or less in the service of space. On the first day, the first days, the gods, God, make a world by separating: the elements. This world is then peopled, and a rhythm is established among its inhabitants. God would be time itself, lavishing or exteriorizing itself in its action in space, in places.

Philosophy then confirms the genealogy of the task of the gods or God. Time becomes the *interiority* of the subject itself, and space, its *exteriority* (this problematic is developed by Kant in the *Critique of Pure Reason*). The subject, the master of time, becomes the axis of the world's ordering, with its something beyond the moment and eternity: God. He effects the passage between time and space.

Which would be inverted in sexual difference? Where the feminine is experienced as space, but often with connotations of the abyss and night (God being space and light?), while the masculine is experienced as time.

The transition to a new age requires a change in our perception and conception of *space-time*, the *inhabiting of places*, and of *containers*, or *envelopes of identity*. It assumes and entails an evolution or a transformation of forms, of the relations of *matter* and *form* and of the interval *between*: the trilogy of the constitution of place. Each age inscribes a limit to this trinitary configuration: *matter, form, interval*, or *power, act, intermediary-interval*.

Desire occupies or designates the place of the *interval*. Giving it a permanent definition would amount to suppressing it as desire. Desire demands a sense of attraction: a change in the interval, the displacement of the subject or of the object in their relations of nearness or distance.

The transition to a new age comes at the same time as a change in the economy of desire. A new age signifies a different relation between:

- man and god(s),
- man and man,
- man and world,
- man and woman

Our age, which is often thought to be one in which the problematic of desire has been brought forward, frequently theorizes this desire on the basis of observations of a moment of tension, or a moment in history, whereas desire ought to be thought of as a changing dynamic whose outlines can be described in the past, sometimes in the present, but never definitively predicted. Our age will have failed to realize the full dynamic reserve signified by desire if it is referred back to the economy of the *interval*, if it is situated in the attractions, tensions, and actions occurring between *form* and *matter*, but also in the *remainder* that subsists after each creation or work, *between* what has already been identified and what has still to be identified, and so on.

In order to imagine such an economy of desire, one must reinterpret what Freud implies by *sublimation* and observe that he does not speak of the sublimation of genitality (except in reproduction? But, if this were a successful form of sublimation, Freud would not be so pessimistic about parental child-rearing practices) or of the sublimation of the *partial drives in relation to the feminine* but rather of their repression (little girls speak earlier and more skillfully than little boys; they have a better relationship to the social; and so on—qualities or aptitudes that disappear without leaving any creative achievements that capitalize on their energy, except for the task of becoming a woman: an object of attraction?)[1]

In this possible nonsublimation of herself, and by herself, woman always tends *toward* without any return to herself as the place where something positive can be elaborated. In terms of contemporary physics, it could be said that she remains on the side of the electron, with all that this implies for her, for man, for their encounter. If there is no double desire, the positive and negative poles divide themselves between the two sexes instead of establishing a chiasmus or a double loop in which each can go toward the other and come back to itself.

If these positive and negative poles are not found in both, the same one always attracts, while the other remains in motion but lacks a "proper" place. What is missing is the double pole of attraction and support, which excludes disintegration or rejection, attraction and decomposition, but which instead ensures the separation that articulates every encounter and makes possible speech, promises, alliances.

In order to distance oneself, must one be able to take? To speak? Which in a certain way comes to the same thing. Perhaps in order to take, one needs a fixed container or place? A soul? Or a spirit? Mourning nothing is the most difficult. Mourning the self in the other is almost impossible. I search for myself, as if I had been assimilated into maleness. I ought to reconstitute myself on the basis of a disassimilation. . . . Rise again from the traces of a culture, of works already produced by the other. Searching through what is in them—for what is not there. What allowed them to be, for what is not there. Their conditions of possibility, for what is not there.

Woman ought to be able to find herself, among other things, through the images of herself already deposited in history and the conditions of production of the work of man, and not on the basis of his work, his genealogy.

If traditionally, and as a mother, woman represents *place* for man, such a limit means that she becomes *a thing*, with some possibility of change from one historical period to another. She finds herself delineated as a thing. Moreover, the maternal-feminine also serves as an *envelope*, a *container*, the starting point from which man limits his things. The *relationship between envelope and things* constitutes one of the aporias, or the aporia, of Aristotelianism and of the philosophical systems derived from it.

In our terminologies, which derive from this economy of thought but are impregnated with a psychologism unaware of its sources, it is said, for example, that the woman-mother is *castrating*. Which means that, since her status as envelope and as thing(s) has not been interpreted, she remains inseparable from the work or act of man, notably insofar as he defines her and creates *his* identity with her as his starting point or, correlatively, with this determination of her being. If after all this, she is still alive, she continuously undoes his work—distinguishing herself from both the envelope and the thing, ceaselessly creating there some interval, play, something in motion and unlimited which disturbs his perspective, his world, and his/its limits. But, because he fails to leave her a subjective life, and to be on occasion her place and her thing in an intersubjective dynamic, man remains within a master-slave dialectic. The slave, ultimately, of a God on whom he bestows the characteristics of an absolute master. Secretly or obscurely, a slave to the power of the maternal-feminine which he diminishes or destroys.

The maternal-feminine remains the *place separated from "its" own place*, deprived of "its" place. She is or ceaselessly becomes the place of the other who cannot separate himself from it. Without her knowing or willing it, she is then threatening because of what she lacks: a "proper" place. She would have to reenvelop herself with herself, and do so at least twice: as a woman and as a mother. Which would presuppose a change in the whole economy of space-time.

In the meantime, this ethical question comes into play in matters of *nudity* and *perversity*. Woman must be nude because she is not situated, does not situate herself in her place. Her clothes, her makeup, and her jewels are the things with which she tries to create her container(s), her envelope(s). She cannot make use of the envelope that she is, and must create artificial ones.

Freud's statement that woman is identified with orality is meaningful, but it still exiles her from her most archaic and constituent site. No doubt orality is an especially significant measure for her: morphologically, she has two mouths and two pairs of lips. But she can act on this morphology or make something of it only if she preserves her relation to *spatiality* and to the *fetal*. Although she needs these dimensions to create a space for herself (as well as to maintain a receptive place for the other), they are traditionally taken from her to constitute man's nostalgia and everything that he constructs in memory of this first and ultimate dwelling-place. An obscure commemoration. . . . Centuries will perhaps have been needed for man to interpret the meaning of his work(s): the endless construction of a number of substitutes for his prenatal home. From the depths of the earth to the highest skies? Again and again, taking from the feminine the tissue or texture of spatiality. In exchange—but it isn't a real one—he buys her a house, even shuts her up in it, places limits on her that are the opposite of the unlimited site in which he unwittingly situates her. He contains or envelops her with walls while enveloping himself and his things with her flesh. The nature of these envelopes is not the same: on the one hand, invisibly alive, but with barely perceivable limits; on the other, visibly limiting or sheltering, but at the risk of being prisonlike or murderous if the threshold is not left open.

We must, therefore, reconsider the whole question of our conception of place, both in order to move on to another age of difference (each age of thought corresponds to a particular time of meditation on difference), and in order to construct an ethics of the passions. We need to change the relations between form, matter, interval, and limit, an issue that has never been considered in a way that allows for a relationship between two loving subjects of different sexes.

Once there was the enveloping body and the enveloped body, the latter being the more mobile through what Aristotle termed *locomotion* (since maternity does not look much like "motion"). The one who offers or allows desire moves and envelops, engulfing the other. It is moreover a danger if no third term exists. Not only to serve as a limitation. This third term can occur within the one who contains as a relation of the latter to his or her own limit(s): relation to the divine, to death, to the social, to the cosmic. If a third term does not exist within and for the container, he or she becomes *all-powerful*.

Therefore, to deprive one pole of sexual difference, women, of a third term also amounts to putting them in the position of omnipotence: this is a danger for men, especially in that it suppresses an interval that is both entrance and space between. A place for both to enter and exit the envelope (and on the same side, so as not to perforate the envelope or assimilate it into the digestive process); for both, a possibility of unhindered movement, of peaceful immobility without the risk of imprisonment.

To arrive at the constitution of an ethics of sexual difference, we must at least return to what is for Descartes the first passion: *wonder*. This passion has no opposite or contradiction and exists always as though for the first time. Thus man and woman, woman and man are always meeting as though for the first time because they cannot be substituted one for the other. I will never be in a man's place, never will a man be in mine. Whatever identifications are possible, one will never exactly occupy the place of the other—they are irreducible one to the other.

When the first encounter with some object surprises us, and we judge it to be new, or very different from what we formerly knew, or from what we supposed that it ought to be, that causes us to wonder and be surprised; and because that may happen before we in any way know whether this object is agreeable to us or is not so, it appears to me that wonder is the first of all the passions; and it has no opposite, because if the object which presents itself has nothing in it that surprises us, we are in nowise moved regarding it, and we consider it without passion. (René Descartes, *The Passions of the Soul*, article 53)

Who or what the other is, I never know. But the other who is forever unknowable is the one who differs from me sexually. This feeling of surprise, astonishment, and wonder in the face of the unknowable ought to be returned to its locus: that of sexual difference. The passions have either been repressed, stifled, or reduced, or reserved for God. Sometimes a space for wonder is left to works of art. But it is never found to reside in this locus: *between man and woman*. Into this place came attraction, greed, possession, consummation, disgust, and so on. But not that wonder which beholds what it sees always as if for the first time, never taking hold of the other as its object. It does not try to seize, possess, or reduce this object, but leaves it subjective, still free.

This has never existed between the sexes since wonder maintains their autonomy within their statutory difference, keeping a space of freedom and attraction between them, a possibility of separation and alliance.

This might take place at the time of the first meeting, even prior to the betrothal, and remain as a permanent proof of difference. The *interval* would never be *crossed*. Consummation would never take place, the idea itself being a delusion. One sex is not entirely consumable by the other. There is always a *remainder*.

Up until now this remainder has been entrusted to or reserved for *God*. Sometimes a portion was incarnated in the *child*. Or was thought of as being *neuter*. This neuter (in a different way, like the child or God?) suggests the possibility of an encounter but puts it off, deferring it until later, even when it is a question of a secondary revision. It always stays at an insurmountable distance, a respectful or deadly sort of no-man's-land: no alliance is forged; nothing is celebrated. The immediacy of the encounter is annihilated or deferred to a future that never comes.

Of course, the neuter might signify an alchemical site of the sublimation of "genitality," and the possibility of generation, of the creation of and between different genders and genres. But it would still have to be receptive to the advent of difference, and be understood as an anticipation from this side and not as a beyond, especially an ethical one. Generally the phrase *there is* upholds the present but defers celebration. There is not, there will not be the moment of wonder of the *wedding*, an ecstasy that remains *in-stant*. The *there is* remains a present that may be subject to pressure by the god, but it does not form a foundation for the triumph of sexual fecundity. Only certain oriental traditions speak of the energizing, aesthetic, and religious fecundity of the sexual act: the two sexes give each other the seed of life and eternity, the growing generation of and between them both.

We must reexamine our own history thoroughly to understand why this sexual difference has not had its chance to develop, either empirically or transcendentally. Why it has failed to have its own ethics, aesthetic, logic, religion, or the micro- and macrocosmic realization of its coming into being or its destiny.

It is surely a question of the dissociation of body and soul, of sexuality and spirituality, of the lack of a passage for the spirit, for the god, between the inside and the outside, the outside and the inside, and of their distribution between the sexes in the sexual act. Everything is constructed in such a way that these realities remain separate, even opposed to one another. So that they neither mix, marry, nor form an alliance. Their wedding is always being put off to a beyond, a future life, or else devalued, felt and thought to be less worthy in comparison to the marriage between the mind and God in a transcendental realm where all ties to the world of sensation have been severed.

The consequences of the nonfulfillment of the sexual act remain, and there are many. To take up only the most beautiful, as yet to be made manifest in the realm of time and space, there are *angels*. These messengers who never remain enclosed in a place, who are also never immobile. Between God, as the perfectly immobile act, man, who is surrounded and enclosed by the world of his work, and woman, whose task would be to take care of nature and procreation, *angels* would circulate as mediators of that which has not yet happened, of what is still going to happen, of what is on the horizon. Endlessly reopening the enclosure of the universe, of universes, identities, the unfolding of actions, of history.

The angel is that which unceasingly *passes through the envelope(s)* or *container(s)*, goes from one side to the other, reworking every deadline, changing every decision, thwarting all repetition. Angels destroy the monstrous, that which hampers the possibility of a new age; they come to herald the arrival of a new birth, a new morning.

They are not unrelated to sex. There is of course Gabriel, the angel of the annunciation. But other angels announce the consummation of marriage, notably all the angels in the Apocalypse and many in the Old Testament. As if the angel were a representation of a sexuality that has never been incarnated. A light, divine gesture (or tale) of flesh that has not yet acted or flourished. Always fallen or still awaiting parousia. The fate of a love still torn between here and elsewhere. The work of a love that is the original sinner, since the first garden, the lost earthly paradise? The fate of all flesh which is, moreover, attributable to God![2]

These swift angelic messengers, who transgress all enclosures in their speed, tell of the passage between the envelope of God and that of the world as micro- or macrocosm. They proclaim that such a journey can be made by the body of man, and above all the body of woman. They represent and tell of another incarnation, another parousia of the body. Irreducible to philosophy, theology, morality, angels appear as the messengers of ethics evoked by art—sculpture, painting, or music—without its being possible to say anything more than the gesture that represents them.

They speak like messengers, but gesture seems to be their "nature." Movement, posture, the coming-and-going between the two. They move—or stir up?—the paralysis or *apatheia* of the body, or the soul, or the world. They set trances or convulsions to music, or give them harmony.

Their touch—when they touch—resembles that of gods. They are imperious in their grace even as they remain imperceptible.

One of the questions which arises about them is whether they can be found together in the same place. The traditional answer is no. This question, which is similar to and different from that of the colocation of bodies, comes back to the question of sexual ethics. The mucous should no doubt be pictured as related to the angel, whereas the inertia of the body deprived of its relation to the mucous and its gesture is linked to the fallen body or the corpse.

A sexual or carnal ethics would require that both angel and body be found together. This is a world that must be constructed or reconstructed. A genesis of love between the sexes has yet to come about in all dimensions, from the smallest to the greatest, from the most intimate to the most political. A world that must be created or re-created so that man and woman may once again or at last live together, meet, and sometimes inhabit the same place.

The link uniting or reuniting masculine and feminine must be horizontal and vertical, terrestrial and heavenly. As Heidegger, among others, has written, it must forge an alliance between the divine and the mortal, such that the sexual encounter would be a festive celebration and not a disguised or polemical form of the master-slave relationship. Nor a meeting in the shadow or orbit of a Father-God who alone lays down the law, who is the immutable spokesman of a single sex.

Of course, the most extreme progression and regression goes under the name of God. I can only strive toward the absolute or regress to infinity under the guarantee of God's existence. This is what tradition has taught us, and its imperatives have not yet been overcome, since their destruction brings about terrible abandonments and pathological states, unless one has exceptional love partners. And even then. . . . Unhappiness is sometimes all the more inescapable when it lacks the horizon of the divine, of the gods, of an opening onto a beyond, but also a *limit* that the other may or may not penetrate.

How can we mark this limit of a place, of place in general, if not through sexual difference? But, in order for an ethics of sexual difference to come into being, we must constitute a possible place for each sex, body, and flesh to inhabit. Which presupposes a memory of the past, a hope for the future, memory bridging the present and disconcerting the mirror symmetry that annihilates the difference of identity.

To do this requires time, both space and time. Perhaps we are passing through an era when *time must redeploy space*? A new morning of and for the world? A remaking of immanence and transcendence, notably through this *threshold* which has never been examined as such: the female sex. The threshold that gives access to the *mucous*. Beyond classical oppositions of love and hate, liquid and ice—a threshold that is always *half-open*. The threshold of the *lips*, which are strangers to dichotomy and oppositions. Gathered one against the other but without any possible suture, at least of a real kind. They do not absorb the world into or through themselves, provided they are not misused and reduced to a means of consumption or consummation. They offer a shape of welcome but do not assimilate, reduce, or swallow up. A sort of doorway to voluptuousness? They are not useful, except as that which designates a *place*, the very place of uselessness, at least as it is habitually understood. Strictly speaking, they serve neither conception nor *jouissance*. Is this the mystery of feminine identity? Of its self-contemplation, of this very strange word of silence? Both the threshold and reception of exchange, the sealed-up secret of wisdom, belief, and faith in all truths?

(Two sets of lips that, moreover, cross over each other like the arms of the cross, the prototype of the crossroads *between*. The mouth lips and the genital lips do not point in the same direction. In some way they point in the direction opposite from the one you would expect, with the "lower" ones forming the vertical.)

In this approach, where the borders of the body are wed in an embrace that transcends all limits—without, however, risking engulfment, thanks to the fecundity of the porous—in the most extreme experience of sensation, which is also always in the future, each one discovers the self in that experience which is inexpressible yet forms the supple grounding of life and language.

For this, "God" is necessary, or a love so attentive that it is divine. Which has never taken place? Love always postpones its transcendence beyond the here and now, except in certain experiences of God. And desire fails to act sufficiently on the porous nature of the body, omitting the communion that takes place through the most intimate mucous membranes. In this exchange, what is communicated is so subtle that one needs great perseverance to keep it from falling into oblivion, intermittency, deterioration, illness, or death.

This communion is often left to the child, as the symbol of the union. But there are other signs of union which precede the child—the space where the lovers give each other life or death? Regeneration or degeneration: both are possible. The intensity of desire and the filiation of both lovers are engaged.

And if the divine is present as the mystery that animates the copula, the *is* and the *being* in sexual difference, can the force of desire overcome the avatars of genealogical destiny? How does it manage this? With what power does it reckon, while remaining nevertheless incarnate? Between the idealistic fluidity of an unborn body that is untrue to its birth and genetic determinism, how do we take the measure of a love that changes our condition from mortal to immortal? Certain figures of gods become men, of God become man, and of twice-born beings indicate the path of love.

Has something of the achievement of sexual difference still not been said or transmitted? Has something been held in reserve within the silence of a history in the feminine: an energy, a morphology, a growth and flourishing still to come from the female realm? An overture to a future that is still and always open? Given that the world has remained aporetic about this strange advent.

Notes

1. Cf. Luce Irigaray, *Speculum of the Other Woman*, trans. Gillian C. Gill (Ithaca, NY: Cornell University Press), 9–129.
2. See Luce Irigaray, "Epistle to the Last Christians," *Marine Lover of Friedrich Nietzsche*, trans. Gillian C. Gill (New York: Columbia University Press, 1991).

25

HÉLÈNE CIXOUS
(1937–)

Hélène Cixous was born in Algeria in 1937. At the age of eighteen, she moved to France to study English literature, receiving her doctorate in 1968 from the University of Sorbonne for a thesis on the writings of James Joyce. In the same year, she became professor of English literature at the University of Vincennes and cofounded the journal *Poétique*. During this time, Cixous became deeply involved in feminist political struggles, participating in the activities of the feminist political group Psychanalyse et Politique, and publishing her writings with Éditions des femmes, a feminist publishing house. As an extension of this work, in 1974, she established the Centre de recherches en etudes féminines, which offered the first doctoral program in women's studies in France. Although she subsequently distanced herself from mainstream feminist politics in France, Cixous remained politically active throughout the 1980s and 1990s, addressing not only feminist issues, but also broader social concerns, including the struggle against apartheid and human rights violations. She is currently professor of English literature and director of the women's studies program at the University of St. Denis.

Cixous's distinctive poetico-philosophical mode of feminist writing began to take shape in the mid-1970s with such writings as "The Laugh of the Medusa" (1975), "Castration or Decapitation?" (1976), and *The Newly Born Woman* (1975). In these works, Cixous, under the influence of Derrida's deconstructive analyses of Western metaphysics, carried out an extensive critique of the various sexed oppositions (man/woman, passive/active, nature/culture) that organize society in a hierarchical manner. In their place, she proposed a more fluid, differential economy of the feminine that reflected the nonoppositional and "bisexual" disposition of "woman." Beginning in the late 1970s, a discernable shift occurred in Cixous's work that can be traced to her reading of Brazilian novelist Clarice Lispector. Cixous found in Lispector not only a literary and poetical companion but also an embodiment of the form of "*écriture féminine*" or feminine writing that she attempted to articulate in her earlier writings. Her readings of Lispector (*Reading with Clarice Lispector* [1990] and *Readings: The Poetics of Blanchot, Joyce, Kafka, Lispector, Tsvetayeva* [1992]) were instrumental in helping Cixous to formulate her own style of ethical "writing-thinking," which was subsequently developed in various fictional (*To Live the Orange* [1979]) and theoretical (*Three Steps on the Ladder of Writing* [1993]) works. Cixous's most recent projects include a series of plays on the political history of Third World countries (for example, *The Terrible but Unfinished Story of Norodum Sihanouk, King of Cambodia* [1985]), and reflections on her youth and Jewish roots (*Hélène Cixous, Rootprints* [1994]).

In our reading, "The Laugh of the Medusa," Cixous examines the ethical and political dimensions of *écriture féminine*. For Cixous, writing as such is a "springboard for subversive thought," and thereby marks "the very possibility of change." Since women have for the most part been forbidden to write in their own voice, symbolic and cultural structures have been dominated by a masculine and phallocentric economy. The only way to disrupt this economy, Cixous argues, is for woman to write her "self" and her "body" in its abundance and multiplicity. Although the project of feminine writing would seem to implicate Cixous in an untenable essentialist theory of women's identity, she is careful to note that the space of feminine writing can be occupied by either women or men. Hence, what is at stake in the elaboration of a specifically feminine libidinal economy of writing is less the establishment of a new, proper identity for women but rather refiguring the identity of "woman" in terms of an ethical logic of the gift, expropriation, and radical openness to alterity.

Select Bibliography of Cixous's Works in English

The Book of Promethea. Trans. Betsy Wing. Lincoln, NE: University of Nebraska Press, 1991.

"Coming to Writing" and Other Essays. Ed. Deborah Jenson. Cambridge, MA: Harvard University Press, 1991.

The Exile of James Joyce or the Art of Replacement. Trans. Sally Purcell. New York: David Lewis, 1980.

The Hélène Cixous Reader. Ed. Susan Sellers. New York: Routledge, 1994.

Hélène Cixous, Rootprints: Memory and Life Writing (with Mireille Calle-Gubar). Trans. Eric Prenowitz. London: Routledge, 1997.

Manna: For the Mandelstams for the Mandelas. Trans. Catherine A.F. MacGillivray. Minneapolis, MN: University of Minnesota Press, 1994.

The Newly Born Woman (with Catherine Clement). Trans. Betsy Wing. Minneapolis, MN: University of Minnesota Press, 1986.

Reading with Clarice Lispector. Trans. Verena Andermatt Conley. Minneapolis, MN: University of Minnesota Press, 1990.

Readings: The Poetics of Blanchot, Joyce, Kafka, Lispector, Tsvetayeva. Trans. Verena Andermatt Conley. Minneapolis, MN: University of Minnesota Press, 1992.

The Terrible but Unfinished Story of Norodom Sihanouk, King of Cambodia. Trans. Juliet Flower MacCannell, Judith Pike, and Lollie Groth. Lincoln, NE: University of Nebraska Press, 1994.

Three Steps on the Ladder of Writing. Trans. Sarah Cornell and Susan Sellers. New York: Columbia University Press, 1993.

To Live the Orange. Trans. Ann Liddle and Sarah Cornell. Paris: Éditions des femmes, 1979.

THE LAUGH OF THE MEDUSA

I shall speak about women's writing: about *what it will do*. Woman must write her self: must write about women and bring women to writing, from which they have been driven away as violently as from their bodies—for the same reasons, by the same law, with the same fatal goal. Woman must put herself into the text—as into the world and into history—by her own movement.

The future must no longer be determined by the past. I do not deny that the effects of the past are still with us. But I refuse to strengthen them by repeating them, to confer upon them an irremovability the equivalent of destiny, to confuse the biological and the cultural. Anticipation is imperative.

Since these reflections are taking shape in an area just on the point of being discovered, they necessarily bear the mark of our time—a time during which the new breaks away from the old, and, more precisely, the (feminine) new from the old. Thus, as there are no grounds for establishing a discourse, but rather an arid millennial ground to break, what I say has at least two sides and two aims: to break up, to destroy; and to foresee the unforeseeable, to project.

I write this as a woman, toward women. When I say "woman," I'm speaking of woman in her inevitable struggle against conventional man; and of a universal woman subject who must bring women to their senses and to their meaning in history. But first it must be said that in spite of the enormity of the repression that has kept them in the "dark"—that dark which people have been trying to make them accept as their attribute—there is, at this time, no general woman, no one typical woman. What they have *in common* I will say. But what strikes me is the infinite richness of their individual constitutions: you can't talk about *a* female sexuality, uniform, homogeneous, classifiable into codes—any more than you can talk about one unconscious resembling another. Women's imaginary is inexhaustible, like music, painting, writing: their stream of phantasms is incredible.

I have been amazed more than once by a description a woman gave me of a world all her own which she had been secretly haunting since early childhood. A world of searching, the elaboration of a knowledge, on the basis of a systematic experimentation with the bodily functions, a passionate and precise interrogation of her erotogeneity. This practice, extraordinarily rich and inventive, in particular as concerns masturbation, is prolonged or accompanied by a production of forms, a veritable aesthetic activity, each stage of rapture inscribing a resonant vision, a composition, something beautiful. Beauty will no longer be forbidden.

I wished that that woman would write and proclaim this unique empire so that other women, other unacknowledged sovereigns, might exclaim: I, too, overflow; my desires have invented new desires, my body knows unheard-of songs. Time and again I, too, have felt so full of luminous torrents that I could burst—burst with forms much more beautiful than those which are put up in frames and sold for a stinking fortune. And I, too, said nothing, showed nothing. I didn't open my mouth, I didn't repaint my half of the world. I was ashamed. I was afraid, and I swallowed my shame and my fear. I said to myself: You are mad! What's the meaning of these waves, these floods, these outbursts? Where is the ebullient, infinite woman who, immersed as she was in her naïveté, kept in the dark about herself, led into self-disdain by the great arm of parental-conjugal phallocentrism, hasn't been ashamed of her strength? Who, surprised and horrified by the fantastic tumult of her drives (for she was made to believe that a well-adjusted normal woman has a . . . divine composure), hasn't accused herself of being a monster? Who, feeling a funny desire sitting inside her (to sing, to write, to dare to speak, in short, to bring out something new), hasn't thought she was sick? Well, her shameful sickness is that she resists death, that she makes trouble.

And why don't you write? Write! Writing is for you, you are for you; your body is yours, take it. I know why you haven't written. (And why I didn't write before the age of twenty-seven.) Because writing is at once too high, too great for you, it's reserved for the great—that is for "great men"; and it's "silly." Besides, you've written a little, but in secret. And it wasn't good, because it was in secret, and because you punished yourself for writing, because you didn't go all the way, or because you wrote, irresistibly, as when we would masturbate in secret, not to go further, but to attenuate the tension a bit, just enough to take the edge off. And then as soon as we come, we go and make ourselves feel guilty—so as to be forgiven; or to forget, to bury it until the next time.

Write, let no one hold you back, let nothing stop you: not man; not the imbecilic capitalist machinery, in which publishing houses are the crafty, obsequious relayers of imperatives handed down by an economy that works against us and off our backs; and not *yourself*. Smug-faced readers, managing editors, and big bosses don't like the true texts of women—female-sexed tests. That kind scares them.

I write woman: woman must write woman. And man, man. So only an oblique consideration will be found here of man; it's up to him to say where his masculinity and femininity are at: this will concern us once men have opened their eyes and seen themselves clearly.[1]

Now women return from afar, from always: from "without," from the heath where witches are kept alive; from below, from beyond "culture"; from their childhood which men have been trying desperately to make them forget, condemning it to "eternal rest." The little girls and their "ill-mannered" bodies immured, well-preserved, intact unto themselves, in the mirror. Frigidified. But are they ever seething underneath! What an effort it takes—there's no end to it—for the sex cops to bar their threatening return. Such a display of forces on both sides that the struggle has for centuries been immobilized in the trembling equilibrium of a deadlock.

Here they are, returning, arriving over and again, because the unconscious is impregnable. They have wandered around in circles, confined to the narrow room in which they've been given a deadly brainwashing. You can incarcerate them, slow them down, get away with the old Apartheid routine, but for a time only. As soon as they begin to speak, at the same time as they're taught their name, they can be taught that their territory is black: because you are Africa, you are black. Your continent is dark. Dark is dangerous. You can't see anything in the dark, you're afraid. Don't move, you might fall. Most of all, don't go into the forest. And so we have internalized this horror of the dark.

Men have committed the greatest crime against women. Insidiously, violently, they have led them to hate women, to be their own enemies, to mobilize their immense strength against themselves, to be the executants of their virile needs. They have made women an antinarcissism! A narcissism which loves itself only to be loved for what women haven't got! They have constructed the infamous logic of antilove.

We the precocious, we the repressed of culture, our lovely mouths gagged with pollen, our wind knocked out of us, we the labyrinths, the ladders, the tramped spaces, the bevies—we are black and we are beautiful.

We're stormy, and that which is ours breaks loose from us without our fearing any debilitation. Our glances, our smiles, are spent; laughs exude from all our mouths; our blood flows and we extend ourselves without ever reaching an end; we never hold back our thoughts, our signs, our writing; and we're not afraid of lacking.

What happiness for us who are omitted, brushed aside at the scene of inheritances; we inspire ourselves and we expire without running out of breath, we are everywhere!

From now on, who, if we say so, can say no to us? We've come back from always.

It is time to liberate the New Woman from the Old by coming to know her—by loving her for getting by, for getting beyond the Old without delay, by going out ahead of what the New Woman will be, as an arrow quits the bow with a movement that gathers and separates the vibrations musically, in order to be more than her self.

I say that we must, for, with a few rare exceptions, there has not yet been any writing that inscribes femininity; exceptions so rare, in fact, that, after plowing through literature across languages, cultures, and ages,[2] one can only be startled at this vain scouting mission. It is well known that the number of women writers (while having increased very slightly from the nineteenth century on) has always been ridiculously small. This is a useless and deceptive fact unless from their species of female writers we do not first deduct the immense majority whose workmanship is in no way different from male writing, and which either obscures women or reproduces the classic representations of women (as sensitive—intuitive—dreamy, etc.).[3]

Let me insert here a parenthetical remark. I mean it when I speak of male writing. I maintain unequivocally that there is such a thing as *marked* writing; that, until now, far more extensively and repressively than is ever suspected or admitted, writing has been run by a libidinal and cultural—hence political, typically masculine—economy; that this is a locus where the repression of women has been perpetuated, over and over, more or less consciously, and in a manner that's frightening since it's often hidden or adorned with the mystifying charms of fiction; that this locus has grossly exaggerated all the signs of sexual opposition (and not sexual difference), where woman has never *her* turn to speak—this being all the more serious and unpardonable in that writing is precisely *the very possibility of change,* the space that can serve as a springboard for subversive thought, the precursory movement of a transformation of social and cultural structures.

Nearly the entire history of writing is confounded with the history of reason, of which it is at once the effect, the support, and one of the privileged alibis. It has been one with the phallocentric tradition. It is indeed that same self-admiring, self-stimulating, self-congratulatory phallocentrism.

With some exceptions, for there have been failures—and if it weren't for them, I wouldn't be writing (I-woman, escapee)—in that enormous machine that has been operating and turning out its "truth" for centuries. There have been poets who would go to any lengths to slip something by at odds with tradition—men capable of loving love and hence capable of loving others and of wanting them, of imagining the woman who would hold out against oppression and constitute herself as a superb, equal, hence, "impossible" subject, untenable in a real social framework. Such a woman the poet could desire only by breaking the codes that negate her. Her appearance would necessarily bring on, if not revolution—for the bastion was supposed to be immutable—at least harrowing explosions. At times it is in the fissure caused by an earthquake, through that radical mutation of things brought on by a material upheaval when every structure is for a moment thrown off balance and an ephemeral wildness sweeps order away, that the poet slips something by, for a brief span, of woman. Thus did Kleist expend himself in his yearning for the existence of sister-lovers, maternal daughters, mother-sisters, who never hung their heads in shame. Once the palace of magistrates is restored, it's time to pay: immediate bloody death to the uncontrollable elements.

But only the poets—not the novelists, allies of representationalism. Because poetry involves gaining strength through the unconscious and because the unconscious, that other limitless country, is the place where the repressed manage to survive: women, or as Hoffmann would say, fairies.

She must write her self: because this is the invention of a *new insurgent* writing which, when the moment of her liberation has come, will allow her to carry out the indispensable ruptures and transformations in her history, first at two levels that cannot be separated.

a) Individually. By writing her self, woman will return to the body which has been more than confiscated from her, which has been turned into the uncanny stranger on display—the ailing or dead figure, which so often turns out to be the nasty companion, the cause and location of inhibitions. Censor the body and you censor breath and speech at the same time.

Write your self. Your body must be heard. Only then will the immense resources of the unconscious spring forth. Our naphtha will spread, throughout the world, without dollars—black or gold—non-assessed values that will change the rules of the old game.

To write. An act which will not only "realize" the decensored relation of woman to her sexuality, to her womanly being, giving her access to her native strength; it will give her back her goods, her pleasures, her organs, her immense bodily territories which have been kept under seal; it will tear her away from the superegoized structure in which she has always occupied the place reserved for the guilty (guilty of everything, guilty at every turn: for having desires, for not having any; for being frigid, for being "too hot"; for not being both at once; for being too motherly and not enough; for having children and for not having any; for nursing and for not nursing . . .)—tear her away by means of this research, this job of analysis and illumination, this emancipation of the marvelous text of her self that she must urgently learn to speak. A woman without a body, dumb, blind, can't possibly be a good fighter. She is reduced to being the servant of the militant male, his shadow. We must kill the false woman who is preventing the live one from breathing. Inscribe the breath of the whole woman.

b) An act that will also be marked by woman's *seizing* the occasion to *speak,* hence her shattering entry into history, which has always been based *on her suppression*. To write and thus to forge for herself the antilogos weapon. To become *at will* the taker and initiator, for her own right, in every symbolic system, in every political process.

It is time for women to start scoring their feats in written and oral language.

Every woman has known the torment of getting up to speak. Her heart racing, at times entirely lost for words, ground and language slipping away—that's how daring a feat, how great a transgression it is for a woman to speak—even just open her mouth—in public. A double distress, for even if she transgresses, her words fall almost always upon the deaf male ear, which hears in language only that which speaks in the masculine.

It is by writing, from and toward women, and by taking up the challenge of speech which has been governed by the phallus, that women will confirm women in a place other than that which is reserved in and by the symbolic, that is, in a place other than silence. Women should break out of the snare of silence. They shouldn't be conned into accepting a domain which is the margin or the harem.

Listen to a woman speak at a public gathering (if she hasn't painfully lost her wind). She doesn't "speak," she throws her trembling body forward; she lets go of herself, she flies; all of her passes into her voice, and it's with her body that she vitally supports the "logic" of her speech. Her flesh speaks true. She lays herself bare. In fact, she physically materializes what she's thinking; she signifies it with her body. In a certain way she *inscribes* what she's saying, because she doesn't deny her drives the intractable and impassioned part they have in speaking. Her speech, even when "theoretical" or political, is never simple or linear or "objectified," generalized: she draws her story into history.

There is not that scission, that division made by the common man between the logic of oral speech and the logic of the text, bound as he is by his antiquated relation—servile, calculating—to mastery. From which proceeds the niggardly lip service which engages only the tiniest part of the body, plus the mask.

In women's speech, as in their writing, that element which never stops resonating, which, once we've been permeated by it, profoundly and imperceptibly touched by it, retains the power of moving us—that element is the song: first music from the first voice of love which is alive in every woman. Why this privileged relationship with the voice? Because no woman stockpiles as many defenses for countering the drives as does a man. You don't build walls around yourself, you don't forgo pleasure as "wisely" as he. Even if phallic mystification has generally contaminated good relationships, a woman is never far from "mother" (I mean outside her role functions: the "mother" as nonname and as source of goods). There is always within her at least a little of that good mother's milk. She writes in white ink.

Woman for women.—There always remains in woman that force which produces/is produced by the other—in particular, the other woman. In her, matrix, cradler; herself giver as her mother and child; she is her own sister-daughter. You might object: "What about she who is the hysterical offspring of a bad mother?" Everything will be changed once woman gives to the other woman. There is hidden and always ready in woman the source; the locus for the other. The mother, too, is a metaphor. It is necessary and sufficient that the best of herself be given to woman by another woman for her to be able to love herself and return in love the body that was "born" to her. Touch me, caress me, you the living no-name, give me my self as myself. The relation to the "mother," in terms of intense pleasure and violence, is curtailed no more than the relation to childhood (the child that she was, that she is, that she makes, remakes, undoes, there at the point where, the same, she mothers herself). Text: my body—shot through with streams of song; I don't mean the overbearing, clutchy "mother" but, rather, what touches you, the equivoice that affects you, fills your breast with an urge to come to language and launches your force; the rhythm that laughs you; the intimate recipient who makes all metaphors possible and desirable; body (body? bodies?), no more describable than god, the soul, or the Other; that part of you that leaves a space between yourself and urges you to inscribe in language your woman's style. In women there is always more or less of the mother who makes everything all right, who nourishes, and who stands up against separation; a force that will not be cut off but will knock the wind out of the codes. We will rethink womankind beginning with every form and every period of her body. The Americans remind us, "We are all Lesbians"; that is, don't denigrate woman, don't make of her what men have made of you.

Because the "economy" of her drives is prodigious, she cannot fail, in seizing the occasion to speak, to transform directly and indirectly *all* systems of exchange based on masculine thrift. Her libido will produce far more radical effects of political and social change than some might like to think.

Because she arrives, vibrant, over and again, we are at the beginning of a new history, or rather of a process of becoming in which several histories intersect with one another. As subject for history, woman always occurs simultaneously in several places. Woman unthinks the unifying, regulating history that homogenizes and channels forces, herding contradictions into a single battlefield. In woman, personal history blends together with the history of all women, as well as national and world history. As a militant, she is an integral part of all liberations. She must be farsighted, not limited to a blow-by-blow interaction. She foresees that her liberation will do more than modify power relations or toss the ball over to the other camp; she will bring about a mutation in human relations, in thought, in all praxis: hers is not simply a class struggle, which she carries forward into a much vaster movement. Not that in order to be a woman-in-struggle(s) you have to leave the class struggle or repudiate it; but you have to split it open, spread it out, push it forward, fill it with the fundamental struggle so as to prevent the class struggle, or any other struggle for the liberation of a class or people, from operating as a form of repression, pretext for postponing the inevitable, the staggering alteration in power relations and in the production of individualities. This alteration is already upon us—in the United States, for example, where millions of night crawlers are in the process of undermining the family and disintegrating the whole of American sociality.

The new history is coming; it's not a dream, though it does extend beyond men's imagination, and for good reason. It's going to deprive them of their conceptual orthopedics, beginning with the destruction of their enticement machine.

It is impossible to *define* a feminine practice of writing, and this is an impossibility that will remain, for this practice can never be theorized, enclosed, coded—which doesn't mean that it doesn't exist. But it will always surpass the discourse that regulates the phallocentric system; it does and will take place in areas other than those subordinated to philosophico-theoretical domination. It will be conceived of only by subjects who are breakers of automatisms, by peripheral figures that no authority can ever subjugate.

Hence the necessity to affirm the flourishes of this writing, to give form to its movement, its near and distant byways. Bear in mind to begin with (1) that sexual opposition, which has always worked for man's profit to the point of reducing writing, too, to his laws, is only a historico-cultural limit. There is, there will be more and more rapidly pervasive now, a fiction that produces irreducible effects of femininity. (2) That it is through ignorance that most readers, critics, and writers of both sexes hesitate to admit or deny outright the possibility or the pertinence of a distinction between feminine and masculine writing. It will usually be said, thus disposing of sexual difference: either that all writing, to the extent that it materializes, is feminine; or, inversely—but it comes to the same thing—that the act of writing is equivalent to masculine masturbation (and so the woman who writes cuts herself out a paper penis); or that writing is bisexual, hence neuter, which again does away with differentiation. To admit that writing is precisely working (in) the in-between, inspecting the process of the same and of the other without which nothing can live, undoing the work of death—to admit this is first to want the two, as well as both, the ensemble of the one and the other, not fixed in sequences of struggle and expulsion or some other form of death but infinitely dynamized by an incessant process of exchange from one subject to another. A process of different subjects knowing one another and beginning one another anew only from the living boundaries of the other: a multiple and inexhaustible course with millions of encounters and transformations of the same into the other and into the in-between, from which woman takes her forms (and man, in his turn; but that's his other history).

In saying "bisexual, hence neuter," I am referring to the classic conception of bisexuality, which, squashed under the emblem of castration fear and along with the fantasy of a "total" being (though composed of two halves), would do away with the difference experienced as to operation incurring loss, as the mark of dreaded sectility.

To this self-effacing, merger-type bisexuality, which would conjure away castration (the writer who puts up his sign: "bisexual written here, come and see," when the odds are good that it's neither one nor the other), I oppose the *other bisexuality* on which every subject not enclosed in the false theater of phallocentric representationalism has founded his/her erotic universe. Bisexuality: that is, each one's location in self of the presence—variously manifest and insistent, according to each person, male or female—of both sexes, nonexclusion either of the difference or of one sex, and, from this "self-permission," multiplication of the effects of the inscription of desire, over all parts of my body and the other body.

Now it happens that at present, for historico-cultural reasons, it is women who are opening up to and benefiting from this vatic bisexuality which doesn't annul differences but stirs them up, pursues them, increases their number. In a certain way, "woman is bisexual"; man—it's a secret to no one—being poised to keep glorious phallic monosexuality in view. By virtue of affirming the primacy of the phallus and of bringing it into play, phallocratic ideology has claimed more than one victim. As a woman, I've been clouded over by the great shadow of the scepter and been told: idolize it, that which you cannot brandish. But at the same time, man has been handed that grotesque and scarcely enviable destiny (just imagine) of being reduced to a single idol with clay balls. And consumed, as Freud and his followers note, by a fear of being a woman! For, if psychoanalysis was constituted from woman, to repress femininity (and not so successful a repression at that—men have made it clear), its account of masculine sexuality is now hardly refutable; as with all the "human" sciences, it reproduces the masculine view, of which it is one of the effects. . . .

The Dark Continent is neither dark nor unexplorable.—It is still unexplored only because we've been made to believe that it was too dark to be explorable. And because they want to make us believe that what interests us is the white continent, with its monuments to Lack. And we believed. They riveted us between two horrifying myths: between the Medusa and the abyss. That would be enough to set half the world laughing, except that it's still going on. For the phallologocentric sublation is with us, and it's militant, regenerating the old patterns, anchored in the dogma of castration. They haven't changed a thing: they've theorized their desire for reality! Let the priests tremble, we're going to show them our sexts!

Too bad for them if they fall apart upon discovering that women aren't men, or that the mother doesn't have one. But isn't this fear convenient for them? Wouldn't the worst be, isn't the worst, in truth, that women aren't castrated, that they have only to stop listening to the Sirens (for the Sirens were men) for history to change its meaning? You only have to look at the Medusa straight on to see her. And she's not deadly. She's beautiful and she's laughing. . . .

Almost everything is yet to be written by women about femininity: about their sexuality, that is, its infinite and mobile complexity, about their eroticization, sudden turn-ons of a certain miniscule-immense area of their bodies; not about destiny, but about the adventure of such and such a drive, about trips, crossings, trudges, abrupt and gradual awakenings, discoveries of a zone at one time timorous and soon to be forthright. A woman's body, with its thousand and one thresholds of ardor—once, by smashing yokes and censors, she lets it articulate the profusion of meanings that run through it in every direction—will make the old single-grooved mother tongue reverberate with more than one language.

We've been turned away from our bodies, shamefully taught to ignore them, to strike them with that stupid sexual modesty; we've been made victims of the old fool's game: each one will love the other sex. I'll give you your body and you'll give me mine. But who are the men who give women the body that women blindly yield to them? Why so few texts? Because so few women have as yet won back their body. Women must write through their bodies, they must invent the impregnable language that will wreck partitions, classes, and rhetorics, regulations and codes, they must submerge, cut through, get beyond the ultimate reserve-discourse, including the one that laughs at the very idea of pronouncing the word "silence," the one that, aiming for the impossible, stops short before the word "impossible" and writes it as "the end."

Such is the strength of women that, sweeping away syntax, breaking that famous thread (just a tiny little thread, they say) which acts for men as a surrogate umbilical cord, assuring them—otherwise they couldn't come—that the old lady is always right behind them, watching them make a phallus, women will go right up to the impossible. . . .

A feminine text cannot fail to be more than subversive. It is volcanic; as it is written it brings about an upheaval of the old property crust, carrier of masculine investments; there's no other way. There's no room for her if she's not a he. If she's a her-she, it's in order to smash everything, to shatter the framework of institutions, to blow up the law, to break up the "truth" with laughter.

For once she blazes *her* trail in the symbolic, she cannot fail to make of it the chaosmos of the "personal"—in her pronouns, her nouns, and her clique of referents. And for good reason. There will have been the long history of gynocide. This is known by the colonized peoples of yesterday, the workers, the nations, the species off whose backs the history of men has made its gold; those who have known the ignominy of persecution derive from it an obstinate future desire for grandeur; those who are locked up know better than their jailers the taste of free air. Thanks to their history, women today know (how to do and want) what men will be able to conceive of only much later. I say woman overturns the "personal," for if, by means of laws, lies, blackmail, and marriage, her right to herself has been extorted at the same time as her name, she has been able, through the very movement of mortal alienation, to see more closely the inanity of "propriety," the reductive stinginess of the masculine-conjugal subjective economy, which she doubly resists. On the one hand she has constituted herself necessarily as that "person" capable of losing a part of herself without losing her integrity. But secretly, silently, deep down inside, she grows and multiplies, for, on the other hand, she knows far more about living and about the relation between the economy of the drives and the management of the ego than any man. Unlike man, who holds so dearly to his title and his titles, his pouches of value, his cap, crown, and everything connected with his head, woman couldn't care less about the fear of decapitation (or castration), adventuring, without the masculine temerity, into anonymity, which she can merge with, without annihilating herself: because she's a giver.

I shall have a great deal to say about the whole deceptive problematic of the gift. Woman is obviously not that woman Nietzsche dreamed of who gives only in order to take.[4] Who could ever think of the gift as a gift-that-takes? Who else but man, precisely the one who would like to take everything?

If there is a "propriety of woman," it is paradoxically her capacity to depropriate unselfishly, body without end, without appendage, without principal "parts." If she is a whole, it's a whole composed of parts that are wholes, not simple partial objects but a moving, limitlessly changing ensemble, a cosmos tirelessly traversed by Eros, an immense astral space not organized around any one sun that's any more of a star than the others.

This doesn't mean that she's an undifferentiated magma, but that she doesn't lord it over her body or her desire. Though masculine sexuality gravitates around the penis, engendering that centralized body (in political anatomy) under the dictatorship of its parts, woman does not bring about the same regionalization which serves the couple head/genitals and which is inscribed only within boundaries. Her libido is cosmic, just as her unconscious is worldwide. Her writing can only keep going, without ever inscribing or discerning contours, daring to make these vertiginous crossings of the other(s) ephemeral and passionate sojourns in him, her, them, whom she inhabits long enough to look at from the point closest to their unconscious from the moment they awaken, to love them at the point closest to their drives; and then further, impregnated through and through with these brief, identificatory embraces, she goes and passes into infinity. She alone dares and wishes to know from within, where she, the outcast, has never ceased to hear the resonance of fore-language. She lets the other language speak—the language of a thousand tongues which knows neither enclosure nor death. To life she refuses nothing. Her language does not contain, it carries; it does not hold back, it makes possible. When id is ambiguously uttered—the wonder of being several—she doesn't defend herself against these unknown women whom she's surprised at becoming, but derives pleasure from this gift of alterability. I am spacious, singing flesh, on which is grafted no one knows which I, more or less human, but alive because of transformation.

Write! and your self-seeking text will know itself better than flesh and blood, rising, insurrectionary dough kneading itself, with sonorous, perfumed ingredients, a lively combination of flying colors, leaves, and rivers plunging into the sea we feed. "Ah, there's her sea," he will say as he holds out to me a basin full of water from the little phallic mother from whom he's inseparable. But look, our seas are what we make of them, full of fish or not, opaque or transparent, red or black, high or smooth, narrow or bankless; and we are ourselves sea, sand, coral, seaweed, beaches, tides, swimmers, children, waves. . . . More or less wavily sea, earth, sky—what matter would rebuff us? We know how to speak them all.

Heterogeneous, yes. For her joyous benefits she is erogenous; she is the erotogeneity of the heterogeneous: airborne swimmer, in flight, she does not cling to herself; she is dispersible, prodigious, stunning, desirous and capable of others, of the other woman that she will be, of the other woman she isn't, of him, of you.

Notes

1. Men still have everything to say about their sexuality, and everything to write. For what they have said so far, for the most part, stems from the opposition activity/passivity from the power relation between a fantasized obligatory virility meant to invade, to colonize, and the consequential phantasm of woman as a "dark continent" to penetrate and to "pacify." (We know what "pacify" means in terms of scotomizing the other and misrecognizing the self.) Conquering her, they've made haste to depart from her borders, to get out of sight, out of body. The way man has of getting out of himself and into her whom he takes not for the other but for his own, deprives him, he knows, of his own bodily territory. One can understand how man, confusing himself with his penis and rushing in for the attack, might feel resentment and fear of being "taken" by the woman, of being lost in her, absorbed or alone.
2. I am speaking here only of the place "reserved" for women by the Western world.
3. Which works, then, might be called feminine? I'll just point out some examples: one would have to give them full readings to bring out what is pervasively feminine in their significance. Which I shall do elsewhere. In France (have you noted our infinite poverty in this field?—the Anglo-Saxon countries have shown resources of distinctly greater consequence), leafing through what's come out of the twentieth century—and it's not much—the only inscriptions of femininity that I have seen were by Colette, Marguerite Duras, . . . and Jean Genet.
4. Reread Derrida's text, "Le style de la femme," in *Nietzsche aujourd'hui* (Union Générale d'Editions, Coll. 10/18), where the philosopher can be seen operating an *Aufhebung* of all philosophy in its systematic reducing of woman to the place of seduction: she appears as the one who is taken for; the bait in person, all veils unfurled, the one who doesn't give but who gives only in order to (take).

26

JULIA KRISTEVA
(1941–)

Born in 1941 in Bulgaria, Julia Kristeva moved to Paris at the age of twenty-four to study French liter-ature. Within a year of her arrival, Kristeva's writings began appearing in such distinguished journals as *Langages*, *Critique*, and *Tel Quel*. Soon thereafter, Kristeva became actively involved with *Tel Quel*, and served on its editorial board along with Philippe Sollers. She went on to receive a doctorate for her thesis, *Revolution in Poetic Language* (published in 1974), and was awarded the chair of linguis-tics at the University of Paris VII, as well as a visiting position at Columbia University in the United States. During the 1970s, she attended Jacques Lacan's seminars and eventually became an impor-tant theoretician and practitioner of psychoanalysis in her own right. Kristeva currently divides her time between teaching linguistics and her psychoanalytic practice.

Kristeva's early writings, such as *Séméiotiké: Recherches pour une sémanalyse* (1969) and *Revo-lution in Poetic Language* (1974), introduced the central concern of all her major writings—namely, the concern to examine the effects *within* discourse of that which *exceeds* discourse. For Kristeva, the standard approaches to linguistics available at the time were largely formal and regarded lan-guage primarily as a vehicle for communication. As such, they failed to take into account the pre-discursive, or "material," register of language. This prompted Kristeva to develop her own form of linguistic analysis, which she called "semanalysis," a combination of Saussurean semiology and Freudian psychoanalysis. Semanalysis allowed Kristeva to analyze both aspects of the signifying process: the communicative aspects of language ("the symbolic") as well as the material and bodily register ("the semiotic") that precedes and conditions communication. As Lacanian psychoanalysis came to figure more prominently in her writings during the 1980s, Kristeva began examining this twofold distinction within the context of the constitution of human subjectivity. Thus, in such works as *Tales of Love* (1983) and *Black Sun* (1987), she sought to demonstrate that various forms of irre-ducible otherness (the unconscious, drives, social relations, etc.) lie at the heart of the conscious subject. A particularly explicit example of this notion of the "subject in process" can be found, Kris-teva argued, in the maternal body, which already bears the other within it. The maternal body would eventually become the model for the establishment of a new outlaw ethics, what Kristeva called "herethics" (*heréthique*), in which the subject and the other are bound together by love rather than by an ethical law imposed from the outside.

Although she is best known in the United States as one of the three primary "French feminists" (along with Cixous and Irigaray), Kristeva has always had a rather uneasy and critical relation to femi-nism. This is evident in our selection, "Women's Time," in which Kristeva distinguishes between, and eventually distances herself from, the two dominant generations of feminism in this century. The first, pre-1968 generation is the feminism associated with suffragists and existentialists. These feminists sought to create a space for women within the "linear time" of men's history—which is to say, they aimed at giving women the same rights, and political, legal, and moral status that men are granted by society. The second, post-1968 generation of feminism derives from those philosophers, psychoanalysts, and artists who are "interested in the specificity of female psychology and its symbolic realizations." As such, the second generation contests the attempt of the first generation to erase feminine specificity in the name of equality with men. Although she acknowledges the necessity and advances that each generation of feminism has made, Kristeva advocates a third type of feminism that displays an "attitude of retreat from sexism (male as well as female)." This avant-garde feminism poses the demand for a new ethics and politics in which the "singularity of each woman," "her multiplicities," and "her plural languages" are embraced as a means of moving beyond the narrow constraints of the ideologies and identity politics governing previous generations of feminism.

Select Bibliography of Kristeva's Works in English

About Chinese Women. Trans. Anita Barrow. New York: Marion Boyars, 1977.

Black Sun: Depression and Melancholy. Trans. Leon Roudiez. New York: Columbia University Press, 1989.

Desire in Language: A Semiotic Approach to Literature and Art. Trans. Thomas Gora, Alice Jardine, and Leon Roudiez. New York: Columbia University Press, 1980.

The Kristeva Reader. Ed. Toril Moi. New York: Columbia University Press, 1986.

New Maladies of the Soul. Trans. Ross Guberman. New York: Columbia University Press, 1995.

The Portable Kristeva. Ed. Kelly Oliver. New York: Columbia University Press, 1998.

Powers of Horror: An Essay on Abjection. Trans. Leon Roudiez. New York: Columbia University Press, 1982.

Revolution in Poetic Language. Trans. Margaret Waller. New York: Columbia University Press, 1984.

Strangers to Ourselves. Trans. Leon Roudiez. New York: Columbia University Press, 1991.

Tales of Love. Trans. Leon Roudiez. New York: Columbia University Press, 1987.

WOMEN'S TIME

Two Generations

In its beginnings, the women's movement, as the struggle of suffragists and of existential feminists, aspired to gain a place in linear time as the time of project and history. In this sense, the movement, while immediately universalist, is also deeply rooted in the socio-political life of nations. The political demands of women; the struggles for equal pay for equal work, for taking power in social institutions on an equal footing with men; the rejection, when necessary, of the attributes traditionally considered feminine or maternal insofar as they are deemed incompatible with insertion in that history—all are part of the *logic of identification* with certain values: not with the ideological (these are combated, and rightly so, as reactionary) but, rather, with the logical and ontological values of a rationality dominant in the nation-state. Here it is unnecessary to enumerate the benefits which this logic of identification and the ensuing struggle have achieved and continue to achieve for women (abortion, contraception, equal pay, professional recognition, etc.); these have already had or will soon have effects even more important than those of the Industrial Revolution. Universalist in its approach, this current in feminism *globalizes* the problems of women of different milieus, ages, civilizations, or simply of varying psychic structures, under the label "Universal Woman." A consideration of *generations* of women can only be conceived of in this global way as a succession, as a progression in the accomplishment of the initial program mapped out by its founders.

In a second phase, linked, on the one hand, to the younger women who came to feminism after May 1968 and, on the other, to women who had an aesthetic or psychoanalytic experience, linear temporality has been almost totally refused, and as a consequence there has arisen an exacerbated distrust of the entire political dimension. If it is true that this more recent current of feminism refers to its predecessors and that the struggle for socio-cultural recognition of women is necessarily its main concern, this current seems to think of itself as belonging to another generation—qualitatively different from the first one—in its conception of its own identity and, consequently, of temporality as such. Essentially interested in the specificity of female psychology and its symbolic realizations, these women seek to give a language to the intrasubjective and corporeal experiences left mute by culture in the past. Either as artists or writers, they have undertaken a veritable exploration of the *dynamic of signs*, an exploration which relates this tendency, at least at the level of its aspirations, to all major projects of aesthetic and religious upheaval. Ascribing this experience to a new generation does not only mean that other, more subtle problems have been added to the demands for socio-political identification made in the beginning. It also means that, by demanding recognition of an irreducible identity, without equal in the opposite sex and, as such, exploded, plural, fluid, in a certain way non-identical, this feminism situates itself outside the linear time of identities which communicate through projection and revindication. Such a feminism rejoins, on the one hand, the archaic (mythical) memory and, on the other, the cyclical or monumental temporality of marginal move-

...inly not by chance that the European and trans-European problematic has been
...t the same time as this new phase of feminism.

...n⁶ the mixture of the two attitudes—*insertion* into history and the radical *refusal* of the
...mitations imposed by this history's time on an experiment carried out in the name of the ir-
...difference—that seems to have broken loose over the past few years in European feminist
...nts, particularly in France and in Italy.

...e accept this meaning of the expression "a new generation of women," two kinds of questions
...t then be posed: What sociopolitical processes or events have provoked this mutation? What are
problems; its contributions as well as dangers?

Socialism and Freudianism

One could hypothesize that if this new generation of women shows itself to be more diffuse and perhaps less conscious in the United States and more massive in Western Europe, this is because of a veritable split in social relations and mentalities, a split produced by socialism and Freudianism. I mean
by *socialism* that egalitarian doctrine which is increasingly broadly disseminated and accepted as
based on common sense, as well as that social practice adopted by governments and political parties in
democratic regimes which are forced to extend the zone of egalitarianism to include the distribution of
goods as well as access to culture. By *Freudianism* I mean that lever, inside this egalitarian and socializing field, which once again poses the question of sexual difference and of the difference among subjects who themselves are not reducible one to the other.

Western socialism, shaken in its very beginnings by the egalitarian or differential demands of its
women (e.g., Flora Tristan), quickly got rid of those women who aspired to recognition of a specificity
of the female role in society and culture, only retaining from them, in the egalitarian and universalistic
spirit of Enlightenment humanism, the idea of a necessary identification between the two sexes as the
only and unique means for liberating the "second sex." I shall not develop here the fact that this "ideal"
is far from being applied in practice by these socialist-inspired movements and parties and that it was
in part from the revolt against this situation that the new generation of women in Western Europe was
born after May 1968. Let us just say that in theory, and as put into practice in Eastern Europe, socialist
ideology, based on a conception of the human being as determined by its place in *production* and the
relations of production, did not take into consideration this same human being according to its place in
reproduction, on the one hand, or in the *symbolic order*, on the other. Consequently, the specific character of women could only appear as non-essential or even non-existent to the totalizing and even totalitarian spirit of this ideology.[1] We begin to see that this same egalitarian and in fact censuring
treatment has been imposed, from Enlightenment humanism through socialism, on religious specifici-
ties and, in particular, on Jews.[2]

What has been achieved by this attitude remains nonetheless of capital importance for women, and
I shall take as an example the change in the destiny of women in the socialist countries of Eastern
Europe. It could be said, with only slight exaggeration, that the demands of the suffragists and existential feminists have, to a great extent, been met in these countries, since three of the main egalitarian demands of early feminism have been or are now being implemented despite vagaries and
blunders: economic, political and professional equality. The fourth, sexual equality, which implies
permissiveness in sexual relations (including homosexual relations), abortions and contraception, remains stricken by taboo in Marxian ethics as well as for reasons of state. It is, then, this fourth equality which is the problem and which therefore appears *essential* in the struggle of a new generation.
But simultaneously and as a consequence of these socialist accomplishments—which are in fact a
total deception—the struggle is no longer concerned with the quest for equality but, rather, with dif-

ference and specificity. It is precisely at this point that the new generation encounters what might be called the *symbolic* question. Sexual difference—which is at once biological, physiological, and relative to reproduction—is translated by and translates a difference in the relationship of subjects to the symbolic contract which *is* the social contract: a difference, then, in the relationship to power, language, and meaning. The sharpest and most subtle point of feminist subversion brought about by the new generation will henceforth be situated on the terrain of the inseparable conjunction of the sexual and the symbolic, in order to try to discover, first, the specificity of the female, and then, in the end, that of each individual woman.

A certain saturation of socialist ideology, a certain exhaustion of its potential as a program for a new social contract (it is obvious that the effective realization of this program is far from being accomplished, and I am here treating only its system of thought) makes way for . . . Freudianism. I am, of course, aware that this term and this practice are somewhat shocking to the American intellectual consciousness (which rightly reacts to a muddled and normatizing form of psychoanalysis) and, above all, to the feminist consciousness. To restrict my remarks to the latter: Is it not true that Freud has been seen only as a denigrator or even an exploiter of women? as an irritating phallocrat in a Vienna which was at once puritan and decadent—a man who fantasized women as submen, castrated men?

Castrated and/or Subject to Language

Before going beyond Freud to propose a more just or more modern vision of women, let us try, first, to understand his notion of castration. It is, first of all, a question of an *anguish* or *fear* of castration, or of correlative penis *envy*; a question, therefore, of *imaginary* formations readily perceivable in the *discourse* of neurotics of both sexes, men and women. But, above all, a careful reading of Freud, going beyond his biologism and his mechanism, both characteristic of his time, brings out two things. First, as presupposition for the "primal scene," the castration fantasy and its correlative (penis envy) are hypotheses, *a priori* suppositions intrinsic to the theory itself, in the sense that these are not the ideological fantasies of their inventor but, rather, logical necessities to be placed at the "origin" in order to explain what unceasingly functions in neurotic discourse. In other words, neurotic discourse, in man and woman, can only be understood in terms of its own logic when its fundamental causes are admitted as the fantasies of the primal scene and castration, even if (as may be the case) nothing renders them present in reality itself. Stated in still other terms, the reality of castration is no more real than the hypothesis of an explosion which, according to modern astrophysics, is at the origin of the universe: nothing proves it, in a sense it is an article of faith, the only difference being that numerous phenomena of life in this "big-bang" universe are explicable only through this initial hypothesis. But one is infinitely more jolted when this kind of intellectual method concerns inanimate matter than when it is applied to our own subjectivity and thus, perhaps, to the fundamental mechanism of our epistemophilic thought.

Moreover, certain texts written by Freud (*The Interpretation of Dreams*, but especially those of the second topology, in particular the *Metapsychology*) and their recent extensions (notably by Lacan), imply that castration is, in sum, the imaginary construction of a radical operation which constitutes the symbolic field and all beings inscribed therein. This operation constitutes signs and syntax; that is, language, as a *separation* from a presumed state of nature, of pleasure fused with nature so that the introduction of an articulated network of differences, which refers to objects henceforth and only in this way separated from a subject, may constitute *meaning*. This logical operation of separation (confirmed by all psycho-linguistic and child psychology) which preconditions the binding of language which is already syntactical, is therefore the common destiny of the two sexes, men and women. That certain biofamilial conditions and relationships cause women (and notably hysterics) to deny this separation and the language which ensues from it, whereas men (notably obsessionals) magnify both and, terrified, attempt to master them—this is what Freud's discovery has to tell us on this issue.

The analytic situation indeed shows that it is the penis which, becoming the major referent in this operation of separation, gives full meaning to the *lack* or to the *desire* which constitutes the subject during his or her insertion into the order of language. I should only like to indicate here that, in order for this operation constitutive of the symbolic and the social to appear in its full truth and for it to be understood by both sexes, it would be just to emphasize its extension to all that is privation of fulfillment and of totality; exclusion of a pleasing, natural and sound state: in short, the break indispensable to the advent of the symbolic.

It can now be seen how women, starting with this theoretical apparatus, might try to understand their sexual and symbolic difference in the framework of social, cultural, and professional realization, in order to try, by seeing their position therein, either to fulfill their own experience to a maximum or—but always starting from this point—to go further and call into question the very apparatus itself.

Living the Sacrifice

In any case, and for women in Europe today, whether or not they are conscious of the various mutations (socialist and Freudian) which have produced or simply accompanied their coming into their own, the urgent question on our agenda might be formulated as follows: *What can be our place in the symbolic contract?* If the social contract, far from being that of equal men, is based on an essentially sacrificial relationship of separation and articulation of differences which in this way produces communicable meaning, what is our place in this order of sacrifice and/or of language? No longer wishing to be excluded or no longer content with the function which has always been demanded of us (to maintain, arrange and perpetuate this socio-symbolic contract as mothers, wives, nurses, doctors, teachers . . .), how can we reveal our place, first as it is bequeathed to us by tradition, and then as we want to transform it?

It is difficult to evaluate what in the relationship of women to the symbolic as it reveals itself now arises from a socio-historical conjuncture (patriarchal ideology, whether Christian, humanist, socialist or so forth), and what arises from a structure. We can speak only about a structure observed in a socio-historical context, which is that of Christian, Western civilization and its lay ramifications. In this sense of psycho-symbolic structure, women, "we" seem to feel that they are the casualties, that they have been left out of the socio-symbolic contract, of language as the fundamental social bond. They find no affect there, no more than they find the fluid and infinitesimal significations of their relationships with the nature of their own bodies, that of the child, another woman or a man. This frustration, which to a certain extent belongs to men also, is being voiced today principally by women, to the point of becoming the essence of the new feminist ideology. A therefore difficult, if not impossible, identification with the sacrificial logic of separation and syntactical sequence at the foundation of language and the social code leads to the rejection of the symbolic—lived as the rejection of the paternal function and ultimately generating psychoses.

But this limit, rarely reached as such, produces two types of counterinvestment of what we have termed the socio-symbolic contract. On the one hand, there are attempts to take hold of this contract, to possess it in order to enjoy it as such or to subvert it. How? The answer remains difficult to formulate (since, precisely, any formulation is deemed frustrating, mutilating, sacrificial) or else is in fact formulated using stereotypes taken from extremist and often deadly ideologies. On the other hand, another attitude is more lucid from the beginning, more self-analytical which—without refusing or sidestepping this socio-symbolic order—consists in trying to explore the constitution and functioning of this contract, starting less from the knowledge accumulated about it (anthropology, psychoanalysis, linguistics) than from the very personal affect experienced when facing it as subject and as a woman. This leads to the active research,[3] still rare, undoubtedly hesitant but always dissident, being carried out by women in the human sciences; particularly those attempts, in the wake of contemporary art, to break the code, to shatter language, to find a specific discourse closer to the body and emotions, to the unnameable repressed by the social contract. I am not speaking here of a "woman's language," whose (at least syntactical) existence is highly problematical and whose apparent lexical specificity is perhaps more the product of a social marginality than of a sexual-symbolic difference.

Nor am I speaking of the aesthetic quality of productions by women, most of which—with a few exceptions (but has this not always been the case with both sexes?)—are a reiteration of a more or less euphoric or depressed romanticism and always an explosion of an ego lacking narcissistic gratification. What I should like to retain, nonetheless, as a mark of collective aspiration, as an undoubtedly vague and unimplemented intention, but one which is intense and which has been deeply revealing these past few years, is this: the new generation of women is showing that its major social concern has become the socio-symbolic contract as a sacrificial contract. If anthropologists and psychologists, for at least a century, have not stopped insisting on this in their attention to "savage thought," wars, the discourse of dreams or writers, women are today affirming—and we consequently face a mass phenomenon—that they are forced to experience this sacrificial contract against their will. Based on this, they are attempting a revolt which they see as a resurrection but which society as a whole understands as murder. This attempt can lead us to a not less and sometimes more deadly violence. Or to a cultural innovation. Probably to both at once. But that is precisely where the stakes are, and they are of epochal significance. . . .

Creatures and Creatresses

The desire to be a mother, considered alienating and even reactionary by the preceding generation of feminists, has obviously not become a standard for the present generation. But we have seen in the past few years an increasing number of women who not only consider their maternity compatible with their professional life or their feminist involvement (certain improvements in the quality of life are also at the origin of this: an increase in the number of day care centers and nursery schools, more active participation of men in child care and domestic life, etc.), but also find it indispensable to their discovery, not of the plenitude, but of the complexity of the female experience, with all that this complexity comprises in joy and pain. This tendency has its extreme: in the refusal of the paternal function by lesbian and single mothers can be seen one of the most violent forms taken by the rejection of the symbolic outlined above, as well as one of the most fervent divinizations of maternal power—all of which cannot help but trouble an entire legal and moral order without, however, proposing an alternative to it. Let us remember here that Hegel distinguished between female right (familial and religious) and male law (civil and political). If our societies know well the uses and abuses of male law, it must also be recognized that female right is designated, for the moment by a blank. And if these practices of maternity, among others, were to be generalized, women themselves would be responsible for elaborating the appropriate legislation to check the violence to which, otherwise, both their children and men would be subject. But are they capable of doing so? This is one of the important questions that the new generation of women encounters, especially when the members of this new generation refuse to ask those questions seized by the same rage with which the dominant order originally victimized them.

Faced with this situation, it seems obvious—and feminist groups become more aware of this when they attempt to broaden their audience—that the refusal of maternity cannot be a mass policy and that the majority of women today see the possibility for fulfillment, if not entirely at least to a large degree, in bringing a child into the world. What does this desire for motherhood correspond to? This is one of the new questions for the new generation, a question the preceding generation had foreclosed. For want of an answer to this question, feminist ideology leaves the door open to the return of religion, whose discourse, tried and proved over thousands of years, provides the necessary ingredients for satisfying the anguish, the suffering and the hopes of mothers. If Freud's affirmation—that the desire for a child is the desire for a penis and, in this sense, a substitute for phallic and symbolic dominion—can be only partially accepted, what modern women have to say about this experience should nonetheless be listened to attentively. Pregnancy seems to be experienced as the radical ordeal of the splitting of the subject: redoubling up of the body, separation and coexistence of the self and of an other, of nature and consciousness, of physiology and speech. This fundamental challenge to identity is then accompanied by a fantasy of totality—narcissistic completeness—a sort of instituted, socialized, natural psychosis. The arrival of the child, on the other hand, leads the mother into the labyrinths of an experience that, without the child, she would only rarely encounter: love for an other. Not for herself, nor for an identical being, and still less for another person with whom "I" fuse (love or sexual passion). But the slow, difficult, and delightful apprenticeship in attentiveness, gentleness, forgetting oneself. The ability to succeed in this path without masochism and without annihilating one's affective, intellectual, and professional personality—such would seem to be the stakes to be won through guiltless maternity. It then becomes a creation in the strong sense of the term. For this moment, utopian?

On the other hand, it is in the aspiration towards artistic and, in particular, literary creation that woman's desire for affirmation now manifests itself. Why literature?

Is it because, faced with social norms, literature reveals a certain knowledge and sometimes the truth itself about an otherwise repressed, nocturnal, secret, and unconscious universe? Because it thus redoubles the social contract by exposing the unsaid, the uncanny? And because it makes a game, a space of fantasy and pleasure, out of the abstract and frustrating order of social signs, the words of everyday communication? Flaubert said, "*Madame Bovary, c'est moi.*" Today many women imagine, "*Flaubert, c'est moi.*" This identification with the potency of the imaginary is not only an identification, an imaginary potency (a fetish, a belief in the maternal penis maintained at all costs), as a far too normative view of the social and symbolic relationship would have it. This identification also bears witness to women's desire to lift the weight of what is sacrificial in the social contract from their shoulders, to nourish our societies with a more flexible and free discourse, one able to name what has thus far never been an object of circulation in the community: the enigmas of the body, the dreams, secret joys, shames, hatreds of the second sex.

It is understandable from this that women's writing has lately attracted the maximum attention of both "specialists" and the media. The pitfalls encountered along the way, however, are not to be minimized: for example, does one not read there a relentless belittling of male writers whose books, nevertheless, often serve as "models" for countless productions by women? Thanks to the feminist label, does one not sell numerous works whose naïve whining or marketplace romanticism would otherwise have been rejected as anachronistic? And does one not find the pen of many a female writer being devoted to phantasmic attacks against Language and Sign as the ultimate supports of phallocratic power, in the name of a semi-aphonic corporality whose truth can only be found in that which is "gestural" or "tonal"?

And yet, no matter how dubious the results of these recent productions by women, the symptom is there—women are writing, and the air is heavy with expectation: What will they write that is new?

In the Name of the Father, the Son . . . and the Woman?

These few elements of the manifestations by the new generation of women in Europe seem to me to demonstrate that, beyond the socio-political level where it is generally inscribed (or inscribes itself), the women's movement—in its present stage, less aggressive but more artful—is situated within the very framework of the religious crisis of our civilization.

I call "religion" this phantasmic necessity on the part of speaking beings to provide themselves with a *representation* (animal, female, male, parental, etc.) in place of what constitutes them as such, in other words, symbolization—the double articulation and syntactic sequence of language, as well as its preconditions or substitutes (thoughts, affects, etc.). The elements of the current practice of feminism that we have just brought to light seem precisely to constitute such a representation which makes up for the frustrations imposed on women by the anterior code (Christianity or its lay humanist variant). The fact that this new ideology has affinities, often revindicated by its creators, with so-called matriarchal beliefs (in other words, those beliefs characterizing matrilinear societies) should not overshadow its radical novelty. This ideology seems to me to be part of the broader antisacrificial current which is animating our culture and which, in its protest against the constraints of the socio-symbolic contract, is no less exposed to the risks of violence and terrorism. At this level of radicalism, it is the very principle of sociality which is challenged.

Certain contemporary thinkers consider, as is well known, that modernity is characterized as the first epoch in human history in which human beings attempt to live without religion. In its present form, is not feminism in the process of becoming one?

Or is it, on the contrary and as avant-garde feminists hope, that having started with the idea of difference, feminism will be able to break free of its belief in Woman, Her power, Her writing, so as to channel this demand for difference into each and every element of the female whole, and, finally, to bring out the singularity of each woman, and beyond this, her multiplicities, her plural languages, beyond the horizon, beyond sight, beyond faith itself?

A factor for ultimate mobilization? Or a factor for analysis?

Imaginary support in a technocratic era where all narcissism is frustrated? Or instruments fitted to these times in which the cosmos, atoms, and cells—our true contemporaries—call for the constitution of a fluid and free subjectivity?

The question has been posed. Is to pose it already to answer it?

Another Generation Is Another Space

If the preceding can be *said*—the question whether all this is true belongs to a different register—it is undoubtedly because it is now possible to gain some distance on these two preceding generations of women. This implies, of course, that a *third* generation is now forming, at least in Europe. I am not speaking of a new group of young women (though its importance should not be underestimated) or of another "mass feminist movement" taking the torch passed on from the second generation. My usage of the word "generation" implies less a chronology than a *signifying space*, a both corporeal and desiring mental space. So it can be argued that as of now a third attitude is possible, thus a third generation, which does not exclude—quite to the contrary—the *parallel* existence of all three in the same historical time, or even that they be interwoven one with the other.

In this third attitude, which I strongly advocate—which I imagine?—the very dichotomy man/woman as an opposition between two rival entities may be understood as belonging to *metaphysics*. What can "identity," even "sexual identity," mean in a new theoretical and scientific space where the very notion of identity is challenged? I am not simply suggesting a very hypothetical bisexuality which, even if it existed, would only, in fact, be the aspiration towards the totality of one of the sexes and thus an effacing of difference. What I mean is, first of all, the demassification of the problematic of *difference*, which would imply, in a first phase, an apparent de-dramatization of the "fight to the death" between rival groups and thus between the sexes. And this not in the name of some reconciliation—feminism has at least had the merit of showing what is irreducible and even deadly in the social contract—but in order that the struggle, the implacable difference, the violence be conceived in the very place where it operates with the maximum intransigence, in other words, in personal and sexual identity itself, so as to make it disintegrate in its very nucleus.

It necessarily follows that this involves risks not only for what we understand today as "personal equilibrium" but also for social equilibrium itself, made up as it now is of the counterbalancing of aggressive and murderous forces massed in social, national, religious, and political groups. But is it not the insupportable situation of tension and explosive risk that the existing "equilibrium" presupposes which leads some of those who suffer from it to divest it of its economy, to detach themselves from it and to seek another means of regulating difference?

To restrict myself here to a personal level, as related to the question of women, I see arising, under the cover of a relative indifference towards the militancy of the first and second generations, an attitude of retreat from sexism (male as well as female) and, gradually, from any kind of anthropomorphism. The fact that this might quickly become another form of spiritualism turning its back on social problems, or else a form of repression ready to support all status quos, should not hide the radicalness of the process. This process could be summarized as an *interiorization of the founding separation of the socio-symbolic contract*, as an introduction of its cutting edge into the very interior of every identity whether subjective, sexual, ideological, or so forth. This in such a way that the habitual and increasingly explicit attempt to fabricate a scapegoat victim as foundress of a society or a counter-society may be replaced by the analysis of the potentialities of *victim/executioner* which characterize each identity, each subject, each sex.

What discourse, if not that of a religion, would be able to support this adventure which surfaces as a real possibility, after both the achievements and the impasses of the present ideological reworkings, in which feminism has participated? It seems to me that the role of what is usually called "aesthetic practices" must increase not only to counterbalance the storage and uniformity of information by present-day mass media, data-bank systems, and, in particular, modern communications technology, but also to demystify the identity of the symbolic bond itself, to demystify, therefore, the *community* of language as a universal and unifying tool, one which totalizes and equalizes. In order to bring out—along with the *singularity* of each person and, even more, along with the multiplicity of every person's possible identifications (with atoms, e.g., stretching from the family to the stars)— the *relativity of his/her symbolic as well as biological existence*, according to the variation in his/her specific symbolic capacities. And in order to emphasize the *responsibility* which all will immediately face of putting this fluidity into play against the threats of death which are unavoidable whenever an inside and an outside, a self and an other, one group and another, are constituted. At this level of interiorization with its social as well as individual stakes, what I have called "aesthetic practices" are undoubtedly nothing other than the modern reply to the eternal question of morality. At least, this is how we might understand an ethics which, conscious of the fact that its order is sacrificial, reserves part of the burden for each of its adherents, therefore declaring them guilty while immediately affording them the possibility for *jouissance*, for various productions, for a life made up of both challenges and differences.

Spinoza's question can be taken up again here: Are women subject to ethics? If not to that ethics defined by classical philosophy—in relationship to which the ups and downs of feminist generations seem dangerously precarious—are women not already participating in the rapid dismantling that our age is experiencing at various levels (from wars to drugs to artificial insemination) and which poses the *demand* for a new ethics? The answer to Spinoza's question can be affirmative only at the cost of considering feminism as but a *moment* in the thought of that anthropomorphic identity which currently blocks the horizon of the discursive and scientific adventure of our species.

Notes

1. See D. Desanti, "L'autre sexe des bolcheviks," *Tel Quel* 76 (1978); Julia Kristeva, *On Chinese Women*, trans. Anita Barrows (London: Marion Boyars, 1977).
2. See Arthur Hertzberg, *The French Enlightenment and the Jews* (New York: Columbia University Press, 1968); *Les Juifs et la révolution française,* ed. B. Blumenkranz and A. Seboul (Paris: Éditions Privat, 1976).
3. This work is periodically published in various academic women's journals, one of the most prestigious being *Signs: Journal of Women in Culture and Society*, University of Chicago Press. Also of note are the special issues: "Ecriture, féminité, féminisme," *La Révue des Sciences Humaines* 4 (1977); and "Les femmes et la philosophie," *Le Doctrinal de sapience* 3 (1977).

INDEX